Parole Board Hearings

law and practice

Hamish Arnott is a partner at Bhatt Murphy Solicitors in London. He specialises in public law and human rights with a particular focus on the civil liberties of prisoners and those detained under immigration laws.

Simon Creighton is a partner at Bhatt Murphy Solicitors and has specialised in prison law since 1993 when he was appointed as the first solicitor at the Prisoners' Advice Service.

Hamish Arnott and Simon Creighton are the authors of *Prisoners: law and practice* (LAG, 2009).

The purpose of the Legal Action Group is to promote equal access to justice for all members of society who are socially, economically or otherwise disadvantaged. To this end, it seeks to improve law and practice, the administration of justice and legal services.

Parole Board Hearings

law and practice

SECOND EDITION

Hamish Arnott and Simon Creighton

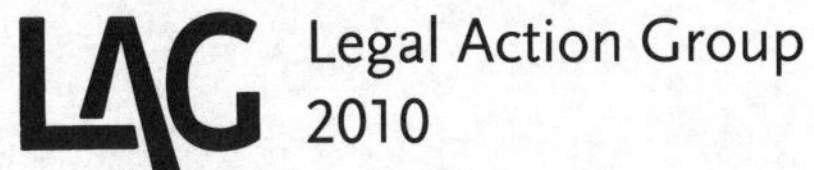

Legal Action Group
2010

2nd edition published in Great Britain 2010
by LAG Education and Service Trust Limited
242 Pentonville Road, London N1 9UN
www.lag.org.uk

British Library Cataloguing in Publication Data
a CIP catalogue record for this book is available from the British Library.

ISBN 978 1 903307 64 9

Typeset by Regent Typesetting, London.
Printed in Great Britain by Hobbs the Printer, Totton, Hampshire

Foreword

Sir David Latham, Chairman of the Parole Board for England and Wales

This is an essential book for anyone concerned, in any capacity, with the work of the Parole Board. It collates all the relevant statutory and other legal material relevant to the Board, and gives detailed practical guidance as to the way in which the Board works. It has been published at a particularly appropriate time. The future of the Board is now being debated. This book therefore provides perhaps the fullest description of the Board's present position in the criminal justice system, and the way in which it carries out its functions. It is therefore a secure foundation from which the debate as to its future can be carried forward.

The authors' clear understanding of their subject matter, and their practical experience of the way in which the Board operates makes their invigorating comments all the more authoritative. This book is therefore extremely welcome.

Sir David Latham
Chairman of the Parole Board for England and Wales
December 2009

Preface

In recent years, the slow passage of the Board from advisory body to court has picked up pace. In the 35 years after the Criminal Justice Act 1967 first established the Board, parole had remained a small niche area only to coming to public attention with the occasional high profile decision. However, as sentencing policy places more and more emphasis on the assessment of risk both at the time of sentence and the time of release, the role of the Board has increased exponentially. In simple numerical terms, the number of prisoners serving indeterminate sentences has doubled since the publication of the first edition of this book, the recall rate for all prisoners has risen and the Board's workload has spiralled, almost to the point of being out of control. These developments have resulted in the role of the Board coming under closer scrutiny by the courts and the procedural safeguards of article 5(4) in the release process being re-evaluated.

It has been four years since the first edition of this book and during that time there have been highly significant developments in the parole review process. The new Parole Board Rules have made oral hearings for indeterminate prisoners discretionary rather than a requirement and the House of Lords ruling on IPP prisoners and delays in the parole process has arguably emptied much of the substance from reviews. At the same time, the future of the Parole Board itself is being considered with a consultation underway seeking to decide if it should reside in the Tribunals or Court Service.

As with many areas of the criminal justice system, the concern for prisoners and for the Board itself is that many of these changes are occurring on the hoof in response to various crises. The danger with developments in the law occurring in response to problems rather than in anticipation to those problems is that expedient options may be adopted rather than principled decisions. It is perhaps time for some genuine 'blue sky' thinking about the future of the Board, such as the ideas put forward in the JUSTICE report, *A New Parole System for England and Wales* (JUSTICE, October 2009) where the Board's role in sentence planning and categorisation has been discussed.

The fluidity of the current situation has meant that we have attempted to analyse not just the changes that have already taken place, but also to look at the possible future outcomes in this edition. We have received enormous assistance from Terry McCarthy, the Head of Casework at the Parole Board, in this task. We are extremely grateful to Sir David Latham, the Chief Executive of the Board, not only for writing the foreword to this edition, but also for promoting the discussion and debate that has been needed in these areas which has included the open exchange of information between the Board and its users. We have also been greatly assisted in understanding and interpreting these developments by our colleagues and clients.

Against this background, the importance of the parole system to the criminal justice system and its impact on individuals must not be forgotten. With over 12,000 prisoners serving indeterminate and life sentences – a figure higher than the rest of Western Europe combined – the human impact of uncertainty and delays must not be forgotten. Where the liberty of the subject is stake, society is entitled to expect a clarity and precision in the review and release process. We hope that this book contributes to the task of explaining the system to everyone involved in parole, whether directly as prisoners and decision-makers, or indirectly such as family members, report writers, witnesses at hearings and victims.

Hamish Arnott
Simon Creighton
Bhatt Murphy Solicitors, London

December 2009

Contents

APPENDICES

Table of cases

References in the right-hand column are to paragraph numbers.

A v United Kingdom (Application No 3455/05) (2009) 49 EHRR 625, [2009] All ER (D) 203 (Feb), ECtHR	10.47
AT v United Kingdom (1995) 20 EHRR CD 50	11.104, 14.26
Ashingdane v United Kingdom (1985) 7 EHRR 528	9.12
Attorney-General v English [1983] 1 AC 116, [1982] 2 All ER 903, HL, *reversing* [1982] 2 WLR 959, QBD	4.1
Blackstock v United Kingdom (Application No 59512/00) (2005) 42 EHRR 55, [2005] All ER (D) 218 (Jun), [2005] 2 Prison Law Reports 85, (2006) 42 EHRR 2, ECtHR	9.12, 11.104
C v Secretary of State for Justice [2009] EWHC 2671 (Admin)	12.25
Cowl v Plymouth City Council [2001] EWCA Civ 1935, [2002] 1 WLR 803, CA, *affirming* [2001] EWHC 734 (Admin)	14.1
Curley v United Kingdom (Application No 32340/96) (2000) *Times*, 5 April, (2001) 31 EHRR 14	11.104, 14.26
Dv Secretary of State for Northern Ireland Intervening, *see* R (on the application of D)	
De Wilde, Ooms and Versyp v Belgium (Application Nos 2832/66, 2835/66, 2899/66) (1972) 1 EHRR 438, ECtHR	1.19
Doorson v Netherlands (Application No 20524/92) (1996) 22 EHRR 330, [1996] ECHR 20524/92, ECtHR	10.42, 11.79
Gebura v Poland (Application No 63131/00) (unreported)	1.28
Gibson v Secretary of State for Justice, *see* R (on the application of Kelly) v Secretary of State for Justice, Re Gibson	
H and R (minors) (sexual abuse: standard of proof), Re [1996] AC 563	11.77, 11.78

Table of statutes

References in the right-hand column are to paragraph numbers.

Table of statutory instruments

References in the right-hand column are to paragraph numbers.

Abbreviations

Legislation

AJA 1999	Access to Justice Act 1999
CDA 1998	Crime and Disorder Act 1998
CJA 1967	Criminal Justice Act 1967
CJA 1991	Criminal Justice Act 1991
CJA 2003	Criminal Justice Act 2003
CJCSA 2000	Criminal Justice and Courts Services Act 2000
CJIA 2008	Criminal Justice and Immigration Act 2008
C(S)A 1997	Crime (Sentences) Act 1997
CPR	Civil Procedure Rules 1998
DPA 1998	Data Protection Act 1998
DVCVA 2004	Domestic Violence, Crime and Victims Act 2004
HRA 1998	Human Rights Act 1998
MHA 1983	Mental Health Act 1983
PCC(S)A 2000	Powers of the Criminal Courts (Sentencing) Act 2000

Other

ACO	Assistant Chief Officer
ACR	Automatic conditional release
ART	Aggression Replacement Therapy
AUR	Automatic unconditional release
CALM	Controlling Anger and Learning to Manage it
CARATS	Counselling, Assessment and Throughcare Services
CDS	Criminal Defence Service
CLS	Community Legal Service
CRD	Conditional Release Date
CSAP	Correctional Services Accreditation Panel
CSCP	Cognitive Self Change Programme
DCR	Discretionary conditional release
DSPD	Dangerous and Severe Personality Disorder
DTO	Detention and Training Order
ECHR	European Convention on Human Rights
ECtHR	European Court of Human Rights
ERS	Early Release Scheme
ETS	Enhanced Thinking Skills
GCC	General Criminal Contract
HCR-20	Historical, Clinical Risk Management

HDC	Home Detention Curfew
HEO	Higher Executive Officer
HMP lifer	Detained at Her Majesty's Pleasure
HRP	Healthy Relationships Programmes
HSF	Healthy Sexual Functioning
JR	Judicial review
LED	Licence expiry date
LRC	Local review committee
LRRS	Lifer Review and Recall Section
LSC	Legal Services Commission
LSP	Life sentence plan
MAPPA	Multi-agency Public Protection Arrangements
MAPPP	Multi-agency Public Protection Panel
MHRT	Mental Health Review Tribunal
NDPB	Non-Departmental Public Body
NOMS	National Offender Management Service
NPD	Non parole date
OASys	Offender Assessment System
OCPA	Office of the Commissioner for Public Appointments
OGRS	Offender Group Reconviction Scale
PAR	Parole Assessment Report
PB	Parole Board
PBR	Parole Board Rules
PC	Probation Circular
PCL-R	Psychopathy Checklist – Revised
PED	Parole eligibility date
PPG	Penile Plethysmograph
PPCS	Public Protection Casework Section
PPO	Prolific and Priority Offender
PPP	Public Protection Panel
PSI	Prison Service Instruction
PSO	Prison Service Order
R&R	Reasoning and Rehabilitation
RAPt	Rehabilitation of Addicted Prisoners Trust
RM 2000	Risk Matrix 2000
ROTL	Release on Temporary Licence
RRS	Release and Recall Section
SACJ	Structured Anchored Clinical Judgment
SARN	Structured Assessment of Risk and Needs
SDS	Standard Determinate Sentence
SED	Sentence expiry date
SOTP	Sex Offender Treatment Programme
SPPU	Sentencing Policy and Penalties Unit
TC	Therapeutic community
VPS	Violence Prediction Scheme
VRAG	Violence Risk Assessment Guide

CHAPTER 1

The Parole Board

Introduction

1.1 All sentences of imprisonment, save for those few cases where a whole life order is made,[1] include a possibility of early release. As a response to prison overcrowding, there are a bewildering array of early release schemes that may apply to a sentence depending on its type and length. The vast majority of those serving normal determinate sentences are automatically released on licence at the half-way point of the sentence. Many such prisoners may also be eligible for release prior to the halfway point on electronic tagging, or on what is known as 'end of custody licence'. These mechanisms of release do not involve the Parole Board. The changes to the Board introduced by the Criminal Justice Act (CJA) 2003 and the Criminal Justice and Immigration (CJIA) Act 2008 focused its role on the release of prisoners who may pose a risk of committing offences of serious harm, most notably those serving life or indeterminate sentences. These changes coincided with an increase in concern over the Board's identity, crucially whether its current constitution enables it to operate sufficiently as a court-like body. A further concern has been an exponential increase in the backlog of cases waiting an oral hearing, which during 2008–09 has led to a systematic failure to ensure that prisoners' rights to a speedy review of their cases under article 5(4) of the European Convention on Human Rights (ECHR) are met. At the time of writing this edition, these concerns have led the Ministry of Justice to commissioning a consultation paper on the future of the Board, which is discussed further below.

Background to the Board's creation

1.2 There have been varying kinds of early release schemes in England and Wales long before the creation of the Parole Board, although these were always at the discretion of the executive.[2] The Board itself

1 A whole life term following a murder conviction is provided for in the circumstances set out in CJA 2003 Sch 21 para 4; the possibility of a whole life order following the imposition of a discretionary life sentence or IPP remains, although as the tariff is meant to be set at one half of the equivalent determinate term in such cases, it is difficult to envisage circumstances where this could be lawfully imposed.

2 For a summary of the history and philosophy behind parole and remission in England and Wales see Part 1 of *The parole system in England and Wales* Cm 532, 1988 (the Carlisle Committee Report).

was created by the Criminal Justice Act 1967, at the same time as there was a comprehensive statutory regime brought in to deal with the early release of prisoners for the first time. The white paper leading to the Act[3] had proposed a system of early release for fixed-term prisoners by which those who showed 'promise or determination to reform' could earn a further period of parole of up to one-third over and above the existing automatic one-third remission. While the wording of the white paper suggests that the key reason for the introduction of a parole system was rehabilitative, there were also pressures on the prison system (overcrowding and prison discipline) that also made it attractive for managerial reasons.[4]

1.3 While there was general support for a system of selective early release, debate in parliament prior to the passing of the CJA 1967 focused on what process should be adopted to decide who should benefit. The then Labour government had proposed that the discretion should lie wholly with the Home Secretary, but this was resisted both by the Opposition and the judiciary.[5] The concerns raised in debates included the fact that if prisoners sentenced to identical terms by the courts were to be released on different dates, then something more than a purely executive decision was required. There was also concern that without some check on executive discretion, parole could be granted too readily when needed to ease the pressure of prison overcrowding.[6]

1.4 In the end, the CJA 1967 created a system whereby the newly created Parole Board (along with local review committees (LRCs) located in the prisons, which were subsequently abolished by the CJA 1991) was consulted by the Home Secretary as to the suitability of prisoners for release on parole. Accordingly, the Parole Board's role in recommending release, including that of life sentence prisoners,[7] was advisory only (although its recommendations in relation to recall cases had to be followed).[8] The Board initially consisted of 17 members, including the chair, High Court judges, recorders, psychiatrists, principal probation officers and criminologists.[9]

3 *The adult offender* Cmnd 2852, 1965.

4 Carlisle Committee Report, Part 1, para 22.

5 See Richardson, *Law, process and custody: prisoners and patients*, Weidenfeld and Nicolson, 1993, p175.

6 Carlisle Committee Report, Part 1, para 22.

7 CJA 1967 s61.

8 CJA 1967 s62. See HOC 66/68 para 4.

9 See HOC 66/68 para 4.

1.5 The procedures involved in parole applications from the creation of the Board until after the coming into force of the CJA 1991, despite the involvement of judges, were far from judicial and are unrecognisable from the procedural safeguards that have since developed. Decisions relating to initial release were all conducted on paper by panels of the Board – there was no disclosure of the material upon which the decisions were made and so no real opportunity to make representations, and no reasons were given (except in recall cases). The standard response given to fixed-term prisoners refused parole stated:[10]

> Your case for early release on licence under the parole scheme has been has been fully and sympathetically considered but the Secretary of State regrets to have to inform you that parole has not been authorised.

Current legal framework of the Board

Constitution

1.6 The Parole Board was reconstituted by the CJA 1991 and the CJA 2003. Since 1996 it has been an executive non-departmental public body (NDPB).[11] NDPBs are designed to permit functions to be carried out at a remove from ministerial control, and so in the Parole Board's case the aim was to bolster its independence from the executive (see further discussion below). Its mission statement states:[12]

> [t]he Parole Board is an independent body that works with its criminal justice partners to protect the public by risk assessing prisoners to decide whether they can be safely released into the community.

1.7 The Board is not to be considered a servant or agent of the Crown[13] and as a statutory corporation it has power to do such things as are incidental or conducive to the carrying out of its functions in relation to deciding on the early release and recall of prisoners.[14]

10 Carlisle Committee Report, para 139.

11 Facilitated by an amendment to the CJA 1991 making it a corporate body – Criminal Justice and Public Order Act 1994 s149.

12 Parole Board Business Plan 2009–10, para 1 at www.paroleboard.gov.uk/servefile.aspx?docid=851.

13 CJA 2003 Sch 19 para 1(1).

14 CJA 2003 Sch 19 para 1(2).

1.8 The Board is to consist of a chair and no less than four other members who are appointed by the Justice Secretary.[15] As an NDPB it has both a chair and a chief executive who retains overall responsibility for management. Members must include someone who has held judicial office, a psychiatrist, someone with experience of after-care services for released prisoners and someone who has made a 'study of the causes of delinquency or the treatment of offenders'.[16] As at 1 May 2009 the Board had 163 members. Most of these are part-time (including the part-time Chair and Vice-Chair) and combine their work on the Parole Board with work in another profession. The membership of the Board includes judges, consultant psychiatrists, forensic psychologists, probation officers and independent members.[17]

1.9 Board members are appointed by the Justice Secretary in accordance with guidance issued by the Office of the Commissioner for Public Appointments (OCPA). The current tenure is six years, split into two three-year terms. Re-appointment is subject to a satisfactory level of performance.[18]

1.10 The Parole Board website[19] states that part-time psychiatrist and forensic psychologist members are expected to commit to a minimum of 35 days a year, part-time judicial members 15 days a year and part-time probation officer members 50 days a year. Non-specialist part-time independent members are expected to commit to an equivalent of 2½ days work per week (115 days per year).[20] For all part-time members it is recognised that much of the work is background, including reading reports and drafting preparatory notes, which can be undertaken at home during the evening and at weekends. Details of the core competencies expected from all members are also set out on the Board's website.[21]

1.11 The Board is serviced by a secretariat of about 100, a figure that has almost doubled since 2004.[22] The part of the secretariat dealing

15 CJA 2003 Sch 19 para 2(1).

16 CJA 2003 Sch 19 para 2(2).

17 Ministry of Justice Consultation Paper 14/09, *The Future of the Parole Board*, para 33.

18 Ibid paras 33 and 48.

19 www.paroleboard.gov.uk/recruitment/members_of_the_parole_board/specialist_members/.

20 www.paroleboard.gov.uk/recruitment/members_of_the_parole_board/part_time_independent_members/.

21 www.paroleboard.gov.uk/recruitment/members_of_the_parole_board/core_competancies/.

22 www.paroleboard.gov.uk/recruitment/secretariat_staff/.

with casework is divided into different teams reflecting the various aspects of the parole process. The contact details for the various casework teams are available on the Board's website:

- Oral hearings – responsible for all casework relating to oral hearings for release on licence of indeterminate sentence prisoners. The casework teams that deal with oral hearings are allocated cases by reference to the prison in which the prisoner is held. This practice is mirrored in the casework teams within the Public Protection Casework Section at the Ministry of Justice;
- Paper hearings – responsible for the processing of determinate sentence cases where there is no oral hearing, including checking dossiers, obtaining additional paperwork and managing deferred cases;
- Recalls – responsible for recall cases decided on the papers and for arranging oral hearings to consider representations for re-release from determinate and indeterminate sentence prisoners;
- Post panel – responsible for all post-panel casework related to Parole Board decisions and recommendations, including judicial reviews and complaints regarding decisions; and
- Listing – responsible for the listing and rescheduling of all oral hearings and allocating members to panels.

1.12 As an executive NDPB, the Board must have a sponsoring department which is responsible, through its ministers, for its funding and can account to Parliament to ensure that funding is justified and used appropriately. As a result of the *Brooke* judgment (see below), from 1 April 2008 the sponsor department of the Board has been the Access to Justice Group in the Ministry of Justice. The implications of sponsorship, both in relation to the need for the Board to be independent, and to its future are also discussed below.

Legal powers and duties

1.13 The Board now derives its powers from section 239 of the CJA 2003.[23] As noted above, the Board remains a corporate body.[24] It is under a duty to advise the Justice Secretary 'with respect to any matter referred to it by him which is to do with the early release or recall of prisoners'.[25] There is a requirement that the Board deals with cases

23 In force from 4 April 2004 – Criminal Justice Act 2003 (Commencement No 8 and Transitional and Saving Provisions) Order 2005 SI No 950.

24 CJA 2003 s239(1).

25 CJA 2003 s239(2).

referred to it on consideration of all such evidence as may be adduced before it.[26]

1.14 The Justice Secretary is given the power to make rules with respect to the proceedings of the Board[27] and also the power to make directions as to the matters the Board should take into account in discharging its functions.[28] Its powers in relation to its decisions as to the release of all classes of indeterminate sentence prisoners are contained in the Crime (Sentences) Act (C(S)A) 1997, as amended; and in relation to determinate sentence prisoners in the Criminal Justice Acts 1991 and 2003 (as amended by the CJIA 2008). These powers are dealt with in detail where relevant in the following chapters of this book.

1.15 The Board, when acting as a court-like body, remains a statutory corporation, not a court of inherent jurisdiction. As such, it can only adopt procedures expressly or impliedly authorised by the statutory framework.[29]

Evolution of the Board's functions

1.16 The changes to the Board's legal powers and in the way it makes its decisions since its creation have been dramatic. The Board now holds oral hearings at which the prisoner is entitled to disclosure and publicly funded legal representation in most indeterminate sentence cases involving potential release on or after the expiry of the punishment phase (or 'minimum term') and in many cases where extended sentence or determinate sentence prisoners are recalled to custody. When considering such cases, the Board's decision to release the prisoner is final. Where there is no right to an oral hearing, the Board's decisions are made after the prisoner has had an opportunity to make representations following disclosure of the material upon which the decision will be based, and full reasons for decisions are given.

1.17 This dramatic shift from an advisory role where decisions were made with virtually no procedural safeguards for the prisoner, to one where the Board is often acting in a judicial manner in deciding on

26 CJA 2003 s239(4).

27 CJA 2003 s239(5); see Parole Board Rules (PBR) 2004 as amended.

28 CJA 2003 s239(6). For discussion on effect of directions, see below and chapter 10.

29 *R (on the application of Roberts) v Parole Board* [2005] UKHL 45 para 65.

release, has been effected primarily by numerous legal challenges by prisoners. These challenges have enhanced the standards of fairness in parole proceedings both by reference to the requirements of the European Convention on Human Rights, and to what is required under common law standards.

Administration of sentences and the ECHR

Article 5

1.18 The major impact on the development of the Board's role, especially in the right to oral hearings, has been brought about in cases involving breaches of the ECHR. The key article that has been invoked in order to enhance the fairness of Parole Board decision making is article 5, which prohibits arbitrary detention. The parts of the article relevant to the parole process are:

> **Article 5**
>
> 1. Everyone has the right to liberty and security of person. No one shall be deprived of his liberty save in the following cases and in accordance with a procedure prescribed by law:
> (a) the lawful detention of a person after conviction by a competent court;
>
> ...
>
> 4. Everyone who is deprived of his liberty by arrest or detention shall be entitled to take proceedings by which the lawfulness of his detention shall be decided speedily by a court and his release ordered if the detention is not lawful.
>
> 5. Everyone who has been the victim of arrest or detention in contravention of the provisions of this article shall have an enforceable right to compensation.

1.19 The key parts of article 5 in relation to release procedures are paras (1)(a) and (4). Prisoners serving sentences imposed by criminal courts are considered to be lawfully detained within the meaning of article 5(1)(a), and so the question arises as to when does article 5(4) requires access to a further review process to decide whether that detention remains lawful?

> At first sight, the wording of Article 5(4) might make one think that it guarantees the right of the detainee always to have supervised by a court the lawfulness of a previous decision which has deprived him of his liberty ... Where [this] decision ... is one taken by an administrative body, there is no doubt that Article 5(4) obliges the Contracting States to make available to the person detained a right of recourse to

a court; but there is nothing to indicate that the same applies when the decision is made by a court at the close of judicial proceedings. In the latter case the supervision required by Article 5(4) is incorporated in the decision; this is so, for example, where a sentence of imprisonment is pronounced after 'conviction by a competent court' (Article 5(1)(a) of the Convention).[30]

1.20 This principle applies where detention remains for the purpose contemplated by the sentencing court. So, where a normal determinate sentence is imposed by a criminal court as punishment, the review required by article 5(4) is already incorporated by the imposition of the sentence. Detention cannot become arbitrary for the purposes of article 5 because, at any time during such a sentence, it remains justified as what the court thought appropriate for punishment and as such satisfies article 5(1)(a).[31]

1.21 It follows that if, in the case of the gravest murders, the sentence is genuinely one of lifelong detention as punishment, article 5(1)(a) will be satisfied for the whole of the prisoner's life.[32]

Article 5 and indeterminate sentences

1.22 In 1983 the Home Secretary issued a ministerial statement[33] that clarified how he intended to exercise his discretion in releasing life sentence prisoners. The life sentence was effectively divided into two: the 'tariff' phase, that is the punitive term that the lifer has to serve for reasons of retribution and deterrence; and the post-tariff phase, when detention is based on whether the lifer is deemed to pose a risk to the public. In setting the tariff the Home Secretary consulted the judiciary, and in deciding to release the Home Secretary consulted the Parole Board. This statement applied to all lifers.

1.23 The European Court of Human Rights (ECtHR) in Strasbourg first analysed the discretionary life sentence when a prisoner, who had been released and recalled before the procedures for tariff setting were clarified, challenged the procedures relating to his recall to custody.[34] The court noted that the discretionary life sentence was

30 *De Wilde, Ooms and Versyp v Belgium* (1972) 1 EHRR 438.

31 *R (on the application of Black) v Secretary of State for Justice* [2009] UKHL 1 paras 81–5; *R (on the application of Giles) v Parole Board* [2003] UKHL 42 paras 51–2; *R (on the application of Smith) v Parole Board* [2005] UKHL 1 para 36.

32 Such sentences can be imposed under the criteria contained in CJA 2003 Sch 21; *R v Bieber (aka Coleman)* [2008] EWCA Crim 1601.

33 30 November 1983.

34 *Weeks v UK* (1988) 10 EHRR 293.

only imposed under domestic law where the offender was assessed as being dangerous and unstable, and these characteristics were by their very nature susceptible to change.[35] Therefore, after release, re-detention required a review under article 5(4) to confirm that there was a 'causal link' with the objectives of the sentencing court.[36] The sentencing court could not predict whether an offender needed to be detained when the punitive phase of the sentence expired, and so a further judicial assessment was required at that stage to ensure detention could be justified under article 5(1)(a).

1.24 There followed a number of domestic challenges that confirmed that for discretionary life sentence prisoners, as dangerousness was the criterion for imposition of the sentence, detention after the tariff (the punitive phase or 'minimum term') required an assessment of dangerousness.[37] The requirement under article 5(4) for this assessment to be carried out by a court-like body, even for the initial release of those sentenced to life imprisonment for very serious crimes, was subsequently confirmed by the ECtHR.[38]

1.25 These decisions led to a divergence in the way that the different life sentences were administered. For example, the ECtHR initially accepted the government's argument that, although the 1983 statement applied to all lifers, the mandatory life sentence for murder, imposed automatically irrespective of dangerousness, was in reality a sentence of lifelong punitive detention[39] and so any release mechanisms could properly remain in the hands of the executive.[40]

1.26 Notwithstanding these comments, the ECtHR later decided that the mandatory indeterminate sentence for those convicted of murder when under 18 (the HMP life sentence) (see para 7.2) required an article 5(4) hearing to determine detention after the tariff phase on the basis that the sentence (which involved considerations of the offender's welfare) could only justify this following a finding of dangerousness.[41] Eventually the ECtHR accepted that its earlier finding that the sentence for adults convicted of murder was one of lifelong punitive detention could no longer be sustained as the domestic arrangements had clearly divided the sentence up into two phases

35 Ibid para 46.

36 Ibid paras 42 and 48.

37 *R v Secretary of State for the Home Department ex p Benson* [1989] COD 329; *R v Secretary of State for the Home Department ex p Bradley* [1991] 1 WLR 134.

38 *Thynne Wilson and Gunnell v UK* (1990) 13 EHRR 666.

39 Statement of Angela Rumbold, 16 July 1991.

40 *Wynne v UK* (1994) 19 EHRR 333.

41 *Singh and Hussain v UK* (1996) 22 EHRR 1.

as with any other life sentence, with dangerousness being the key to detention in the post-tariff phase.

> The Government maintained that the mandatory life sentence was nonetheless an indeterminate sentence which was not based on any individual characteristic of the offender, such as youth and dangerousness, and therefore there was no question of any change in the relevant circumstances of the offender that might raise lawfulness issues concerning the basis for his continued detention. However, the Court is not convinced by this argument. Once the punishment element of the sentence (as reflected in the tariff) has been satisfied, the grounds for the continued detention, as in discretionary life and juvenile murderer cases, must be considerations of risk and dangerousness.[42]

1.27 Accordingly, mandatory lifers became entitled to article 5(4) compliant reviews on tariff expiry. The whole process of life sentences moving from being wholly administered by the executive to being judicially controlled, therefore, took about 20 years. Release arrangements for all indeterminate sentences were eventually harmonised by the coming into force of the relevant parts of the CJA 2003 in January 2004.

Article 5 and determinate sentences

1.28 The starting point for analysing how article 5 applies to determinate sentences is that article 5(1) is satisfied for the whole of the fixed-term sentence imposed as punishment (see para 1.20 above). The exception to this principle is where a prisoner is wrongfully detained beyond a statutory early release date that carries a right to be released. Such detention has been held to constitute the tort of false imprisonment, and accordingly is a breach of article 5(1).[43] The same principle applies where entitlement to release under a conditional release scheme is established, as there is no longer lawful authority to detain, although this does not mean that the procedure leading to a decision that such a prisoner should be released needs to comply with article 5(4).[44]

1.29 As the structure of article 5 logically links the need for a review under paragraph (4) with the potential lawfulness of detention under paragraph (1)(a), it might be thought that determinate sentence prisoners are not entitled to an article 5(4) compliant review at any stage

42 *Stafford v UK* (2002) 35 EHRR 32.

43 *R v Governor of Brockhill Prison ex p Evans (No 2)* [2001] 2 AC 19.

44 *Gebura v Poland* (Application No 63131/00) (unreported); *R (on the application of Black) v Secretary of State for Justice* [2009] UKHL 1 para 70.

of their sentence, even where they have been released and recalled. The domestic courts have, however, drawn a distinction between the position of a prisoner who is seeking their initial release from prison at the parole eligibility date halfway through the sentence, and a prisoner whose recall to prison is being considered by the Board. In the latter case, even though article 5(1)(a) is satisfied by the original sentence in its entirety, the House of Lords in the *Smith and West* case held that article 5(4) is engaged when the Parole Board considers recall.[45] The rationale behind this finding was not entirely clear. In a subsequent case Lord Brown stated:[46]

> Inescapably it follows from [*Smith and West*] that contrary to the view expressed in the Strasbourg court's admissibility decision in Brown, a prisoner's recall for breach of his licence conditions *does* raise, 'new issues affecting the lawfulness of the detention' such as to engage article 5(4). And that seems to me clearly correct: it would not be lawful to recall a prisoner unless he *had* breached his licence conditions and there could well be an issue as to this.

The fact that recall raises fresh issues as to the legality of detention would appear to be self-evident. But this is difficult to reconcile with the decision that detention can never become unlawful under article 5(1)(a) during the currency of a determinate sentence where the prisoner is recalled. The language of 'new issues affecting lawfulness' of detention suggests that the need for an article 5(4) review is precisely to prevent detention becoming arbitrary.

1.30 This apparent conflict raised by *Smith and West*, that article 5(4) could be engaged even where there was no risk of detention in breach of article 5(1), subsequently led the Divisional Court and Court of Appeal in a series of cases to hold that article 5(4) *was* engaged when the Parole Board was considering the *initial* release of determinate sentence prisoners.[47] These cases accepted an analysis that the release of determinate sentence prisoners involved an assessment of risk by the Parole Board, which was analogous to its function when deciding whether to release indeterminate sentence prisoners at the end of the minimum term.

1.31 However, this line of cases was overruled when *Black* reached the House of Lords. The Lords reaffirmed the analysis that article

45 *R (on the application of Smith) v Parole Board* [2005] UKHL 1.

46 *R (on the application of Black) v Secretary of State for Justice* [2009] UKHL 1 para 74.

47 *R (on the application of Johnson) v Secretary of State for the Home Department* [2007] EWCA Civ 247; *R (on the application of Black) v Secretary of State for Justice* [2008] EWCA Civ 359; *R (on the application of O'Connell) v Parole Board* [2007] EWHC 2591 (Admin).

5(4) had no part to play in the initial release of determinate sentence prisoners (see para 1.20 above). Therefore, in principle early release mechanisms can be left wholly to the executive without offending article 5(4), and that position is not altered simply because the decision is in fact entrusted to a court-like body such as the Board.[48]

1.32 Although the position for determinate sentences and article 5 is generally as set out above, extended sentences (that is, sentences comprising a punitive 'custodial term' together with an 'extension period' of supervision in the community imposed to protect the public) are different. Although not strictly indeterminate, similar considerations as for life sentences apply to detention during the extension period. As the extension period is not imposed punitively, but to protect the public, whether detention is necessary for this purpose requires examination under article 5(4).[49]

Article 6

1.33 It has been decided that when considering whether it is appropriate to release a prisoner that the Parole Board is not determining a 'criminal charge' within the meaning of article 6 of the ECHR (even when considering a recall based on further misconduct).[50] Whether article 6 applies in so far as liberty is a 'civil right' remains undecided,[51] although in cases where article 5 applies it is difficult to see what article 6 in its 'civil right' aspect would add in terms of fair procedure.

Consequences of the applicability of article 5

1.34 Article 5(4) requires review of the legality of detention by a 'court'. However, the court referred to in article 5(4):

- does not necessarily have to be a court of law of the classic kind integrated within the standard judicial machinery of the country; but
- must be independent of the executive and any parties to the case; and
- needs to provide a judicial procedure appropriate to the kind of deprivation of liberty in question; and
- must have the power to direct, not only advise on, release.[52]

48 *R (on the application of Black) v Secretary of State for Justice* [2009] UKHL 1 paras 82–3.

49 *R (on the application of Sim) v Parole Board* [2003] EWCA Civ 1845.

50 *R (on the application of Smith) v Parole Board* [2005] UKHL 1.

51 Ibid.

52 *Weeks v UK* (1988) 10 EHRR 293 paras 59 and 61.

1.35 The need for the review to be 'wide enough to bear on those conditions that, under the ECHR, are essential for the lawful detention of a person in the situation of the particular detainee'[53] necessitates the reviewing body to be fact-sensitive and rule on the essential question of risk to the public. Accordingly, when first analysing its requirements the ECtHR considered that the availability of judicial review of a non-ECHR compliant parole procedure did not remedy the breach of article 5(4), as the grounds for judicial review were traditionally too narrow.[54] The Parole Board, as an expert quasi-judicial body set up to examine risk, was clearly suited to the task of carrying out such reviews, subject to amendments to its powers and procedures.

1.36 However the House of Lords has rejected a suggestion that the Board is required by article 5(4) to take steps to ensure that it has detailed reports before it that present a full assessment of the risk posed by the prisoner. Lord Brown, in an analysis that he acknowledged suggests that article 5(4) is all about form rather than substance, stated:[55]

> I have concluded that article 5(4) requires no more than that 'a court' (the Parole Board) shall speedily decide whether the prisoner continues to be lawfully detained, and this will indeed be the case unless and until the Board is satisfied of his safety for release (or so long has elapsed without any effective review of his dangerousness that the article 5(1) causal link must be presumed broken as discussed above). I accept that article 5(4) requires the basic rule 6 dossier to be made available: without this the Board simply cannot function. But I cannot accept that article 5(4) requires anything more in the way of enabling the Board to form its judgment.

1.37 The Lords accordingly overturned the very purposive decision of the Court of Appeal that considered that what might amount to an 'empty exercise' might well breach article 5(4). The need for the Board's decision to be made 'speedily' to satisfy article 5(4) is dealt with in chapter 14.

53 *R (on the application of Smith) v Parole Board* [2005] UKHL 1 para 37.

54 *Weeks v UK* (1988) 10 EHRR 293 para 69 – despite the fact that now the HRA may require the judicial review court to decide itself whether a decision is proportionate (*R (on the application of Daly) v Secretary of State for the Home Department* [2001] 2 AC 532) as the Parole Board is an expert body entrusted by Parliament to assess risk, the court will not review the merits of its decisions but rather whether it was entitled to come to its view: *R (on the application of Wyles) v Parole Board and Secretary of State for the Home Department* [2006] EWHC 493 (Admin) para 32.

55 *R (on the application of James, Lee, Wells) v Parole Board* [2009] UKHL 22 para 60;*R (on the application of Smith) v Parole Board* [2005] UKHL 1 para 37.

Oral hearings, disclosure and the power to release

1.38 At the time of the first case in which article 5 was held to apply to the administration of discretionary life sentences by the ECtHR, the Board did not have directive powers of release in periodic reviews, and even in recall cases the procedure adopted did not provide for full disclosure of any adverse material. Accordingly, article 5(4) was held to have been breached without consideration as to whether an oral hearing was required.[56] However, when the CJA 1991 introduced procedures to consider the post-tariff release and recall of discretionary lifers, and gave the Board the power to direct release, procedures for disclosure and the holding of oral hearings were also introduced into the parole process for the first time.[57] The Board now clearly has powers to direct release in nearly all the cases where it is considering release, and certainly in all cases where it has been held that article 5(4) applies. The Parole Board Rules and the policies applied by the Board in determinate sentence cases also mandate the disclosure, subject to specific exceptions, of the reports it considers.

1.39 When the first edition of this book was written it did not seem in doubt that where article 5(4) was engaged when the Parole Board was considering whether to release a prisoner that there was a right to an oral hearing. As the release of successive categories of life-sentenced prisoners was held to engage article 5(4) the Rules governing hearings were amended to include the right of the prisoner to require the Board to hold an oral hearing.[58]

1.40 This assumption was given compelling support by a succession of decisions of the ECtHR. For example when the ECtHR confirmed that an article 5(4) review was necessary to review the post-tariff release of HMP lifers, it stated:

> The Court is of the view that, in a situation such as that of the applicant, where a substantial term of imprisonment may be at stake and where characteristics pertaining to his personality and level of maturity are of importance in deciding on his dangerousness, Article 5 para 4 requires an oral hearing in the context of an adversarial procedure involving legal representation and the possibility of calling and questioning witnesses.[59]

56 *Weeks v UK* paras 63–68.

57 The Parole Board Rules 1992.

58 PBR 1992 r10; PBR 1997 r10 included the right to an oral hearing for HMP and automatic lifers, and PBR 2004 r12(2) for mandatory lifers and extended sentence prisoners recalled during the extension period.

59 *Hussain and Singh v UK* (1996) 22 EHRR 1 para 60.

1.41 When the ECtHR came to examine the cases of adult mandatory lifers at a time when the Board could not direct their release, it appeared to mandate an oral hearing where article 5(4) was engaged even where there were no disputed facts, and no prospect of release:[60]

> While the Parole Board reviewed the applicant's case in 2001, it did not have any power to order his release and could only make recommendations to the Secretary of State. Nor did any oral hearing take place, with the opportunity to examine or cross-examine witnesses relevant to any allegations that the applicant remained a risk to the public.

1.42 It is further of note that in a parliamentary answer[61] in January 2006, Baroness Ashton of Upholland (then Under-Secretary of State at the Department of Constitutional Affairs) stated that in response to these cases:

> The Government have submitted information to the Committee of Ministers on these provisions, the new Parole Board Rules (under which all life-sentence prisoners will be entitled to insist on an oral hearing), and information on the applicants' personal situations.

1.43 However, it was a case which primarily examined the procedural requirements of fairness under the common law rather than those of article 5(4) which led to a challenge to the accepted view that article 5(4), where the Board is assessing risk, necessitates an oral hearing. Prior to incorporation of the ECHR the common law had been slow to enhance the fairness of parole processes. For example, in *Payne,* when holding that a mandatory lifer was not even entitled to the reasons as to why release was being refused, Lord Denning stated:

> But, so far as I can judge of the matter, I should think that in the interests of the man himself, as a human being facing indefinite detention, it would be better for him to be told the reasons. But, in the interests of society at large, including the due administration of the parole system, it would be best not to give them.[62]

1.44 The justification for what now seems like an astonishing assertion was rooted in the notion of early release being a privilege, not a right, and the spurious assumption that for prisoners to know the reasons for decisions would both inhibit the candour of reports and lead to

60 *Von Bulow v United Kingdom* (Application No 75362/01), 7 January 2004 para 24: in this case the prisoner was in category C conditions and none of the reports before the Board supported release. In *Wynne v United Kingdom (No 2)* (2004) 38 EHRR 42 the prisoner was in a high security prisoner, yet the court's decision finding a breach of article 5(4) referred to a lack of an oral hearing in similar terms.

61 10 January 2006 col WA37.

62 *Payne v Lord Harris of Greenwich and another* [1981] 2 All ER 842.

unmeritorious litigation by prisoners. Nevertheless, the judgment bound the courts for many years in relation to how natural justice was held to apply to parole processes. It took another ten years until a discretionary lifer finally managed to obtain an order to disclose parole reports under common law standards of fairness,[63] by which time the article 5 cases had achieved the same result. *Payne* was eventually overruled when the House of Lords decided that in the tariff setting process for mandatory lifers (which at the time remained an executive decision of the Home Secretary) fairness required disclosure sufficient to make meaningful representations, and also reasons for the decision.[64] In relation to determinate sentence prisoners, the Carlisle Committee Report that led to the changes brought in by the CJA 1991 recommended that there should be disclosure of the dossier and reasons given for decisions and this became practice after the Act came into force in 1992.

1.45 However, the increasing judicial role of the Board, necessitated by the need to carry out article 5(4) compliant reviews, has impacted on how the courts now view the Board's duties to act fairly in accordance with the common law. When two determinate sentence prisoners in the *Smith and West* case challenged the refusal of the Board to hold oral hearings to determine whether they had been correctly recalled, the House of Lords decided there may be entitlement right to an oral hearing in such circumstances, even though there was no possibility of detention in breach of article 5(1).[65] The decision was surprising, as in terms of what the common law requires it marked a significant shift from *Doody*.[66]

1.46 In *Smith and West* the Lords did not decide that common law fairness always required an oral hearing. As the case is now the leading domestic authority on the need for oral hearings in the parole process it is worth quoting all three Lords who delivered opinions. Lord Bingham:[67]

> The common law duty of procedural fairness does not, in my opinion, require the board to hold an oral hearing in every case where a

63 *R v Parole Board, ex p Wilson* [1992] QB 740.

64 *R v Secretary of State for the Home Department, ex p Doody* [1994] 1 AC 531.

65 *R (on the application of Smith) v Parole Board* [2005] UKHL 1 – although the Lords stated that the right was not absolute, the circumstances in which it was considered hearings should be allowed were so wide that it is difficult to see how a hearing cannot be held when requested by the prisoner. Accordingly, the practice adopted after this case was to offer hearings in all cases where an initial paper review did not result in release.

66 See note 64 above.

67 At para 35.

> determinate sentence prisoner resists recall, if he does not decline the offer of such a hearing. But I do not think the duty is as constricted as has hitherto been held and assumed. Even if important facts are not in dispute, they may be open to explanation or mitigation, or may lose some of their significance in the light of other new facts. While the board's task certainly is to assess risk, it may well be greatly assisted in discharging it (one way or the other) by exposure to the prisoner or the questioning of those who have dealt with him. It may often be very difficult to address effective representations without knowing the points which are troubling the decision-maker. The prisoner should have the benefit of a procedure which fairly reflects, on the facts of his particular case, the importance of what is at stake for him, as for society.

Lord Slynn:[68]

> There is no absolute rule that there must be an oral hearing automatically in every case. Where, however, there are issues of fact, or where explanations are put forward to justify actions said to be a breach of licence conditions, or where the officer's assessment needs further probing, fairness may well require that there should be an oral hearing. If there is doubt as to whether the matter can fairly be dealt with on paper then in my view the board should be predisposed in favour of an oral hearing. On any view the applicant should be told that an oral hearing may be possible though it is not automatic; if having been told this the applicant clearly says he does not want an oral hearing then there need not be such a hearing unless the board itself feels exceptionally that fairness requires one.

Lord Hope:[69]

> I agree therefore that the common law test of procedural fairness requires that the board re-examine its approach. A screening system needs to be put in place which identifies those cases where the prisoner seeks to challenge the truth or accuracy of the allegations that led to his recall, or seeks to provide an explanation for them which was not taken into account or was disputed when his recall was recommended by his supervising probation officer. Consideration then needs to be given to the question whether it is necessary to resolve these issues before a final decision is made as to whether or not the prisoner is suitable for release. If it is, an oral hearing should be the norm rather than the exception.

1.47 As noted above (see paras 1.29–1.30) the Lords did not merely hold that common law fairness may necessitate an oral hearing in the

68 At para 50.
69 At para 68.

context of the recall of determinate sentence prisoners. They also held that article 5(4) would be breached if the Board did not hold one where it was required by the common law even if the question it was considering was not capable of determining whether detention was lawful under article 5(1).[70] The *Smith and West* decision was not criticised by the House of Lords in *Black* even though its conclusion on article 5(4) appears to fall precisely into the error identified by Lord Brown, that of saying that article 5(4) is engaged because of the identity of the decision-maker, rather than by the nature of the decision (see para 1.31).

1.48 *Smith and West* established that the common law may not always require an oral hearing, but that where it does the Board will also breach article 5(4) by not holding one. It does not obviously follow, especially in light of the cases referred to above, that where article 5(4) is necessarily engaged that an oral hearing is optional. However, following *Smith and West* the courts have held that the engagement of article 5(4) does not mandate an oral hearing and that the test for whether one is required is the same as that under the common law.[71] This has led to amendments to the Parole Board Rules that for the first time permit the Board to deny oral hearings to life sentenced prisoners at the end of the tariff or minimum term.[72] This change to the Rules has not yet been challenged in the courts, but there is an obvious concern that it conflicts with what the ECtHR has expressed as the minimum requirements of article 5(4) where the Board is assessing whether a prisoner should not be released because of their dangerousness. The Board now has policies on when it will hold oral hearings for both determinate and indeterminate prisoners, which are examined in the appropriate chapters below.

1.49 The change to the Parole Board Rules has obviously been prompted by the Board's inability to deal with the increase in numbers of hearings that it is required to hold. The expediency involved in this should not ignore the insight that in the absence of an oral hearing:

> assumptions based on general knowledge and experience tend to favour the official version as against that which the prisoner wishes to put forward. Denying the prisoner of the opportunity to put forward his own case may lead to a lack of focus on him as an individual. This

70 Lord Bingham at para 37; Lord Hope at para 75.

71 *R (on the application of O'Connell) v Parole Board* [2008] 1 WLR 979 para 21, although the Court of Appeal subsequently overruled the finding that article 5(4) was engaged in the context of this case.

72 Parole Board (Amendment) Rules 2009 SI No 408.

can result in unfairness to him, however much care panel members may take to avoid this.[73]

Independence of the executive

1.50 The ECtHR, even at a time when the Board's powers and procedures were insufficient to meet the requirements of article 5(4), considered that it was sufficiently independent and impartial:

> The Parole Board sits in small panels, each of which in the case of life prisoners includes a High Court judge and a psychiatrist. The manner of the appointment of the Board's members does not, in the Court's opinion, establish a lack of independence on the part of the members. Furthermore, the Court is satisfied that the judge member and the other members of the Board remain wholly independent of the executive and impartial in the performance of their duties.
>
> There remains the question whether the Board presents an appearance of independence, notably to persons whose liberty it considers. On this point, as the Government stated, the functions of the Board do not bring it into contact with officials of the prisons or of the Home Office in such a way as to identify it with the administration of the prison or of the Home Office.[74]

1.51 A subsequent complaint to the ECtHR raising similar issues was rejected at the admissibility stage in 2000.[75] However, domestically concerns grew about the Board's independence and in particular its close relationship with the precise department of the executive whose decisions it had to review. When the Board became an NDPB in 1996 its sponsoring department was the Home Office department responsible for release and recall decisions (this was before the creation of the Ministry of Justice). When the issue of sponsorship was reviewed in 2001, the primary purposes of sponsorship were identified as including:

- providing ministers with advice on the overall efficiency and effectiveness of the Parole Board and its usefulness as an instrument of government policy; and
- monitoring the Board's performance and providing support and advice and, if necessary, imposing sanctions to ensure efficient and effective delivery of required services.[76]

73 *R (on the application of Smith) v Parole Board* [2005] UKHL 1 para 66.

74 *Weeks v UK* (1988) 10 EHRR 293, para 62.

75 *Hirst v UK* (Application No 40787/98), 21 March 2000.

76 *Comprehensive review of parole and lifer processes*, October 2001, para 5.4.3.

1.52 Although the review identified sponsorship as a potential problem in relation to perceived independence, it stated that it was 'unclear how far public or prisoner concerns about the Board's independence are a problem in practice, rather than theory',[77] and the conclusion was that the Board could remain sponsored by a department whose decisions it was required to review. However in 2008 the Court of Appeal in *Brooke* upheld a decision of the Divisional Court that the Board's relationship with its sponsoring department did unlawfully breach its requirement to be independent both in relation to article 5(4) and the common law.[78]

1.53 The Court of Appeal did not consider that sponsorship by a department in the Ministry of Justice itself would be fatal, but that it was not appropriate that the Board should be sponsored by the body responsible for preparing prisoners for release, and whose views on suitability were to be judicially assessed by it. A number of instances led the Board to this conclusion, most importantly:

- in exercising his power to give directions to the Board the Secretary of State had intended to go beyond giving mere guidance about relevant matters, and had sought to direct the Board as to how it should carry out its judicial functions;
- he had also sought to influence the way in which the Board reached decisions by deciding in 2006 that victims, or those with involvement in victim support organisations, should be appointed to the Board as a response to murders committed by two offenders on licence;
- in 2004 there was also improper use of the power to control the Board's budget in order to limit the numbers of interviews it carried out with prisoners as part of the parole process, even though the Board considered that such interviews were necessary; and
- the declared purpose of sponsorship, that the Board should be an 'instrument of government policy' was clearly inappropriate when considering how a court should function.

The Court stated:[79]

> [t]he close working relationship between the board and the unit acting as its sponsor has tended to blur the distinction between the executive role of the former and the judicial role of the latter.

77 Ibid para 5.4.5.

78 *R (on the application of Brooke, O'Connell and Murphy) v Parole Board and the Secretary of State for Justice* [2008] EWCA Civ 29.

79 Ibid para 79.

1.54 The Court of Appeal did not consider that either the method or length of tenure of Parole Board members in themselves were incompatible with due independence as long as the Justice Secretary did not have any significant input into their selection. However the power to terminate a member's appointment for failure to perform their duties would at the least need to be restricted by a procedure to ensure that termination was not without good cause and subject to a fair process.

1.55 The outcome of the case was that sponsorship of the Board was from 1 April 2008, transferred from the National Offender Management Service Agency (NOMS) to the Access to Justice Group in the Ministry of Justice. This group plays no direct part in decision-making in relation to the early release of prisoners.

1.56 The power of the Justice Secretary to issue directions to the Board (see para 1.14 above) had been earlier raised in the *Girling* case.[80] When the procedures to provide discretionary lifers with article 5(4) compliant reviews were introduced in 1992, the Home Secretary accepted that it was not appropriate to issue directions to the Board. This was on the basis that it was the Board's responsibility, in acting as an independent court, to apply the appropriate test for release.

1.57 However, when release procedures for indeterminate sentence prisoners were harmonised in 2004, the Home Secretary's view changed.[81] He issued directions as to matters the Board was required to take into account. This Court of Appeal in *Girling* held that as long as the directions were not instructing the Board as to how to carry out its judicial function, but were limited to guidance on the matters to which, as a matter of law, the Board is in any event required to have regard, then the use of the power was not objectionable. The only direction found by the Court of Appeal to breach this requirement was where the directions purported to restate in different language the statutory test for release to be applied by the Board. This was the instance later relied on in *Brooke* to demonstrate that the Secretary of State through his sponsoring department had gone too far in issuing directions.[82]

80 *Girling v Secretary of State for the Home Department and Parole Board* [2006] EWCA Civ 1779.

81 Perhaps in response to the Comprehensive Review of Parole and Lifer Processes which reported in 2001, which suggested that it would not be unlawful for directions to be issued in relation to the release of lifers.

82 *Girling* (see note 80 above) at para 31. Notwithstanding this, the relevant directions, those issued in August 2004 relating to the release of life sentence prisoners, still include the criticised part, namely para 4 – see appendix F.

Summary of the Board's current functions

1.58 The Board now carries out the following functions, which are examined in greater detail in subsequent chapters:

- It makes binding decisions as to whether all classes of indeterminate sentenced prisoners should be released on licence. The Board will not release such prisoners without holding an oral hearing; but where it appears there is no prospect of a release decision it may decline to hold an oral hearing. Article 5(4) of the Convention is engaged in such decisions.
- It makes binding decisions as to the re-release of recalled indeterminate sentenced prisoners who make representations against recall. Such decisions will be made at an oral hearing. Article 5(4) is engaged in such decisions.
- It makes recommendations to the Justice Secretary as to whether indeterminate sentence prisoners should be transferred to open conditions as a prelude to release. Article 5(4) is not engaged, but the Board will not make a positive recommendation without an oral hearing.
- In relation to the initial release of determinate sentence prisoners, the Board's role is limited to making decisions in relation to prisoners serving sentences of four or more years for specified sexual or violent offences[83] committed prior to 4 April 2005. All other determinate sentence prisoners are released automatically on licence. The Board's decisions are binding except for prisoners serving 15 years or more where the Justice Secretary can decide to reject them (although the Coroners and Justice Act 2009 s145 removes this power to veto, but is not yet in force). In these cases the Parole Board will normally hold an oral hearing for under 18-year-olds. Otherwise the Board will hold an oral hearing only where it assesses that this is necessary to fairly make its decision. Article 5(4) is not engaged.
- Where determinate sentence prisoners are recalled the Board makes binding decisions as to whether they should be released. Such decisions are initially made on the papers and if the prisoner is unhappy with the outcome they can make representations that an oral hearing should be held. The Board will decide whether fairness requires this according to the principles set out in *Smith and West* (see para 1.46 above). Article 5(4) is engaged.

83 Those contained in CJA 2003 Sch 15.

- For those serving extended sentences for offences committed before 4 April 2005, the Board only makes decisions as to initial release where the custodial term is four or more years for a specified sexual or violent offence.[84] For extended sentences imposed after that date but before 14 July 2008 the Board makes a binding decision on initial release. An oral hearing will only be held in such cases where the prisoner is under 18 or where the Board considers fairness requires it. For extended sentences imposed on or after 14 July 2008 initial release is now automatic. Article 5(4) is not engaged.
- Where extended sentence prisoners are recalled the Board makes a binding decision as to whether they should be released. This will be normally be at an oral hearing. Article 5(4) is engaged.
- The Board is also consulted by the Justice Secretary where there is time as to whether prisoners, serving both determinate and indeterminate sentences, should be released on compassionate grounds. Article 5(4) is not engaged, but article 8 may be (see further chapter 12).

Future of the Parole Board

1.59 Developments such as challenges to the Board's independence, and its current inability to deal with its case-load due to insufficient resources, and most particularly a lack of judicial members has resulted in debate as to whether it is right that it should continue with its present constitution. A detailed consultation paper was issued by the Ministry of Justice in July 2009.[85] The key issue the paper addresses is whether, in its current form, the Board is capable of dealing with the demands created by its transformation from an advisory body, to a court making binding judicial decisions. In summary the options covered in the consultation are:[86]

- leaving existing sponsorship arrangements as they are, or transferring sponsorship of the Parole Board to Her Majesty's Court Service (HMCS) or the Tribunals Service;
- integrating the Parole Board fully into the Courts Service;
- integrating the Parole Board fully into the Tribunals Service.

84 CJA 2003 Sch 15.

85 www.justice.gov.uk/consultations/docs/future-parole-board-consultation.pdf.

86 Ibid, para 8 of the Executive Summary.

1.60 The organisation Justice has recommended that the Board in its current form is abolished, and a Parole Tribunal established within the Tribunal Service, which would also allow for an appeal to a dedicated chamber within the Upper Tier.[87] While there is emerging consensus that the Board cannot remain with its current constitution, the other option would be to establish it as a specialist court within the Courts Service. This would have the advantage of giving the Board a status equal to the sentencing court, whose decision on risk it will be revisiting. It may also ensure better availability of judicial members. Whichever option is pursued there will be an opportunity to radically overhaul its procedures to include, for example, sanctions for breaches of its directions, and the possibility of issuing of witness summonses.

87 *A new parole system for England and Wales*, Justice, October 2009.

CHAPTER 2

Other agencies involved in the parole process

2.1 Beyond the individual prisoner and the Parole Board there are a number of other agencies involved in the policy, administration and decision-making in parole processes.

The Ministry of Justice

2.2 The Ministry of Justice was created in May 2007. The Secretary of State for Justice then took over from the Home Secretary the various statutory responsibilities in respect of prisons and probation. Also transferred were the statutory powers and duties contained in the various Criminal Justice Acts relating to the referral of prisoners' cases to the Parole Board, and to the release and recall of prisoners. References to the 'Secretary of State' in this book therefore refer to the Justice Secretary unless stated otherwise. In practice the Secretary of State's powers are delegated to officials in the NOMS agency (see below).

The National Offender Management Service Agency

2.3 The National Offender Management Service Agency (NOMS)[1] is an agency within the Ministry of Justice that now has responsibility for the management of both the Prison and Probation Services. It was created in 2004 following the publication of the Carter Review *Managing offenders, reducing crime*, which recommended greater integration between the agencies dealing with offenders. The creation of NOMS has not been without criticism, as there was little consultation before the effective merger of the services was carried out, and there are also concerns that the move was made as a means of facilitating the privatisation of services (the principle of 'contestability'). The NOMS agency operates under a framework document that was last issued in July 2008.[2]

2.4 Recent developments have streamlined the management of the Prison and Probation Services so that the NOMS Director General is responsible for both and they now share the same headquarters. Since April 2009 the Director General in turn manages regional

1 www.noms.justice.gov.uk.

2 www.justice.gov.uk/noms-agency-framework.pdf.

Directors of Offender Management (DOMS) who are responsible for the provision of both prison and probation services in their respective areas. From 1 August 2009 there has been a single system of issuing policy guidance throughout NOMS. NOMS now issues central policy guidance in the form of agency instructions ('AIs').[3]

The Public Protection Casework Section

2.5 The Public Protection Casework Section (PPCS) is part of the Public Protection Unit, the department within NOMS that now has responsibility for the Secretary of State's functions in relation to the release and recall of prisoners. It has overall responsibility for parole policy and procedures. However it is no longer the sponsoring body of the Parole Board (see para 1.12). Previously there were separate departments that dealt with indeterminate and determinate prisoners. The PPCS now deals with both. Therefore in indeterminate cases it has responsibility for: referring cases to the Parole Board; presenting the Secretary of State's view to the Board; making decisions as to whether to accept recommendations that prisoners are transferred to open conditions; implementing release directions and preparing the licence; and making decisions as to recall.

2.6 In relation to determinate sentence cases dealt with by the Board the PPCS similarly makes decisions on release where the Secretary of State has the final say (that is in cases where the prisoner is serving a sentence of 15 years or more for an offence committed before 4 April 2005). It makes decisions as to whether determinate prisoners should be recalled and has casework responsibility for recall hearings.

The Prison Service

2.7 The Prison Service is a separate executive agency, managed by the NOMS agency Director General. The Prison Service issues policy guidance in the form of prison service instructions (PSIs) and prison service orders (PSOs). Individual prisons are subject to supervision by DOMs and Prison Service headquarters retains policy responsibility for matters such as offending behaviour programmes and management of category A prisoners.

3 AI 1/2009.

2.8 The governor of the prison holding the prisoner retains responsibility for issuing the licence in relation to determinate sentence prisoners. Prisons will also have offender management units (OMU). These will contain staff responsible for collating reports for parole reviews and disclosing the dossier to the prisoner and forwarding it to the Board.

2.9 Individual prisons have responsibility for the transfer of life sentence prisoners (except where the move involves category A prisoners, or is a move to open conditions that can only be authorised by PPCS following a Parole Board recommendation). Contact details for all prisons in England and Wales can be found on the Prison Service website, as can copies of most PSIs and PSOs.[4]

The Probation Service

2.10 The Probation Service is in transition. Although the Probation Service is managed under the NOMS agency, it is a statutory body. The National Probation Service was created by the Criminal Justice and Court Services Act (CJCSA) 2000. This statutory framework divided the service into local probation boards[5] that cover the same geographical area as the different police areas. The aim of this was to better facilitate multi-agency working such as that under the MAPPA (see para 2.17) arrangements (see below). However the local probation boards are now in the process of being replaced with 'probation trusts' created under the Offender Management Act (OMA) 2007. Under the Act the 'probation purposes' for which the Secretary of State has ultimate responsibility, include 'the supervision and rehabilitation of persons charged with or convicted of offences'.[6] Although the 'probation purposes' include providing accommodation in probation hostels (known as 'approved premises') this is a target duty. Individual prisoners cannot therefore insist on being provided with a place by the Probation Service if suitable accommodation is not available.[7]

2.11 Probation trusts created by the Offender Management Act have statutory power to contract the provision of probation services from the private or voluntary sector.[8] The aim is to complete the transfer of

4 See www.hmprisonservice.gov.uk/prisoninformation.

5 CJCSA 2000 s4.

6 OMA 2007 s1(1)(c).

7 *R (on the application of Irving) v London Probation Board* [2005] EWHC 605 (Admin).

8 OMA 2007 s5(3).

the remaining 34 into trusts by April 2010. There remains a Director of Probation in NOMS who reports to the Director General. The National Probation Service issues central policy guidance in the form of probation instructions ('PIs', these were formally known as 'probation circulars').[9] Probation officers also act under Offender Management National Standards (issued under OMA 2007 s7 – last issued in 2007).

2.12 Under the Offender Management Model ('OMM') prisoners will have allocated to them an offender manager ('OM': this role has replaced that of the 'home probation officer'). The OM will be a probation officer based in the prisoner's local probation area whose function is to manage the sentence from imposition until the sentence expiry date. The OM will therefore be responsible for developing the sentence plan, drafting key reports such as those required in the parole process, and also enforcing the licence (recommending recall where considered necessary). Individual prisons also have probation staff seconded from the Probation Service who also will contribute to sentence planning, the delivery of offending behaviour courses or treatment, and the provision of reports for parole or other processes. Although the OMM has not explicitly been extended to all life sentence prisoners, its terminology is now commonly used in respect of all parole reviews

2.13 Under 18-year-olds are supervised by officers from youth offending teams ('YOTs'), which local authorities are required to set up in their areas.[10]

Victims

2.14 There is a statutory duty on probation boards and trusts to ascertain whether victims of crimes, where the offender receives a sentence of 12 or more months for a sexual or violent offence, wish to make representations to the courts or the Parole Board as to whether a prisoner should be subject to any particular licence conditions on release, and further whether they want to receive information about licence conditions actually imposed,[11] If the victim does wish to make such representations it is the duty of the probation board or trust to

9 PI 1/2009. They are available at the Probation Service website www.probation.homeoffice.gov.uk/output/page31.asp.

10 Crime and Disorder Act 1998.

11 Domestic Violence, Crime and Victims Act (DVCVA) 2004 s35.

ensure that they are forwarded to the court or the Parole Board.[12] A detailed Code of Practice relating to the treatment of victims in the criminal justice system has been in force since 2006[13] giving guidance on these powers.[14]

2.15 The degree to which victims should be involved in the parole process has raised some controversy. The Secretary of State's attempt to require the Board to recruit victim members contributed to the Court of Appeal's decision that it was insufficiently independent at the time its sponsoring department was in NOMS.[15] The Parole Board now has a practice guide to victim participation in parole hearings.[16] This adopts a definition of victim as 'someone who was harmed or who has suffered physical or emotional damage as a result of the offence or offences'. The policy is that victims can put a written victim personal statement ('VPS') to the Board when it is considering whether to release prisoners. The Probation Service has responsibility for assisting the victim in preparation of the VPS. The statement should normally be disclosed to the prisoner (subject to the general rules on witholding information – see paras 10.45 and 10.51). At an oral hearing the victim can ask to present the VPS themselves or have it read to the panel. If the victim attends they will be asked to leave once they have read the statement.

2.16 The policy states that those preparing a VPS should

> bear in mind that the Parole Board's primary role is to protect the public by risk assessing prisoners to decide whether or not they can be safely released into the community. Victim personal statements should therefore contain information that helps the Board assess the current risk the offender presents.

Whilst victim concerns over potential contact with released prisoners should clearly inform potential licence conditions, it is unclear in what circumstances victims will have relevant information to give regarding the prisoner's current risk to the public. The concern is that victims will almost inevitably believe that they have some degree of say over whether a prisoner should be released, when the Board would be acting unlawfully if they did so.

12 DVCVA 2004 s35(6).

13 Issued under DVCVA 2004 s32.

14 See www.homeoffice.gov.uk/documents/victims-code-of-practice

15 See para 1.53.

16 www.paroleboard.gov.uk/victims_and_families/practice_guide_on_victim_participation/

Multi-agency Public Protection Arrangements

2.17 There is a statutory duty for area chief police officers, local probation boards or trusts and the Prison Service to establish arrangements to assess the risks posed by serious sexual and violent offenders.[17] These arrangements are known as Multi-Agency Public Protection Arrangements ('MAPPA'). The Secretary of State has, through the Public Protection Unit at NOMS, issued statutory guidance under s325(8) of the CJA 2003 on how the various bodies are to exercise their functions under their MAPPA functions. The third version of the MAPPA guidance was issued in 2009.[18] The Prison Service has also issued a Public Protection Manual which also gives guidance on MAPPA.[19]

2.18 The statutory framework of MAPPA places duties on the 'responsible authority' ('RA'), which collectively consists of the police, prison and probation services.[20] The relevant RA will be determined by the location of the prisoner's offender manager.[21] Other public bodies have a duty to co-operate with the RA[22] including local social services departments, NHS trusts, YOTs, local authority housing and education departments, and social landlords. The MAPPA guidance includes sections on when MAPPA agencies will share and disclose information regarding offenders.[23]

2.19 The purpose of MAPPA is to facilitate multi-agency working in order to devise and implement risk management plans for specific categories of sexual and violent offenders.[24] There is a specific electronic database that holds details of all MAPPA-managed offenders, and onto which MAPPA meeting minutes are entered. This is the Violent and Sexual Offenders Register, or ViSOR.[25] The relationship between MAPPA meetings and parole hearings is discussed in later chapters.

17 CJA 2003 ss325–326.

18 www.probation.homeoffice.gov.uk/files/pdf/MAPPA%20Guidance%202007%20v2.0.pdf.

19 This was last updated in 2009 – the Manual has replaced PSO 4745.

20 CJA 2003 s325(1).

21 MAPPA Guidance, para 4.19.

22 CJA 2003 s325(3).

23 Sections 5 and 6.

24 See MAPPA Guidance, para 1.2.

25 MAPPA Guidance, para 2.5. ViSOR is available to all police, probation and prison services.

2.20 MAPPA cover three categories of offender:[26]

- Category 1 offenders – registered sexual offenders. This group are those who have been convicted or cautioned of a sexual offence and have therefore become subject to the statutory registration requirements under Part 2 of the Sexual Offences Act 2003.
- Category 2 offenders – violent and other sexual offenders. In short this category includes violent offenders and other sexual offenders who receive a sentence of imprisonment of 12 months or more (including extended and indeterminate sentences) for specified offences.[27]
- Category 3 offenders – other dangerous offenders. This category is comprised of offenders, not in either category 1 or 2 but who are considered by the responsible authority to pose a risk of serious harm to the public which requires active inter-agency management.

2.21 Each MAPPA area then applies three levels of management of relevant offenders:[28]

- Level 1 – ordinary agency management. This is the level used in cases where the risks posed by the offender can be managed by the agency responsible for supervision/case management of the offender (such as the Probation Service). Category 3 cases cannot by their nature be managed at this level. Other agencies might be involved but referral to a MAPP meeting is not required.
- Level 2 – active multi-agency management. Cases should be managed at level 2 where the offender:
  - is assessed under OASys (or ASSET) (see para 4.24 below) as being high risk of causing serious harm;
  - requires active involvement and co-ordination of interventions from other agencies to manage the presenting risks of harm; or
  - has been previously managed at level 3 and the seriousness of risk has diminished, and/or the complexity of the multi-agency management of the risks have been brokered, and a RMP for level 2 has been firmly established.

26 MAPPA Guidance, Section 4.

27 Those contained in CJA 2003 Sch 15.

28 MAPPA Guidance, Section 10 and the Prison Service Public Protection Manual, PC 15/2006, Section 2.

- Level 3 – active multi-agency management. The criteria for referring a case to a level 3 MAPP meeting are where the offender:
  - is assessed under OASys (or ASSET) as being a high or very high risk of causing serious harm; and
  - presents risks that can only be managed by a plan that requires close co-operation at a senior level due to the complexity of the case and/or because of the unusual resource commitments it requires; or
  - although not assessed as a high or very high risk, there is a high likelihood of media scrutiny and/or public interest in the management of the case and there is a need to ensure that public confidence in the criminal justice system is maintained.

2.22 Accordingly it is only for level 2 and 3 cases that regular MAPP meetings are held in order to make decisions as to risk, and the content of any RMP. For serving prisoners the guidance states that the appropriate MAPPA level should be set six months before the anticipated release date, or immediately if the release date is less than six months ahead.[29] It will be for the offender manager initially to determine the prisoner's level in consultation with other relevant agencies.

29 Public Protection Manual, para 3.1.

CHAPTER 3

Public funding

3.1 Prison law as a category is funded by the Legal Services Commission (LSC) as part of the Criminal Defence Service (CDS) that was established together with the Community Legal Service (CLS) by the Access to Justice Act (AJA) 1999.[1] Firms can have either a general criminal contract (to cover police station advice and criminal defence work) under which they can take on prison law cases, or a 'stand-alone' prison law contract if the firm does not undertake criminal defence work. For a 'stand-alone' contract the supervisor standard includes having carried out 350 hours prison law work in each of the preceding three years.[2]

3.2 Extensive consultations have been conducted by the LSC with a view to introducing a new specialist prison law contract as from June 2010. Additionally, the Ministry of Justice has commenced a further review of public funding for prison work and so there are likely to be major changes to the funding regime as set out in this book. The position as at 30 October 2010 is addressed in detail and even though that regime is unlikely to remain in existence beyond June 2010, it still provides some guidance on the likely parameters of the new regulations in relation to matters such as instructing counsel and the sufficient benefit test.

The future funding proposals

3.3 The proposals for future public finding of prison law work are that from June 2010:

- prison law will become a specialist stand-alone contract rather than being part of the general criminal contract;
- a stricter supervisor standard will be put in place for practitioners to obtain a prison law contract requiring the supervisor to practice in prison law for 350 hours a year;
- hourly rates will be replaced by fixed or standard fees;
- future methods of service delivery should include assessing the viability of duty solicitor and telephone advice schemes.

3.4 The document published by the LSC at the close of the consultation[3] confirmed that three different levels of funding will be available for the different prison law cases. For advice and assistance cases there

1 AJA s12.

2 See LSC Manual, 2B-138.

3 https://consult.legalservices.gov.uk/inovem/gf2.ti/f/157314/2828453.1/pdf/-/prison_law_responseIA_150709%20%20793kb.pdf.

will be a fixed fee, with an escape clause at three times the fixed fee. For advocacy assistance at disciplinary hearings and parole hearings there will be a standard lower and standard upper fee, also with escape clauses. As it is intended to deal with more parole cases by way of paper reviews without an oral hearing, these will remain as advice and assistance cases and so will attract only the smaller fixed fees.

3.5 The proposed fee rates are:

Advice and assistance		
	Including VAT	*Excluding VAT*
Fixed fee	£253	£220
Escape limit	£759	£660
Disciplinary hearings		
Standard lower fee	£257	£223.48
Lower fee limit	£450	£391.30
Standard higher fee	£711	£618.26
Escape limit	£2,132	£1,853.91
Parole hearings		
Standard lower fee	£551	£479.13
Lower fee limit	£1,177	£1,023.48
Standard higher fee	£1,833	£1,593.91
Escape limit	£5,498	£4,780.87

3.6 Cases that reach the escape limits in the different categories will be paid at the current national hourly (out of London) rate. However, in keeping with other fixed and standard fee regimes, although time spent waiting can be counted towards meeting the exceptional escape limits, travel time will not as this catered for in the fixed fee. Once the exceptional case escape limit has been reached, however, travel time is then included in the final costs at hourly rates. Disbursements will cover the same range of activities as previously, for example travel costs and experts' reports. Disbursements above £500 will need prior authority from the LSC.

3.7 The situation is further complicated by the subsequent Ministry of Justice consultation on the refocusing of public funding on priority cases. [4] The proposals for prison law funding in this consultation appear to have been a direct ministerial response to those aspects of

4 www.justice.gov.uk/consultations/legal-aid-refocusing-priority-cases.htm.

the LSC consultation that had achieved an outcome contrary to the preferred path of removing whole swathes of prisoners' legal issues from the scope of public funding, in particular 'treatment' issues. The consultation does not define what treatment matters are, but it would appear that this will include anything that is not parole, prison discipline or related to sentence calculation and categorisation. This would potentially encompass matters as diverse as all issues relating to contact with outside world through letters, visits and telephone calls, access to the courts, searching, complaints about discrimination and segregation, and CSC decisions.

3.8 Public funding for treatment issues will only be available within the Community Legal Service through the actions against the police and public law contracts, thereby seeking to limit any public funding to cases where there is a potential claim for damages or judicial review. In addition, it is proposed that prisoners will only be able to obtain publicly funded advice once the internal complaints procedures have been utilised. These are envisaged to include, the formal complaints process; the independent monitoring boards and the Prisons and Probation Ombudsman.

Scope of prison law

3.9 Regulation 4 of the Criminal Defence Service (General) (No 2) Regulations 2001[5] confirms that the LSC will provide funding, which in practice is provided through contracts with approved firms, to any individual who:

> (f) requires advice and assistance regarding his treatment or discipline in prison (other than in respect of actual or contemplated proceedings regarding personal injury, death or damage to property);
> (g) is the subject of proceedings before the Parole Board;
> (h) requires advice and assistance regarding representations to the Home Office in relation to a mandatory life sentence or other parole review; ...

3.10 The general criminal contract (GCC), by which individual firms are bound by when carrying out work under the CDS, determines the circumstances in which advice and assistance and advocacy assistance can be given. This[6] is now somewhat outdated as the specifica-

5 SI No 1437.

6 See Contract Specification, Part A 5.2.

tion has not managed to keep up with the changes in the law, such as the harmonisation of early release procedures for lifers. However, the specification explicitly permits advice and assistance and advocacy assistance to be provided to prisoners within all Parole Board procedures.

3.11 The current eligibility limits set out on the CDS Keycard No 44a, issued in April 2008, are:

- Advocacy assistance is available where weekly disposable income does not exceed £209 and disposable capital does not exceed £3,000 (for those with no dependants; £3,335 for those with one dependant, £3,535 for those with two dependants with a £100 increase in the limit for each further dependant).
- Advice and assistance is available where weekly disposable income does not exceed £99 and disposable capital does not exceed £1,000 (for those with no dependants; £1,335 for those with one dependant, £1,535 for those with two dependants with a £100 increase in the limit for each further dependant).

3.12 Evidence of capital is accepted as being the prisoner's certification by signing the form. In terms of income, prisoners will not be able to supply pay slips (as prison work is not contractual) or proof of benefits (not being eligible), and so usually the only evidence of what income they are receiving will be what they certify on the CDS 2 or 3.[7]

3.13 Although prisoners are separated from their spouses/partners by the fact of imprisonment, this does not necessarily prevent the aggregation of means. Regulations require the aggregation of the means of the prisoner and his/her partner (defined as 'a person with whom the person concerned lives as a couple, and includes a person with whom the person concerned is not living but from whom he is not living separate and apart'),[8] unless the partner has a contrary interest in the matter or where 'in all the circumstances of the case it would be inequitable or impractical to do so'.[9] The guidance from the LSC on this issue confirms that the fact that one partner is in prison does not mean that the couple are living 'separate and apart'. For this definition to be satisfied there must be a breakdown in the relationship, so at least one of them needs to regard it as at an end.[10] Prisoners serving long or life sentences may have someone with whom they intend

7 Contract Specification, Part B 2.6.

8 Criminal Defence Service (General) (No 2) Regulations 2001 Sch 1 para 1.

9 Criminal Defence Service (General) (No 2) Regulations 2001 Sch 1 para 6.

10 LSC Manual 4E-004.

to live eventually, but might be required to reside in a hostel rather than a home address on release. In these circumstances there is a strong argument that they should not be treated as having a partner for the purpose of aggregation of means.

Advice and assistance

3.14 This is the kind of funding that will be used where there is either no oral hearing, or where it is unclear at the initial stages of a case whether there will be one. The forms that must be completed are CDS 1 and CDS 2. The forms can be completed by post as the solicitor can exercise a devolved power to accept a postal application where there is 'good reason' to do so,[11] which the guidance in the contract states will include where the client is in prison. Similarly a claim for telephone advice prior to the signing of the form can be claimed for where there is good reason.[12]

3.15 As with other kinds of CDS advice and assistance, there is a sufficient benefit test:

> Advice and Assistance may only be provided on legal issues concerning English law and where there is sufficient benefit to the Client, having regard to the circumstances of the Matter, including the personal circumstances of the Client, to justify work or further work being carried out.[13]

3.16 The payment rates for advice and assistance are:[14]

	National	*London*
Preparation and attendance	£46.90 per hour	£49.70 per hour
Travel and waiting	£26.30 per hour	£26.30 per hour
Letters and phone calls	£3.70 per item	£3.85 per item

3.17 The upper limit of the amount of work that can be undertaken without applying for an extension is £300.[15] Beyond this limit, prior authority to carry out further work can be applied for from the relevant area office on form CDS 5. If authority is granted further work 'actually

11 Contract Specification, Part B 2.1.
12 Contract Specification, Part B 2.3.
13 See Contract Specification, Parts A 5.3 and Part B 2.5.
14 See Contract Specification, Part E 2.1.
15 Contract Specification, Part B 5.5.

and reasonable carried out in accordance with the Sufficient Benefit test' can be claimed for up to the maximum agreed extension.[16]

3.18 As noted above, a case may start as an advice and assistance matter at a stage at which it is unclear as to whether there will be an oral hearing (for example, where representations are made to the single member in the ICM process for lifers), but then proceed to an oral hearing. In these circumstances the matter proceeds as a single case but the solicitor can grant advocacy assistance as long as the applicable benefit test is met (see below), and the limit on the work that can be carried out will be the higher of either the initial advocacy assistance limit, or any extension to the advice and assistance limit obtained on CDS 5. When the matter concludes, it should be reported as an advocacy assistance matter and all work can be claimed at advocacy assistance rates. This is so even where the Parole Board decides to convene an oral hearing but that hearing does not subsequently take place, provided that the relevant qualifying criteria were met.[17]

Advocacy assistance

3.19 This is the type of public funding used in relation to the preparation for, and advocacy at, oral hearings. The forms that have to be used are CDS 1 and CDS 3, although if there has already been provision of advice and assistance in the matter (see above) only a CDS 3 needs to be signed by the client. The solicitor can then grant advocacy assistance under devolved powers. As with advice and assistance, it is possible to accept a postal application for advocacy assistance where there is good reason and to claim for prior telephone advice.[18]

3.20 In relation to Parole Board applications and hearings, the applicable merits test is that advocacy assistance may not be provided if 'it appears unreasonable that approval should be granted in the particular circumstances of the case'.[19] This is clearly not dependent on the prospects of success, which reflects the fact that Parole Board hearings are the way in which the state is satisfying the duty to have detention based on a perceived risk to the public reviewed in accordance with article 5 of the European Convention on Human Rights

16 Contract Specification, Part B 2.8.

17 See guidance in *Focus* on CDS LSC, issue 11, April 2003.

18 Contract Specification, Part B 4.1.

19 Contract Specification, Part B 4.3.

(ECHR). There may also be many reasons that it may be in the interests of the prisoner for representation to be provided where there is no prospect of release.

3.21 The payment rates for work carried out as advocacy assistance are:[20]

	National	*London*
Preparation and attendance	£56.15 per hour	£60.00 per hour
Advocacy	£68.25 per hour	£68.25 per hour
Travel and waiting	£26.30 per hour	£26.30 per hour
Letters and phone calls	£4.05 per item	£4.05 per item

3.22 The upper limit of the amount of work that can be undertaken without applying for an extension is £1,500.[21] As with advice and assistance, beyond this limit, prior authority on form CDS 5 can be applied for from the relevant area office, and the same rules as for advice and assistance apply for claiming for work carried out under an extension. Extensions will nearly always be needed where an expert report – for example, from an independent psychologist – is obtained, especially where the expert is to attend the hearing to give evidence.

3.23 Counsel can be instructed to represent the prisoner at the hearing under devolved powers, although counsel can only be paid at the same rates that apply to solicitors.[22] If counsel is instructed, the contract specification states that the solicitor cannot claim for any time spent at, or travelling to and from, the hearing to accompany counsel (although the LSC have conceded that there may be very exceptional cases where payment in these circumstances would be appropriate – where, for example, this might be necessary for 'equality of arms'; however, prior authority for this should be sought).

Limits on allowed work

3.24 Unlike with police station or criminal defence work in the courts, there is very little guidance on what the LSC will consider as an appropriate amount of time for specified units of work (the contract specification contains no guidance on specific units of work in relation

20 Contract Specification, Part E 5.2.
21 Contract Specification, Part B 5.5.
22 Contract Specification, Part B 4.8.

to parole applications or hearings). Clearly it is extremely important to ensure that attendances on the file justify the amount of time recorded for any work claimed for.[23]

3.25 In relation to travel time to visit prisoners, the contract suggests that travel time of up to three hours one way may be justified to visit a prisoner if the solicitor is already acting and either:

- there is no other local contactor available (including, if necessary, at short notice); or
- the client's problem is so specialised that, in the solicitor's reasonable view, there is no more local contractor with the expertise to deal with the case; or
- the solicitor has significant previous knowledge of the case or dealings with the client in relation to the issues raised by the case so as to justify renewed involvement even though the client is at a distance.[24]

Judicial review

3.26 Public funding for judicial review applications arising from any matter within the prison law category can be carried out as associated CLS work under crime contracts.[25] Initial work can be carried out as legal help, but public funding certificates need to be applied for to issue judicial review claims on form CLS App 1 and the appropriate means form (usually MEANS 1 as the prisoner will not be on benefits). Financial eligibility for full representation under the CLS is more complicated (as certificates can be granted subject to contributions). However, a prisoner with disposable capital of £8,000 or below and disposable income of less than £300 will be financially eligible with no contribution.

3.27 The merits test is set out in part 7 of the Funding Code. Full representation may be refused if the prospects of successfully obtaining the result sought are poor or unclear. If the prospects of success are borderline, funding will be refused unless there is a significant wider public interest, or overwhelming importance to the client, or significant human rights issues in the case.[26] Furthermore, even where the

23 See LSC Manual 4H-019.
24 Contract Specification, Part B 7.9.
25 Contract Specification, Part F 1.1.
26 Funding Code, para 7.4.5.

prospects of success are good, in terms of cost benefit analysis the likely benefits of the proceedings should justify the costs, having regard to the prospects of success and all other circumstances.[27]

27 Funding Code, para 7.4.6.

CHAPTER 4

Assessment of risk

continued

Introduction

4.1 The Parole Board is required to undertake a risk assessment in each case that it considers. Indeed, the task of evaluating and assessing risk is the key to the entire review process. The Board's duty was described in the following manner in one case:

> assessing a risk is not the same as reaching a conclusion about a factual event. A risk, as Lord Diplock observed,[1] is a noumenon. If I may have the temerity to amplify, a noumenon is the opposite of a phenomenon, it is an object of intellectual intuition, not something which may be observed.[2]

4.2 A fuller discussion of the legal issues around the appropriate test for release and the manner in which the Board must approach that test follows in chapter 9. This section aims to explore the methods by which the Board will seek to arrive at an assessment of risk.

An overview of risk assessment[3]

4.3 There is no empirically tested, scientific method of assessing risk and there is no definitive psychological consensus on how risk can be controlled and managed. However, since the introduction of the sex offenders treatment programme in the 1990s, the Prison Service and the Parole Board have placed increasing reliance on the use of offending behaviour programmes based on a cognitive behavioural treatment model as the primary tool for reducing risk in people with criminal convictions. The number of programmes has proliferated and shows no sign of decreasing. In order for these programmes to be targeted effectively, there has been a corresponding increase in the use of risk assessment tools that seek to identify areas of criminogenic need, or risk factors, and then to assess whether these have been reduced when a programme has been undertaken.

1 See *Attorney-General v English* [1983] 1 AC 116.

2 *R (on the application of Hirst) v Parole Board and Home Secretary* [2002] EWHC 1592 (Admin) para 83.

3 Most of the information in this section is taken from Hazel Kemshall, *Risk management of serious and violent offenders*, 2002, prepared for the Scottish Executive and available on their website; Hazel Kemshall, *Risk assessment and management of known sexual and violent offenders*, Home Office Police Research series, Paper 140, 2001; and Harper and Chitty (eds) *The impact of corrections on re-offending: a review of what works*, Home Office Research Study 291, 2005.

4.4 As the Prison Service's reliance on this approach to identifying and reducing offending behaviour has become almost absolute, prisoners are increasingly concerned that the offending behaviour programmes run by the Prison Service are untested, ineffective or that they are based largely upon evidence obtained from the US and Canada where offending behaviour programmes are delivered in a different manner and environment. These arguments often have validity and it will usually be possible to find reputable psychologists who support these views. For example, the research findings that the main thinking skills programmes run by the Probation Service appeared to have the effect of increasing reoffending rates[4] received a great deal of media coverage.

4.5 However, it is mistaken to assume that the decision taken by the Prison Service to make use of risk assessment tools and of cognitive offending behaviour programmes as the key intervention to achieve risk reduction does not have a respectable academic and well-researched basis. Meta-analyses of risk assessment tools have indicated that structured methods of predicting future behaviour tend to be more accurate than relying on clinical judgment.[5] One Home Office study provides an overview of the difficulties that arise in researching and monitoring the effectiveness of these programmes – not least due to the lack of reliable long-term evidence from this country – but concludes that:

> International evidence from systematic reviews of practice on reducing re-offending tends to support the use of cognitive-behavioural offending programmes and interventions with offenders.[6]

4.6 The current policy has been made with the full knowledge that despite the 'robust' evidence from around the world about the effectiveness of these programmes, 'in Britain the evidence is mixed and limited'.[7] The aim of the policy is to draw on the international evidence and domestic research to try to ensure that interventions and programmes can be more effective in identifying and targeting the needs of individuals. Interestingly, as more and more studies are conducted, the evidence appears to be less than clear. Recent studies for the Ministry of Justice have shown a still emerging picture of what 'works'. For example, a study following released prisoners over a period of

4 Harper and Chitty, pxiii.

5 Simon, J, 'Reversal of fortune: the resurgence of individual risk assessment' in 1 *Criminal Justice Annual Review of Law and Science*, 2005, pp397–421.

6 Harper and Chitty, pxii.

7 Harper and Chitty, p77.

12 months showed that receiving family visits, having contact with a probation officer and completing a victim awareness programme had a positive impact on reducing reoffending, whereas undertaking offending behaviour and drug programmes did not.[8] As it is accepted that risk assessment is 'highly fallible', the emphasis has tended to focus on whether it is defensible, being the extent to which decisions can be considered reasonable based on an understanding and evaluation of decisions where there has been a negative outcome.[9]

4.7 As risk assessment can never be truly scientific, the policy approach adopted by the Prison Service is ultimately political and the prevalent political theory is that the management of dangerous offenders should be undertaken through the 'precautionary principle', an approach that requires any possible risk of harm to be avoided; 'unambiguous' evidence of risk is therefore not required before pursuing a course of action designed to ensure public safety. Instead, the emphasis is upon making defensible decisions in relation to risk assessment.[10] Risk assessment and risk management are now considered to be the core tasks of NOMS and the Prison Service and this includes a requirement to address risky behaviour through intervention programmes.[11] The difficulty with this approach to risk assessment is that it can be never-ending, with the ever-present possibility that new risk factors will be uncovered or better interventions devised. In cases where there is uncertainty about the existence of a risk or the extent to which it has diminished, the default position will be one of caution. Indeed, NOMS is quite clear that when seeking to balance the tension between the rights of a prisoner to a fresh start after release against the rights of the wider public to be protected from harm '[t]he general principle is that public and victim protection should outweigh offender and prisoner rights.'[12] This leads to the question of whether it is rational and lawful for the Parole Board to rely upon this view of risk assessment and risk management in its decision-making process.

4.8 It is unsurprising that the Parole Board has largely adopted the risk-averse approach favoured by the Prison Service, not least

8 May and others, *Factors linked to reoffending*, Ministry of Justice Research, 2008, Summary 5.

9 Kemshall, 2001, p21.

10 For a discussion of the principle and its limits, see Hebenton and Seddon, 'From dangerousness to precaution: managing sexual and violent offenders in an uncertain age', *British Journal of Criminology*, 2009, 343.

11 Public Protection Manual, Version 4, para 2.

12 Public Protection Manual, para 8.3.

because, ultimately, it is the Board that will make the final decision whether or not to release a prisoner. In the absence of any conclusive scientific evidence about the efficacy and accuracy of risk assessment, the courts have approved the view that it is reasonable to rely on the cognitive behavioural method. In one case where there was a strong divergence between a prison and independent psychologist about whether a particular risk-assessment tool should be relied upon, the court ruled in the following terms:

> The position may be summarised in this way. There clearly is a body of professional opinion that has grave reservations about the utility of SARN [Structured Assessment of Risk and Need]. On the other hand, there is another body of professional opinion which does not share those reservations, and which considers it to be a useful tool, not of course the be all and end all, but a useful exercise. There is also a respectable body of professional opinion, with which the defendant was entitled to agree, that it would be of advantage for the claimant to undertake the SARN. Against this background, the claimant's challenge comes nowhere near surmounting the irrationality threshold.[13]

4.9 In the light of this background, it is highly unlikely that it will assist a prisoner's application for parole to seek to undermine the principles that underpin this method of risk assessment. As a very general guide, in cases where a prisoner has valid reasons for believing that the conventional risk assessment and treatment programmes used by the Prison Service are not suitable in his or her particular case, it will usually be more productive to concentrate on the specific features of the individual that might justify a different type of approach. The risk-assessment tools can do little more than provide the statistical likelihood of reoffending in a particular way and this can never be truly determinative; otherwise prisoners with very high static risk factors could never hope to be released. A clinical assessment of risk is still necessary in every case. In all such cases, independent expert evidence will usually be essential. It is also extremely difficult to validate the tools that require statistical evidence for offences that occur with very low frequency, such as murder. Therefore, although the completion of courses and the level of risk ascribed by psychological assessment tools are very influential with the Board, they are not conclusive. The Board's duty is always to consider the totality of the evidence before it and to reach its own view on risk.

13 *R (on the application of Bealey) v Home Secretary* [2005] EWHC 1618 (Admin) 27.

What is risk?

4.10 Risk within the criminal justice system encompasses:

- the risk of reoffending within a particular timescale;
- the risk of reconviction (ie the risk of detected reoffending);
- the risk of harm that will arise if a prisoner reoffends.[14]

For the purposes of parole, the critical period for assessing these risks is during the time that the prisoner is on licence. In the case of prisoners serving life or indeterminate sentences the time period is indefinite but for those serving determinate – including extended – sentences, the appropriate timescale is during the licence period.

4.11 The purpose of the various risk-assessment tools utilised by the Prison Service is therefore to assess the likelihood that further offences or harmful acts will be committed and the impact that this might have in terms of the harm that will be caused. The categories currently utilised for the likelihood or reoffending are: low; medium; high; and, very high. Within each category the aim is also to assess what level of harm will be caused, ranging from low through to serious harm. Serious harm is defined by the OASys Manual as 'a risk which is life threatening and/or traumatic and from which recovery, whether physical or psychological can be expected to be difficult or impossible'.[15]

4.12 Once the risk has been identified, the task is then to prepare a risk-management strategy. This is intended to:

- minimise the motivation to offend;
- identify and minimise circumstances that might be risk for the individual;
- minimise the likelihood of a further offence occurring;
- minimise the impact of any harm that might be caused.[16]

Methods of risk assessment

4.13 As risk assessment requires a calculation of the frequency or likelihood of reoffending and the impact that any reoffending will have on potential victims,[17] the aim is therefore not just to try to predict whether someone will reoffend, but also, if they do, the types of

14 Public Protection Manual, para 2.1.

15 Chapter 8 – NOMS have a rather patchy approach to disclosure of this Manual although it is expected to become more widely available in the future.

16 Public Protection Manual, para 2.2.

17 Kemshall, 2002, para 3.1.

offence that will be committed. This is an important component of the assessment process and has particular application to lifers as it is necessary to distinguish between offending that causes serious harm to the public and other possible non-violent or sexual offending.[18]

4.14 A full assessment of risk will normally require:

- an actuarial risk assessment;
- a clinical risk assessment.

4.15 Research indicates that the actuarial method of risk assessment is the most accurate in pure predictive terms. However, there are significant limits to the extent that it is possible to apply general information to an individual. Consequently, the advice is that:

> The combined use of clinical and actuarial methods in an holistic approach to risk assessment is now advocated as the approach most likely to enhance both the predictive accuracy and usefulness of risk assessments or sexual and dangerous offenders.[19]

Actuarial risk assessment

4.16 Actuarial risk assessment is based upon the statistical probability that people will reoffend. The factors that are used to make this actuarial assessment are usually referred to as static risk factors. They are static as they are the features pertaining to the individual that are not susceptible to change with treatment. The types of features that are analysed to arrive at the static risk assessment are:

- date of birth;
- previous convictions including types of previous convictions (eg sexual or violent);
- current conviction (often referred to as the 'index offence' in life sentence cases);
- employment history;
- relationship history.

4.17 The static risk assessment will usually identify an individual as being either a low, medium, high or very risk of future offending. The predicted likelihood of future offending will then inform the extent to which intervention is necessary through offending behaviour programmes.

18 The test for release is whether the lifer still poses a risk to the safety of the public – see chapter 9.

19 Kemshall, 2001, p60.

Clinical risk assessment

4.18 Clinical risk assessment is a far more subjective method of assessing risk and is based much more on the traditional medical and mental health diagnostic techniques:

> It is based upon detailed interviewing and observation by the clinician in order to collect information on the social, environmental, behavioural and personality factors that have resulted in harmful behaviour(s) in the past.[20]

4.19 The clinical assessment will assist in the identification of the dynamic risk factors, those factors that are susceptible to change with treatment or over the passage of time. Within OASys, now the main risk predicting tool utilised by the NOMS and which is discussed further below, dynamic risk factors are referred to as 'criminogenic needs'. These will encompass the following features:

- the current situation of the individual, including employment and whether there is ongoing substance misuse;
- offence-supporting attitudes;
- social networks;
- pro-criminal associations;
- poor emotional management;
- mental health issues;
- grievance issues;
- resistance to rules.

4.20 The identification of these factors is intended to enable treatment needs to be focused more effectively, such as through housing and employment support or drug and alcohol work. For violent offenders, the ageing process itself will often be a key dynamic risk factor, as a major dynamic risk factor in violent offending is the existence of antisocial attitudes that are very often higher in young people.

4.21 When assessing sex offenders, a number of further and more focused dynamic risk factors have been identified as follows:

- impaired relationships with adults;
- lack of victim empathy;
- extent and nature of anger, particularly whether instrumental or expressive;
- cognitive distortions and rationalisations for offending;
- sexual fantasy and deviant sexual arousal;

20 Kemshall, 2002, para 3.25.

- anti-social personality;
- impulsivity.[21]

4.22 The dynamic features will not all be present in every case and it is the task of the clinical assessment to try and extrapolate which of these features are present and/or have been modified by intervention.

Risk-assessment tools

4.23 A number of assessments are used by the Prison and Probation Services to undertake the assessment of risk. The key tools are as follows.

OASys

4.24 OASys is the joint Prison/Probation Service Offender Assessment System[22] and is now the key risk-assessment tool for the purposes of sentence management. It is designed to provide continuity in identifying and treating risk from conviction through to release and should be updated annually. It is based on both documentary records and an interview with the prisoner and is designed to identify static risk factors and the progress through treatment of dynamic risk factors. A similar system known as ASSET is used for those under 18 years of age. It is a computer-based system that will structure sentence planning and resettlement plans. OASys has not replaced all other risk-assessment tools and once broad areas of risk are identified, other more specific risk-assessment methods will still be utilised.

4.25 PSO 2205 states that the key aims of OASys are to:

- assess how likely an offender is to be reconvicted;
- identify and classify offending-related needs;
- assess risk of harm (to self and others);
- assist with management of risk of harm;
- link assessments, supervision and sentence plans;
- indicate any need for further specialist assessments;
- measure how an offender changes during the period of supervision/sentence.

4.26 The likelihood of reconviction is given a numerical score of between 0–168. A score of 0–40 is considered to be a low risk; 41–99 a medium

21 Kemshall, 2001 pp20–21.

22 See PSO 2205.

risk; and 100–168 a high risk. The statistical risk of reconviction must also be accompanied by a more subjective assessment of the risk of harm that might be caused if the prisoner reoffends. This is necessarily a more subjective view based on the nature and circumstances of previous offending.

4.27 The levels of risk of harm used in OASys are:

- *Low* – No significant, current indicators of risk of harm.
- *Medium* – There are identifiable indicators of risk of harm. The offender has the potential to cause harm but is unlikely to do so unless there is a change in circumstances, for example failure to take medication, loss of accommodation, relationship breakdown, drug or alcohol misuse.
- *High* – There are identifiable indicators of risk of harm. The potential event could happen at any time and the impact would be serious.
- *Very high* – There is an imminent risk of harm. The potential event is more likely than not to happen imminently and the impact would be serious.

4.28 As the OASys is designed to be used both at the very start of the prison sentence and then annually thereafter, the initial OASys assessment is likely to be used as a starting point to help determine whether more focused risk assessment is necessary. As the prisoner progresses through the sentence, or where other risk assessment tools are available, they will be incorporated into the OASys report.

Offender Group Reconviction Scale (OGRS)

4.29 This predicts, from a number of purely static factors such as criminal history and demography, the probability that an offender will be reconvicted within two years of release from custody or the start of a community sentence. It is often used as a starting point for risk assessment for programmes such as FOCUS (see below) to help guide the level of intervention that will be necessary. The assessment produces a percentage figure that predicts the likelihood of reoffending and is considered to be one of the most accurate methods of risk assessment.[23] The most recent version was introduced in 2009 as OGRS 3. This replaced OGRS 2 and OGRS – Sexual and Violent as it was considered that the previous model might under-predict the risk of

23 Ministry of Justice Research Summary 6/07.

violent and sexual offending by only applying this tool to those with previous convictions for such offences, thus missing out on people who are at risk of committing such offences even though they do not have previous convictions of that type.[24]

Violent Risk Assessment Guide (VRAG)

4.30 This is the most widely used actuarial tool for assessing violent recidivism and will assign people to one of nine risk categories for future offending. It is limited to the extent that it does not contain any assessment of the nature, severity or frequency of future violence. It involves analysing features ranging from age at the time of the index offence, performance at school and history of substance abuse, through to existence of psychopathy and personality disorders. There is a more refined version of VRAG designed to address the levels of dangerousness in high risk men called the Violence Prediction Scheme (VPS).

HCR-20

4.31 Historical, Clinical Risk Management takes into account 20 items[25] and is a tool for assessing risk of future violent reoffending, taking into account both static and dynamic factors. The different areas assessed are historical items (H), clinical items (C) and risk management (M). It will measure an individual's motivation to change and coping mechanisms, and although it was originally developed as a case-management tool, it is increasingly seen as an accurate predictor of future violent behaviour. However, research indicates that the risk-management item is a less accurate predictive tool than the historical assessment.[26]

Psychopathy Checklist – Revised (PCL-R)

4.32 The PCL-R[27] is the most widely used tool in relation to the identification of psychopathy. The identification of psychopathy and psychopathic traits is considered to be central to risk prediction and management as high PCL-R scores are closely related to the com-

24 Ministry of Justice Research Summary 7/09.

25 These can be found in Kemshall, 2001, pp11–12.

26 Ministry of Justice Research Summary 6/07.

27 PCL-R, or Hare's psychopathy checklist.

mission of violent and sexual crime, predatory offending, criminal diversity, the speed of reconviction and failure on supervision. It is not a risk-predictive tool in isolation but is considered to be particularly valuable when utilised in conjunction with other tools, such as VRAG or the HCR-20. It has 20 items that are rated on a three-point scale, and a high score (above 25) may suggest that the offender's risk will not be reduced by normal accredited offending behaviour programmes. It is usual to apply the term psychopath to anyone scoring above 30. A high score may also mean a prisoner is assessed by the Dangerous and Severe Personality Disorder Unit (DSPD) for the presence of personality disorders. The PCL-R is also being increasingly used to identify certain personality traits that might be relevant to offending even where the overall score does not indicate especially high levels of psychopathy. So, for example, if a prisoner has high scores in relation to grandiosity or superficial charm, these can be taken into account when assessing the success of interventions.

Risk Matrix 2000

4.33 An actuarial-based assessment of future risk of sexual and violent offending that has been developed from the Structured Anchored Clinical Judgment (SACJ), which is based on empirical research into recidivism amongst sex offenders. While the SACJ contained an extensive clinical assessment, the Risk Matrix 2000 was developed from a shortened version concentrating on static risk factors that had been developed to address those situations where the necessary dynamic and clinical data were not available. Although this risk-assessment tool can be used for both sexual and violent offenders, it is used far more extensively for sex offenders.

Structured Assessment of Risk and Need (SARN)

4.34 More akin to clinical assessment, SARN has been developed by Dr David Thornton of the Prison Service and combines the actuarial assessment of risk with the SACJ. This is an instrument that is currently being used within the national prison Sex Offenders Treatment Programme (SOTP), and which is described in the SOTP Accreditation documentation. In brief, four 'risk domains' are considered, relating to sexual interests, distorted attitudes, socio-affective functioning and self-management. It is used to set treatment targets and to determine the level of intervention required. It does have acknowledged limitations as it cannot quantify changes in static risk and is restricted to covering variables that have been identified in research to date, leaving open the possibility that there are further unidentified predictors.

Personality assessment

4.35 The most common tool used in the Prison Service for the diagnosis of personality disorder is the International Personality Disorder Examination (IPDE). The purpose of using the IPDE is to determine the identity and relevance of personality traits and the possible presence of personality disorder. The IPDE is a semi-structured clinical interview developed to assess personality disorders defined by the *Diagnostic and Statistical Manual of Mental Disorders.*[28] DSM-IV describes ten personality disorder diagnoses, which are organised into three clusters. The first cluster is labelled odd or eccentric and consists of paranoid, schizotypal and schizoid diagnoses. The second cluster is labelled dramatic and unstable and consists of antisocial, narcissistic, histrionic and borderline diagnoses. The third cluster is labelled anxious and fearful and consists of avoidant, dependent and obsessive-compulsive diagnoses. In prisons and secure hospitals, diagnoses in the dramatic and unstable cluster are most commonly observed.

Penile Plethysmograph (PPG)

4.36 This is used to assess deviant sexual interests and is the only risk-assessment tool that requires a degree of physical intrusion. It measures physical arousal to different images as a method for assessing whether there is arousal or interest in deviant sexual behaviour so that treatment can be focused on specific areas and problems. It may be used as part of the assessment for the HSF programme (see below).

Offending behaviour programmes

4.37 The courses provided by the Prison Service are almost exclusively cognitive behavioural therapy (CBT) based offending behaviour programmes. These aim to reduce criminal attitudes and beliefs by addressing deficits in thinking and behaviour. The courses based on CBT will normally be made up of a fixed number of sessions in

28 4th edn (DSM-IV).

groups and seek to address assessed risk in terms of the relationship between thoughts, feelings and behaviour. CBT developed out of cognitive therapy, which is designed to change people's thoughts, beliefs, attitudes and expectations and behavioural therapy, which is designed to change how people act. CBT is based on the assumption that the way people think about a situation affects how they act. In turn, their actions can affect how they both think and feel. It aims to change both the type of thinking and behaviour associated with committing offences.

4.38 Courses are accredited through the Correctional Services Accreditation Panel (CSAP), which is designed to ensure that the principles underpinning effective practice are implemented consistently.[29] CSAP is an advisory non-departmental public body originally established in 1999 and made up of a chair, independent experts, and representatives of the Prison Service, the National Probation Service, and the Ministry of Justice.[30] Programmes that are not fully accredited but are used within individual prisons must nevertheless be subject to the Prison Service's own validation process to ensure that there is some basis for believing that the intervention is effective.[31] Offending behaviour programmes are managed centrally at the Prison Service by the Interventions and Substance Misuse Group.

4.39 Attendance on offending behaviour programmes is always voluntary. The courts have upheld decisions to refuse prisoners enhanced privilege status as a result of sentence planning reviews that set attendance on these courses as targets. This has been upheld even for prisoners who maintain their innocence, the court being of the view that it was appropriate for the Prison Service to encourage prisoners to address their offending.[32]

4.40 Before prisoners can attend programmes, a number of responsivity assessments will be completed. These are intended to ensure that the programme will be effective and it will meet the needs and learning styles of the participants. Responsivity assessments will include:[33]

- an assessment of intellectual ability and learning styles. For more serious offences, an IQ test in the form of the WAIS-III may be administered;

29 CSAP was put in place in 2002, replacing the General Accreditation Panel which had been in operation since 1996.

30 For fuller details of the workings of the CSAP see PSO 4360.

31 PSO 4350.

32 See, eg, *R v Home Secretary ex p Hepworth* [1998] COD 146.

33 *Assessing suitability for offending behaviour programmes*, Offending Behaviour Programmes Unit, HM Prison Service, August 2007.

- language skills including literacy, ability to speak and understand English and dyslexia;
- mental and physical health, to ensure the prisoner is fit to take the programme;
- current drug misuse as it may be necessary to await a detoxification programme before commencing on group work;
- psychopathy, as the presence of psychopathic traits may make prisoners unsuitable for courses (see para 4.32 above);
- motivation to ascertain whether the prisoner is likely to participate and benefit from the programme.

4.41 The Prison Service provides information on the key offending behaviour programmes that it runs[34] and a list of the establishments running the different programmes can be found on the website of the Association of Prison Lawyers.[35] The key programmes that are available are as follows.

General offending behaviour programmes

Enhanced Thinking Skills (ETS)

4.42 The programme addresses thinking and behaviour associated with offending. It targets the following cognitive deficits: impulse control, cognitive style, social perspective taking, values/moral reasoning, critical reasoning and interpersonal problem solving. The programme employs a sequenced series of structured exercises designed to teach interpersonal problem solving skills, impulse control and improve perspective-taking ability. It is targeted at male and female medium to medium-high risk offenders, and can be sequenced with another programme (such as SOTP, CALM and the CSCP). It is usually targetted at prisoners who score 56 or above on OASys, excluding low risk offenders. It does not require prisoners to describe their offences and so it can be undertaken by prisoners who maintain their innocence. The course has 21 sessions of two hours' duration and is usually completed over a five-week period. However, these sessions are followed by completing a series of objectives and post-course reviews meaning that it usually takes 14 weeks to complete in total. A community-based version of the programme, called Think First, is run by the Probation Service and a version of the scheme for juveniles

34 www.hmprisonservice.gov.uk/adviceandsupport/beforeafterrelease/offenderbehaviourprogrammes/.

35 www.associationofprisonlawyers.co.uk/.

(JETS) is also run for those under 18 years of age. There is, at present, little evidence that completing the course has a direct impact on re-offending rates, with one Home Office study indicating that while it reduced reconviction rates for the first year after release, this reduction was not maintained two years after release.[36] For women prisoners, there was no difference in reconviction rates for those who had completed the ETS and those who had not.[37] An earlier version of the ETS, the Reasoning and Rehabilitation programme, was phased out in 2004.

Cognitive Skills Booster (CSB)

4.43 This, as the title suggests, is a programme designed for those who have already completed a course such as the ETS to refresh and put into practice the skills that have been learned. It is available both in prison (usually in open conditions) and through the Probation Service. It consists of ten sessions that can be completed over 3–10 weeks.

FOR

4.44 This is a brief course for those who are within three months of release and are to be supervised in the community. It is a 13-session programme that aims to increase motivation to change so that prisoners will be more likely to engage with services on release. It is designed to be delivered as part of a resettlement programme. Prisoners will normally need an OASys score of 56 or above and have identified needs in the areas of employment, accommodation or substance abuse to be suitable for the course.

Victim empathy

4.45 As is self-evident from the title, these programmes are intended to address deficits in victim empathy and to encourage more understanding of the experiences of victims of crime. Many of the programmes listed above will have components which address victim empathy. Where specific victim empathy courses are not available, prison chaplaincies may provide a non-accredited programme designed to encourage greater victim empathy called the Sycamore Tree Trust programme.

36 *Findings 226*, Home Office RDSD, 2003.
37 *Findings 276*, Home Office RDSD, 2006.

Programmes addressing violent behaviour

Controlling Anger and Learning to Manage it (CALM)

4.46 This programme is aimed at those whose anger or poor emotional control lead to a criminal offence.[38] All participants must meet the criteria of a current or previous offence precipitated by anger or poor emotional control and will usually have an OASys score of 56 or above. The structured interview to assess suitability will examine whether the violence used was expressive and whether there is anger or emotional mismanagement in the offending history. Any offence type may be included but not all violent offenders will be suitable for CALM. Offenders whose use of aggression is only instrumental (ie to achieve another goal) are not suitable for the programme. This may include, for example, armed robbers. Whilst CALM and CSCP are not necessarily mutually exclusive, they are aimed to address different types of violent offending and whilst CALM may sometimes be a precursor for the CSCP where both types of offending are present, it is very unlikely that a prisoner who has completed the CSCP will require the CALM. The course is made up of 24 sessions including up to three individual sessions.

Aggression Replacement Training (ART)

4.47 A Probation Service programme designed to reduce aggressive behaviour by improving social skills, anger management and moral reasoning.

Cognitive Self-Change Programme (CSCP)

4.48 Using a rolling format, this intensive programme aims to reduce instrumental violence and related offending behaviour in adult men defined as being at high risk of reconviction. The programme addresses the individual's anti-social thinking patterns, violent fantasy, lack of insight into violent behaviour, poor management of increased arousal or anger and socio-cognitive skills deficit. It is aimed at those with a pattern of convicted and unconvicted violence throughout their life span and whose violence is not resultant of substance misuse alone. The normal criteria for entry requires an OASys score of 100 or above and four or more convictions for violence (including actual, attempted or threatened harm). However, these criteria are not

38 The course has replaced the ad hoc anger management programmes which were previously run by many prisons, and is also now run by many probation areas.

rigid and prisoners with a smaller number of very severe convictions or a history of unconvicted violent behaviour may also be eligible. It is not aimed at people with a history of predominately sexual offending or domestic violence. Participants will usually have to complete the ETS or be assessed as not requiring it before commencing the CSCP. The core elements of the programme take approximately one year to complete but is dependent on an individual's progress though treatment. CSCP continues post completion, where skills are practised and maintained, for the remainder of the individual's time in custody and on licence.

Healthy Relationships Programme (HRP)

4.49 This programme is designed for men who have committed abusive and violent behaviour in the home and its aim is to reduce the risk of violence towards intimate partners. Suitable participants are usually identified through section 6, question 6.7 of OASys concerning evidence of domestic violence. There are two versions of the HRP – the High Intensity HRP consists of ten modules involving about 68 sessions. The Moderate Intensity HRP consists of six modules and involves about 24 sessions.

CHROMIS

4.50 CHROMIS is a relatively new programme currently only run at the Dangerous and Severe Personality Disorder (DSPD) unit at HMP Frankland. It aims to reduce violence in high risk offenders with high levels of psychopathic traits. The criteria for entry to the programme are a history of violent and threatening behaviour, a combination of psychopathic traits that disrupt the ability to engage in CBT programmes and a very high risk of future violence as assessed on the HCR-20 or VRS. The programme comprises five core components that take around two years to complete. As CHROMIS is run in the DSPD, participants also have to meet the criteria for a severe personality disorder, which are a PCL-R of over 30 or a PCL-R of 25-29 together with at least one personality disorder diagnosed other than an anti-social personality disorder or two or more DSIM-IV personality order diagnoses.

Sex Offender Treatment Programmes (SOTP)

4.51 The SOTP is considered suitable for any prisoner with a current or previous conviction for a sexual offence or another offence that has a sexual component, such as a sexually motivated murder. Assessment of suitability is usually undertaken through the SARN and the Risk Matrix 2000. The level of risk identified by the Risk Matrix 2000 and the number of domains that require treatment as identified in the SARN will inform the decision as to which versions of the SOTP should be completed. The main focus on SOTP is for it to be completed in prison in closed conditions, although for prisoners with a low risk and a low number of treatment domains completing the course in the community is viable. All probation areas now run some form of the SOTP.

- *Core Programme*: This is the main treatment programme and is aimed at male medium and high risk offenders and challenges thinking patterns, develops victim empathy and relapse prevention skills. It consists of 86 sessions usually taking place over six months. The treatment goals of this programme include helping offenders develop an understanding of how and why sexual offences were committed to increase awareness of victim harm issues, and to develop meaningful life goals as part of a relapse prevention plan.
- *Extended Programme*: A supplementary programme for high risk offenders covering five treatment need areas: dysfunctional thinking styles; emotion management; offence-related sexual fantasy, intimacy skills; and inadequate relapse prevention plans. It is targeted at male high and very high risk sex offenders and is completed in 73 sessions over a period of around four months.
- *Adapted Programme*: Treatment goals are similar to the core programme, but treatment methods are adapted to suit learning-disabled sex offenders – usually those with an IQ of 80 or under as measured on the WAIIS – across all risk levels. The programme is designed to increase sexual knowledge, modify offence-justifying thinking, develop ability to recognise feelings in themselves and others and to gain an understanding of victim harm, and develop relapse prevention skills.
- *Rolling Programme*: This programme covers the same topics as the core programme but with less emphasis on obtaining an adequate offence account, and more emphasis on relationship skills and attachment deficits. It is targeted at male low and medium risk sex offenders, but sex offenders who have completed primary treatment programmes and who are serving long sentences can attend as a 'top-up' programme.

- *Better Lives Booster Programme*: This programme is designed to provide an opportunity for offenders to refresh and boost their learning from other SOTP programmes and to prepare for additional relapse prevention and release work and, as such, it is only available to those who have successfully completed the SOTP.

Healthy Sexual Functioning (HSF)

4.52 The programme is designed to complement the SOTP for those prisoners considered to have disordered or deviant arousal patterns. It has four modules: understanding sexuality, patterns in sexual arousal, promoting sexual healthy interest and relapse prevention.

Substance abuse programmes

4.53 As well as the accredited offending behaviour programmes, the National Drugs Programme Delivery Unit manages a number of interventions designed to address problems related to drug and alcohol abuse and offending. The key courses and treatments available in prison are the following.

FOCUS

4.54 This is a high intensity programme for adult males with a medium and high risk of reconviction and high or severe drug or alcohol dependence. It comprises 62 sessions delivered over 18 weeks.

Prison Addressing Substance Related Offending (P-ASRO)

4.55 This is a CBT programme that addresses how temperament and socio-economic situations contribute to the development of substance misuse. It is aimed at male prisoners who are 18 or over with a low to medium risk of reconviction. It is made up of 20 sessions delivered over five to six weeks. There is also a version of P-ASRO specifically for women that covers similar areas.

Short Duration Programme (SDP)

4.56 This is a programme for male and female prisoners who are serving short sentences, or who are approaching release. It is designed as a stepping stone to further drug treatment both in prison and the community. It consists of 20 2½-hour sessions delivered over four weeks.

Substance Treatment and Offending Programme (STOP)

4.57 STOP targets male prisoners who are 21 or older who are medium or high risk dependent offenders. The programme aims to achieve abstinence and consists of 90 one-hour sessions.

12-Step Programme/Rehabilitation of Addicted Prisoners Trust (RAPt)

4.58 RAPt is a charitable foundation working in association with the Prison Service in a number of prisons and aims to treat drug and alcohol addiction through a version of the 12-step programme. The 12 step programme can also be delivered by prison staff. The first 5 steps are completed in prison custody with the remainder in the community. It is only suitable for prisoners who are able to participate in a process based around the existence of a 'higher power'.

Counselling, Assessment and Throughcare Services (CARATS)

4.59 This is designed to address problems of addiction to drugs and alcohol through a mixture of assessment and counselling and seeks to provide continuity of treatment through to the community by establishing links with probation and community-based addiction services. It is a service that is available to prisoners throughout their sentences who have completed other drug interventions.

Therapeutic communities

4.60 The only current alternative to the accredited cognitive behavioural courses is through admission to a therapeutic community (TC) to complete the Prison Partnership Therapeutic Community Programme.[39] There are currently five democratic therapeutic communities for men and one for women. The most well known and the longest established is HMP Grendon. It has 235 places for category B and category C prisoners. It has five 'communities' and an assessment unit. Grendon is also able to offer the SOTP, a move designed to prevent prisoners engaged in therapy having to be moved on to different prisons to address this treatment need. The others are:

- HMP Dovegate (near Uttoxeter) has 200 places for category B prisoners – four communities, an assessment unit and a high intensity programme unit.

39 See PSO 2400 – Democratic Therapeutic Communities.

- HMP Gartree (near Market Harborough) has one community offering 23 places for category B lifers.
- HMP Aylesbury has a young offender institution, part of which contains 22 therapeutic places for young offenders.
- HMP Blundeston (near Lowestoft in Suffolk) opened a therapeutic community in 2004 providing 40 places for category C prisoners.
- HMP Send (in Woking), which has a 40-place therapeutic community for women.

4.61 The special status of TCs is reflected in the admission procedures, which are normally through a referral from the medical officer, although an application for a transfer can also be made directly to Prison Service headquarters.[40] They are described as democratic communities as they are based on an egalitarian model with the community – which includes prisoners, prison staff, probation officers and the psychiatric and psychological teams – setting the boundaries of acceptable behaviour both within therapy and in the general prison environment. This can be difficult, given the very obvious hierarchy that has to exist within any prison.

4.62 Although the communities are very staunchly defended by those who have participated in them, it is often the case that prison psychologists will place greater emphasis on the accredited programmes and will consider that prisoners who have successfully completed their therapy should still attend the accredited programmes. Historically, this often created a major problem for lifers who had successfully completed their therapy at Grendon, which is a category B prison. They would often find that there was enormous reluctance from the Prison Service and Secretary of State to accept that they should move directly from Grendon to open prison conditions. Grendon is now able to hold category C prisoners who have completed therapy so that in appropriate cases they can be considered for transfer directly to open conditions without having to return to the mainstream prison estate.

Dangerous and severe personality disorder units (DSPDs)

4.63 These units are designed to fill the lacuna in the provision of treatment to dangerous prisoners whose dangerousness is linked to a personality disorder. The diagnosis of this condition posed particular

40 See PSO 2400.

problems for the Prison Service, as it had previously been deemed to be untreatable. The consequence of this was that special hospitals could decline to accept people with severe personality disorders on the grounds that no effective treatment could be offered, leaving the Prison Service to attempt to address their treatment and progress. Prisoners are not required to consent to a transfer to a DSPD, but are not under any compulsion to agree to participate in the assessments or treatment once a transfer has taken place.[41]

4.64 The units were set up in 2002 in Whitemoor and HMP Frankland, two high security prisons (alongside similar units in Rampton and Broadmoor) with further units for female prisoners running the Primrose Programme at Durham and Low Newton. The entry criteria for the DSPD units are a PCL-R of over 30 or a PCL-R of 25–29 together with at least one personality disorder diagnosed other than an anti-social personality disorder or two or more DSIM-IV personality order diagnoses.[42]

Prisoners who maintain their innocence

4.65 There has always been a particular problem for prisoners who maintain their innocence to establish that they have satisfactorily addressed their offending behaviour.[43] This need not, however, be an insuperable barrier to attending accredited courses as part of the progress through the life sentence.

4.66 Prisoners convicted of sexual offences, or with a sexual element to their offence, are in the most difficult position, as attendance on the SOTP requires that an active account is given of the offence. Where the prisoner cannot give this account, then it will usually lead to an assessment that they are unsuitable for the programme and guidance from the Prison Service is that prisoners who maintain their innocence will nort normally be accepted on either the SOTP or the HRP.[44] This makes it very difficult to progress, as the Prison Service and the Parole Board find it very difficult to accept that there is any other method of safely assessing risk. Various attempts have been made to allow prisoners to attend versions of the SOTP (for example,

41 For a fuller discussion of DSPD units see Creighton and Arnott, *Prisoners: law & practice*, LAG, 2009, pp133–5.

42 Probation Circular 21/2008, annex D.

43 The legal implications are discussed in chapter 14 on remedies; this section is designed to look at the impact on attending offending behaviour courses.

44 *Assessing suitability for offending behaviour programmes*, above, p12.

in cases where one sexual offence is admitted and another denied), but the trend has been away from this, as it is felt that it is not possible to provide an accurate assessment of risk and progress in treatment while any sexual offences are still denied.

4.67 For violent offenders entry to the CALM and CSCP will usually require an admission of guilt but as the CSCP is usually for prisoners who have more than one conviction, the acceptance of guilt for one or more of the offences might be sufficient.

4.68 The various cognitive skills programmes, such as the ETS or FOR, are not offence-specific, give wider scope for attendance. Prisoners can examine aspects of their choices and thinking that resulted in previous convictions or their general lifestyles at the time of the current conviction through these programmes. Prisoners convicted of murder who consider that a manslaughter conviction was more appropriate should also be able to attend this type of course.

4.69 Drug and alcohol treatment courses are not dependent on a prisoner admitting guilt of a particular offence. Any prisoner who admits to a substance abuse problem is eligible. As prisoners often develop drug problems, or more severe drug problems, in custody, there is no need for these courses to be linked to convictions.

4.70 The Parole Board is very anxious to assure prisoners who maintain their innocence that this is not a barrier to release and has even devoted part of its website to this issue. However, their figures show that the success rate for all parole applications is more than 50 per cent lower for prisoners who maintain their innocence. The Board accepts that in cases involving sexual offending, parole refusal rates are likely to be at their highest. The Board did conduct a survey of 50 mandatory lifers who maintained their innocence and yet achieved release. It was noted that they had all spent lengthy periods of time in open conditions and the majority had undertaken offending behaviour work into areas such as anger management, thinking skills and assertiveness.

CHAPTER 5

Determinate sentences: an overview

continued

Introduction

5.1 A detailed examination of sentencing principles and provisions is outside the scope of this book, as is any comprehensive consideration of early release mechanisms that do not involve the Parole Board.[1] However, an overview is necessary in order to understand the relevant functions of the Parole Board. This chapter deals with the various kinds of fixed term, or determinate, sentences that can be imposed by the courts, and the relevant early release schemes that apply to them.

How determinate sentences are served

5.2 After sentence, prisoners will generally be sent to the nearest local prison that holds a remand population. Then, depending upon the length and seriousness of their offence, they will be placed in one of a number of security categories (ranging from category A for those deemed to pose a high risk to the public, to category D for those considered to be suitable for open prisons). Prisoners will then be allocated to a prison with conditions of security appropriate to their category. Security category is reviewed at regular intervals to enable prisoners to progress to less secure prisons when appropriate. Guidance on initial and subsequent categorisation and allocation is contained in PSO 0900.[2]

5.3 Prisoners will also be subject to sentence planning with a view to identifying risk factors and appropriate offending behaviour work aimed at reducing the assessed risk to the public. For those prisoners whose initial release is not automatic, but depends on the Parole Board assessing the risk to the public as being acceptable for release, the degree to which a prisoner has progressed through the prison system and is seen as having addressed the relevant risk factors through offending behaviour work will clearly be very important.

Summary of release arrangements and the Parole Board role

5.4 How determinate sentences are administered depends on three factors: first the nature of the offence, second the length of the sentence, and third when it was imposed.

1 See Creighton and Arnott, *Prisoners: Law and Practice*, LAG, 2009.

2 Ibid, chapters 3 and 4.

Summary of early release arrangements for determinate sentence prisoners

Length of sentence	**Relevant legislation**	**Automatic release date**	**Parole eligibility date**	**Licence expiry date**
Offences for which sentence was imposed before 1 October 1992				
Any	CJA 1967	⅔	⅓	⅔
Sentence imposed on or after 1 October 1992 and offence committed before 30 September 1998				
<12 months	CJA 1991	½	n/a	n/a
12 months but <4 years	CJA 1991	½	n/a	¾*
4 years +	CJA 1991	⅔ (unless the offence is not a specified offence *and* the PED falls on or after 9 June 2008 in which case the 2003 Act applies)	½	¾* unless recalled on or after 14 July 2008 in which case SED
Offence committed on or after 30 September 1998 but before 4 April 2005				
<12 months	CJA 1991	½	n/a	n/a
>12 months but <4 years	CJA 1991 (as amended by CDA 1998)	½	n/a	¾*
4 years +	CJA 1991 (as amended by CDA 1998)	⅔ (unless the offence is not a specified offence *and* the PED falls on or after 9 July 2008 in which case the 2003 Act applies)	½	¾* unless recalled, in which case SED

Length of sentence	Relevant legislation	Automatic release date	Parole eligibility date	Licence expiry date
Extended sentence – custodial period under 12 months	CJA 1991 (as amended CDA 1998)	½ of custodial term	n/a	Specified extension period commencing from ¾ point of custodial term
Extended sentence – custodial period 12 months and <4 years	CJA 1991 (as amended by CDA 1998)	½ of custodial term	n/a	Specified extension period commencing from ¾ point of custodial term
Extended sentence – custodial period 4 years +	CJA 1991 (as amended by CDA 1998)	⅔ of custodial term	½ of custodial term	Specified extension period commencing from ¾ point of custodial term
Offence committed on or after 4 April 2005				
Any determinate sentence of 12 months or more (except extended sentences)	CJA 2003	½	n/a	SED
Determinate sentence <12 months	CJA 1991	½	n/a	n/a
Extended Sentence	CJA 2003	½ of custodial term	End of custodial term	Specified extension period
Sentence imposed on or after 14 July 2008				
Extended sentence	CJA 2003 (as amended by CJIA 2008)	n/a	½ of custodial term	Specified extension period

* the power always existed for the court to impose an extended licence period up until to SED under CJA 1991 section 44 for those convicted of sexual offences.

5.5 There are now three generations of release arrangements for determinate sentences, under the Criminal Justice Acts (CJAs) 1967, 1991 and 2003, respectively. In summary, the Parole Board is only involved in the following situations:

- Considering the suitability for release on parole licence of prisoners serving sentences of four years or more (including extended sentences with custodial terms of four years or more) where the offence was committed before 4 April 2005, and where the offence is one of the sexual or violent offences contained in Schedule 15 to the Criminal Justice Act 2003 or where parole has been refused prior to 9 June 2008 and the prisoner has a subsequent parole review (see appendix D). Parole eligibility is at the halfway point (of the custodial term for extended sentences), except for those sentenced before 1 October 1992 where it is at the one-third point. The Parole Board will usually decide suitability for release by considering the case only on the papers although an oral hearing will be held if fairness requires. The Board has a practice of holding oral hearings where the referral involves an under 18-year-old. Article 5(4) of the ECHR is not engaged in such referrals.
- Considering the suitability for release on licence of extended sentence prisoners serving sentences for offences committed on or after 4 April 2005 where the sentence was imposed before 14 July 2008 (those given an extended sentence on or after that date are now released automatically). Again the Board may hold an oral hearing if fairness requires it, although the initial decision will be taken on the papers. Article 5(4) is not engaged in such cases.
- Deciding whether recalled determinate sentence prisoners should be re-released on licence whenever the offence was committed. If on an initial consideration of the case on the papers the Board does not direct release the prisoner can request an oral hearing before the Board. The Board no longer grants an oral hearing in all cases but has a policy they should be held to comply with the judgment in *Smith and West*. Article 5(4) is engaged when a recall case is referred to the Board.
- Advising the Secretary of State, where circumstances make it practicable, as to whether the power to release a prisoner early on compassionate grounds should be exercised.

The CJA 1967

5.6 The arrangements under the CJA 1967 apply to prisoners who were sentenced prior to the coming into force of the CJA 1991 on 1 October 1992 (referred to in this book as 'CJA 1967 cases'). Accordingly, they apply to an ever-decreasing number of prisoners. Eligibility for release on parole licence, if recommended by the Parole Board, is set at one-third of the sentence for these prisoners. Unconditional release (with no licence supervision) is set at two-thirds. The coming into force of the CJA 1991 did not affect the administration of these sentences, as transitional arrangements preserved the eligibility dates.[3]

The CJA 1991

5.7 The CJA 1991 came into force on 1 October 1992 and applies to all those sentenced on or after that date, up until the coming into force of the CJA 2003 (and still applies for those sentenced to under 12 months). For sentences of 12 months and over, the CJA 1991 applies except for sentences in relation of offences committed on or after 4 April 2005, the date of commencement of the relevant parts of the CJA 2003.[4] Its provisions have been substantially amended by the Criminal Justice and Immigration Act (CJIA) 2008.

5.8 The commencement of the CJA 1991 on 1 October 1992 was anomalous in that the early release provisions it introduced were applied to prisoners *sentenced* after their coming into force, whenever the offences were committed. This risked offenders, who may have committed similar offences on the same day, being subjected to different release regimes purely on the basis of the date on which the court disposed of their case. By contrast, the amendments brought in by the Crime and Disorder Act (CDA) 1998 and the CJA 2003 apply only to offences *committed* after the relevant commencement dates. The changes brought in by the CJIA 2008 introduced a further element of arbitrariness. For example on commencement, whether a DCR prisoner (see below) was to be released automatically may have depended on whether their parole eligibility date fell before or after

3 CJA 1991 Sch 12 para 8.

4 The Criminal Justice Act 2003 (Commencement No 8 and Transitional and Saving Provisions) Order 2005 SI 2005 No 950 – initial release dates under the CJA 1991 were preserved in relation to sentences imposed for offences committed before 4 April 2005 by para 19.

9 June 2008, rather than because of the date, or seriousness, of their offence. Challenges to the changes on the basis that they breach the necessity for certainty in sentencing arguably implicit in article 6 of the Convention have so far failed.[5]

Release schemes under the CJA 1991

5.9 The CJA 1991 introduced three release schemes administered according to the length of sentence. Those serving fewer than four years are defined as 'short-term prisoners' under the Act, and those four years or more as 'long-term prisoners':[6]

- *Automatic unconditional release (AUR)* – Short-term prisoners serving less than 12 months are released unconditionally at the halfway point.[7]
- *Automatic conditional release (ACR)* – Short-term prisoners serving sentences of 12 months to fewer than four years are released under licence supervision automatically at the halfway point.[8] Licence supervision continues, subject to recall, to the three-quarter point, the licence expiry date (LED).[9]
- *Discretionary conditional release (DCR)* – Long-term prisoners, those serving four or more years, originally became eligible for release on parole licence at the halfway point (the parole eligibility date (PED)) if recommended by the Parole Board[10] and were in any event released automatically on licence at the two-thirds point (the non-parole date, or NPD),[11] the licence expiring, subject to recall, at the three-quarter point. These provisions were amended by the CJIA 2008 so that DCR prisoners are from 9 June 2008 released automatically at the halfway point unless they are serving a sentence for a specified sexual or violent offence contained in Schedule 15 to the CJA 2003.[12] Release of such prisoners is remains subject to a Parole Board recommendation, which the

5 See *R (on the application of Salami) v Secretary of State for Justice* [2009] EWHC 2251 (Admin).
6 CJA 1991 s33(5).
7 CJA 1991 s33(1)(a).
8 CJA 1991 s33(1)(b).
9 CJA 1991 s37(1).
10 CJA 1991 s35(1).
11 CJA 1991 s33(2).
12 CJA 1991 ss33(1B) and 35, as amended by CJIA 2008 s26; guidance to prisons was contained in PSI 17/2008.

Secretary of State treats as binding except where the sentence is 15 years or more.[13] The licence for those released automatically now expires at the end of the entire sentence,[14] whereas the licences for those released by the Board prior to the two-thirds point still expire at the three-quarter point.[15]

- *The 'at risk provisions'* – After release if offenders are convicted of a further offence committed before sentence expiry date (SED) they can be ordered to return to prison by the court sentencing for the new offence. The period of the order to return cannot exceed the length of time between the commission of the new offence and sentence expiry of the original offence.[16] If the return to custody term together with any new sentence is less than 12 months, the prisoner is not released unconditionally at the halfway point but on a three-month licence.[17]

Further provisions for sexual and violent offences under the CJA 1991

Extended licences

5.10 For offences committed up until 30 September 1998[18] the sentencing court can direct, in the case of sexual offences, that the offender be subject to licence supervision for the whole of the sentence.[19]

Extended sentences

5.11 For offences committed on or after 30 September 1998, but before 4 April 2005,[20] the sentencing court can, for certain sexual or violent offences, impose an extended sentence.[21] This combines a custodial term, commensurate with what would have been imposed for the offence had an extended sentence not been appropriate, together with a further period of licence supervision in the community. The

13 CJA 1991 s50(2); Parole Board (Transfer of Functions) Order 1998 SI No 3218 although section 145 of the Coroners and Justice Act will remove this power if brought into force.

14 CJA 1991 s37ZA.

15 CJA 1991 s37(1).

16 Powers of Criminal Courts (Sentencing) Act (PCC(S)A) 2000 s116.

17 CJA 1991 s40A.

18 The date of the coming into force of the relevant parts of the CDA 1998.

19 The power is now under PCC(S)A 2000 s86.

20 The date of the coming into force of the relevant parts of the CJA 2003.

21 Now under PCC(S)A 2000 s85.

length of the custodial term determines the initial release date.[22] Accordingly initial release will be automatically on licence to the end of the extension period, except for cases where the custodial term is for four or more years for an offence contained in Schedule 15 to the CJA 2003. Extended sentence prisoners are not eligible for release on home detention curfew (see para 5.30 below).

Principles of sentence calculation under the CJA 1991

5.12 The way in which multiple and overlapping sentences imposed for offences committed before 4 April 2005 are calculated is complicated and has been the subject of repeated judicial criticism. Individual prison governors as legal custodians of prisoners have a duty to work out release dates correctly where the sentence is administered under the CJA 1991. PSO 6650 contains very detailed guidance on this area.

5.13 In summary, the CJA 1991[23] requires multiple and overlapping determinate sentences to be treated as a 'single term' for the purposes of working out which is the applicable release scheme. Accordingly, where the court imposes consecutive sentences, the single term is the aggregate period of all such sentences – so, for example, two consecutive sentences of two years would result in a four-year single term and the application of the DCR scheme. For concurrent, overlapping sentences, the single term starts with the date of imposition of the first sentence and ends with the sentence expiry date of the last such sentence to be imposed. So if a prisoner, when he/she had served one year of a three-year sentence, was given a further three-year sentence, the result would become a single term of four years.[24]

5.14 In relation to sentences imposed after 30 September 1998, section 51(2) of the CJA 1991 (as amended) confirms that sentences will not be single-termed with any earlier sentence if the prisoner has been released from any of the earlier sentences. This change was brought in to avoid the complications in working out the single term that arose where prisoners who had been recalled to custody received further sentences.

5.15 Under the CJA 1991 the prison is responsible for determining how much remand time falls to be deducted from the sentence.[25]

22 CJA 1991 s44.

23 CJA 1991 s51.

24 See *R v Home Secretary ex p Francois* [1999] 1 AC 43.

25 CJA 1967 s67 (as amended) – see the guidance in PSO 6650 chapter 4.

The CJA 2003

5.16 For determinate sentence prisoners, the main provisions of the 2003 Act came into force on 4 April 2005.[26] The transitional provisions state that the Act's provisions in relation to release only come into force in relation to offences committed on or after 4 April 2005.[27]

5.17 The 2003 Act's provisions in relation to sentences of under 12 months (the 'custody plus' sentence) were not brought into force in April 2005, although pilots were started in January 2004[28] of the 'intermittent custody' sentence,[29] which was designed to allow offenders to maintain employment and family ties while serving a custodial sentence at, for example, weekends. The pilots related to courts within the catchment area of two 'intermittent custody centres' at HMP Kirkham for men, and HMP Morton Hall for women. At present, the CJA 2003's provisions only then relate to sentences of 12 months or more.

Release arrangements under the CJA 2003

5.18 The CJA 2003 has, to an extent, simplified release arrangements for determinate sentence prisoners, as the distinction between long-term and short-term prisoners is removed and all offenders (including extended sentence prisoners who are sentenced on or after 14 July 2008) will now be released automatically at the halfway point. In summary, the position for those sentenced for offences committed on or after 4 April 2005 is as follows:

- Those sentenced to less than 12 months (unless in an intermittent custody pilot area) are still dealt with under the AUR arrangements (see para 5.9 above) of the CJA 1991 including the 'at risk' provisions.[30]
- Those sentenced to 12 months or more (now referred to as the 'standard determinate sentence' (SDS)) are released automatically on licence at the halfway point (the conditional release date

26 See the Criminal Justice Act 2003 (Commencement No 8 and Transitional and Saving Provisions) Order 2005 SI 2005 No 950.

27 Ibid Sch 2 para 4.

28 Criminal Justice Act 2003 (Commencement No 2 and Saving Provisions) Order 2004 SI No 81.

29 CJA 2003 s183.

30 Criminal Justice Act 2003 (Commencement No 8 and Transitional and Saving Provisions) Order 2005 SI No 950 Sch 2 paras 14 and 29.

(CRD))[31] and the licence will remain in force until the SED.[32] For SDS prisoners released on licence there are no 'at risk' provisions.

- Where an offender commits a specified sexual or violent offence[33] that has a maximum sentence of less than ten years, and where the court considers the offender at significant risk of causing serious harm by the commission of further such offences, the court is required to impose an extended sentence.[34] As with extended sentences administered under the CJA 1991, this comprises a custodial term, commensurate with the seriousness of the offence, and an extension period to be served on licence, imposed to protect the public. Those serving extended sentences under the CJA 2003 imposed before 14 July are eligible for release halfway through the custodial term if the Parole Board directs,[35] and are only automatically released once the custodial term has been served in full.[36] Those whose sentence was imposed on or after 14 July 2008 are now released automatically even though the imposition of an extended sentence from that date requires a minimum custodial term of four years.[37] On release, all extended sentence prisoners remain under licence supervision until the end of the entire extended sentence.

Sentence calculation under the CJA 2003

5.19 Under the CJA 2003[38] sentences imposed for offences committed on or after 4 April 2005 that are wholly or partly concurrent have their release dates calculated separately. The offender will not be released until the latest release date and will remain on licence until the latest sentence expiry date.[39]

31 CJA 2003 s244(3)(a).
32 CJA 2003 s249(1).
33 Listed in CJA 2003 Sch 15.
34 CJA 2003 ss227 and 228.
35 CJA 2003 s247(2).
36 CJA 2003 s247(4).
37 CJA 2003 s247(2) as amended from 14 July 2008 by CJIA 2008 Sch 28 para 2(1) – there is an obvious contradiction between increasing the seriousness threshold for imposition of the sentence, and then making release at the halfway point of the custodial term automatic, rather than dependent on the Board's assessment of risk.
38 See PSO 6650 chapter 18 for guidance.
39 CJA 2003 s263.

5.20 Sentences imposed consecutively are aggregated so that, for example, where an offender receives two SDSs of three years to run consecutively, the automatic release date will be three years after the imposition of the sentences.[40]

5.21 Under the CJA 2003, remand time is not calculated by the prison but rather the sentencing court makes a direction specifying the amount of remand time to be deducted from the sentence.[41] The court does not need to make a direction if it considers it just in all the circumstances not to do so.[42]

Effect of additional days added as punishment

5.22 If prisoners are given additional days as punishment by independent adjudicators in the prison disciplinary process[43] then both under the CJA 1991[44] and CJA 2003[45] the additional days must be served in full. The relevant release dates, licence expiry and sentence expiry dates are put back by the total number of days given as punishment.

Young and child offenders

Detention and training orders (DTOs)

5.23 For those under 18 the normal determinate sentence will be a DTO imposed under section 100 of the PCC(S)A 2000. The maximum sentence is 24 months and generally half is served in custody and half in the community.

5.24 If during the supervision period of the DTO the offender fails to comply with the requirements of supervision, the court may order the offender to be detained.[46] The Parole Board does not play any part in the release or recall of those serving DTOs.

40 CJA 2003 s264.

41 CJA 2003 s240.

42 CJA 2003 s240(4)(b).

43 For detailed examination see Creighton and Arnott, *Prisoners: law and practice*, Legal Action Group, 2009, chapter 9.

44 CJA 1991 s42.

45 CJA 2003 s257.

46 PCC(S)A 2000 s104.

Other sentences

5.25 If the offence is sufficiently serious, those under 18 at the time of its commission can receive a determinate sentence imposed under section 91 of the PCC(S)A 2000. For those aged 18 and above but under 21, the sentence of detention in a young offender institution can be imposed.[47] There is no restriction (except the available maximum for the offence) on the length of such sentences. These sentences are administered in the same way as determinate sentences for adults. Release dates and liability to recall will depend on the offence, length of sentence and when it was imposed.

5.26 Those serving these sentences who are released before they are 22 years old are subject to a minimum three months' licence supervision.[48] This does not just apply to sentences of under 12 months where otherwise there would be no supervision, but may require the offender to remain on licence beyond the expiry date of the sentence imposed by the court (if not released until sentence expiry because of, for example, the imposition of additional days). This possibility of supervision beyond the SED has been held not to breach article 5 of the European Convention on Human Rights, on the basis that it constitutes a restriction on, not a deprivation of, liberty.[49]

5.27 Section 228 of the CJA 2003 allows the court to impose an extended sentence on those under 18 on conviction for offences committed after 4 April 2005.

Effect of transfer under the Mental Health Act 1983

5.28 Prisoners may be transferred from prison to hospital at any stage in their sentence under the Mental Health Act (MHA) 1983.[50] Transfer does not affect automatic release dates for determinate sentence prisoners. So for ACR and SDS prisoners the prison remains responsible for issuing a licence at the appropriate time, the conditions of which are amended to take into account the fact that the person is detained under the MHA 1983.[51]

47 PCC(S)A 2000 s96.

48 CJA 1991 s65.

49 *R (Davies) v Home Secretary* [2005] EWCA Civ 461. It is of note that breach of this licence cannot result in executive recall but is punishable on conviction by the courts: see CJA 1991 s65(6).

50 MHA 1983 s47.

51 See guidance in PSO 6000 chapter 11.

5.29 Cases where the Parole Board are responsible for the initial release decision are different, as those detained in hospitals are not eligible for review by the Parole Board. However, if a prisoner is parole eligible and the hospital, or a Mental Health Review Tribunal (MHRT), advises the Ministry of Justice Mental Health Unit that treatment is no longer required (or that no effective treatment can be given), then a parole application can be made.[52] The PPCS is responsible for preparing a dossier for the Board rather than the prison. If release is at the NPD, then the PPCS takes responsibility for issuing the licence.[53]

Other mechanisms of early release

Home detention curfew

5.30 Also introduced by the CDA 1998 was the possibility of early release on electronic tag.[54] This provides that most short-term prisoners (those serving less than four years) serving three months or more can be released earlier than the halfway point of the sentence on a curfew condition. The curfew remains in force until what would have been the automatic release date.[55] Those serving extended sentences are excluded from the scheme.[56]

5.31 This scheme is known as home detention curfew (HDC) and is generally at the discretion of the governor of the prison.[57] The scheme is complex although, broadly, those serving sentences for sexual or violent offences are excluded. If the curfew condition is breached prisoners can be recalled, and any representations against recall for this reason will be considered by the PPCS on behalf of the Secretary of State.[58] The Parole Board has no role to play in granting HDC or reviewing recall for breach of the curfew condition. If the recall is upheld on review the prisoner will then be released automatically on licence at the halfway point of the sentence.[59]

52 MHA 1983 s50; PSO 6000 para 11.3.

53 PSO 6000 para 11.4.

54 CJA 1991 s34A (as amended).

55 CJA 1991 s37A(3).

56 CJA 1991 s34A(1).

57 See PSO 6700, PSI 9/2001, PSI 19/2002, PSI 39/2002 and PSI 31/2003 for guidance on the scheme.

58 CJA 1991 s38A(4).

59 CJA 1991 s33A.

5.32 For those sentenced for offences committed on or after 4 April 2005 the CJA 2003 re-enacts entitlement to consideration for early release on HDC.[60] The maximum period remains 135 days and the guidance in PSO 6700 and related PSIs will continue to be relevant. Although the Act has removed the distinction between short-term and long-term prisoners, guidance has been issued[61] to the effect that those serving four years or more (who were not eligible for HDC under CJA 1991) will be 'presumed unsuitable' for HDC, and will only be released under the scheme in exceptional circumstances.

The early release scheme

5.33 Prisoners who are 'liable to removal' from the UK within the meaning of section 46(3) of the CJA 1991, or section 259 of the CJA 2003 for those whose offences were committed on or after 4 April 2005[62] may qualify for the early release scheme (ERS).

5.34 Prisoners liable to removal are not eligible for HDC, but the ERS provides for early release up to 270 days before what would otherwise be the earliest date of release.[63] Guidance on the scheme is contained in PSI 27/2004 and chapter 9 of PSO 6000. There is a presumption in favour of release, subject to refusal by the prison governor if there are 'exceptional or compelling' reasons to refuse.[64] Decision making is primarily delegated to individual governors[65] and the Parole Board does not play any role in this. Unlike with HDC, the length of sentence does not affect eligibility.

Compassionate release

5.35 The CJA 1991 s36 and CJA 2003 s248 contain power for the Secretary of State to release determinate sentence prisoners early on compassionate grounds where there are 'exceptional circumstances'.

60 CJA 2003 s246.

61 Note from the Chief Executive of NOMS, April 2005.

62 Those liable to removal are where there has been a decision or court recommendation to deport, a refusal of leave to enter, illegal entry, or those liable to administrative removal because of, for example, overstaying of leave to remain.

63 See PSI 19/2008 para 7 for details of eligibility dates.

64 PSI 45/2008.

65 See guidance in PSO 6000 chapter 9.

5.36 Detailed guidance on the circumstances in which the power will be exercised is contained in chapter 12 of PSO 6000. The policy makes clear that the exceptional circumstances test is a stringent one (for example, terminal illness where death is likely to occur soon[66]). In CJA 1991 cases, the Secretary of State is expected to consult the Parole Board before releasing long-term prisoners unless circumstances make such consultation impracticable[67] and a similar proviso applies under the CJA 2003 for post 4 April 2005 offences in relation to those serving extended sentences.[68] Such consultation will be on the papers and the Board's remit will essentially be related to consideration as to whether there is any ongoing risk to the public.

Special remission

5.37 Part 13 of PSO 6650 contains the policy of when special remission will be granted. This is where the royal prerogative of mercy is used to reduce a sentence because of the prisoner's meritorious conduct, or where a prisoner has been persistently misled to his/her disadvantage as to his/her correct release date. This again is a power that is exercised rarely, as it requires the granting of a royal warrant to effect the sentence reduction.[69] The Parole Board plays no part in the process.

Temporary release and end of custody licence

5.38 Prisoners can request release on temporary licence (ROTL) for certain purposes including resettlement.[70] Such periods of temporary release do not impact on the prisoners' actual release dates and it is for the governors of individual prisons to carry out the necessary risk assessments and grant the licences. The Parole Board plays no role in this process.

5.39 In a further attempt to ease prison overcrowding, an additional form of release on temporary licence was introduced by the Lord Chancellor on 19 June 2007.[71] End of custody licence (ECL) authorises release up to 18 days before what would otherwise be the automatic

66 PSO 6000 para 13.4.

67 CJA 1991 s36(2).

68 CJA 2003 s248(2).

69 PSO 6000 para 13.1.6.

70 PR 9, YOIR 5 and guidance in PSO 6300.

71 See PSI 42/2007.

release date for prisoners serving sentences of four weeks or more but less than four years. Certain prisoners are excluded.[72] As ECL is a type of release on temporary licence, recall for breach of the licence conditions is a decision as the governor's discretion and the Parole Board does not play any part in release or recall decisions. If recalled from ECL prisoners will be released at the normal release date (which will be delayed by any time spent unlawfully at large).

72 PSI 42/2007 para 4.4.

CHAPTER 6

The release of determinate sentence prisoners

Introduction

Parole eligible prisoners and eligibility dates

6.1 The Parole Board now only makes the decision as to the initial release (for the situation on recall see chapter 13) of determinate sentence prisoners in the following cases:

- Where the sentence was imposed before 1 October 1992 prisoners are eligible for release on licence following a recommendation by the Board (the parole eligibility date (PED)) at the one-*third* point.[1] Such prisoners are automatically released unconditionally at the two-thirds point.[2]
- Where the sentence is of four or more years imposed on or after 1 October 1992,[3] for an offence committed before 4 April 2005, where the offence is also included in Schedule 15 to the CJA 2003, or where the prisoner was refused parole prior to 9 June 2008. The PED is at the *halfway point* of the sentence.[4] Release for such prisoners is automatic at the two-thirds point (the non-parole date (NPD)) on licence to the three-quarter point,[5] although before 30 September 1998 CJA 1991 s44 allowed the sentencing court to order that the licence last until sentence expiry in the case of sexual offences.
- Where an extended sentence has been imposed for an offence committed on or after 30 September 1998 but before 4 April 2005, where the custodial term is four or more years and the offence is included in Schedule 15 to the CJA 2003. The PED is at the *halfway* point of the *custodial term.*[6] The prisoner is automatically released at the two-thirds point of the custodial term on licence to the end of the extension period.[7]
- Where an extended sentence is imposed before 14 July 2008 for an offence committed on or after 4 April 2005. The prisoner is eligible for release on licence at the *halfway* point of the custodial

1 CJA 1991 Sch 12 para 8(6)(a); CJA 1991 s35.
2 CJA 1991 Sch 12 para 8(6)(b); CJA 1991 s37(1).
3 Including where multiple sentences give rise to a 'single term' of four or more years.
4 CJA 1991 ss33(1B) and 35.
5 CJA 1991 ss33(2) and 37(1).
6 CJA 1991 ss44(2) and 35.
7 CJA ss33(2) and 44(4).

term.[8] The prisoner is released automatically on licence at the end of the custodial period on licence to the end of the sentence.[9]

6.2 All other determinate sentence prisoners are initially released automatically without any consideration by the Board. The changes introduced by the CJIA 2008, which now differentiate between DCR prisoners convicted of sexual or violent offences, and others, who are released automatically but on licence to sentence expiry, have been held not to unlawfully interfere with the sentence of the court so as to breach article 6 of the ECHR.[10]

6.3 Extensive guidance on the arrangements for parole reviews for determinate sentence prisoners whose release is dependent on a Parole Board decision is contained in PSO 6000 chapter 5, which was extensively revised to coincide with the coming into force of relevant parts of the CJA 2003 on 4 April 2005. Its terminology has not been updated since the creation of the Ministry of Justice or the transfer of responsibility for parole policy to the PPCS in NOMS. References to the release and recall section in the policy should therefore be taken as referring to the PPCS. The Parole Board Rules 2004 do not apply where the Parole Board is considering the initial release of determinate sentence prisoners.

The review process

6.4 The parole review process is essentially the same in all the above cases.[11] The timetable for consideration of cases is set out in appendix B to PSO 6000 chapter 5 (see below).

Beginning of the parole process

6.5 The parole review process begins 26 weeks before the first PED or subsequent anniversaries, as PSO 6000 confirms that for those serving long enough sentences (or custodial terms in the case of extended

8 CJIA 2008 s25, which amended the CJA 2003 to provide for automatic release at the same point for extended sentence prisoners, was not applied to prisoners sentenced prior to that date: CJIA 2008 (Commencement No 2 and Transitional and Saving Provisions) Order 2008 SI No 1586 Sch 2 para 2.

9 CJA 2003 ss247 and 249.

10 *R (on the application of Poku) v Secretary of State for Justice* [2009] EWHC 1380 (Admin).

11 See PSO 6000 para 8.4.5.

sentences) there is a right to an annual review of parole eligibility.[12] The timetable starts with the prisoner applying for parole on a prescribed form.[13] The prisoner is able to opt out of the process if he/she does not wish to apply for parole.[14]

6.6 The prison holding the prisoner is responsible for preparing the dossier.[15] In order to avoid disruption to the parole process, prisoners whose parole process is underway should not be transferred to another prison before their dossier is completed unless there are exceptional circumstances, such as where a move is required on the grounds of security, good order or discipline, health or other compassionate factors, or to avoid severe overcrowding.[16] Where such a transfer does take place, responsibility for compilation of the dossier rests with the prison with 'the greater knowledge of the prisoner' and such responsibility should be agreed at the time of the transfer.[17]

The dossier

6.7 If the prisoner applies for parole it is the responsibility of the offender management unit ('OMU') in the prison to request reports from prison staff and outside agencies including the PAROM 1 (see para 6.19 below) from the supervising probation officer or offender manager. These are then compiled into a dossier, and form the basis of the material upon which the Parole Board will make its assessment of risk to the public. What the dossier should contain is outlined in PSO 6000 chapter 5 appendix F (see box on page 98).

Disclosure of the dossier

6.8 The reports in the dossier should be written with a view to open reporting.[18] Before the dossier is sent to the Parole Board the prisoner must be given access to a copy (subject to the restrictions on disclosure set out below) so that he/she has the opportunity to make representations on its contents. The timetable states that the dossier

12 PSO 6000 para 5.9.2.
13 At PSO 6000 chapter 5 appendix C.
14 PSO 6000 para 5.13.
15 PSO 6000 para 5.14.1.
16 PSO 6000 para 5.11.1.
17 PSO 6000 para 5.11.2.
18 PSO 6000 para 5.15.1.

should be disclosed at 17 weeks before the parole eligibility date.[19] The prisoner is not given a copy of the dossier, although copies can be obtained by the prisoner or his/her legal representative on payment of the administrative charges involved in the copying.[20]

6.9 When instructed in relation to parole reviews, legal representatives can provide advice and assistance under the CDS general criminal contract. It is important to obtain a copy of the dossier as soon as it is available so that instructions on its contents can be obtained and representations forwarded to the parole clerk for inclusion prior to its being sent to the Board. However, the dossier is often disclosed much later than the timetable prescribes, and sometimes only after it has been forwarded to the Parole Board with the prisoner's own representations. In these circumstances further representations can be made directly to the Parole Board. If the dossier has been sent to the Board it is important to ascertain when a panel is due to consider the case to ensure any further representations are received in time.

6.10 PSO 6000 makes clear that 'in the interests of fairness, the presumption must be that all reports are disclosed'.[21] However, it also sets out five grounds upon which, exceptionally, reports may be withheld from the prisoner.[22] These are:

- in the interests of national security;
- for the prevention of disorder or crime – this includes information relevant to prison security;
- for the protection of information that may put a third party at risk;
- where, on medical and/or psychiatric grounds, it is felt necessary to withhold information where the mental and/or physical health of the prisoner could be impaired; and
- where the source of the information is a victim, and disclosure without their consent would breach any duty of confidence owed to that victim, or would generally prejudice the future supply of such information.

6.11 The decisions on withholding information should be made by the governor or a nominated senior officer[23] and the relevant decision-maker is encouraged to seek guidance from PPCS on such decisions.

19 PSO 6000 chapter 5 appendix B.
20 PSO 6000 para 5.15.1.
21 PSO 6000 para 5.16.
22 PSO 6000 para 5.16.1.
23 PSO 6000 para 5.16.2.

If a request is made to not disclose any material the governor or nominated senior officer must:

- consider whether the information is relevant;
- if it is relevant, consider whether it could be rewritten to exclude information that is not disclosable without reducing its impact. Any decision on rewriting such documents should be made in consultation with the author of the material;.
- if rewriting is not possible, consider whether a gist of the document can be produced. If it is not possible to produce a gist, consider whether it meets the criteria for non-disclosure (see above).[24]

6.12 When it has been decided that a document is not for disclosure, the prisoner must be informed on a prescribed form that information has been withheld, and under which limb of the non-disclosure criteria, but must not be given any information about the non-disclosed material itself.[25] Where there has been a request for non-disclosure of relevant information, if the non-disclosure criteria are not met it should not be included in the dossier unless the author or source agrees it may be disclosed.[26]

6.13 The policy notes that it will only be in 'rare' cases that information is so sensitive that no part of it can be disclosed on application of the non-disclosure criteria. In these circumstances the prisoner must be advised and 'his representative (recognised barrister or solicitor) may apply to have sight of the information. Permission would normally be given only after having first received a written undertaking that they will not disclose the information, in full or in part, to the prisoner'. A request by the representative should only be refused after consultation with PPCS.[27]

6.14 The potential unfairness of partial or non-disclosure of material that may be relevant to the Board's assessment is obvious, as the prisoner's right to make meaningful representations will be affected. There are also potential ethical problems in a legal representative receiving material that is not disclosed to the client (although this course can be adopted if the client agrees).

6.15 The provisions in the determinate parole process now largely mirror those in the Parole Board Rules (PBR) 2004 and comments

24 PSO 6000 para 5.16.3.
25 PSO 6000 para 5.16.5.
26 PSO 6000 para 5.16.6.
27 PSO 6000 para 5.16.10.

on disclosure issues under the PBR[28] are relevant (although in relation to the release of a prisoner early during the currency of the sentence imposed as punishment article 5 of the European Convention on Human Rights is not directly engaged). Accordingly, as in cases under the PBR, once disclosure of material is made to a representative it would be open to the representative to make further representations to the governor and/or the PPCS as to further disclosure to the prisoner. There has been at least one case in relation to a determinate sentence prisoner, where there has been non-disclosure both to the prisoner and the legal representative, in which the Administrative Court has ordered that fairness requires the use of a special advocate, who has no contact with the prisoner after receiving the material, but who can make representations in relation to it to the Board in closed session.[29]

Contents of the dossier

6.16 Further guidance on the dossier contents is contained in PSO 6000 chapter 5 appendix G. This guidance confirms that it is important that the summary of the offence accurately reflects the sentencing court's findings. The guidance states that, where possible, a report should be obtained from the police as soon as possible after sentence, but that material that may not reflect the findings of the sentencing court, such as pre-trial prosecution evidence, bail summaries and witness statements 'must not be included in the dossier as they do not necessarily set out the circumstances of the offence as established in court: they are liable to challenge by the prisoner and could mislead the Parole Board'.[30]

6.17 This is a common problem, and if there is such erroneous and prejudicial material in the dossier representations should be made to the parole clerk to have it removed before the dossier is sent to the Board. If the parole clerk is unwilling to do so then the matter can be referred to the PPCS. The Board is under a duty to consider any documents provided to it in the dossier[31] and it has been held

28 See paras 10.34–10.42.

29 *R (Patel) v Home Secretary and Parole Board* CO/2588/2004 Order 15, June 2004, a model approved by the House of Lords in lifer cases in *R (on the application of Roberts) v Parole Board; sub nom Roberts v Parole Board* [2005] UKHL 45.

30 PSO 6000 chapter 5 appendix G para 2.

31 See CJA 2003 s239(3)(a).

PSO 6000 Chapter 5 Appendix F

Parole dossiers must include (where applicable)

	Contents of parole dossier	*Source*
1.	Front cover sheet and index	Parole clerk/OMU
2.	Summary of offence from *one* or all of the following sources • Police report • Pre-sentence report (probation) • Pre-sentence psychiatric report • Court transcription of sentencing remarks	PPCS
3.	Court papers (including Form 5089 and 5035) (including, if the offender has appealed, *the appeal papers must be included*)	Sentencing court/Court of Appeal
4.	Court transcription of sentencing remarks	Prison/PPCS
5.	List of previous convictions	Police/Court/Probation
6.	Pre-sentence medical, psychological or psychiatric reports (if applicable)	Probation/Healthcare/ prison psychology
7.	Copy of previous parole dossiers (if applicable)	Parole clerk/OMU
8.	Copy of previous parole refusal notice(s) (if applicable)	Parole clerk/OMU
9.	Sentence planning and OASys documentation	Prison/Probation
10.	Adjudications and ADAs (if applicable)	Prison
11.	Prison parole assessment	Prison
12.	Seconded probation officer's report	Seconded probation officer
13.	Report(s) on offence related work (if any)	Prison
14.	Prison medical/psychiatric/psychological reports (if applicable)	Prison/other
15.	Post-sentence psychology report (if any)	Prison psychology
16.	Category A review report (if applicable)	Category A clerk
17.	Security report	Security Manager
18.	Victim personal statement (if available)	Offender manager/police
19.	PAROM 1 (formerly PAR)	Offender manager
20.	Prisoner's disclosure form/representations	Prison
21.	Parole board member interview report (if carried out)	Parole board member
22.	Disclosure form/representations	Prisoner/legal representative

The Parole Clerk must check that dossiers contain these reports.

The Secretariat WILL return dossiers to establishments if they do not contain the reports.

The dossier may also contain other relevant information such as pre-sentence reports, Prison Chaplain's report or job offers or letters of support. Letters/Other Papers – these may be included in the dossier but none of these documents are essential for the parole review.

that this means that it is unable to remove such material itself.[32] In cases where there are only minor errors or concerns in the dossier it may be simpler, rather than entering into time-consuming correspondence about what the dossier should contain, to deal with the issues in the representations submitted to the Board. PSO 6000 confirms that complaints about the contents of the dossier can be made through the normal prison complaints procedure[33] but that consideration by the Board will not normally be deferred pending the complaint's investigation. Even where there is evidence that previous convictions may be unsafe, the Board cannot go behind such convictions and make its decision on the basis that they are correct unless quashed.[34]

The key reports

6.18 As the Board's focus will be on the risk the offender poses to the public, the key reports will be from those from the probation officers and any psychology report completed during the sentence (a psychology report compiled in the prison is not mandatory and will only be completed if the prisoner has had contact with a psychologist[35]).

6.19 The dossier will contain two probation reports. One from a seconded probation officer based in the prison, and one from the home probation officer, now known as the offender manager, in the community, who will be responsible for the supervision of the prisoner if released on licence. Since the implementation of Phase III of the Offender Management Model ('OMM') on 7 January 2008 the report of the offender manager for determinate sentence cases is in the same format as that used in lifer cases. This is the PAROM 1 report and detailed guidance has been given to probation officers as to what this report should contain, namely:[36]

- an account of the index offence, including the offender's attitude and motivation;
- an analysis of any previous offending history, including patterns of offending and the risks of serious harm and of reoffending at the time of the offence;

32 *R v Parole Board ex p Harris* [1998] COD 223.

33 PSO 6000 para 5.15.3.

34 *R (on the application of Solomon) v Parole Board* [2006] EWHC 2639 (Admin).

35 See PSO 6000 chapter 5 appendix G para 14.

36 See PC 7/2008 the PAROM 1 is now used instead of what used to be known as the Parole Assessment Report or 'PAR'.

- any relevant victim information, including subsequent contact by the probation service with the victim;
- relevant information about the personal circumstances of the offender;
- details of interventions engaged during the prison sentence which have addressed both the risk of harm and of reoffending, and an analysis of their impact;
- details of the offender's behaviour in prison, including any adjudications and drug test results;
- a current risk assessment, including a summary of different staff views;
- an analysis of the evidence from assessment tools that have been used such as OASys, RM 2000 or SARA;
- a summary from sentence planning reviews;
- where relevant, a resettlement and sentence plan, which must include an assessment of the risks the offender poses if released now; the key relapse indicators; and a risk management plan. It should include any MAPPA involvement and relevant multi-agency planning undertaken or to be undertaken;
- a clear proposal as to suitability for open conditions or release on licence; or the work that needs to be undertaken before such moves could be considered.

6.20 Whilst the Probation Service is required to draft a resettlement plan where appropriate this does not require it to provide a release address if no suitable accommodation in approved premises is available.[37] Similarly, where a release plan depends on actions of a local authority, such as provision of foster care, where that authority believes that the plan is unsuitable it is under no duty (either by application of article 5 or the common law) to make such provision.[38]

6.21 Probation service guidance recognises that the seconded probation officer and offender manager should provide complimentary but distinct assessments of the prisoner.[39] In relation to the seconded probation officer's report, guidance specifies the matters that should be included:[40]

- an interpretation and analysis of prison behaviour, including sentence plan, adjudications, impact of offending behaviour work

37 See para 2.10.

38 *R (on the application of S) v Halton BC and the Parole Board* [2008] EWHC 1982 (Admin).

39 PC 34/2004 para 5.1.

40 PC 34/2004 para 6.2.

and other relevant risk reduction work such as literacy and vocational qualifications;

- an analysis of the offender's motivation to change and sustain an offence-free lifestyle upon release. This assessment must be based not only on prisoner's stated intent but should include some analysis of his/her ability to achieve this;
- an assessment of whether licence conditions might strengthen and sustain a prisoner's motivation to change.

6.22 The prison parole assessment is completed either by the prisoner's personal officer, or an officer with personal knowledge of the prisoner. The report should be completed following an interview with the prisoner, consultation with other relevant members of staff and consideration of the prisoner's records.[41]

Representations

6.23 The disclosure form that the prisoner is invited to sign when a copy of the dossier is given to him/her includes a section upon which the prisoner can write his/her own representations or comments on the dossier. The timetable in PSO 6000 states that representations should be submitted to the OMU at the prison 13 weeks before the parole eligibility date. There is no set format for representations submitted by legal representatives. As noted above, to ensure that representations are considered by the Board they should be sent to the parole clerk so that they are attached to the dossier prior to its being forwarded to the Board. However, if time constraints make this impossible representations can be forwarded to the Board. If this is done it is sensible to confirm their receipt and obtain an assurance from the Board that the representations will be forwarded to the panel considering the prisoner's case.

Contents of representations

6.24 The content of representations will obviously depend upon the contents of the dossier. If there are disputed facts in the dossier and these have not been amended in correspondence with the prison and/or PPCS prior to representations being submitted, a further statement from the prisoner can be included together with other evidence of the true facts. Prior authority can be obtained from the LSC on form CDS 5 to obtain independent expert reports (such as from

41 PSO 6000 chapter 5 appendix G para 10.

an independent psychologist) if necessary. Other common issues that may need to be addressed in representations are:

- providing background information on matters such as disciplinary findings of guilt, and custodial history;
- providing information about offending behaviour programmes or other activities in prison that have not been dealt with, or dealt with sufficiently, in the reports contained in the dossier;
- further information about release plan (supporting statements/letters from family, those providing a release address/job offers) especially if the offender manager's report is not particularly detailed in these respects;
- details of outside activities that prisoners have been allowed that might demonstrate trustworthiness (such as town visits, community work or periods of resettlement leave).

Where appropriate factors which demonstrate that fairness may require the Board to either interview the prisoner or hold an oral hearing before reaching its decision (see paras 6.28–6.31 below).

6.25 Representations should focus on risk to the public, and the directions the Board have to consider (see paras 6.32–6.40 below) provide a guide as to the issues upon which the Board will focus.[42]

Parole Board member's interview

6.26 Up until 1 April 2004 DCR prisoners were interviewed by a Parole Board member as part of the parole process. When this was first introduced after the coming into force of the CJA 1991, it was seen as a way of ensuring that prisoners, in the absence of oral parole hearings, had an opportunity to meet a representative of the body that would be making the decision as to whether they should be released.

6.27 In fact the interviewing member's role was never particularly clear. The joint Prison Service/Probation Service Comprehensive Review of Parole and Lifer Processes, which reported in 2001, noted that it was not clear whether the purpose was to enhance procedural fairness for the prisoner, or to allow the Board better to assess the risk to the public. From April 2004[43] the Parole Board only carry out an interview (which the prisoner cannot be compelled to attend) where it considers that without one there is insufficient information to make a decision. The interviewing member used to advise on

42 See also para 10.64 on written representations in lifer cases, as many of the points raised there will also be relevant to determinate sentence parole reviews.

43 See PSI 29/2004 and PSO 6000 para 5.17.

whether the panel considering the prisoner's case should include a psychiatrist. This role in the absence of an interview is delegated to the governor. In fact it transpired in evidence that was put before the Court of Appeal in the *Brooke* case[44] that the Parole Board did consider that such interviews were of value and the impetus to restrict their use was due to the executive's desire to cut costs. This evidence contributed to the Court of Appeal's finding that the Board was insufficiently independent from its sponsoring department.

Decision making

Procedure

6.28 The Parole Board initially consider determinate sentence cases on the papers before a three-member panel of the Board. The timetable in PSO 6000 states that this consideration should take place seven weeks before the parole eligibility date. In most cases the final decision will be made on the basis of the paper consideration. However, it has been held that even where article 5(4) of the Convention does not apply the Board retains a discretion to hold one where fairness requires.[45] Oral hearings in determinate cases used to be extremely rare. Whilst the vast majority of determinate sentence release decisions are made on the papers, oral hearings have become more common.

6.29 The Parole Board does not have a stated policy as to when oral hearings will be held in determinate sentence initial release cases. However the Board accepts that fairness may require a hearing where there is a dispute of fact that can only be fairly resolved by hearing evidence, or where there is conflicting expert evidence. The courts when considering the entitlement to an oral hearing in cases involving the initial release of determinate sentence prisons have also held that similar factors as those identified by the House of Lords in *Smith and West*[46] weigh in favour of an oral hearing even where article 5(4) is not engaged. For example, when considering whether the Board should hold oral hearings to determine the initial release of extended sentence prisoners the Court of Appeal stated:

> It seems to me that the Parole Board should be predisposed to holding an oral hearing in such cases. That would certainly be the case

44 See para 1.52.

45 Under CJA 1991 s32(3); see *R v Parole Board ex p Davies* HC, 27/11/96 unreported; CJA 2003 s239(3) is in the same terms.

46 See para 1.46.

where there is any dispute of fact, or any need to examine the applicant's motives or state of mind.[47]

6.30 While requesting an oral hearing may be necessary to ensure that a prisoner's case is fairly considered, prisoners and their representatives should be aware that, so long as the Board remains severely under-resourced, demanding a hearing may lead to a delay in the case being heard.

Hearings for children

6.31 The position for under 18-year-olds is different. The Board currently has a policy of considering these cases, of which there are relatively few, at an oral hearing.[48] The procedure is that an Intensive Case Management (ICM) member of the Board will consider the dossiers of such prisoners 12 weeks before the parole eligibility date in order to identify witnesses with a view to a hearing taking place no later than five weeks before the PED. The Board's policy on under 18s was changed following a case that decided that it had acted unfairly in failing to consider whether to hold a hearing when considering whether to release a 15-year-old serving an extended sentence. The court stated that the Board had to be 'particularly scrupulous in observing its obligations of fairness in a case concerning the liberty of one so young'.[49] Under 18-year-old prisoners should also have the assistance of an adult in making representations. Children in the dedicated units in Young Offenders' Institutions (YOIs) should have access to the advocacy services located within them for help in making representations and for referrals to solicitors where necessary.

47 *R (on the application of O'Connell) v Parole Board* [2008] 1 WLR 979 para 24, although this decision was overruled by the Court of Appeal ([2009] EWCA Civ 575) on the applicability of article 5(4) to the initial release of extended sentence prisoners. As the court held that the test as to when an oral hearing was required was the same under the common law as under article 5(4) its finding on this issue is presumably still good law. See also *R (on the application of Hopkins) v Parole Board* [2008] EWHC 2312 (Admin) where the Administrative Court quashed a decision refusing release of a determinate sentence prisoner where no hearing was held as there were disputed facts, and very strong support for release from probation officers.

48 See *Intensive case management oral hearings general guidance*, Parole Board, July 2008, Section 10.

49 *R (on the application of K) v Parole Board* [2006] EWHC 2413 (Admin) para 28: the court did not suggest that fairness will always require an oral hearing for this group of prisoners and the Board has perhaps overreacted by always insisting on one.

The test for release

6.32 As noted above, this section is dealing with the initial release of determinate sentence prisoners, where such a decision is subject to a Parole Board decision. This therefore includes DCR prisoners where the offence is contained in Schedule 15 to CJA 2003, CJA 1991 extended sentence prisoners where the custodial term is four or more years for an offence in Schedule 15, and CJA 2003 extended sentence prisoners where the sentence was imposed before 14 July 2008. In practice, the Parole Board considers the release of all three classes of prisoner by reference to the same directions issued by the Secretary of State. However the different sentences do potentially raise different issues as to how the Board should approach the test it applies.

CJA 1991 DCR cases

6.33 DCR prisoners have been sentenced to a term of imprisonment that is commensurate with the seriousness of the offence.[50] As the sentencing court has decided that the whole of the term should be imposed as punishment, no fresh issues as to the legality of detention pursuant to the sentence can arise under article 5 of the European Convention on Human Rights.[51] Accordingly, within the statutory scheme, initial release is at the discretion of the executive.[52] In practice the Secretary of State has delegated the final decision on DCR release cases to the Board for all prisoners serving sentences of less than 15 years.[53] There have been two attempts to challenge the lawfulness of this retention of the power to decide whether determinate sentence prisoners serving 15 years or more should be released. In *R on the application of Clift v Secretary of State for the Home Department*[54] it was argued that as parole falls within the ambit of article 5, the difference in treatment between prisoners serving under and over 15 years was discriminatory under article 14. Although the Lords were sympathetic to the argument and accepted that parole does fall within the ambit of article 5, they did not accept that the sentence

50 PCC(S)A 2000 s80(2)(a).

51 See *R (on the application of Giles)* [2004] 1 AC 1 paras 51–52.

52 CJA 1991 s35(1) states that after a DCR prisoner has served half the sentence 'the Secretary of State may, if recommended by the Board, release him on licence'.

53 Parole Board (Transfer of Functions) Order 1998 SI No 3218.

54 [2007] 1 AC 484.

length could be considered a personal characteristic capable of being subject to discriminatory treatment.[55]

6.34 In a subsequent case, a prisoner in the same position unsuccessfully argued that the retention of the power by the executive was a direct breach of article 5(4), the Lords holding that release on licence for a prisoner serving a determinate sentence does not engage a convention right.[56] The Coroners and Justice Act 2009 contains an amendment to the CJA 1991 section 35 giving the Board directive power even for this group of prisoners (although this had not been enacted at the time of writing).[57]

6.35 This framework means that when it comes to the test for release of DCR prisoners, the Secretary of State is entitled to issue directions[58] to the Board as to matters it should take into account.[59] The most recent directions came into force on 1 May 2004.[60] The directions include great detail as to the matters the Board should take into account when coming to their decision (and as such can provide a guide as to matters to deal with in written representations).

6.36 The Board is directed to consider 'primarily' whether:

> the risk to the public of a further offence being committed at a time when the offender would otherwise be in prison and whether such risk is unacceptable. This must be balanced against the benefit, both to the public and the offender, of early release back into the community under a degree of supervision which might help rehabilitation and so lessen the risk of re-offending in the future.[61]

It is not necessarily the risk of the similar kind of offending that led to the imposition of the sentence that will justify the refusal of parole.

6.37 The changes to the CJA 1991 brought in by the CJIA 2008 do raise an issue as to whether the proper test in these cases should be referable to a risk of committing any offence. Since 9 June 2008 it is

55 Although Lord Bingham described it as an 'indefensible anomaly' that the Secretary of State retained the final decision-making power in this context: para 38.

56 *R (on the application of Black) v Secretary of State for Justice* [2009] UKHL 1.

57 Coroners and Justice Act 2009 s14.

58 Under CJA 1991 s32(6).

59 This is in contrast to the position where article 5 of the Convention requires the Board to have directive powers of release, where the courts have held that such directions cannot be binding as they interfere with the Board's independence as a court – *R (on the application of Girling)* [2005] EWHC 546 (Admin).

60 See ministerial statement of Paul Goggins, 18 March 2004, and appendix F.

61 Ibid.

only DCR prisoners who are convicted of sexual or violent offences (contained in Schedule 15 to CJA 2003) who are not automatically released at the halfway point of their sentence. There is therefore an argument that it is only the risk of the commission of such sexual or violent offences that should justify detention between the PED and the NPD.[62]

CJA long-term extended sentences

6.38 Those sentenced to an extended sentence for an offence contained in Schedule 15 to the CJA 2003, committed between 30 September 1998 and 4 April 2005, where the custodial term is four or more years, are eligible for release at the halfway point of the custodial term.[63] As the custodial term will be the same as the sentence commensurate with the seriousness of the offence, release at the halfway point can be on the same criteria as for DCR cases. As noted in the section on recalls,[64] article 5 of the Convention is engaged where there is a recall during the extension period, as that element of the sentence is not imposed punitively, but in order to protect the public and secure rehabilitation. This means the test the Board must pose when considering recalls is different.[65] However, for practical reasons the Board does not appear to distinguish between the test applicable to those recalled prior to the statutory commencement of the extension period, and those recalled afterwards.

CJA 2003 extended sentence prisoners

6.39 The guidance in PSO 6000 suggests that when the initial release of CJA 2003 extended sentence prisoners is considered by the Board, the procedures adopted should be the same as those applicable to CJA 1991 DCR cases outlined above, including the application of the

62 A similar argument in the context of CJA 2003 extended sentence cases was left unresolved in *O'Connell* (see note 70 below). Prior to the coming into force of the CJIA 2008 an attempt to establish that DCR prisoners should have their release considered by reference to a serious harm test failed in *R (on the application of Pilgrim) v Parole Board and Secretary of State for Justice* [2008] EWHC 1019 (Admin), the judge commenting on the 'unlikely consequences' that a result that the Board would be required to release a DCR prisoner who had an open intent to commit thefts on release.

63 CJA 1991 ss44(2) and 35(1).

64 See chapter 12.

65 The situation is complicated by the fact that the extension period in CJA 1991 extended sentence cases commences at the three-quarter point of the custodial term: CJA 1991 s44(5)(a).

same statutory directions.[66] The assumption that release at the halfway point of the custodial term of a CJA 2003 extended sentence case should be treated the same as release at the halfway point of a CJA 1991 DCR case relies on the fact that in both cases the prisoner is applying for release during the currency of term of imprisonment commensurate with the seriousness of the offence.

6.40 As noted above, those serving an SDS of 12 months or more under the CJA 2003 are automatically released on licence at the halfway point.[67] By contrast, extended sentence prisoners sentenced before 14 July 2008 are eligible for release halfway through the custodial term only where the Parole Board directs release.[68] The Board can only make a direction where 'it is satisfied that it is no longer necessary for the protection of the public that the prisoner should be confined'.[69] There is therefore an argument that as, but for the finding of the sentencing court of dangerousness, the offender would have been released automatically at the halfway point of the custodial term, the ongoing justification for detention beyond this point can only be continued dangerousness. An argument asserting that this analysis should lead to a finding that article 5(4) is engaged in such cases failed in the Court of Appeal.[70] However the case did not determine the issue as to what test for release should be adopted by the Board.

Parole Board decisions

6.41 The Board will issue decisions to the prison in all cases except DCR cases where the sentence is 15 years or longer. In those cases the Parole Board decision is treated as a recommendation[71] by officials in the PPCS who make the final decision on behalf of the Secretary of State.[72] The Board may defer a decision if it considers further information is necessary.[73] The Board will give reasons for its decision.

66 PSO 6000 para 8.4.5.

67 CJA 2003 s244.

68 CJA 2003 s247(2).

69 CJA 2003 s247(3).

70 *R (on the application of O'Connell) v Parole Board and another* [2009] EWCA Civ 575, which held that the Lords in *Black* had ruled out the applicability of article 5(4) to the initial release of all determinate sentence prisoners (see note 58).

71 Under CJA 1991 s35(1) but see para 6.34 above.

72 Parole Board (Transfer of Functions) Order 1998 SI No 3218.

73 PSO 6000 para 5.18.2.

If the decision is to refuse parole, and where the sentence is long enough, the prisoner will be informed of any entitlement to further annual reviews.[74] For examination of the licence conditions that will be imposed and length of licence see chapter 12.

6.42 If the outcome is a release decision, the governor or director (in private prisons) should ensure that the release arrangements (such as a hostel place arranged by the Probation Service) are in place[75] and once the release date has been agreed the governor must issue the licence on behalf of the Secretary of State.[76] The governor or authorised officer must sign the licence to confirm that its conditions have been explained to the prisoner. If the prisoner refuses to sign the licence, this will be reported to the Parole Board or PPCS as a refusal to comply with the conditions of release and could lead to suspension of release on licence.[77]

6.43 The release decision, even after it has been communicated to the prison by the Board can be suspended at any point up to the moment of departure 'if new information comes to light which would cause the Parole Board or Secretary of State to review its/his decision'.[78] The policy gives examples of the prisoner facing disciplinary charges or where the release plan breaks down. The prison is required to inform the Parole Board or PPCS (in DCR cases where the sentence is 15 or more years), which will either confirm the release decision or invite further representations from the prisoner in light of the changed circumstances as to whether parole should be withdrawn.

Further reviews

6.44 If parole is refused, the prisoner is entitled to further annual reviews, as long as at the beginning of the review process there are at least 13 months until the date of automatic release on licence at the two-thirds point of the sentence/custodial term (for DCR and CJA 1991 extended sentence cases) or the automatic release date at the end of the custodial term (for CJA 2003 extended sentence cases).[79]

74 PSO 6000 para 5.19.1.

75 PSO 6000 para 5.19.3.

76 PSO 6000 para 5.25.

77 PSO 6000 para 5.25.2 – compare with the position on automatic release dates where a refusal to sign the licence cannot prevent release, for example in relation to the SDS sentence: see PSO 6000 para 4.10.5.

78 PSO 6000 para 5.21.1.

79 PSO 6000 para 5.9.3.

6.45 Beyond these annual reviews, PSO 6000 paragraph 5.10.1 contains the policy on when early or special reviews may be agreed outside the normal timetable:

> The [PPCS] (on behalf of the Secretary of State) has the power to authorise special or early reviews in exceptional circumstances. The Secretary of State has delegated to the Parole Board the authority to determine whether to reconsider an earlier decision in the light of representations. If the Board declines to reconsider a case, the prisoner or his representative may apply to the [PPCS] to re-refer the case back to the Board. Exceptionally, the [PPCS] may ask for an early review. The Board and/or the [PPCS] will advise the Governor if a special or early review is ordered by letter, when appropriate. *In such cases any subsequent reviews must commence 26 weeks after the special/early review panel date.*

6.46 The courts, when examining the policy on special or early reviews have held that it is not just a change of circumstances, such as completion of an offending behaviour course, that will justify a special review as such a change will not always be 'exceptional'. However, the court stated that the Board should have a flexible approach to what does constitute 'exceptional circumstances' and not merely limit itself to instances where the reasons for the decision were flawed, or where there had been procedural errors, or decisions made due to a material basis of fact.[80] A common situation where the Board will agree to a further review is if material that should have been placed before the Board, such as a report on an offending behaviour course completed before its decision was made, is for some reason not included in the dossier.

6.47 Where a decision of the Board has indicated that progress in a particular area may lead to a favourable decision at the next review, such an indication is not binding on the panel that subsequently considers the prisoner's case. It will have to make its own decision on risk based on the material available at the time of its decision.[81]

Non-parole release

6.48 If not released on the recommendation of the Board at the halfway point of the sentence or at any subsequent reviews:

80 *R (on the application of McCalla)* [2001] EWHC 396 (Admin).

81 *R (on the application of Atkinson) v Parole Board* [2008] EWHC 1215 (Admin).

- existing CJA 1967 prisoners are released unconditionally at the two-thirds point;
- DCR and CJA 1991 extended sentence prisoners with a custodial term of four or more years are released at the two-thirds point of the sentence or custodial term;[82]
- DCR prisoners are released on licence to the three-quarter point;[83]
- CJA 1991 extended sentence prisoners are released on licence to the end of the extension period;
- CJA 2003 extended sentence prisoners are released at the end of the custodial term on licence to sentence expiry.

Prisoners liable to removal

6.49 Prisoners who are liable to removal and are not released under the ERS scheme[84] and who are serving sentences which fall to be administered under the CJA 1991 (imposed for offences committed before 4 April 2005) are subject to the normal early release schemes that depend on sentence length.

6.50 Prior to the coming into force of the CJIA 2008, in the case of DCR prisoners liable to removal no referral was made to the Board and the Secretary of State was responsible for the release decision. The position was changed after the House of Lords held that this unlawfully discriminated against prisoners liable to removal.[85] Now such prisoners are treated in the same way as all others. If not released on the ERS scheme they will be released automatically at the halfway point of the sentence unless serving a DCR sentence of four or more years for an offence contained in Schedule 15 to the CJA 2003. In that situation their cases will be referred to the Parole Board.[86] The UK Border Agency may of course seek to detain those subject to immigration control under the Immigration Act 1971 if released from the criminal sentence.

82 CJA 1991 s33(2).

83 CJA 1991 s37(1), unless for sexual offences committed before 30 September 1998, the court ordered that the licence extend to sentence expiry under PCC(S)A 2000 s86.

84 See paras 5.33–5.34.

85 *R (n the application of Clift, Headley and Hindawi) v Secretary of State for the Home Department* [2006] UKHL 54.

86 CJIA 2008 s27; PSI 14/2009.

CHAPTER 7

Indeterminate sentences: an overview

The various types of life and indeterminate sentences

7.1 There are a number of different life and indeterminate sentences available to the courts. While all of these sentences are administered by the Prison Service and the Parole Board in the same manner, the legal basis for the imposition of the sentence can have relevance when assessing risk issues for the purposes of parole, and so it is important to be aware of which life sentence has been imposed. The various life sentences available to the courts are listed below.

Murder

7.2 Following a conviction for murder it is a mandatory statutory requirement to impose a life sentence. The three sentences that can be imposed are:

- the life sentence that is imposed automatically on persons convicted of murder who are aged 21 or over when the offence is committed.[1] This is commonly referred to as the 'mandatory life sentence' and people serving the sentence are often described as 'mandatory lifers';
- custody for life, which is imposed automatically on people convicted of murder who are aged 18 or over but under 21 when the offence was committed.[2] For practical purposes, there is no real legal distinction to be made between this class of lifers and adult mandatory lifers;
- detention at Her Majesty's Pleasure (HMP) is imposed on people convicted of murder who were under the age of 18 when the offence was committed.[3] This sentence has a complex history, originally being introduced at the start of the twentieth century to replace the death penalty for minors with indefinite detention. When the death penalty was abolished for adults, the sentence effectively became subsumed into the adult mandatory life sentence, but a series of cases over the past 15 years has allowed the courts to reaffirm the distinctive nature of HMP detention. The relevance of these differences is discussed as they arise in context,

1 Murder (Abolition of Death Penalty) Act 1965 s1.
2 PCC(S)A 2000 s93.
3 PCC(S)A 2000 s90, which replaced the Children and Young Persons Act 1933 s53(1).

but the fundamental distinction is that this sentence contains an intrinsic welfare element as well as the normal punitive and protective elements in sentences imposed on adults.

Life sentences for other serious offences

Discretionary life sentences

7.3 The discretionary life sentence can be imposed where life is the maximum sentence – eg for a range of offences such as attempted murder, manslaughter, arson with intent to endanger life or where there is recklessness, rape, buggery where the victim is under 16, armed robbery or other serious offences of violence. It is currently imposed under CJA 2003 section 225 for offences committed on or after 4 April 2005 (this requires the imposition of a life sentence where the offence attracts a maximum of life, and the court considers that the seriousness of the offence is such to justify the imposition of a life sentence). Before the enactment of the CJA 2003, the statutory authority for the sentence was found in section 80 of the PCC(S)A 2000.

7.4 The sentencing court is justified in imposing a discretionary life sentence where it believes that the offender is dangerous. It is therefore meant to be reserved for offenders whose mental state makes it difficult to predict future risk or where the offences are so serious that there may be ongoing risk. *R v Hodgson*[4] established the following criteria for the imposition of a discretionary life sentence:

- where the offence or offences in themselves are grave enough to require a very long sentence; and
- when it appears from the nature of the offences or from the defendant's history that he/she is a person of unstable character likely to commit such offences in the future; and
- where, if further offences are committed, the consequences to others may be especially injurious, as in the case of sexual offences or cases of violence.

7.5 However, subsequent case-law has suggested that the sentence is available in cases where the severity of the offence justifies it, even if there is no direct evidence of mental instability. This development seems to have been particularly concentrated on sexual offending. The Court of Appeal has also confirmed that a discretionary life sentence remains appropriate rather than that a sentence of Indeterminate

4 [1968] 15 CAR 13.

Public Protection (IPP) in cases where the offending crosses the appropriate level of seriousness.[5] Judge LCJ stated that:

> Without being prescriptive, we suggest that the sentence should come into contemplation when the judgment of the court is that the seriousness is such that the life sentence would have what Lord Bingham observed in *Lichniak* [2003] 1 AC 903, would be a 'denunciatory' value, reflective of public abhorrence of the offence, and where, because of its seriousness, the notional determinate sentence would be very long, measured in very many years.

Automatic lifers

7.6 The automatic life sentence ceased to be available to the sentencing courts from 4 April 2005, when it was replaced by the sentence of imprisonment for public protection (see below). However, the sentence was so prevalent for while that there are large numbers of automatic lifers serving the sentence in custody and on licence.

7.7 The sentence was originally introduced by the C(S)A 1997 section 2 (subsequently replaced by the PCC(S)A 2000 section 109). It required the courts to impose a life sentence on anyone convicted for the second time of the following offences specified by the statute:

(a) attempted murder, incitement or conspiracy or soliciting to commit murder;
(b) manslaughter;
(c) wounding or committing GBH with intent;
(d) rape or attempted rape;
(e) sexual intercourse with a girl under 13;
(f) possession of a firearm with intent to injure;
(g) use of a firearm with intent to resist arrest;
(h) carrying a firearm with criminal intent;
(i) armed robbery.

7.8 Although the second conviction must have been after the Act came into force, the first conviction can have occurred at any time.

7.9 The automatic life sentence, after an uncertain start, to a large extent eventually came to mirror the discretionary life sentence. The rationale for the sentence is founded on the premise that persons convicted of a second serious offence are presumed to be dangerous, unless exceptional circumstances displace that presumption. In the early days of the sentence, the Court of Appeal created a very narrow test of exceptional circumstances. However, following the applica-

5 *R v Bennett* [2009] EWCA Crim 1925.

tion of the European Convention on Human Rights to the sentence,[6] the Court of Appeal accepted that this construction breached article 5(1) of the Convention in that it rendered the sentence arbitrary. As a consequence, the Court of Appeal stated that if an offender could establish that they did not pose a continuing danger to the public, the exceptional circumstances criterion would be met. The result is that persons subject to this sentence will have been found to present a potential for continuing danger to the public at the outset, albeit to a lesser extent in many cases than persons receiving discretionary life sentences.

Sentence of imprisonment for public protection

7.10 This has replaced the automatic life sentence for offences committed on or after 4 April 2005[7] and has been one of the most contentious sentences of modern times. To qualify for one of the new sentences, the offender must be convicted of a 'specified offence', that is one of the 153 categories of violent or sexual offences listed in Parts 1 or 2 of Schedule 15 to the CJA 2003. Violent offences range from murder to affray and threats of various kinds and sexual offences from rape to indecent exposure.

7.11 A specified offence may or may not be serious (section 224). It will be serious if it is punishable, in the case of a person aged 18 or over, with 10 years' imprisonment or more (section 224(2)(b)). If serious, it may attract life imprisonment or imprisonment for public protection for an adult (section 225) or detention for life or detention for public protection for those under 18 on the day of conviction (section 225). It will attract such a sentence if the court is of opinion that there is a significant risk to members of the public of serious harm by the commission of further specified offences and if the minimum term to be imposed for the offence would be two years or more (sections 225(1), (3) and 226(1)).

7.12 Significant risk must be shown in relation to two matters: first, the commission of further specified, but not necessarily serious, offences; and, secondly, the causing thereby of serious harm to members of the public. If there is a significant risk of both, either a life sentence or indeterminate imprisonment for public protection must be imposed on an adult (section 225(2) and (3)). It must be a life sentence if the offence is one for which the offender is liable to life

6 *R v Offen* [2001] 1 WLR 253.

7 CJA 2003 s224(2) and Criminal Justice Act 2003 (Commencement No 8 and Transitional and Saving Provisions) Order 2005 SI No 950.

imprisonment and the seriousness of the offence, or of the offence and one or more offences associated with it, is such as to justify imprisonment for life (section 225(2)); otherwise it must be imprisonment for public protection. For sentences passed on or after 14 July 2008, it is a requirement that the offence is serious enough to justify a minimum term of at least two years (section 225(3)).

7.13 The requirement for a two-year minimum term was as a qualifying feature was introduced by the CJIA 2008 to try and halt the explosion in the numbers of prisoners serving IPP and was a response to the Home Affairs' Justice Committee critical report on the sentence and the lack of thought and planning that had preceded its introduction.[8] However, the Court of Appeal has made it clear that the change in the law is not to be applied retrospectively and that appeals against sentence for those who received minimum terms of less than two years prior to 14 July 2008 will not be allowed.[9]

7.14 For those under 18, there are similar provisions in relation to sentences of detention for life and detention for public protection subject, in the latter case, to an additional criterion which requires the court to consider the adequacy of an extended sentence under section 228 (section 226(2) and (3)). By section 229(3), where an offender aged 18 or over has previously been convicted of a specified offence, the court must assume there is a significant risk under sections 225 and 227 unless this would be unreasonable after taking into account information about the nature and circumstance of each offence, any pattern of behaviour of which any offence forms part and the offender.

7.15 The Court of Appeal has, notwithstanding the complexity of the new provisions, held that essentially the sentencing court, as with the old sentences, will really be making a decision as to whether the offender is 'dangerous'.[10] The practical problem that this regime creates, however, is that as the index offence does not have to reach a particular threshold of seriousness (as is the case in the discretionary life sentence for example), the sentencing court has to engage in a predictive exercise in relation to risk. The lack of certainty that exists in making such predictions combined with the lack of empirical evidence that exists for the reduction of risk after sentence, means that ever increasing numbers of people are receiving relatively short preventative sentences for less serious offences and become subject

8 *Towards effective sentencing*, HC-184-1, 22 July 2008.

9 *R v Ellis* [2009] EWCA Crim 164.

10 *R v Lang* [2005] EWCA Crim 2864.

to a release regime that was originally designed for the most serious crimes and the longest prison sentences.[11]

7.16 The only key difference between the life and indeterminate sentence is that IPP detainees can apply for their licence to be terminated after 10 years in the community whereas a life licence continues indefinitely, even after the reporting requirements have ended.[12] The custodial part of the sentence is served in precisely the same manner as any other life sentence and the possibility of terminating the licence altogether is the only distinguishing factor.

The length of the sentence

7.17 The period of time that a lifer must spend in custody before the Parole Board can consider suitability for release is known as the 'minimum term'. This is the punitive part of the sentence that is imposed for the purposes of retribution and deterrence. Historically, this part of the sentence was referred to as the 'tariff', but was changed on the advice of the Sentencing Advisory Panel as it was felt that 'minimum term' would convey more clearly that release at the end of this period is not automatic but dependent on risk being reduced sufficiently. The terms 'tariff' and 'minimum term' are now used interchangeably, although minimum term is the correct expression.

7.18 Although the detailed history and the precise mechanics for setting the minimum term are outside the scope of this book, a basic understanding of the principles applied by the courts when imposing a life or indeterminate sentence can be important to the parole process in terms of the assessment of how the sentencing court was required to assess the original offence.[13]

Minimum term for murder

7.19 Since 18 December 2003, the CJA 2003 section 269 has required the court that imposes a mandatory life sentence to set the minimum term. Statutory guidelines for determining the length of the minimum term are contained in CJA 2003 Schedule 21. In the event

11 The distinction that has been preserved between sentences justifying a discretionary life sentence and IPP in *Bennett* (note 5 above) would seem to indicate that there remains a qualitative difference between the two sentences.

12 CJA 2003 Sch 18.

13 For a detailed discussion of the history and practice pertaining to life sentences see Creighton and Arnott, *Prisoners: law and practice*, LAG, 2009, chapter 10.

that the offender is aged over 21 when the offence was committed, the court has the power to impose a whole life term.[14] There are three statutory starting points for the length of the term, and aggravating and mitigating features then add to, or subtract from, those starting points.

7.20 The sentencing court is also required to specify whether allowance is being given for time spent on remand and, if so, how much time has been allowed.[15] The term that is imposed is subject to the normal provisions for an appeal, either by the prisoner or on an Attorney-General's reference, to the Court of Appeal against sentence.[16]

Whole life terms

7.21 A whole life order is to be imposed in cases where the offender is over 21 at the time the offence was committed and the offence involves:

(a) the murder of two or more persons, where each murder involves any of the following –
  (i) a substantial degree of premeditation or planning,
  (ii) the abduction of the victim, or
  (iii) sexual or sadistic conduct,
(b) the murder of a child if involving the abduction of the child or sexual or sadistic motivation,
(c) a murder done for the purpose of advancing a political, religious or ideological cause, or
(d) a murder by an offender previously convicted of murder.[17]

30-year starting point

7.22 A starting point of 30 years is deemed appropriate for persons aged 18 years or over who are convicted of the following offences:

(a) the murder of a police officer or prison officer in the course of his duty,
(b) a murder involving the use of a firearm or explosive,
(c) a murder done for gain (such as a murder done in the course or furtherance of robbery or burglary, done for payment or done in the expectation of gain as a result of the death),
(d) a murder intended to obstruct or interfere with the course of justice,
(e) a murder involving sexual or sadistic conduct,

14 CJA 2003 s269(4).
15 CJA 2003 s269(3).
16 CJA 2003 ss270–271 which also amends Criminal Appeal Act 1968 s9(1).
17 CJA 2003 Sch 21 para 4.

(f) the murder of two or more persons,
(g) murder that is racially or religiously aggravated or aggravated by sexual orientation, or
(h) a murder falling within [CJA 2003 Schedule 21] paragraph 4(2) committed by an offender who was aged under 21 when he committed the offence.[18]

15-year starting point

7.23 The starting point for any case that does not fall within these two categories and where the offender was aged 18 years or over at the time of the offence is 15 years.[19]

Aggravating features

7.24 The factors which will justify a higher sentence being imposed are:

(a) a significant degree of planning or premeditation,
(b) the fact that the victim was particularly vulnerable because of age or disability,
(c) mental or physical suffering inflicted on the victim before death,
(d) the abuse of a position of trust,
(e) the use of duress or threats against another person to facilitate the commission of the offence,
(f) the fact that the victim was providing a public service or performing a public duty, and
(g) concealment, destruction or dismemberment of the body.[20]

Mitigating factors

7.25 The relevant factors which mitigate the length of the sentence are:

(a) an intention to cause serious bodily harm rather than to kill,
(b) lack of premeditation,
(c) the fact that the offender suffered from any mental disorder or mental disability which (although not falling within section 2(1) of the Homicide Act 1957 (c 11)), lowered his degree of culpability,
(d) the fact that the offender was provoked (for example, by prolonged stress) in a way not amounting to a defence of provocation,
(e) the fact that the offender acted to any extent in self-defence,
(f) a belief by the offender that the murder was an act of mercy, and
(g) the age of the offender.[21]

18 CJA 2003 Sch 21 para 5(2).
19 CJA 2003 Sch 21 para 6.
20 CJA 2003 Sch 21 para 10.
21 CJA 2003 Sch 21 para 11.

7.26 The full impact of these sentencing guidelines has yet to be realised but it is already apparent that there are an increasing number of people convicted of murder who are serving extremely long minimum terms in excess of 30 years and that the number of people serving whole life terms has dramatically increased. The lawfulness of the whole life term has been upheld both domestically[22] and by the European Court of Human Rights.[23]

Transitional cases

7.27 There are very large numbers of prisoners serving life sentences for murder that were imposed prior to 18 December 2003. These comprise one group who had minimum terms set by the Secretary of State when he still retained this power, and a smaller group who never had a minimum term set by the Secretary of State as their convictions occurred after it was decided it was in breach of article 6 of the European Convention on Human Rights for him to fix these sentences.[24] Both groups of lifers will now have a judicially set minimum term. The difference between the two groups is that those who never had a minimum term fixed will have had their cases considered by a High Court judge automatically, whereas those who did have a tariff or minimum term set by the Secretary of State must apply to the court if they wish it to be reset by a High Court judge[25] (providing the previously set tariff has not already expired). The court is prohibited from setting a minimum term greater than the previously notified tariff or the term that would have been set by the Secretary of State at the time – but must have regard to the term previously set, the judicial recommendations and the guidance contained in CJA 2003 Schedule 21 for current sentences.[26]

7.28 The procedure for setting the minimum terms is a written one, although the final decision is given in open court.[27] All decisions are published on the Court Service's website.[28] Once the High Court has

22 *R v Bieber* [2008] EWCA Crim 1601.

23 *Kafkaris v Cyprus* (2008) 25 BHRC 591.

24 This occurred in December 2002 when the House of Lords ruled in *R (Anderson) v Home Secretary* [2003] AC 837.

25 CJA 2003 Sch 22 paras 6 and 3(1)–(2).

26 CJA 2003 Sch 22 para 4.

27 See also *R (Hammond) v Home Secretary* [2004] EWHC 2753 (Admin) where the Divisional Court held that the judge setting the term should have the discretion to convene an oral hearing if necessary. At the time of writing, this decision was awaiting the outcome of an appeal to the House of Lords.

28 See www.hmcourts-service.gov.uk.

given a decision, there remains a right of appeal by either the prisoner or the Attorney-General to the Court of Appeal.[29]

All other life sentences

7.29 For all other lifers and indeterminate sentence prisoners, the minimum term is fixed in open court at the conclusion of the trial. The power to set these sentences was transferred from the executive to the judiciary many years ago (1992 for discretionary lifers and 1998 for HMP detainees) and so there are unlikely to be any outstanding transitional cases.[30]

HMP detainees

7.30 The minimum term for this group is set according to the principles applied in CJA 2003 Schedule 21 paragraph 7, which specifies that the starting point will be 12 years. The normal aggravating and mitigating factors specified in the Act should then be applied to the sentence.

Discretionary lifers, automatic lifers and IPP detainees

7.31 All of these prisoners have their minimum terms set by the trial judge in the same manner as any other. A succession of cases over the years has established that the sentencing judge should address the following matters when imposing the sentence:

- specify the determinate sentence that would have been imposed if a sentence of life imprisonment had not been imposed;
- proceed to set the minimum term at a point between one-half and two-thirds of the determinate sentence;
- specify the amount of remand time that will be allowed against the minimum term.

7.32 There have been a large number of cases over the years that have looked at the relationship between the minimum term and the notional determinate sentence. The decision that it should be somewhere between one-half and two-thirds is to reflect the point at which a determinate sentence prisoner will be considered for parole or, eventually, released automatically. By setting the minimum term in this way, the

29 CJA 2003 Sch 22 paras 14 and 15 amend the Criminal Appeal Act 1968 to include this type of case in the normal procedures for an appeal against sentence.

30 The last group of transitional HMP detainees had their position clarified in July 2005 in *R (Smith and Dudson) v Home Secretary* [2005] UKHL 51 and 52.

lifer will not be disadvantaged in the punitive part of the sentence in relation to prisoners serving determinate sentences. While the norm has been for the sentence to be one-half of the determinate sentence, the Court of Appeal has refused to be too prescriptive, allowing leeway up to the two-thirds point in more serious cases.[31]

Compassionate release

7.33 The Secretary of State retains the power to release prisoners serving life sentences on compassionate grounds at any time during the life sentence.[32] The purpose of compassionate release for lifers is ordinarily restricted to medical grounds and the guidance on the use of this power states that it may be exercised where:

- the prisoner is suffering from a terminal illness and death is likely to occur very shortly (although there are no set time limits three months may be considered to be an appropriate period for an application to be made to the PPCS), or the lifer is bedridden or similarly incapacitated, for example they are paralysed or suffering from a severe stoke; and
- the risk of reoffending (particularly of a sexual or violent nature) is minimal; and
- further imprisonment would reduce the prisoner's life expectancy; and
- there are adequate arrangements for the prisoner's care and treatment outside prison; and
- early release will bring some significant benefit to the prisoner or his/her family.[33]

7.34 The power is somewhat narrower than for prisoners serving determinate sentences where release on compassionate grounds is permitted where there are tragic family circumstances as well as on medical grounds and it is normally authorised to allow the prisoner to die outside of prison. However, this narrow construction cannot act as a fetter on the discretion of the executive and, in the case of prisoners serving determinate sentences, it has been held that compas-

31 The two cases which clarify these principles are: *R v Home Secretary ex p Furber* [1998] 1 All ER 23 and *R v Marklew* [1999] 1 Cr App R (S) 6. This has survived the introduction of automatic release at the halfway point in all determinate sentence cases: *R v Szczerba* [2002] 2 Cr App R (S) 86.

32 C(S)A 1997 s30.

33 PSO 4700 para 12.2.1.

sionate grounds can extend beyond medical issues and tragic family circumstances.[34]

7.35 The Secretary of State is required to consult the Parole Board, where practicable, before exercising this power and authorising release[35] but the exercise of this power is entirely discretionary and does not engage article 5. Although the statute requires the Board to be consulted where release is being contemplated, there is no such requirement in cases where the Secretary of State does not consider that compassionate release is appropriate[36] The logic behind this is that the Board's remit is restricted to advising on risk issues and not the substantive merits of the application itself.

34 *R (on the application of A) v Governor of Huntercombe YOI and Secretary of State for the Home Department* [2006] EWHC 2544 (Admin).

35 C(S)A 1997 s30(2).

36 *R (on the application of Spinks) v Secretary of State for the Home Department* [2005] EWCA Civ 275.

CHAPTER 8

Serving the life sentence

How indeterminate sentences are served

8.1 The primary policy guidance on how life and indeterminate sentences will be served is the Indeterminate Sentence Manual (ISM), issued as PSO 4700.[1] A copy should also be available to all lifers in prison libraries. All lifers will normally be expected to follow a similar path from conviction to release, although there will obviously be scope for individual cases to vary from the core structure. The policy mainly deals with adults serving relatively long minimum terms whose entire sentences will be served in the adult estate, although the revised ISM has attempted to be more explicit about the progress of IPP prisoners and those serving short minimum terms.

Ministry of Justice structure

8.2 The method by which the Ministry of Justice organises decision-making for lifers has been in a state of constant flux ever since it was created in May 2007. The background to the current position needs some explanation so that lifers' parole dossiers can be properly understood both in respect of decision-making and the jargon they contain. Historically, lifers posed a particular organisational problem for the government due to the tension between the desire of ministers to maintain control over the life sentence and the practicalities of decision-making about individuals serving the sentence. In the past, when there was more direct ministerial control over the release of mandatory lifers and when the numbers of lifers was far smaller, all decisions pertaining to life sentence prisoners were made by a central department acting under delegated authority form the relevant minister. This specialist unit at the Prison Service, the Lifer Unit, was responsible for making decisions on lifers' categorisation and allocation and for dealing with parole reviews and recalls to prison custody. The department was initially split into two arms, with the *Lifer Review Unit* taking responsibility for decisions on progress and release and the *Lifer Management Unit* addressing transfer and allocation issues. These two arms were amalgamated in 2000 so that one team dealt with all aspects of the lifer's

1 PSO 4700 used to be known as the Lifer Manual but was revised and renamed in July 2009. It can be found on the Prison Service's website at: http://pso.hmprisonservice.gov.uk/PSO_4700_lifer_manual.doc.

progress. Prisons would simply submit reports and recommendations to this department, as opposed to making final decisions on these matters.

8.3 In February 2004, the Lifer Unit moved to become directly managed by NOMS rather than remaining as part of the Prison Service. The decision was taken at this time to devolve the day-to-day operational decisions previously taken by the Lifer Management Unit back to the prisons in which the individual lifers are held. However, the Lifer Review and Recall Section (LRRS) at NOMS retained responsibility for co-ordinating parole reviews, compiling parole dossiers and dealing with recalls to custody. LRRS was subsequently renamed the Public Protection Casework Section (PPCS). The one major difference is that while PPCS will prepare the core historical part of a lifers' parole dossier, the addition of up-to-date reports and the disclosure of the dossier now rests with the prison itself.

8.4 As at November 2009, the PPCS has the following responsibilities:[2]

- to monitor the whole parole review process for all lifers;
- to refer cases for review to the Parole Board;
- to prepare the skeleton dossier and disclose it to the prison;
- to provide the Secretary of State's view
- to consider and, where appropriate, to refer cases to the Parole Board for advice on a lifer's continued suitability for open conditions;
- to process Parole Board directions for release;
- to make decisions on recommendations for movement to open conditions and to set the timing of future reviews;
- to monitor the progress of life licencees in the community, including their recall to custody and cancellation of supervision where appropriate;
- to oversee and develop policy in respect of lifers in the above areas;
- to liaise with the Prison Service on operational lifer policy development.

8.5 Until June 2004, LRRS would also be asked to give final approval on matters relating to high profile prisoners, such as decisions on temporary release, but this is now dealt with by DOMs and not PPCS.

8.6 As PPCS is a department of NOMS, it falls under the direct jurisdiction of the Ministry of Justice and not the Prison Service.

2 See PSO 6010 chapter 1 and PSI 8/2004.

Throughout the course of 2009 it has gradually been moved from offices at Prison Service headquarters to its own offices within the Ministry of Justice. It is divided into a number of teams that deal with lifers on a geographic division that mirrors the allocation of prisoners to caseworkers at the Parole Board (see appendix G).

8.7 All operational decisions – save for decisions pertaining to category A prisoners – are made by the prison in which the lifer is held. Therefore, all inquiries about matters such as categorisation, transfers, access to courses, prison discipline and temporary release should be made to the lifer manager of that prison. In difficult cases, or in situations where the matter may have direct relevance to a parole review, PPCS may sometimes be able to intervene to try to broker a resolution to the problem. This most commonly occurs when a prison approves a progressive transfer but cannot find another prison to accept the individual. Although PPCS does not have any operational powers, it can sometimes assist in seeking to persuade a new prison to accept the lifer.

8.8 With category A prisoners, there is another level of administration to negotiate. Categorisation decisions for this group are made by the Director of High Security Prisons under devolved authority from the Secretary of State. The Directorate of High Security Prisons[3] has casework teams that deal with category A reviews and the allocation and movement of category A prisoners.

Sentence planning: an overview

8.9 The number of prisoners serving life and indeterminate sentences has increased massively since the introduction of the IPP sentence in April 2005. In the decade between 1998 and 2008 numbers trebled from around 4,000 to over 12,000, of which over 5,000 were serving IPP.[4] As IPP prisoners now make up such a large percentage of the lifer population, there are also large numbers of this class of prisoner serving relatively short minimum terms. This has created particular problems for their management, as the old lifer system had been largely designed to accommodate prisoners serving very lengthy tariffs which allowed for slow and measured sentence planning before the minimum term would expire. In April 2009, 33 per cent of

3 Based at Prison Service Headquarters, Cleland House, Page Street, London SW1P 4LN.

4 Prison Reform Trust, *Bromley Briefing: Prison Factfile*, June 2009, p11.

IPPs were being held over their tariffs and only 60 had actually been released from sentences of IPP.[5]

8.10 PSO 4700 explains that the aim of NOMS in relation to those serving life sentences is as follows:

> The Prison Service, working in accordance with its statement of purpose, vision, goals and values, and jointly with the Probation Service, aims to work constructively with life sentence prisoners by:
>
> - keeping them in custody and ensuring the safety and protection of the public;
> - allocating them to prisons whose regimes best meet individual needs;
> - helping them come to terms with their offence;
> - assisting them to identify, address and modify their problem behaviour and attitudes; and
> - ensuring their suitability for release is objectively assessed by staff in a range of settings.[6]

8.11 All life-sentenced prisoners are required to have a life sentence plan, the purpose of which is to structure the sentence from remand to release. The intention of this single-sentence planning framework is to allow all information on risk assessment and progress to be integrated and properly monitored. This requires all of the different risk-assessment systems to be considered and summarised. In addition, it allows the individual to understand what objectives have been set. There are currently two overlapping systems in place. The original system was a sentence planning model which provided for annual sentence plan reviews to be completed at the prison with more formal sentence planning to be conducted at regular intervals with a backstop of at least five years. This model is discussed in greater detail below. It is gradually being replaced by the Offender Management Model ('OMM')[7] covering IPP prisoners convicted after 7 January 2008 and gradually being rolled out to include all IPP prisoners and other lifers. For those IPP prisoners already in custody on 7 January 2008 and for other lifers, transition to this new scheme is determined on a case-by-case basis.

8.12 The OMM places far more emphasis on the offender manager ('OM') right at the outset and requires that an OASys is completed

5 Ibid.

6 Paragraph 1.8.

7 Available at http://noms.justice.gov.uk/news-publications-events/publications/guidance/phase_III_implementation_guide/Phase_III_Specification_doc?view=Binary.

prior to the pre-sentence report and that both these documents are provided to the prison for the first sentence planning review following sentence. This review should take place within either 8 or 16 weeks of the sentence depending on the length of the minimum term. If the minimum term is two years or under, the shorter time scale is applied. If the OASys was not completed before sentencing, a post-sentence report and OASys should be provided within that time. Additionally, as part of the induction process and within ten days of the sentence a 'promoting protective factors' assessment – covering accommodation, employment, family ties and healthcare – should be completed by prison service staff and an interview conducted by the offender supervisor ('OS'). The feedback from that interview should be conveyed back to the OM.

8.13 Under this new model, the OASys becomes the primary tool for sentence planning within the prison and the OS has responsibility for assisting the OM in obtaining sentence planning and review (SPR) reports for sentence planning review meetings to aid the sentence-planning process. The OS is tasked with 'driving forward' the plan during the custodial period. The OM, following consultation with the OS, reviews and revises the OASys risk of reconviction, risk of serious harm and sentence plan no more than 12 months after the last review while the offender is in custody. A review meeting is chaired by the OM, either in person or by video link, and involves the offender, OS and any relevant key workers or specialist staff working with the offender. This review meeting must be held at a minimum once every year.

8.14 This new system is in stark contrast with the old sentence-planning model, which very often did not allow for much contact with the OM (or home probation officer) until far later in the sentence, often once the resettlement stage had started. This was not appropriate for prisoners with short minimum terms as it meant that work on resettlement plans might not be prompted until the punitive part of the sentence was complete. However, whilst the OMM has many advantages in terms of multi-agency involvement and planning, it does require the OM to be proactive to commence the sentence-planning process and there are concerns that information generated at the prison about a prisoner's progress is not adequately conveyed back to the OM.

8.15 For IPP prisoners who were already in custody on 7 January 2008 and for other lifers transition to the OMM scheme is determined on a case-by-case basis. Until then, the existing sentence-planning scheme remains in place for this group, although it should be noted that, although this still remains in PSO 4700, it would appear that it is slowly being assimilated into the categorisation and allocation process adopted for determinate prisoners. This sentence-planning scheme in PSO 4700 requires that, after conviction, the following forms are to be completed by the local prison:[8]

LSP 1A Post conviction immediate needs assessment
LSP 1B Initial allocation to first stage prison
LSP 1C Post conviction induction report
LSP 1D Local prison lifer profile
LSP 1E Multi-agency lifer risk assessment panel report
LSP 1F Pre-transfer report to first stage prison
LSP 1G Pre-first stage report.

8.16 The forms LSP 1B and LSP 1G are sent to PPCS. For all lifers other than IPP prisoners, the prison should then identify three potential options for allocation and notify these options to the Population Management Section – the department at NOMS that organises the physical movement of prisoners. The special arrangements for IPP prisoners are set out below. PMS then make arrangements for the move to take place.

8.17 The police will also be asked to supply information about each convicted lifer and this usually consists of a summary of the evidence in a case and permits the senior investigating officer to attend a meeting at the prison to discuss the case if necessary. It is intended that the written document will be received at the prison within two months of the sentence and, rather worryingly, it is treated as a confidential document. The document should then be considered by a multi-agency lifer risk assessment panel (MALRAP) that is convened by the lifer manager and should include the following staff as a minimum: the lifer manager, the wing lifer officer or personal officer, the home probation officer and the police investigating officer(s). This panel is intended to inform the home probation officer's post sentence report (LSP 1F) and will also generate a confidential document to be placed on the individual's file with risk factors entered into the life sentence plan. This procedure is potentially quite worrying for lifers as it involves a mechanism for the police to feed concerns into the sentence-planning process without any check or balance in the system. Police reports that have routinely appeared in determinate parole dossiers (police forms MG5) have tended to contain an account of the police investigation including reference to police

8 PSO 4700 para 8.3.

suspicions and unconvicted allegations. The prospect of sentence planning and risk factors being based on undisclosed material does have the potential to undermine the general principle of openness in the reporting process and may in some cases breach basic standards of administrative fairness.

Allocation

8.18 On conviction, adult male lifers will be sent to a prison with a stage 1 main lifer centre. There are several of these around the country and all are in either category B training prisons or high security prisons (formerly known as 'dispersals' after the policy of dispersing high risk prisoners around the system). For female lifers, there are a number of designated stage 1 lifer prisons.[9] This initial decision is made by the lifer manager of the prison in which the lifer is held at the time of conviction. A form LSP 1 should be completed and forwarded to the PMS, the relevant case work team at PPCS. This transfer request should include a list of suitable prisons to which the lifer could be transferred.

8.19 All category A prisoners will be allocated to a high security prison, of which there are currently five. Non-category A prisoners can also be allocated to a high security prison if it is felt that the offence or the lifer's history justifies these conditions. For category A prisoners, the LSP 1B form should be used and marked 'high security allocation'. This is processed by the Directorate of High Security Prisons at Prison Service headquarters. In all cases, allocation decisions should be made within 28 days of the transfer request being received.

8.20 Under-18-year-olds will be allocated to a secure training centre or a local authority secure children's home if under 16 years of age.[10] At 16 years or over, allocation will ordinarily be to one of the four long-term closed YOIs at Aylesbury, Castington, Moorland and Swinfen Hall. On reception, an immediate review should be held to determine whether the young offender should be allocated to education or employment and this is followed by a more comprehensive review after six months that is intended to address personal and training and remedial needs as well as identifying areas of concern and risk that need to be addressed.[11] It is usual practice to transfer young offenders to an adult prison between the ages of 21 and 22, although for those

9 For a fuller discussion of the establishments which can hold life sentenced prisoners see *Prisoners: law and practice* LAG, 2009.

10 Although the number of places available at secure children's homes has been reduced making places harder to find.

11 PSO 4700 para 10.5.

serving long sentences this can often occur earlier. Transfer can be to any category of prison depending on the length of the sentence left and the progress made. On transfer, responsibility for management reverts to the normal adult system.

8.21 Female lifers will ordinarily be allocated to a first stage lifer prison. Women's prisons are formally allocated as first and second stage lifer establishments, the first stage prisons usually being Buckley Hall, Bullwood Hall, Durham and Holloway. The second stage prisons are Buckley Hall, Cookham Wood, Durham, Foston Hall, Holloway and Styal. As there is an overlap between the prisons holding first and second stage lifers, it is important for female lifers to ensure that it is noted on their sentence plans when they have moved onto the second stage, as there is a greater chance that they will remain in the same establishment despite the progression.

8.22 Guidance on the factors that should inform allocation decisions, both initially and at subsequent transfers, can be found in PSO 4700.[12] These include:

- security issues relating to escape risk;
- control issues, including behaviour and progress in custody;
- risk assessment based on work completed in respect of offending behaviour;
- regime issues to ensure that the suggested prison can meet the prisoner's treatment, healthcare and resettlement needs;
- life sentence issues that will take account of overall progress through the sentence, public interest in the case and the proximity to or outcome of parole hearings.

Short tariff IPPs and lifers

8.23 As the categorisation of all male lifers was premised upon initial placement in at least category B conditions, it was considered that this might be inappropriate for those serving IPP sentences where the average tariff in 2008 was under four years. The prison service recognised that this group of lifers would previously have been likely to receive determinate sentences and may have been eligible for category C conditions at the outset. To address the problem, an amended form ICA 1 was introduced in February 2008[13] which identifies those with tariffs of under three years so that they can be assessed for suitability to be moved directly to category C conditions. NOMS have

12 At para 21.

13 PSI 07/2008.

also been working on replacing the staged approach to progression and release with the concept of new pathways to release for IPP and short tariff prisoners. In proposed revisions to PSO 0900, it is suggested that lifers and IPP prisoners who have minimum terms of less than four years should be subject to six-monthly recategorisation reviews until they reach category C conditions and those with terms of four years or more will have annual recategorisation reviews. The draft PSO suggests that this review is completed on a form RC 1.[14] However, indications are that in practice this system is only considered appropriate for those serving short minimum terms and that mandatory lifers and any indeterminate sentence of six years or more will continue to be dealt with by way of the life sentence plan (LSP) system.

Progress reviews

Annual sentence planning and interim reviews

8.24 A LSP will be produced after conviction at the prison to which the lifer is allocated immediately after conviction (the first stage).[15] After an OASys assessment (currently not mandatory) and completion of the core life sentence plan document (LSP 2), the lifer should progress to the second stage (either a category B or C prison). This is where the majority of the work on addressing the risk factors identified in the LSP will be carried out. From 1 October 2007 initial risk factors will be set by using the OASys 2 report supplemented by the form OASys 7A instead of the LSP 2.[16]

8.25 There should be annual reviews of the life sentence plan (with reports known as LSP 3B reports) and more intense reviews at significant points of the sentence, such as the completion of a relevant piece of offending behaviour work and at least every five years. The more intensive reviews are completed on forms LSP 3E reports and are the same as the format used for compiling reports for Parole Board reviews.[17] During their time in category B or high security

14 For further discussion of the categorisation and recategorisation of determinate prisoners, see Creighton and Arnott, *Prisoners: law and practice*, LAG, 2009.

15 See PSI 26/2006.

16 PSI 13/2007.

17 These used to be known as F75 reports and older parole dossiers may still contain references to F75s.

prisons, male lifers will usually carry out the bulk of the offending behaviour work identified on the life sentence plan. It is quite common, particularly for those serving longer sentences, to spend time in a number of different category B prisons.

8.26 Once a lifer is considered suitable for the second stage, they can be moved to either another category B prison (the second stage ones are: Albany, Bristol, Cardiff, Dovegate, Dovegate Therapeutic Community, Garth, Gartree, Grendon, Kingston main, Parkhurst, Rye Hill, Swaleside) or, if their categorisation is reduced to category C, onto a category C prison.[18]

8.27 Guidance on the factors to be taken into account on the allocation decision are set out in PSI 26/2006, annex A. These encompass issues regarding security, control, life sentence, risk assessment and regime, and consideration will be given to the nature of the offence, any history of escape planning, custodial behaviour, the location of co-defendants, OASys assessments, family and resettlement matters. The proximity of the prisoner's Parole Board review is also of importance and, more controversially, ministerial public or media interest may be taken into account. The PSI recognises the general public law duty to give proper and reasoned decisions in relation to allocation and categorisation.[19]

8.28 The LSP 3E reports follow the same pro forma as the reports used for full parole reviews except they will obviously not comment on release or a transfer to open conditions as the prisoner will be too early in the sentence for this to take place. They will usually comprise reports prepared by the lifer manager, personal officer, seconded and home probation officers and the prison psychologist. The purpose of the LSP 3E review is to:

- enable the prisoner's progress and life sentence plan to be monitored;
- provide an opportunity for staff to comment on progress or other circumstances that might justify a transfer or change in security categorisation;
- provide information on any reduction of risk that has been achieved.[20]

8.29 LSP 3 E reports will be disclosed to the prisoner and a period of seven days should be allowed for any comments to be made. Lifers may take

18 As at February 2009, 26 category C prisons accepted lifers – a full list can be found in PSO 4700 at appendix 4.

19 Paragraph 17.

20 PSO 4700 para 5.4.1.

legal advice on this and representations may be made by a solicitor on their behalf.

8.30 The movement of adult lifers to category C conditions is of particular significance as it represents the stage at which the majority of offending behaviour work has been completed and represents the opportunity for further testing. The Prison Service states that there is a significantly higher degree of trust in category C prisons and, as such, a 'proper assessment of a lifer's trustworthiness and escape potential must remain a key factor in the recategorisation decision'.[21] Transfer will not take place until there are no outstanding or security concerns to justify retention in category B conditions.

Accessing offending behaviour courses

8.31 Prisoners' attendance on offending behaviour courses has become more problematic with the rapid rise in the lifer population. Difficulties first arose after the introduction of the automatic life sentence in 1997 and then reached crisis point when the IPP sentence was introduced in 2005. In the case of *R (on the application of Cawser) v Secretary of State for the Home Department*[22] an automatic lifer who was significantly over tariff and had been told that he would have to wait several years for a place on a sex offender's course sought to challenge the delay. The Secretary of State accepted that there was a public law duty to provide courses that were needed to reduce risk and allow for release, although he argued that it was a rational policy to target resources at prisoners who were serving determinate sentences and so would be released anyway as this would place the public at less risk. An argument that the failure to provide courses could also breach article 5(1) on the grounds that the purpose of the detention was being defeated was rejected by the Court of Appeal.[23]

8.32 The issue was revisited for IPP prisoners in *Secretary of State v Walker and James*.[24] Although the Court of Appeal considered that the failure to provide courses was unlawful, that did not necessarily render the detention itself unlawful. The finding of dangerousness

21 PSI 26/2006 para 20.

22 [2003] EWCA Civ 1522.

23 Although Arden LJ dissented considering that, in principle, a continued failure to provide courses needed to satisfy the test for release might break the causal link with the original purposes of the sentence and render the detention unlawful (para 47).

24 [2008] EWCA Civ 30.

at the time the sentence was imposed did not mean that the prisoner would remain dangerous indefinitely and so it could not be assumed that there remained a danger. If the Parole Board was unable to make that assessment because relevant course work had not been provided, then this is where there might be a breach of article 5(1), although that position had not been reached in those two cases. This view was not shared by the House of Lords where a far more restrictive approach to the application of article 5 was taken. The Lords were very critical of the 'systemic failures' to provide the necessary facilities and resources for these prisoners but considered that this had not resulted in a breach of either article 5(1) or (4).[25] Whilst this decision has a very restrictive interpretation of article 5, the affirmation of the common law duty to provide treatment does leave scope for challenges, albeit on a more limited basis.[26]

First parole review

Timing

8.33 The first formal review of a lifer's case by the Parole Board takes place approximately three years before the expiry of the minimum term. In cases where the minimum term is less than six years, the start date will be adjusted (see the section on short tariffs below).[27] The purpose of this review is to enable consideration to be given as to whether the lifer has made sufficient progress to be moved to open conditions. The review time is set at three years before the earliest release date, in order to allow for the lifer to spend some time in open conditions before the minimum term expires. This is to reflect the requirement that before most lifers can be released, they will need to spend time in open conditions to establish a release plan and to demonstrate that they can be trusted to comply with supervision on

25 *R (on the application of James (formerly Walker), Lee and Wells) v Secretary of State for Justice* [2009] UKHL 22.

26 *R (on the application of Mehmet) v Secretary of State for Justice* [2009] EWHC 1202 (Admin) where the failure to provide a written report to the Board for over a year was held to be unlawful.

27 Interestingly, the new policy on town visits in category C conditions restricts these to lifers who have served ten continuous years in custody, which seems to indicate that the need for community readjustment is less important for sentences even longer than six years.

life licence in the community.[28] The ISM explains the rationale of the policy as follows:

> A period in open conditions is essential for most life sentenced prisoners ('lifers'). It allows the testing of areas of concern in conditions which are nearer to those in the community than can be found in closed prisons. Lifers have the opportunity to take home leave from open prisons and, more generally, open conditions require them to take more responsibility for their actions.[29]

8.34 The date of this review can be brought forward by six months in cases where the prisoner has been in a category C prison – or a second stage female prison – for at least one year before it is reached (ie for 12 months before the three-and-a-half years prior to the expiry of the minimum term).[30] Generally speaking, it will be extremely rare to find a case where a referral to the Board will take place earlier than this, and the one attempt to challenge the normal 'three-year policy' – in a case where a lifer argued that she had completed all necessary work in closed conditions and would benefit from a longer period of time in open conditions – was rejected by the Administrative Court.[31]

The statutory grounds for referral

8.35 There is no requirement in statute for cases to be referred at the pre-tariff stage, nor for a move to open conditions to be dependent on a recommendation from the Parole Board. This practice has arisen solely as a matter of policy. However, the statutory authority for cases actually to be referred to the Board and considered under this policy can be found in CJA 2003 section 239(2), which requires the Board to advise the Secretary of State on matters relating to the early release of prisoners where the Secretary of State has requested advice.

8.36 As the review is to examine progress prior to release, it does not fall within the ambit of article 5(4) of the European Convention on Human Rights. There is extensive case-law, both domestically and before the European Court of Human Rights, that makes it clear that

28 Ministerial statement of 7 November 1994. This policy was affirmed by the Court of Appeal in *R v Secretary of State for the Home Department ex p Stafford* [1998] 1 WLR 503 and this part of the judgment was not criticised by either the House of Lords or the European Court of Human Rights.

29 ISM, appendix 7 p4.

30 See *R v Secretary of State for the Home Department ex p Roberts* [1998] 8 July, unreported and the ministerial statement of 9 July 1998.

31 *R (on the application of Payne (Kelly)) v Secretary of State for the Home Department* [2004] EWHC 581 (Admin).

decisions on the movement of prisoners to open conditions do not engage article 5 rights, as the concept of liberty is absolute in this context. The transfer of a prisoner to an open prison remains a decision taken on the conditions of imprisonment as opposed to one that engages liberty.[32] The Board does retain the discretionary power to convene an oral hearing if it feels it necessary as a matter of fairness on a case-by-case basis.[33]

The review process

8.37 The pre-tariff review process has been formally amalgamated with end-of-tariff and post-tariff parole reviews since April 2009.[34] The rationale for the amalgamation of the review processes has two sources. The first is the policy adopted by the Parole Board of only permitting lifers to move to open conditions after an oral hearing.[35] This policy was adopted in response to recommendations made by the Chief Inspector of Probation in his report, *An independent review of a further serious offence: Anthony Rice* where it was suggested the critical point of risk assessment for lifers is the decision to move them to an open prison, as once the lifer is in open conditions, the assumption had tended to be that all future work is purely concerned with resettlement issues and the presumption in sentence planning shifts to release.[36] The second underlying factor was the amendment to the Parole Board Rules 2004 in April 2009 that removed the automatic right to an oral hearing for lifers who have served their minimum term. Once the entitlement to an oral hearing became a matter of discretion rather than of right, there was no longer any distinction between the pre-tariff and post-tariff lifers. The unified procedures are therefore set out in chapter 10.

8.38 Although the review process is the same for all lifers, there are a number of legal distinctions to be drawn between the reviews. As noted above, article 5(4) does not apply to pre-tariff reviews as release is not an option and the reference to the Board is solely to advise on suitability for open conditions. Strictly speaking, where an oral

32 *R (on the application of Hill) v Secretary of State for the Home Department* [2007] EWHC 2164 (Admin); *R (on the application of Day) v Secretary of State for the Home Department* [2004] EWHC (Admin) 1742.

33 *R v Parole Board ex p Davies* (1996) 27 November, unreported.

34 PSO 6010 on the Generic Parole Process, para 1.1.2.

35 www.paroleboard.gov.uk/policy_and_guidance/lifer_oral_hearings/.

36 www.justice.gov.uk/inspectorates/hmi-probation/docs/anthonyricereport-rps.pdf.

hearing is convened the Parole Board Rules do not apply to the review process, although the Board chooses to use them as the template for hearing cases.[37] Lastly, the Secretary of State is still entitled to issue directions to the Board in relation to this category of review that set out the test to be applied, not just matters to be taken into account.

The Secretary of State's directions

8.39 The Secretary of State has issued directions to the Parole Board setting out the matters they should take into account when deciding whether to authorise a transfer to open conditions. It has been held that the practice of issuing directions to the Parole Board breaches the concept of judicial independence and so impinges on article 5(4).[38] Nonetheless, as the court also held that the directions related to considerations that any sensible Parole Board would take into account in any event, it is necessary to bear these in mind when drafting representations to the Board. Also, as the review at this stage does not engage article 5, there is no reason why the Secretary of State should not issue directions.

8.40 The directions state that:

> [a] move to open conditions should be based on a balanced assessment of risk in benefits. However the Parole Board's emphasis should be on the risk reduction aspect is particular, on the need for the life to have made significant progress In charging his or her attitudes and tackling behavioural problems in closed conditions, without which a move to open conditions will not generally be considered.

8.41 The detailed guidance is that the following should be considered:

(a) the extent to which the lifer has made sufficient progress during sentence in addressing and reducing risk to a level consistent with protecting the public from harm, in circumstances where the lifer in open conditions would be in the community, unsupervised, under licensed temporary release;
(b) the extent to which the lifer is likely to comply with the conditions of any such form of temporary release;
(c) the extent to which the lifer is considered trustworthy enough not to abscond;

37 See para 10.1.

38 *R (on the application of Girling) v Parole Board and Home Secretary* [2005] EWHC 546 (Admin).

(d) the extent to which the lifer is likely to derive benefit from being able to address areas of concern and to be tested in a more realistic environment, such as to suggest that a transfer to open conditions is worthwhile at that stage.

8.42 The directions also set out a number of factors to be taken into account when balancing the risks of transfer against the benefits.

8.43 The Board is also specifically instructed that advice is only sought on the suitability of a move to an open prison – or, for lifers at the end of their minimum term, release – and it is not required to comment on the timing of the next review or moves to other categories of prison.[39]

Special considerations

Short tariff lifers

8.44 When the automatic life sentence was first introduced, the Prison Service was suddenly confronted with large numbers of life-sentenced prisoners with short tariffs, in some cases as short as 12–18 months. As the life sentence had previously been reserved for very serious offending, the normal structure of the life sentence did not translate properly to people who would become eligible for release before they even had their first full internal review. In order to address the difficulties this created, special directions were put in place for those with tariffs of under five years. These are:

- The Parole Board confirmed that there was no absolute requirement for short tariff lifers to go to open conditions, with an assessment being made on the merits of each case.
- On conviction, priority should be given to allocating this group to main lifer centres.
- Where the tariff is under five years, initial progress reports should be prepared after six months at the first stage prison.
- Pre-tariff parole reviews will generally only be feasible in cases where the tariff is three years or more. However, if the six-month review considers that a move to open conditions might be appropriate, steps will be taken by PPCS to try to facilitate a pre-tariff expiry parole review.

39 *R (on the application of Spence) v Secretary of State for the Home Department* [2003] EWCA Civ 732.

Deportees

8.45 Prisoners who are to be deported at the end of their life sentence should, in theory, not face any difference in their progress through the sentence and their parole reviews. For many years the Secretary of State did not permit this group of lifers to take town visits from category C conditions or to move to open conditions. Now, in theory, there is no reason why deportees should not go to open conditions. In practice, they will find this more difficult to achieve than lifers not facing deportation, as they will need to overcome any concerns that they might seek to abscond from open conditions to avoid deportation. PPCS will also consult with the immigration authorities so that any objections they might have can be considered. In cases where it is decided that the lifer is not suitable for open conditions, release and deportation will normally take place from a category C prison.

Mental Health Act detainees

8.46 The Secretary of State can direct that a prisoner should be transferred to a psychiatric hospital if, on receipt of reports from at least two registered medical practitioners, he is satisfied that the prisoner is suffering from a mental disorder; and the mental disorder is of a nature or degree that makes it appropriate for him to be detained in a hospital for medical treatment; and appropriate medical treatment is available for him.[40]

8.47 Prisoners are usually transferred under restriction directions pursuant to MHA 1983 section 49.[41] Where a restricted transfer has been made, if the Secretary of State is advised that the prisoner no longer requires treatment in hospital for mental disorder or that no effective treatment for his disorder can be given in the hospital to which he has been transferred, the Secretary of State can order either that the prisoner is returned to prison or that the prisoner is released on licence.[42] If no restriction order is made because, for example, the prisoner is approaching release at the time of the transfer, the prisoner is treated as having been released from prison custody on licence.

8.48 It is the invariable practice of the Secretary of State to make restricted transfer directions for prisoners serving a life sentence. The

40 Mental Health Act 1983 ss47–48.

41 This makes the prisoner subject to the restrictions contained in MHA 1983 ss40–41, which ensure that the Secretary of State has a continuing role over matters such as temporary releases and discharge.

42 MHA 1983 s50.

effect of a restricted transfer in such circumstances is that once the prisoner is discharged from Mental Health Act detention, a direction is still required from the Parole Board before release from custody can take place. The logic behind this is that there may be offending behaviour issues that are not necessarily linked to the prisoner's mental health and which still require consideration by the Parole Board. In such cases, the normal procedure would be for the individual to be returned to custody for a parole hearing, although it may be appropriate in some cases for the person to remain in hospital pending a parole review to be conducted at the secure unit if a transfer back to prison would be detrimental to their health.

Prisoners transferred to other UK jurisdictions

8.49 Prisoners serving life sentences may be transferred to other UK jurisdictions, such as Scotland or Northern Ireland.[43] Such transfers can either be unrestricted or restricted. An unrestricted transfer gives all authority for the administration of the sentence and release to the receiving jurisdiction whereas a restricted transfer requires that the prisoner remains subject the parole and licence schemes from the sending jurisdiction. Prisoners serving life and indeterminate sentences in England and Wales who are granted such transfers are invariably subject to a restricted transfer meaning that the Parole Board continues to have the legal power to determine release.[44]

8.50 When a lifer is transferred under these powers, the Scottish prison will take responsibility for preparing the current reports that are added to the skeleton parole dossier that has been prepared by PPCS.[45] The case will otherwise be dealt with by the English Parole Board in the same way as for any other lifer, with the Board travelling to Scotland to conduct any oral hearing that is required. If the prisoner requires public funding for their representation in the review process, this means that the case will have to be dealt with by a legal representative from this jurisdiction as the matter remains one of English law. It should be noted, however, that the restriction only extends to the release of the prisoner and their licence conditions and so internal administrative matters such as temporary release and

43 C(S)A 1997 s41 and Sch 1; for further information on such transfers see Creighton and Arnott, *Prisoners: law and practice*, LAG 2009, pp137–8.

44 C(S)A 1997 s28 continues to apply to prisoners transferred to Scotland by virtue of the Scotland Act 1998 (Functions Exercisable in or as Regards Scotland) Order 1999 SI No 1748 art 8 and Sch 4.

45 See chapter 10.

movement to open conditions are dealt with under the Scottish system. In Scotland, the transfer of lifers to open conditions is solely a matter for the prison governor and so does not require either any involvement from the Parole Board or the Secretary of State.

CHAPTER 9

The test for release

The test for release

9.1 The statutory test for the release of prisoners serving indeterminate sentences that must be applied by the Parole Board in every case is whether:

> the Board is satisfied that it is no longer necessary for the protection of the public that the prisoner should be confined.[1]

9.2 There is an historical background to this statutory test arising from case-law. It is often referred to as the 'life and limb' test, as the danger posed by the lifer must be of reoffending that would cause serious harm to the public, and the *level* of risk that will justify post-tariff detention is a 'substantial' or 'more than minimal' risk.[2] For mandatory lifers, this replaced a much narrower test that authorised detention if they were at risk of committing 'any imprisonable offence' but the current statutory test was applied to this group following the European Court of Human Rights (ECtHR) decision in *Stafford v UK*.[3]

9.3 The 'life and limb' test was first expressed in relation to a challenge by a discretionary lifer. The manner in which it was described by the court was as follows:

> If risk to the public is the test, risk must mean risk of dangerousness. Nothing else will suffice. It must mean there is a risk of Mr Benson repeating the sort of offence for which the life sentence was originally imposed; in other words risk to life and limb.[4]

9.4 These comments might, at first sight, seem to imply that the type of offending has to be the same as for the conviction rendering detention unlawful if the risk was of a different type of offending, but case-law has established that the test relates to risk irrespective of the nature of the risk posed. In *Stafford*, the applicant had been convicted of murder, released on life licence and then recalled to prison following a conviction for fraud. The ECtHR found that the decision to imprison Mr Stafford pursuant to his original life sentence on the grounds that he might commit further non-violent offences was in breach of article 5(1) of the European Convention on Human Rights (ECHR), as there was no causal link between the original conviction and the subsequent detention.[5]

1 C(S)A 1997 s28(6)(b).

2 *R v Parole Board ex p Bradley* [1991] 1 WLR 134.

3 (2002) 35 EHRR 32.

4 From *R v Secretary of State for the Home Department ex p Benson (No 2)* (1988) *Independent* 16 November, but quoted in full in *Bradley* [1991] 1 WLR 134 at 142C.

5 Also see *R v Secretary of State for the Home Department ex p Cox* [1992] COD 72 where the recall of a lifer.

9.5 This lead to an argument that the Board could not detain a lifer who posed a risk of offending that differed from the index offence. The flaw in this argument was that the basis for the original imposition of a life sentence is that the offender is considered to be dangerous.[6] Therefore, any further offending that poses a risk of serious harm to the public is causally connected to the conviction that resulted in the life sentence as it pertains to dangerousness. Under the statutory test that the Board is required to apply, detention is therefore justified. Stanley Burnton J explained the situation in the following terms:

> The causal connection is broken in cases where there is no risk to life and limb after the expiry of the tariff, but not where there is such a risk, albeit from offences of a different kind from those originally committed. ... I conclude that where both the original sentence and the continued detention of a life prisoner are based on the risk of serious harm to the public, there is no inconsistency between the original objectives of the sentencing court and the decision not to release or the decision to re-detain notwithstanding that the sentencing court had in mind a different kind of offence from that subsequently feared.[7]

9.6 Although all lifers will have been considered dangerous at the time of their conviction, there is a distinction to be drawn between those convicted of murder and other lifers. For those convicted of murder, the sentence is mandatory, whereas for all others, there must be some finding of dangerousness based on the individual's behaviour at the time of sentencing. When the case eventually comes before the Board, it should not therefore be assumed that those convicted of murder have any underlying pathology or behavioural traits that render them dangerous:

> It is quite wrong to make any assumptions about the dangerousness of an HMP detainee. When considering whether the prisoner poses a risk to life and limb that is more than minimal, the Board must apply the most careful scrutiny since a fundamental human right, the right to liberty, is at stake. I am prepared to accept the submission [of the Applicant] that the Board require cogent evidence before being satisfied that a prisoner poses more than a minimal risk of danger to life and limb.[8]

6 For discretionary lifers because a finding of dangerousness has been made by the courts; and for mandatory lifers because the offence of murder is inherently so serious that the person convicted can be deemed to pose a risk to the public.

7 *R (on the application of Green) v Parole Board* [2005] EWHC 548 (Admin), para 32.

8 *R v Parole Board ex p Curley* (1999) 22 October, HC, unreported.

9.7 Finally, the Board's duty is to assess risk wherever the release will take place. This is of particular importance to lifers facing deportation at the end of their sentence as it will still be necessary for the Board to reach a decision that they do not pose a risk of harm on release, even when the actual release will be to a different country.[9] This can pose particular problems for lifers being returned to countries where there may have few or no family ties especially as there is no obligation on the receiving country to provide any support or assistance.

The Secretary of State's directions

9.8 Prior to 2004 the Secretary of State only issued directions to the Board in relation to decisions where the Board did not have directive powers (see paras 1.56-1.57 above). When procedures for all lifers were harmonised after the coming into force of the CJA 2003, he issued directions for both lifers and determinate sentenced prisoners. These directions encompass the factors to be taken into account when transferring lifers to open conditions, those factors relevant to release and guidance on the recall of lifers on life licence.[10]

9.9 The practice of issuing directions to the Board in cases where it is acting as a court pursuant to article 5(4) of the ECHR was initially held to be unlawful by the Administrative Court. In *Girling v Parole Board*[11] the Court of Appeal allowed the secretary of state's appeal. It held that the use of the power to issue directions to the Board, even where it was acting as a court was not unlawful as long as such directions only provided guidance on matters to be taken into account. What was not permissible was for directions to state or interpret the statutory test to be applied by the Board. The directions do provide helpful guidance eon the approach to be taken by the Board.

> ...
>
> 6. In assessing the level of risk to life and limb presented by a lifer, the Parole Board shall consider the following information, *where relevant and where available,* before directing the lifer's release, recognising that the weight and relevance attached to particular information may vary according to the circumstances of each case:

9 *R v Parole Board ex p White* (1994) *Times* 30 December.

10 The directions on transfers to open conditions are set out in chapter 10 (pre-minimum term expiry reviews).

11 [2005] EWHC 546 QBD.

(a) The lifer's background, including the nature, circumstances and pattern of any previous offending;
(b) the nature and circumstances of the index offence, including any information provided in relation to its impact on the victim or victim's family;
(c) the trial judge's sentencing comments or report to the Secretary of State, and any probation, medical, or other relevant reports or material prepared for the court;
(d) whether the lifer has made positive and successful efforts to address the attitudes and behavioural problems which led to the commission of the index offence;
(e) the nature of any offences against prison discipline committed by the lifer;
(f) the lifer's attitude and behaviour to other prisoners and staff,
(g) the category of security in which the lifer is held and any reasons or reports provided by the Prison Service for such categorisation, particularly in relation to those lifers held in Category A conditions of security;
(h) the lifer's awareness of the impact of the index offence, particularly in relation to the victim or victim's family, and the extent of any demonstrable insight into his /her attitudes and behavioural problems and whether he/she has taken steps to reduce risk through the achievement of life sentence plan targets;
(i) any medical, psychiatric or psychological considerations (particularly if there is a history of mental instability)
(j) the lifer's response when placed in positions of trust, including any absconds, escapes, past breaches of temporary release or life licence conditions and life licence revocations;
(k) any indication of predicted risk as determined by a validated actuarial risk predictor model, or any other structured assessments of the lifer's risk and treatment needs
(l) whether the lifer is likely to comply with the conditions attached to his or her life licence and the requirements of supervision, including any additional non-standard conditions;
(m) any risk to other persons, including the victim, their family and friends.

7. Before directing release on life licence, the Parole Board shall also consider:
   (a) the lifer's relationship with probation staff (in particular the supervising probation officer), and other outside support such as family and friends;
   (b) the content of the resettlement plan and the suitability of the release address;
   (c) the attitude of the local community in cases where it may have a detrimental effect upon compliance;

(d) representations on behalf of the victim or victim's relatives in relation to licence conditions.[12]

9.10 Although the directions do not add anything to the release test, they do assist in filling in the practical application of that test to the facts of individual cases. As can be seen, the risk assessment must focus on the historical background which resulted in the commission of the offence for which the sentence was imposed, the manner in which the lifer has progressed in custody and the extent to which the resettlement plans will provide sufficient protection for the public.

The limits of the Parole Board's powers

9.11 The only statutory power granted to the Board is to direct the release of life-sentenced prisoners. If the Board is not directing release, its power does not extend beyond giving advice to the Secretary of State.[13] Although the Board is master of its own procedure, it must operate within this statutory framework.[14]

9.12 When lifers' cases are referred to the Board, if the Board does not direct release; the referral note only asks the Board to advise on suitability for open conditions. This referral note specifically instructs the Board not to advise or comment on other matters, such as movement between closed security categories (ie categories A to C) or the timing of the next review. Before the terms of referral were set in this manner, it had not been uncommon for prisoners to ask the Board to comment on matters relating to their general progress and when their next review should be held.[15] It has been held by the domestic courts, and confirmed by the ECtHR, that the requirements of article 5(4) of the ECHR extend only to the need for a court to have the

12 These directions can be found on the website of the Parole Board: www.paroleboard.gov.uk/release. Emphasis in original.

13 CJA 2003 s239(2).

14 See, eg, Lord Woolf in *R (on the application of Roberts) v Parole Board* [2005] UKHL 45 at para 44.

15 One case which demonstrates the importance that used to be attributed to the Board's observations on these issues was *R (on the application of Williams) v Secretary of State for the Home Department* [2002] EWCA Civ 498. In this case a Category A lifer received a recommendation from the Board that he should be downgraded, resulting in a finding that the discrepancy between the Board's view of his case and the view of the Home Secretary justified special procedures being put in place for his Category A review, including the possibility of an oral hearing.

power to direct release. Any other decision, even if it ultimately may have an important bearing on release, does not engage article 5(4). The Board is not, therefore, empowered to:

- direct a move to open conditions – it can only offer advice to the Secretary of State on this issue. In *Ashingdane v UK*[16] the ECtHR held that the movement of a mental health act detainee from a secure hospital to a psychiatric unit did not engage article 5 as the issue concerned the conditions of detention rather than the right to liberty. This has been followed in numerous cases concerning the movement of prisoners to open conditions, both domestically and before the ECtHR;[17]
- set the time between parole reviews – even though the courts have suggested this might be desirable, it is not a requirement of article 5(4);[18]
- comment on moves within the closed prison estate.[19]

Burden of proof

The development of the burden of proof

9.13 The original wording of the 'life and limb' test left open the possibility that there was a burden of proof in lifer parole reviews. It was not clear if there was a burden and, if so, whether it fell on the Home Secretary to prove the necessity for the prisoner to be detained or whether the prisoner needed to prove that he/she is safe for release. This question has not been answered definitively, but there is now a far clearer indication that the courts are unlikely to consider that the traditional concept of a burden of proof is truly relevant to the review process.

9.14 The favoured approach of the courts has been to suggest that the task of the Parole Board is to make a decision based on the material before it. In one case heard fairly soon after the oral parole system had been established, the early judicial indication was that there was no duty on the Secretary of State to 'prove' that the prisoner would

16 (1985) 7 EHRR 528.

17 *Blackstock v UK (Admissibility)* [2005] 2 Prison Law Reports 85 and (2006) 42 EHRR 2 affirming a long line of domestic decisions.

18 *R (on the application of Day) v Home Secretary* [2004] EWHC 1742 (Admin).

19 *R (on the application of Spence) v Secretary of State for the Home Department* [2003] EWCA Civ 732.

pose a risk if released, but that the Board needed to be satisfied that the risk was low enough for release:

> the Board must be satisfied that it is not necessary that he should be kept in prison and not that there would be a substantial risk if he were released. In other words it must be shown that the risk is low enough to release him, not high enough to keep him in prison.[20]

9.15 Although the judgment did not provide a definitive response to the burden of proof question, the clear implication is that the onus is on the prisoner to establish that he/she is safe for release.

The impact of the HRA

9.16 The issue has been reopened several times since the Human Rights Act (HRA) 1998 was enacted. The original discretionary lifer panel scheme was based very closely on the mental health review tribunals, not least because it was often very hard to distinguish between those who received discretionary life sentences and those who received hospital orders. When it was established that the correct post-HRA test in the mental health context was that the burden of proof rested with the Secretary of State to justify detention,[21] it was clear that the issue needed to be resolved in the parole context.

9.17 Lord Bingham commented on this subject[22] in *R v Lichniak and Pyrah*.[23] Parole reviews were touched upon as part of Lord Bingham's finding that the system of review ensured the mandatory life sentence did not breach article 3 and he cast considerable doubt on whether there was actually a place for a burden of proof when considering risk assessments in the parole context:

> I doubt whether there is in truth a burden on the prisoner to persuade the Parole Board that it is safe to recommend release, since this is an administrative process requiring the Board to consider all the available material and form a judgment. There is, inevitably, a balance to be struck between the interest of the individual and the interest of society, and I do not think it objectionable, in the case of someone

20 *R v Parole Board ex p Lodomez* (1994) 26 BMLR 162 at p18.

21 *R (H) v North London and East Region Mental Health Review Tribunal* [2001] 3 WLR 512.

22 Although his comments were obiter dictum as the main decision in the case was that the mandatory life sentence itself was not an arbitrary punishment and so was compatible with article 5(1) and article 3.

23 [2002] UKHL 47.

who has once taken life with the intent necessary for murder, to prefer the latter in case of doubt.[24]

9.18 The judgment left as much open as it resolved, to the extent that it shied away from the burden of proof approach while at the same time hinting that it was not for the prisoner to prove anything. It also dates from a time when the release of mandatory lifers had not been held to fall within the ambit of article 5 and so the Board's duty remained administrative rather than judicial.

9.19 The one case that attempted to confront the problem head on was *R (on the application of Hirst) v Parole Board*.[25] The application was made by a lifer prior to his parole review taking place. A declaration was sought in relation to the burden of proof, but the application was dismissed as being premature. Although the court declined to make a finding, it indicated that, if forced to reach a conclusion, the opinion expressed by Lord Bingham would be most likely to prevail. The position of Mental Health Act (MHA) 1983 detainees was distinguished on the grounds that lifers are only detained once a court has already established that they posed a risk to the public. MHA detainees are subject to executive detention and so there needs to be judicial supervision to determine whether the grounds for detention are made out. In the post-judgment discussion, the court indicated that it did consider the issue to be a serious one that merited full consideration, but that it was simply impossible to reach a decision in a vacuum. In order for a judgment to make any sense, it would need to proceed with a settled factual outcome that would enable the practical application of the arguments to be tested. However, once again, the implication of the judgment was to cast doubt on the very idea that this approach was relevant at all.

9.20 It is important not to confuse the burden of proof with the standard of proof, although when dealing with risk assessment rather than fact finding these boundaries can sometimes become blurred. The Board operates to the civil standard of proof and it has been held that this is a single standard, although the cogency of the evidence needed can vary depending on the nature and seriousness of the allegations in issue.[26] This standard of proof is discussed in detail in chapter 11.

24 At [16].

25 [2002] EWHC 1592 (Admin).

26 *Re D v Life Sentence Comrs for Northern Ireland* [2008] UKHL 33.

Conclusions

9.21 Although it not possible to provide a definitive answer to this question, the very clear indication is that the courts are highly unlikely to hold that it is appropriate to approach the task of risk assessment at a parole review by reference to a burden of proof. The comments of various courts strongly suggest that the Board's duty is to consider all the available material and form a judgment on risk. In order properly to exercise its judgment, the Board will not be requiring either party to 'prove' its case, but will reach a view as to whether the prisoner poses a risk or not.[27]

9.22 There is one exception to this approach and that is where there is a material factual dispute, for example where a prisoner is accused of a criminal act that is denied. This situation will arise most commonly, but not exclusively, at recall hearings. In those cases, it is far harder to envisage the burden of proof not being applicable and it would seem to be grossly at odds with the general principle of fairness if the person making the allegation were not required to stand the burden of proving it.

9.23 The outcome of these judicial observations does allow the Board an extremely wide discretion. As risk assessment is not an exact science, providing decisions are properly reasoned the Board will generally have the leeway to accept any reasonable view on risk assessment that is put to it. Interestingly, the IPP sentence may arguably allow for this issue to be revisited on the basis that the sentence is predictive of dangerousness at the time it is passed and so the threshold for continued detention at the end of the minimum term might conceivably be different than for other lifers. Lord Bingham's comments in *Lichniak* (above) specifically relate the heinous nature of the crime to the burden to be applied on release. While this holds true for murder and offences for which a discretionary life sentence might be passed, the argument is less persuasive for some of the more mundane offences that now attract the sentence of IPP.[28] However, in the event that a case ever does come before the courts that allows this issue to be resolved, the obvious danger is that it will resolve any ambiguity against the prisoner.

27 Although where an extended sentence prisoner is recalled, as the extension period is designed to be served in the community the Board must assume a default position in favour of liberty and so have to be positively satisfied of the need for detention – see chapter 12.

28 In *R (on the application of Bayliss v Parole Board)* [2008] EWHC 3127 (Admin) the Secretary of State agreed that the test for release for IPP sentence prisoners had to relate to the basis upon which the sentence was imposed, that is a significant risk of committing offences occasioning serious harm.

CHAPTER 10

Reviews of life sentences by the Parole Board

continued

The Parole Board Rules and the generic parole process

10.1 The procedure and timetable for oral parole hearings is governed by the Parole Board Rules 2004 (PBR), which were most recently amended in April 2009 by the Parole Board (Amendment) Rules 2009.[1] Somewhat confusingly, the PBR were not laid by statutory instrument but the amendments issued in 2009 were. The reason for this apparent anomaly is that the PBR were originally made under an enabling power contained in CJA 1991 section 32(5) that was repealed in April 2005. CJA 2003 section 239(5) requires the PBR to be made by statutory instrument under the negative resolution procedure. The PBR only formally apply to references made to the Board in connection with the release and recall of prisoners serving life or indeterminate sentences[2] although the Board will use them as a broad template for the correct procedure in any case where an oral hearing is taking place.

10.2 The parole review process is now called the generic parole process[3] and is based around a timetable that splits the review into three stages. The first is a 26-week period to allow for the dossier and reports to be compiled, for the Parole Board to consider the case on the papers and if an oral hearing is to be convened, for the directions to be complied with. The second stage is for the oral hearing itself to take place, the intention being for this to occur on the month after the first stage. Finally, the third stage of the process is to allow two weeks for the receipt of the Parole Board's (PB) decision and to allow this to be processed. In all, this envisages a review process of approximately eight months. Interestingly, the system this has replaced required stages 1 and 2 to be completed within 26 weeks and so one month has been added to the review process. The key stages in the review are set out in the table below:[4]

1 SI 2009 No 408.
2 PBR r2(1).
3 PSO 6010.
4 This table is largely taken from PSO 6010 pp5–6.

Stages in the generic parole process

Week	*Actions*	*Responsibility*
1st stage	**Case administration**	
0	PPCS commences review	PPCS
	PB issues notification of target hearing period (post-tariff only) and letter to prisoner	PB
	Prison request all relevant reports	Prison
	PPCS commence skeleton dossier	PPCS
4	Deadline – PPCS send skeleton dossier to prison	PPCS
5	Deadline for receipt of skeleton dossier	Prison
	Deadline for prisoner to notify PB of legal representative	Prison
8	Relevant reports received	Prison
	Prison compiles and paginates dossier and gives to: • Prisoner • PPCS • PB • Solicitor sends	
9	PB assess dossier – return to prison if incomplete	PB
10	Deadline for prison to return complete dossier to PB	Prison
12	Prisoner to submit written representations	Prison
	PB copies dossier to ICM member	PB
13	ICM issues standard directions on outstanding dossiers	PB
14	PB consider pre- and post-tariff dossiers on papers	PB
	Pre-tariff – PB issues negative recommendation or refers dossier to oral hearing and issues ICM directions	PB

Week	*Actions*	*Responsibility*
	Post-tariff – PB issues negative decision or ICM directions for oral hearing (If negative decision issued, prisoner has 28 days to accept or challenge decision)	PB
16	Prison/PPCS confirms all ICM directions complied with	Prison/PPCS
	PB lists case for oral hearing	PB
18	PB issue oral hearing exact date notification to all parties and identifies panel members and	PB
	Deadline for any challenge to negative decision issued at week 12 to be forwarded to PB by prison/legal representative	Prison
	Secretary of State's view to be provided (where appropriate)	PPCS
20	PB copies dossier to members of panel and chair issues further directions (if required) and rules on applications for non-disclosure, victim and witness attendance	PB
22	Prison/PPCS confirms all outstanding directions complied with	Prison/PPCS
	PB issues timetable for oral hearing to all parties	PB
26	End of 1st stage	
2nd stage	**Calendar month for listing oral hearing**	
	Oral hearing takes place during this calendar month	PB
3rd stage	**Post oral hearing**	
	Deadline for receipt of PB decision (two weeks following oral hearing)	PB
Process ends	Release at tariff expiry/ Consideration of transfer to open conditions/setting new review date	PPCS

10.3 The old review process was designed to be completed entirely within the 26-week period, but the new procedure envisages eight months from start to finish. For end-of-tariff reviews, the aim is to receive and process the decision before the tariff expires. However, PSO 6010 does not contain any timetable for PPCS to process recommendations and directions made by the Board at any other reviews. The implication in the timetable is that the review is to be completed by PPCS within one month of the recommendation or direction being received if the eight-month timetable is to be met.

Referral of cases to the Parole Board

10.4 The C(S)A 1997 section 28(7) allows life-sentenced prisoners to require the Secretary of State to refer their cases to the Parole Board once the minimum term has been served and at least every two years thereafter. Although the statute is worded to place the onus on the prisoner to seek the referral, in practice the referral is made by the Public Protection Casework Section (PPCS) on behalf of the Secretary of State without the prisoner having to make any application. It is arguable that as the duty to review is a positive obligation on the part of the state, any system that in practice actually required the prisoner to make the application would be in breach of article 5(4) of the European Convention on Human Rights (ECHR). Each parole dossier will commence with the document containing the formal referral from the Secretary of State, which reads as follows:[5]

1. This case is hereby referred to the Parole Board by the Secretary of State under section 28(6)(a) of the Act to consider whether or not it would be appropriate to direct the prisoner's release.

2. If, after considering the case, the Board decide to direct the prisoner's release on licence under section 28(5)(b) of the Act, it is invited to make a recommendation to the Secretary of State under section 31(3)(a) in relation to any condition which it considers should be included in the licence. The Board is also asked to comment on any aspects of the prisoner's behaviour which need to be monitored in the period prior to release and on the prisoner's return to the community.

5 For pre-tariff referrals, it is made clear that the referral is pursuant to the CJA 2003 s239(2) and the sole issue on which advice is being sought is suitability for open conditions. The referral basis for recalls is dealt with in chapter 13.

3. If the Board does not consider it appropriate to direct release, it is invited to advise the Secretary of State:
   i) on the prisoner's continued suitability for open conditions, if relevant;
   ii) whether the prisoner, if in closed conditions, should be transferred to open conditions. If the Board makes such a recommendation, it is invited to comment on the degree of risk involved;
   iii) on the continuing areas of risk that need to be addressed.
4. The Board is asked to give full reasons – which will be disclosed to the prisoner – for any decision or recommendation it makes.
5. In any event the Board should note that it is not being asked to comment on or make any recommendation about:
   i) the security classification of the closed prison in which the prisoner may be detained;
   ii) any specific treatment needs or offending behaviour work required;
   iii) the date of the next review.
6. Under the Parole Board Rules 2004, the Board is required to notify the prisoner and the Secretary of State of its decision, and the reasons for it, within 14 days of the hearing.

10.5 Although the referral of cases is made by PPCS, there can be occasions where it is necessary to contact PPCS to make sure that the referral has been made at the appropriate time. This will arise most that in cases where there are concurrent life and determinate sentences which can cause confusion in calculating the correct review dates.

10.6 The obligation on the state is to conduct a review before the end of the minimum term to ensure that release can take place, if appropriate, at the first opportunity. This duty has been held to extend to the Secretary of State's duty to refer cases sufficiently early to allow the Parole Board to complete the review process in time[6] and also to the Parole Board to ensure that they organise their procedures to allow for release to be possible the moment the minimum term ends.[7] During the course of 2008–09, the Parole Board was not able to meet this requirement following the rapid increase in the number of lifers and IPP prisoners eligible for parole reviews. The courts took a pragmatic approach to the issue rather than a principled stance and held

6 *R v Secretary of State for the Home Department and the Parole Board ex p Norney* [1995] Admin LR 861.

7 *R (on the application of Noorkoiv) v Secretary of State for the Home Department (No 2)* [2002] EWCA Civ 770.

that while the delays might breach article 5(4), as the Parole Board had adopted a rational listing priority the courts should only interfere with listing decisions in very exceptional cases.[8] The prospects of release and length of time served over tariff have been held not to be sufficient in themselves to be considered exceptional circumstances.[9] Although the courts rejected the prospect of litigating to shorten the delays, if there is loss or injury caused by the breach of article 5(4) damages can be claimed.[10]

A general note about the Parole Board Rules

10.7 The procedure following the referral of a case to the Board is governed by the PBR. Historically, parole hearings tended to proceed with little attention to the timetables set out in the PBR and as the timetable is entirely dependent on the prompt disclosure of the parole dossier itself, the extent to which it can be followed is largely dictated by prisons making sure reports are written and disclosed on time. One of the key aims of the generic parole process introduced by PSO 6010 is to try and ensure that such delays are eradicated and, to this end, a Parole Process Monitoring Board was established reporting directly to NOMS and the Parole Board which monitors performance against the timetable in table 1 (above). The key performance targets include:

- the provision of skeleton dossiers by PPCS to prisons;
- the disclosure of dossiers to the Board by the prison;
- the issuing of and compliance with ICM directions;
- the receipt of Parole Board decisions.[11]

Regrettably, the issuing of the final decision by PPCS after the oral hearing has concluded has not been included in these performance targets.

10.8 Although the PBR set out a fairly clear timetable, rule 23 ensures that even where there has been a failure to comply with the PBR, this will not undermine the validity of the proceedings provided the panel hearing a case takes such steps as are necessary to avoid there being any prejudice to the parties:

8 *Betteridge v Parole Board* [2009] EWHC 1638 (Admin).

9 Eg, *R (on the application of Alcock) v Parole Board* [2009] EWHC 2401 (Admin).

10 *R (on the application of Pennington) v Parole Board* [2009] EWHC 2296 (Admin).

11 PSO 6010 para 1.12.

23. Any irregularity resulting from a failure to comply with these Rules before the panel has determined a case shall not of itself render the proceedings void, but the panel may, and shall, if it considers that the person may have been prejudiced, take such steps as it thinks fit, before determining the case, to cure the irregularity, whether by the amendment of any document, the giving of any notice, the taking of any step or otherwise.

The discussion of the procedure that follows and the extent to which a deviation from this procedure has any impact on the review itself must be read with this consideration in mind.

10.9 It should also be borne in mind that the prisoner cannot be compelled to participate in a review. The review is to vindicate prisoners' rights to have their detention reviewed by an independent tribunal. If the prisoner does not wish the review to take place at that particular time, it is possible to apply for a deferral. The procedure for applying for a deferral and the considerations taken into account when this request is made are examined in detail below.

Steps following referral

10.10 The PBR apply to all cases that have been referred to the Board by the Secretary of State, where the minimum term has expired or following recall.[12] They are also applied voluntarily by the Board in any pre-tariff care referred to them by the Secretary of State[13] or where the Board has decided to hold an oral hearing for a prisoner serving an extended or other determinate sentence.

10.11 Following referral, the PBR require that cases are allocated to a member of the Board. For cases where the proceedings will be resolved without a hearing, a single member is appointed.[14] For cases where an oral hearing is to take place, one or more members may be appointed and the appointed panel must include a sitting or retired judge for all cases except IPPs.[15] Where there is a judge on a panel, the judge will be the chair.[16] In practice, as the PBR require the case to be considered on the papers alone in the first instance, the normal route will be for a single member to be appointed for the paper review and for the case to be passed onto a panel if an oral hearing is listed.

12 PBR r2.

13 Under the power to seek advice from the Board in CJA 2003 s239(2).

14 PBR r3(1).

15 PBR r3(3).

16 PBR r3(5).

Where a case proceeds from a single member to an oral hearing, the single member must not form part of the oral hearing panel.[17]

10.12 The Board is also required to list the oral hearing for the case and notify the parties – the prisoner and PPCS – within five working days.[18] Where the prisoner has notified the Board of their legal representative, notification will be sent to that person. Cases are not actually given a hearing date at this stage and in practical terms, listing simply refers to the practice of entering the case into the list of cases to be dealt with. A case is only put forward for an actual hearing date once the ICM process is complete and the Board has decided that an oral hearing is necessary.

Legal representation

10.13 Within five weeks of the commencement of the review the prisoner will receive a form asking whether they wish their review to proceed with an oral hearing and notifying the Board of their legal representative and the details of their offender manager. The decision on how the review should proceed is somewhat premature as the prisoner will not have received any disclosure at this stage, but some prisoners may be content that the review is straightforward enough to proceed on the papers. It is not clear what would happen if a prisoner elects for a paper review at this stage but later decides to seek an oral hearing, but the requirements of procedural fairness would seem to indicate that it is open to a prisoner to request an oral hearing at any stage and that it would not be proper for that right to be irrevocably waived at such an early stage of the review.

10.14 It is also envisaged that a prisoner will notify the Board of who is to act as their prisoner's legal representative at this point.[19] This requirement is perhaps the least important in the PBR, as the Board is usually content to allow for representatives to be appointed at any stage of the review process. However, from an administrative point of view, it is in the prisoner's interests to have their representative's details on record with the Board and the prison as early as possible so that all material and any directions are served promptly.

10.15 Although the choice of representation is left to the prisoner, certain persons are prohibited from this role. These are:

17 PBR r3(4).

18 PBR r4.

19 PBR r5(3).

- anyone liable to be detained under the Mental Health Act 1983;
- anyone serving a prison sentence;
- any person currently on licence following release from prison;
- anyone with an unspent previous conviction.[20]

10.16 In cases where the prisoner is unrepresented, it is also possible for the Board to appoint a legal representative if the prisoner consents to this course of action. In practice, it is very difficult to envisage any circumstances where this is likely to happen, other than where a prisoner is unable to find a solicitor and the Board is able to assist or where there are issues of capacity for the prisoner.

10.17 There is one situation where it is possible that the Board may seek to appoint a representative without the prisoner's consent and where this might be held to be permissible. In the rare situations where the Board decides that material cannot be disclosed to either a prisoner or the prisoner's appointed representative, it is possible that the Board may decide that a special advocate should be appointed to protect the prisoner's interests, whether or not the prisoner consents. The extent to which the appointment of a special advocate is possible in any circumstances is discussed further in some detail below.

Contents of the parole dossier

10.18 Within five weeks of the commencement of the review, PPCS are required to prepare and send the skeleton dossier to the prison at which the prisoner is held. The skeleton dossier contains the following information:

- an index sheet;
- the note formally referring the case to the Parole Board for consideration;
- the pro-forma case summary (other than in IPP cases where the prisoner has spent less than eight years in custody) containing the basic details of the case including the period of time the prisoner has served in custody, his or her current location, the dates of remand, sentence and length of tariff, and brief details of the index offence;
- offence-related papers. These must include (where they exist) the summary of offence prepared by PPCS (including reference to sources relied upon), transcript of the trial judge's sentencing

20 PBR r5(2).

remarks, the pre- and post-trial sentence reports prepared by qualified probation staff, a current list of previous convictions as recorded on the police national computer (ie within the last 12 months but more recent if there are convictions within the last 12 months) and any other relevant papers such as psychiatric or psychological reports prepared for trial and/or sentencing, information on any appeals lodged and the trial judge's report to the Secretary of State (for lifers sentenced before 18 December 2003);

- a record of adjudications since remand in custody/sentencing extracted from the Inmate Information System (IIS), including establishment, offence, date of hearing, result (proven or dismissed) and punishment.
- a summary of reports of progress in prison including therapeutic community and dangerous and severe personality disorder (DSPD) unit reports;
- reports from any offending behaviour courses completed in custody;
- previous Parole Board decision if a subsequent review.[21]

10.19 The skeleton dossier is not disclosed to the prisoner at this stage and is only received by the case administration office (now the OMU) at the prison. This is the unit that will then take responsibility for compiling the full dossier with current reports. Any inaccuracies in the skeleton dossier will not, therefore, be known to the prisoner until the full dossier is complete and has been disclosed. This can be problematic if report writers are to then compile their reports based on inaccurate or incomplete material.

10.20 The case administration officer is responsible for contacting the required report writers and the parole dossier should be disclosed within eight weeks of the Board listing a case following referral.[22] The disclosure of the dossier is the key to the progress and timing of the entire review. All the substantive stages of the review can only take effect once the full dossier has been disclosed. It is therefore essential that close attention is paid to the preparation of reports in sufficient time to allow for disclosure to be made promptly.

10.21 The PBR[23] require that the following information is contained in the parole dossier (it is this information that is contained on the skeleton dossier).[24]

21 PSO 6010 para 1.4.1.

22 PBR r6(1).

23 PBR r6(1)(a).

24 See para 10.18 above.

Information relating to the prisoner[25]

10.22 The following information relating to the prisoner must be included in the parole dossier:

(a) the prisoner's full name and date of birth;
(b) the prison in which the prisoner is detained, details of previous prisons where the prisoner has been detained and the dates and reasons for transfer;
(c) details of the offence for which the life sentence was imposed and details of previous convictions;
(d) the trial judge's sentencing comments (if available);
(e) details of any appeal to the Court of Appeal;
(f) the parole history, if any, of the prisoner including any periods spent on licence during the currency of the life licence or extended sentence.

Reports relating to the prisoner[26]

10.23 The following reports relating to the prisoner are required by the PBR to be included in the parole dossier:[27]

(a) pre-trial and pre-sentence reports examined by the sentencing court on the circumstances of the offence;
(b) reports on a prisoner while he was subject to a transfer direction under section 47 of the Mental Health Act 1983;
(c) current reports on the prisoner's risk factors, reduction in risk and performance and behaviour in prison, including views on suitability for release on licence as well as compliance with any sentence plan;
(d) an up-to-date home circumstances report prepared for the Board by an officer of the supervising local probation board, including information on the following where relevant:
   (i) details of the home address, family circumstances and family attitudes towards the prisoner;
   (ii) alternative options if the prisoner cannot return home;
   (iii) the opportunity for employment on release;
   (iv) the local community's attitude towards the prisoner (if known);

25 PBR Sch 1 Part A.
26 PBR Sch 1 Part B.
27 PBR r6(1)(b).

(v) the attitudes and concerns of the victims of the offence (if known);
(vi) the prisoner's attitude to the index offence;
(vii) the prisoner's response to previous periods of supervision;
(viii) the prisoner's behaviour during any temporary leave during the current sentence;
(ix) the prisoner's attitude to the prospect of release and the requirements and objectives of supervision;
(x) an assessment of the risk of reoffending;
(xi) a programme of supervision;
(xii) a view on suitability for release; and
(xiii) recommendations regarding any non-standard licence conditions.

10.24 The PBR do not prescribe who must prepare these reports but PSO 6010 has detailed guidance on the identity of the report writers and the contents of their reports. The guidance requires that the following are prepared, although the SPR K is not required for IPP cases:[28]

- PAROM1: home probation officer's report completed by a qualified probation officer, countersigned by line manager to meet quality standards identified by NSMART (the Probation Service system for monitoring standards);
- SPR K completed by a Prison Service designated staff member (PSDSM). This report will only normally be completed if the offender supervisor is not sufficiently qualified or experienced. If the SPR K is required to be completed it must be undertaken by the PSDSM who is responsible for the assessment, sentence planning and reviews of progress of the prisoner and assesses if there have been any changes to the risk and status of the prisoner. The PSDSM report presents a risk assessment that includes attitudes to offence, victim information, and an assessment of any risks presented by the prisoner during his or her time in custody. The PSDSM must state in their report their level of experience and length of time working with lifers. The PSDSM must also state their qualifications and training courses attended that relate to working with life-sentenced prisoners. Where the report writer is not a qualified probation officer, they should ideally have, as a minimum, successfully completed the Introduction to Risk Assessment and Management (IRAM) and Management of Indeterminate Sentences and Risk (MISaR) training courses or equivalent (eg Life in the 21st Century) to demonstrate their knowledge and

28 PSO 6010 paras 1.5.5–6.

skills in risk assessment and management and have some previous experience of working with life sentence prisoners. This is not a mandatory requirement but governors should plan for it to be so by April 2010. The PSDSM must confirm in the SPR K whether an offender supervisor has been allocated to the lifer concerned and, if so, that an SPR C is included in the dossier before submission. If there is no offender supervisor allocated to the lifer, the PSDSM must address the additional issues that would otherwise have been covered by the offender supervisor (OS).[29] In these cases, the PSDSM must confirm that they have liaised directly with the offender manager and the personal officer or other wing staff who can comment first hand on the behaviour of the lifer;

- SPR C prepared by the OS. In lifer cases if there is a separate OS also working with the prisoner then a SPR C must be included in the dossier. This must be confirmed by the PSDSM in their report. The OS has information and views relevant to the decision on release or about transfer to open conditions. The OS must also state their qualifications and training courses attended that relate to working with life-sentenced prisoners The OS should as a minimum have attended the IRAM training course. All OS staff should also eventually have attended the MISaR course;
- SPR D from any relevant key workers. This includes, where relevant, reports from the Counselling, Assessment, Referral, Advice and Throughcare (CARAT) worker, interventions and activity supervisors, offending behaviour programmes staff, therapeutic community, DSPD staff, personal officer or wing staff;
- The OASys report reviewed within the last 12 months of the target month for the review hearing and countersigned by OASys supervisor.

10.25 In addition to these mandatory reports, there are a range of discretionary reports that can be requested if relevant to the individual case. The request is normally made by the OM or the PSDSM:

- **SPR E** psychologist;
- **SPR F** healthcare;
- **SPR G** psychiatrist;
- **SPR H** security.

10.26 Where these additional reports are not prepared initially, the Parole Board may still request that they be obtained and added following the

29 Sections in the SPR C on Behaviour in Prison and Response to Sentence Plan.

consideration of the case by a single member at the intensive case management (ICM) stage of the review (see below).

10.27 It is not a mandatory requirement for there to be a report from a psychologist or psychiatrist. In cases where there has been recent treatment or assessments by a specialist, then the Board would normally expect that person to prepare a report for inclusion in the dossier. Indeed, it is difficult to see how a valid assessment of risk can be made without such reports. In cases where there is a historical psychological report and no ongoing concerns or treatment needs were identified, it is unlikely to be necessary for there to be a current psychological assessment.

Disclosure of the parole dossier

Initial disclosure and intensive case management

10.28 The responsibility for disclosing the dossier rests with the prison at which the lifer is held at the time of the review. Prior to the dossier being disclosed, a governor should sign off the dossier to confirm that all of the required reports have been obtained from suitably qualified staff and that they are completed to the required standard.[30] The dossier must then be disclosed to the prisoner, to PPCS and the Parole Board. If a prisoner's legal representative requests a copy, this must be provided.[31] In order to ensure that there are no delays in obtaining the dossier, it is advisable to prepare a written authority signed by the prisoner authorising disclosure to the legal representative. The request for disclosure should be addressed to the lifer clerk or parole clerk at the prison. The dossier will also contain a form SPR J, which provides a pro forma for the prisoner to make representations. In cases where there is a legal representative appointed, it is always sensible for the prisoner to take legal advice rather than completing this form on their own behalf.

10.29 The PBR require representations to then be submitted by the prisoner, or their representative, within four weeks.[32] The extent to which this is possible will depend on whether the dossier contains all of the information that the prisoner considers to be relevant and necessary for the review and, if it does not, how long it will take to obtain it. The

30 PSO 6010 para 1.5.2.

31 PSO 6010 para 1.5.3.

32 PBR r7(1).

PBR make provision for a single member of the Board to undertake ICM at any stage of the review and the practice is for dossiers to be placed before a single member for ICM four weeks after disclosure has taken place. A great deal of caution has to be exercised at this stage; if the dossier is complete at the time it is sent to the Board and the ICM does not identify the need for any further information, the Board can proceed directly to the stage of considering the application substantively by a single member pursuant to PBR rule 11 at the same time as the ICM is conducted. Therefore, it is essential that representations are made at this stage even if the case is not ready for a substantive decision to be made. Those representations should either ask for specific directions to be made during the ICM, such as seeking further specialist reports, or request additional time in which to submit substantive representations.

Obtaining further information

10.30 It may prove necessary to obtain further details of a prisoner's record before preparing representations; for example, adverse comments made in respect of wing records may require an application to be made for the prisoner's wing history sheets or security records. It is possible to apply for copies of prison records under the Data Protection Act (DPA) 1998. This enables prisoners to apply subject to the exemptions contained in the Act. An application can be made by a legal representative on behalf of the prisoner by submitting a signed authority from the prisoner. A fee of £10 is payable and the request should be made to the Prison Service's Information Management Section.[33] The DPA requires disclosure to be made within 40 days and requests are dealt with more speedily where specific information is sought as opposed to all prison records. The request might, for example, seek copies of medical records, security intelligence reports, wing history sheets or other information that might not ordinarily be included in the dossier or might not have been disclosed under the normal reporting procedures.

Challenging erroneous information

10.31 There will be occasions when the dossier contains information that is simply factually inaccurate. This arises most commonly in parole

33 Branston Registry Building 16, S & T Store, Burton Road, Branston, Burton Upon Trent, Staffs, DE14 3EG.

reviews for determinate prisoners rather than for lifers where, for example, pre-trial police reports are included rather than accurate information compiled after conviction. Although this does not tend to be a major issue in lifers' reviews, there will be occasions when there is factual information in the dossier that is inaccurate and highly prejudicial.

10.32 When assessing whether information falls into this category, it is important to distinguish between information that may be unproven but relevant (such as disputed risk assessments or details of security concerns that never formed the subject of formal disciplinary proceedings), and information that is simply untrue. In cases where the information falls into the first category, the proper method of challenging it is through the submission of representations and additional evidence during the review itself.

10.33 On the rare occasions when there is material that is factually incorrect and cannot be rectified satisfactorily through representations, the correct procedure to follow will depend on whether the dossier has been supplied to the Board. The Board is under a statutory duty to consider *all* material placed before it[34] and so if the dossier has been sent to the Board, it has no power to remove material from it.[35] This is a function that can only be performed by the Secretary of State and so must be resolved with the prison or PPCS. If it has not been resolved prior to the submission of the dossier to the Board, it will be necessary for the Board to agree to return the dossier for the inaccuracies to be corrected and then resubmitted. As this can be time consuming, it is always worth considering whether the problems can be corrected through representations or whether the material is so prejudicial that it must be removed.

Withholding information

10.34 The normal principle applied to disclosure is that all material to be considered by the Board should also be disclosed to the prisoner. This is a requirement that arises as a matter of common law fairness and as part of the requirements of article 5(4). As such, it is recognised in the PBR that the norm is full disclosure.

34 CJA 2003 s239(3).

35 See *R v Parole Board ex p Harris* [1998] COD 233 and *R v Parole Board ex p Higgins* (1998) 22 September, unreported. Both of these cases concerned determinate prisoners but the principles apply equally to dossiers prepared for life sentenced prisoners.

10.35 PBR rule 6(2) authorises the Secretary of State to withhold material contained in the dossier where:

> its disclosure would adversely affect national security, the prevention of disorder or crime or the health and welfare of the prisoner or others (such withholding being a necessary and proportionate measure in all the circumstances of the case) ...

10.36 Where it is proposed to withhold material under this rule, it must be served upon the Board separately from the dossier itself, together with the reasons for that decision.

10.37 On receipt of this material, the chair of the panel that is to consider the case is required to make arrangements for it to be served on the prisoner's representative providing the representative is a barrister or solicitor, a registered medical practitioner or someone whom the chair considers suitable to receive the material by virtue of their experience or qualifications.[36] This representative is forbidden to disclose the material either directly or indirectly to the prisoner without the consent of the chair.

10.38 If the Board proposes to serve material on a representative in accordance with these provisions, this can create a serious professional problem. Some representatives will not feel that it is ethical to proceed with a review in such circumstances and it may also create problems if the material is received without the client consenting to the representative receiving it under these constraints.[37] To try to minimise these problems, the appropriate procedural step to be followed is for the Board to ask the representative whether he/she is prepared to receive material under PBR rule 6(3). This allows the representative to explain to the client how the rule operates and to obtain the client's consent to receive material that might not be seen by the client at all.

10.39 On a purely practical level, it will normally be in the prisoner's best interests for the representative to accept material under this rule. Very often, the Secretary of State will have taken an overly restrictive view of what cannot be disclosed and may be paying undue deference to the wishes of the person providing the material without giving proper consideration to the overall requirements of fairness and the extent to which non-disclosure can genuinely be justified. It is only if the representative has access to the material that this can be addressed in representations to the Board.

36 PBR r6(3).

37 Solicitors Practice Rule 16-06 states that the solicitor must normally disclose all relevant information to the client.

10.40 The following are examples of cases where material has been initially withheld under PBR rule 6(2) only for it to become apparent that this is not justified when it is passed to the representative:[38]

- where the information was an allegation that had already been the subject of criminal trial (and acquittal);
- where the information in a 'confidential' police report had already been largely disclosed to the prisoner in the lifer manager's report that summarised the police records;
- allegations where there was no evidence of danger to the source but where the source had been given an assurance the allegations would not be disclosed. It was eventually decided that it was appropriate to provide a gist of the material to the prisoner.

10.41 As can be seen from these examples, there will be many instances where a representative can receive material under the restrictions contained in PBR rule 6(3) and can then effectively challenge the decision not to disclose the material to the client. Representations should be made to the chair of the panel dealing with the case and an oral directions hearing requested if necessary. The chair has express power to make directions relating to the disclosure or non-disclosure of this material under rule 8(2). In any case where directions are made in relation to disclosure (eg to disclose the material to the prisoner or to withhold it), it is possible for either the prisoner or the Secretary of State to appeal the decision to the chair of the Parole Board within seven days of the notification.[39] This decision is then final and the only further remedy is by way of judicial review.

10.42 The real ethical difficulties for a representative will arise if the final decision prevents disclosure of the material, or a gist of the allegations, to the prisoner. In such cases the representative will have to make a decision as to whether it is possible properly to represent the prisoner's interests at a 'closed' hearing where the prisoner is not present and, if so, whether the prisoner is prepared to authorise the representative to embark on this course of action. It is necessary to make a decision on a case-by-case basis as to whether it is possible for the prisoner's interests to be safeguarded in these circumstances and whether the procedure, taken as a whole, will comply with the requirements of article 5(4) of the ECHR. Case-law from the ECtHR has tended to approach this issue on a case-by-case basis, with the vast majority of cases concerning criminal trials. The question of

38 There is no reported case-law on this issue; these are examples taken from practical experience.

39 PBR r8(3).

whether such a procedure can guarantee fairness will ordinarily depend on whether the prisoner's case can be adequately presented without instructions being taken on the material and without the prisoner giving evidence.[40] However, in light of developments in relation to special advocates, it is arguable that the limits of this procedure should now be more tightly drawn.[41]

Special advocates

10.43 There may be very rare circumstances where the Board decides that it is impossible safely to disclose to the representative material that has been withheld under PBR rule 6(2). In the case where this first arose, it was decided that the source of the material in question faced a genuine threat to life and limb where there was a risk of inadvertent disclosure of the material to the prisoner if it was disclosed to the representative: *R (on the application of Roberts) v Parole Board*.[42]

10.44 The case of *Roberts* concerned a prisoner serving mandatory life sentences for the murder of three police officers. The Parole Board decided that it was not safe to disclose the material either to the prisoner or his representative and decided that in order to ameliorate the unfairness to the prisoner, the best course of action was to appoint a 'special advocate' to represent his interests at a closed hearing at which neither he nor his legal representatives would be present. The special advocate procedure was imported from the Special Immigration Appeals Commission (SIAC) where there is statutory provision for material to be withheld in this way where national security issues are at stake and for the material to be tested in closed hearings by special advocates who are allowed no contact with the individual or his/her legal team once they have received the material in question.

10.45 It was argued by the prisoner that this decision was ultra vires, as the PBR did not make any provision for a special advocate procedure and that any procedure that allowed for a secret hearing to take place to determine liberty was in breach of article 5(4) of the ECHR. The House of Lords rejected this argument by a 3:2 majority. Underpinning the majority decision was the view that the special advocate procedure is not an infringement of a right but a potential enhancement of rights in a situation where there might otherwise be no other

40 The contrasting decisions in *Doorson v Netherlands* (1996) 22 EHRR 330 and *Kalashnikov v Russia* (2003) 36 EHRR 34 illustrate the fact-specific approach taken by the ECtHR.

41 See paras 10.48–10.49.

42 [2005] UKHL 45.

way of testing the material in question. Lord Steyn and Lord Bingham however were quite trenchant in their views that the procedure was unlawful. Lord Steyn concluded with the opinion that:

> Taken as a whole the procedure completely lacks the essential characteristics of a fair hearing. It is important not to pussyfoot about such a fundamental matter: the special advocate procedure undermines the very essence of elementary justice. It involves a phantom hearing only.[43]

Although he sided with the majority, Lord Woolf's speech appeared to suggest that the role of the special advocate has to be limited to procedural testing of the evidence as a final determination based on a secret hearing would breach article 5(4):

> There are two extreme positions as far as the prisoner is concerned. On the one hand there is full disclosure and on the other hand there is no knowledge of the case against him being made available to the prisoner so that even with a SAA he cannot defend himself. In between there is a grey area and within that grey area is the border which is the parameter between what is acceptable and what is not acceptable ... The Board's existing statutory framework, including the Rules, do not entitle the Board to conduct its hearing in a manner that results in a significant injustice to a prisoner and in view of Article 5(4) I do not anticipate that primary legislation can now be introduced that expressly authorises such a result.[44]

10.46 At the conclusion of the parole proceedings the Board reached a decisive adverse finding based upon the withheld material and the prisoner challenged the compatibility of this outcome with article 5(4). The decision was upheld by the High Court in *R (on the application of Roberts) v Parole Board*[45] with Wynn Williams J considered himself to be bound by the Court of Appeal's decision in *Secretary of State for the Home Department v AF*[46] that there is no core irreducible minimum requirement of disclosure and that 'fairness' is a flexible concept. As he considered there was no such core irreducible minimum he took the view that all that was possible was a balancing exercise 'in which complete fairness to all those interested in the decision in question simply cannot be achieved'.[47]

43 Para 88.
44 Para 77.
45 [2008] EWHC 2714 (Admin).
46 [2008] EWCA Civ 1148.
47 Para 100.

10.47 However, it is extremely doubtful whether this decision can still be considered good law following the Lords' decision to overrule the Court of Appeal in *AF*.[48] The previous Lords' ruling on disclosure in the control orders context had been as unclear as their *Roberts'* decision.[49] However, after the Grand Chamber decision *A v United Kingdom*[50] the Lords unanimously accepted the ECtHR finding that non-disclosure of material that is relevant to continued detention and so cannot be effectively challenged is no longer tenable even in the interests of national security. The natural consequence of this decision is that it is highly unlikely that the special advocate procedure could still be adopted lawfully by the Board to reach a final determination on a prisoner's suitability for release.

10.48 These developments also raise serious concerns about the whole issue of non-disclosure, even where it is to a legal representative as is envisaged in the normal course of PBR rule 6(2). There may well be situations where a prisoner's own legal representative is unable to secure disclosure of the material to the prisoner and feels that it is not possible to contest the allegations properly without instructions. In *AF*, Lord Phillips gave the lead judgment and he referred with approval to Lord Bingham's observations in *MB* about the *Roberts'* situation:

> I do not understand any of my noble and learned friends [in *Roberts*] to have concluded that the requirements of procedural fairness under domestic law or under the Convention would be met if a person entitled to a fair hearing, in a situation where an adverse decision could have severe consequences, were denied such knowledge, in whatever form, of what was said against him as was necessary to enable him, with or without a special advocate, effectively to challenge or rebut the case against him.[51]

10.49 These observations make the point that a closed hearing where the representative is present but not the prisoner may not be any fairer or compliant with article 5(4) than the special advocate procedure. The question to be answered is whether the prisoner is denied the opportunity to challenge or rebut the case against him irrespective of whether or not a special advocate is involved. It is likely that the correct response is for the representative when faced with any rule 6(2) material is to attempt to represent the prisoner's interests as far as possible and then seek to challenge the outcome if it is unfavourable.

48 [2009] UKHL 28.

49 *Secretary of State for the Home Department v MB* [2007] UKHL 46.

50 (2009) 49 EHRR 29.

51 Ibid para 34.

Victims' opinions

10.50 There are two different situations in which victims may come to be involved in the parole process. If the victims or their families have information that is directly relevant to the risk-assessment process, for example if the prisoner has been seeking to make contact or issuing threats, then this evidence should be included in the dossier and any questions of witness protection are dealt with under the PBR rule 6 procedures. However, there is also a process to obtain the input of victims in relation to the impact of the crime upon them and a lifer's licence conditions and this is dealt with somewhat differently as it is not relevant to the actual release decision.

10.51 The Domestic Violence, Crime and Victims Act 2004 requires the Probation Service to enquire of victims whether they wish to make representations to the Parole Board or other bodies responsible for the release of prisoners as to particular licence conditions that may be imposed (see also paras 2.14–2.16). Under the code of practice issued pursuant to this legislation the Parole Board is required to take victims' representations into account in deciding which licence conditions to impose. The Parole Board has begun to adapt its procedures to try and allow for a more formal role in the proceedings for victims and they explain to victims how to submit a victim's impact statement. The guidance states, *inter alia*:[52]

> 3. The Board currently allows victims to make a written statement for consideration by the panel. This may be the statement put forward at trial, or a current statement. This statement is known as a Victim Personal Statement. Under the new arrangements the victim can still choose to have the written statement placed before the panel for the panel members to read for themselves. The victim may request to be present and have the statement read on his or her behalf or; request to be present and read it in person or; request to read the statement via Live-Link or record it on audio/video tape or DVD and played to the panel (only if facilities are available). Normally, a request to attend in person will be granted.
>
> 4. The statement should be concise and normally not take more than about 10 minutes. The audio/video tape or DVD must be limited to a reading by the victim of the written statement. The written statement must accompany the audio/video tape or DVD. The panel chair will have the power to limit the number of victim statements. The Ministry of Justice will be responsible for providing facilities for the

52 www.paroleboard.gov.uk/victims_and_families/practice_guide_on_victim_participation/.

playing of audio/video/DVD recordings and for the provision of Live Link.

6. Those preparing a victim personal statement should bear in mind that the Parole Board's primary role is to protect the public by risk assessing prisoners to decide whether or not they can be safely released into the community. Victim personal statements should therefore contain information that helps the Board assess the current risk the offender presents.

7. This statement and any recording thereof must be sent by the Ministry of Justice to the Board at least 28 days before the date fixed for the panel hearing. The statement will be considered by the panel chair as soon as is practicable thereafter. He/she may then give such directions in relation to the statement as he/she thinks fit. A direction may, for example, provide for the removal of any irrelevant material from the statement: however, if it appears to the panel chair that the statement contains new information potentially relevant to the prisoners risk, the panel chair may request the Secretary of State to submit evidence relating to the matter and/or may direct that that information will only remain within the statement if the victim attends the panel hearing as a witness in order to give evidence (and potentially to be cross-examined) in relation to it.

10.52 The guidance makes it clear that where the information does go beyond a description of the impact of the offence into evidence about risk, that formal evidence will be required and this may also require the victim to give evidence in the proceedings rather than simply to deliver a statement. In those cases where the Board allow victims to present their impact statements in person, the procedures for their attendance are discussed in more detail in chapter 11.

10.53 The reason for the distinction between an impact statement and formal evidence on risk is that the views of the victims cannot have a direct impact on the decision as to whether the prisoner should be released. If the evidence is actually related to risk, it should be dealt with in the same manner as other evidence and not under this specific statutory scheme. In the criminal sphere, it has been confirmed that victims' views should not alter the sentences that are imposed[53] and it was made clear that in the area of tariff setting, the invitation to victims to make representations is limited to the impact of the offence on the individual and does not extend to the appropriate length of the tariff itself.[54] This approach is consistent with the views

53 See, eg, *R v Nunn* [1996] Cr App Rep (S) 136.

54 *R (on the application of Bulger) v Secretary of State for the Home Department and Lord Chief Justice* [2001] EWHC 119 (Admin).

of the ECtHR on release where the complaint made by a relative of a victim that she had been refused the opportunity to have a formal role in the release process was considered to be inadmissible.[55]

MAPPA documents

10.54 The Prison Service Public Protection Manual requires individual prisons to set up interdepartmental risk management teams to provide regular monitoring of prisoners who pose the greatest risk to the public and the vast majority of lifers and indeterminate prisoners will be MAPPA managed.[56] The existence of MAPPA (see further paras 2.17–2.22) does pose some issues of fairness for serving prisoners. The guidance clearly states that one of the purposes of MAPP meetings will be to inform decisions relating to release on temporary licence, the licence conditions that prisoners will be subject to on release, and the decision of the Parole Board.[57] While the MAPP meeting cannot decide any of these matters, it is of concern that its recommendations are made in a process that affords very little in the way of procedural fairness for prisoners.

10.55 Public Protection Panel (PPP) meetings are not open to the prisoner or legal representatives:[58]

> As a general principle, it is important to be clear that the human rights of offenders should never take priority over public protection. In particular, it is considered that the presence of an offender at a MAPP meeting could significantly hinder the core business of sharing and analysing information objectively and making decisions accordingly. Offenders (and their representatives) should therefore be excluded from MAPP meetings. The offender should, however, be allowed the opportunity to present written information to the MAPP meeting through their offender/case manager or for this person to provide information on their behalf.

10.56 This guidance is not specific in relation to the level of disclosure that may be given to prisoners to assist them in making representations. In the absence of some form of disclosure, the right to make such representations may be meaningless as the offender may be unaware of the matters to be considered, and whether the information before

55 *McCourt v United Kingdom* (1993) 15 EHRR CD 110.

56 For an explanation of the different MAPPA levels see chapter 2.

57 MAPPA Guidance, section 14.

58 MAPPA Guidance, para 4.8.

the meeting contains any significant factual errors. It is arguable that fairness does require a basic level of disclosure to an offender prior to a meeting to enable proper representations to be made to address the issues to be considered. The view that, as a minimum, a gist should normally be provided was expressed in *R (on the application of Gunn) v Secretary State for Justice and the Nottinghamshire Multi Agency Public Protection Arrangements Board*.[59] In that case a licensee had actually received quite extensive disclosure but Blake J noted that as a general point of principle:

> Assessment of risk is always an exercise in judgement based on all the available material, some of which may be fragile, hearsay, confidential and disputable. The decision-maker will have to act fairly. Having regard to the nature and purpose of the exercise, it is the duty of those entrusted with making assessments in the absence of a trial or full disclosure to the person concerned to assess such material with care before relying on it. It is necessary for the decision-maker to consider any counter-indicators against the assessment in question, to consider any reason why any particular source of information may be unreliable in some respects, to have regard to what the claimant says in response to the gist of the material and to set the information against what is known, admitted or provable.[60]

10.57 After a MAPPP meeting the guidance states that requests by offenders for disclosure of the minutes must be referred to the meeting chair.[61] An executive summary of the minutes can be prepared and this should be supplied to the Parole Board or to an offender if requested.[62] In practice the executive summary can be an unhelpful and anodyne document and it may be that prisoners who are challenging the recommendations of MAPPP meetings need to make further requests for disclosure.

Independent reports

10.58 Once the dossier has been disclosed, consideration can be given to commissioning independent reports. Independent reports are most likely to be necessary where the client disagrees with an expert assessment made by a psychologist or psychiatrist. Occasionally, reports from independent social workers or probation officers might

59 [2009] EWHC 1812 (Admin).

60 Ibid at para 19.

61 MAPPA Guidance, para 11.18.

62 MAPPA Guidance, paras 6.11 and 14.1.

be helpful if there are concerns about probation reports. If a medical issue is relevant to the assessment of risk, independent medical reports may also be helpful.

10.59 When considering whether an independent report is necessary, it is important to consider the reasons why the prisoner is unhappy with the report under challenge and precisely what an independent expert might be able to address. For example, if a prisoner is unhappy with a sex offender treatment programme (SOTP) report, then it will be necessary to identify whether the prisoner wants to challenge the suggestion that the SOTP is an appropriate treatment method in his particular case or whether the challenge is to the accuracy of the risk assessment itself on the conclusion of the SOTP. The client should always be advised that a favourable expert report is not a guarantee that the Board will be required to prefer that evidence over the Prison Service's experts. Risk assessment is not a precise science and will always carry a degree of subjective interpretation.[63]

10.60 This does mean that it is very important to select an expert with appropriate expertise in the relevant area of risk assessment. It is usually helpful for the expert to have had some experience of prisons, as this will ensure familiarity with the methods and tools used in the contested assessments. Ideally, the expert should also have some experience of treating ex-offenders in the community as this will provide some basis for assessing the extent to which risk levels are manageable under supervision on licence. Prisoners will often suggest particular experts that they perceive as writing reports favourable to prisoners. There can be a risk when instructing experts who may be perceived by the Board as writing stock reports on behalf of prisoners, as there can be tendency to give less weight to their assessments. Clients should always be advised of these risks so that an informed choice can be made as to the appropriate expert. It can often be extremely helpful to contact regional secure units to try to identify expert psychologists and psychiatrists who have experience in treating and managing high risk offenders. It is always essential to discuss the case with the expert before sending written instructions.

10.61 Expert reports can be paid for under the CDS funding scheme as a disbursement where it is considered necessary to progress the case properly. Justification will need to be recorded on the file and it will be necessary to obtain an extension to cover the cost. The guidance operated by the CDS extensions team as at October 2009 was that as a general rule expert fees should be in the region of £85 per hour; if

63 See chapter 4.

the estimate is higher than that, an explanation will need to be given as to why the higher hourly rate is justified.

10.62 Most experts who prepare these reports will contact the prison to make their own arrangements for entry to the prison, although they may occasionally require the legal representative to make the arrangements with the prison to allow them to see the prisoner. The normal practice is for facilities for psychologists and psychiatrists to be provided in the health care centre and the prison medical records will usually be made available for the expert to inspect.

10.63 If the client is unhappy with the views of the independent expert, there is no requirement for this to be disclosed to the Parole Board or PPCS and it can simply not be used in the review process. PPCS had initiated discussions as to whether there should be an obligation in the PBR to disclose all independent expert reports or whether it is possible to implement arrangements for joint experts as exists under the Civil Procedure Rules (CPR) 1998, but this was not accepted. There are occasions where all the parties agree that a particular expert's report should be commissioned and the prisoner and PPCS agree to one expert being instructed. Prisoners should be advised only to agree to this where it is possible to reach a genuine agreement on the appropriate expert.

The prisoner's written representations

Timing

10.64 Following disclosure of the parole dossier, the prisoner has four weeks in which to submit written representations.[64] The four-week deadline is set to enable the case to be considered at the ICM stage although, as noted above, if the dossier is complete and there are no further reports or information required, this can then proceed directly to the full determination of the case on the papers.[65]

10.65 It may not always be possible to submit representations within the four-week period allowed, either because further evidence is needed or simply because it has not proven possible to take instructions. This will arise in virtually every case where an independent psychological or psychiatric report is being obtained, as there are relatively few suitably qualified experts available and they tend to be heavily

64 PBR r7(1).

65 Under PBR r11.

oversubscribed. It may also be the case that further prison reports are necessary, for example if it is clear that a psychological assessment is needed but the prison has not obtained one.

10.66 Where further information is needed on behalf of the prisoner to enable properly informed representations to be prepared, it is appropriate to write to the Parole Board to ask for the case not to be considered at the ICM stage until it has been possible to prepare these representations, with an explanation of the reasons for the delay and a likely timescale. If the administrative section of the Board reject the application and proposes to put the case to ICM in any event, these representations will then need to be addressed directly to the member conducting the ICM. The directions sought would include a timescale for the case to be considered by a single member pursuant to PBR rule 11. For example, if it is considered that further reports are needed from prison or probation staff, then the ICM should be asked to make a direction for the preparation of the report within a set period of time and for the case to be returned for further ICM once it has been disclosed and sufficient time given for representations to be filed.

Format

10.67 There is no standard format for the submission of representations, and representatives are at liberty to adopt the style they find most comfortable. The most common formats are a letter, a document of numbered paragraphs or a statement from the client. Generally, the use of a statement from the client to cover both factual and legal matters can appear slightly artificial and it can lead to the client appearing overbearing or pompous. In cases where a personal statement from the client is going to advance the case, separating this from the more general submissions can work to the client's favour as it allows some room for the expression of their personality and personal views without this being subsumed into observations that may come across as pedantic or even bombastic. A statement is most likely to be needed if there are disputed facts and it is necessary to have the prisoner's version. As in all litigation, the representative will need to be sure that the prisoner can come up to proof should the matter proceed to an oral hearing.

Oral hearings and article 5(4)

10.68 The preparation of these representations is possibly the most critical part of the review process now that the Board has the power to determine the case without an oral hearing.[66] As an oral hearing is necessary in any case where release or a move to open conditions is being sought, these representations will have to make the case for such a direction or recommendation properly in order to establish why a hearing is needed. However, the Board may also choose to convene an oral hearing even when it is clear that neither of these is an option. Guidance is contained in the Bench Book[67] issued by the Board to its members about the circumstances when an oral hearing might be appropriate:

> Aside from there being a likelihood of release or open conditions, the ICM member may have identified that factors are present that require examination before a full oral panel. An example may be where a progressive move is not a realistic outcome, but where live evidence is needed to determine the risk factors. It is envisaged that this will be a rare step to take and would normally only be necessary where experts disagreed about a risk factor; for example, whether or not there was a sexual element to an offence that needed exploring. For whatever reason the case is progressing towards an oral hearing, the ICM member will give brief reasons and make directions for case management.[68]

10.69 The question of whether an oral hearing on the expiry of the minimum term and at subsequent reviews was necessary has not been authoratively decided since the PBR were amended in April 2009 (see also paras 1.39–1.49). Prior to this amendment, the assumption had always been that an oral hearing was a necessary component of article 5(4) and so the right to elect for such a hearing was enshrined in the PBR. This appeared to be supported by the ECtHR, and in the leading judgment on this issue the following findings had been made:

> 59. The Court recalls in this context that, in matters of such crucial importance as the deprivation of liberty and where questions arise which involve, for example, as assessment of the applicant's character or mental state, it has held that it may be essential to the fairness of the proceedings that the applicant be present at an oral hearing.
>
> 60. The Court is of the view that, in a situation such as that of the applicant, where a substantial term of imprisonment may be at stake and where characteristics pertaining to his personality and level of maturity are of importance in deciding on his dangerousness, Article

66 PBR rr11–12.

67 *The Oral hearing guide for chairs* is an Internal Parole Board document which can be obtained by making a Freedom of Information Act request for disclosure to the Board.

68 *The Oral hearing guide for chairs* para 6. The policy can also be found at: www.paroleboard.gov.uk/policy_and_guidance/criteria_for_refusing_an_oral_hearing

5(4) requires an oral hearing in the context of an adversarial procedure involving legal representation and the possibility of calling and questioning witnesses.[69]

10.70 However, a school of judicial thought has gradually moved towards the view that oral hearings are not an absolute requirement of article 5(4) and in a case involving a prisoner serving an extended sentence, Latham LJ (who incidentally was appointed as Chairman of the Parole Board in 2009) held that even where article 5(4) was engaged, an oral hearing might not be necessary:

> The question remains as to whether or not at the end of the day the answer to the question whether or not the claimant poses a relevant risk requires as a matter of fairness his presence at an oral hearing in order to determine the issues raised by his application. I confess that I have not found it an easy question to answer. It seems to me that the Parole Board should be pre-disposed to holding an oral hearing in such cases. That would certainly be the case where there is any dispute of fact, or any need to examine the applicant's motives or state of mind. But in the present case, I do not read the Parole Board decision as being one which could have been affected in any way by anything further that the claimant could have said beyond that which he had set out in his written representation.[70]

10.71 While this view still puts a very strong emphasis on the need for an oral hearing – almost to the extent that there is a presumption in favour of such a hearing – the necessity for a hearing appears to be limited to cases where there is a possibility that that the Board may make a direction or recommendation within the ambit of the referral made by the Secretary of State. Therefore, if a prisoner is, for example, in a high security prison and accepts that release or open conditions are not on the agenda and the case does not raise another significant issue (as set out in para 10.69 above), then there is arguably nothing in issue that requires resolution at an oral hearing (although the standard referral to the Board does invite it to comment on the 'continuing areas of risk that need to be addressed': see para 10.4). The question to be resolved is whether the ECtHR require an oral hearing in all cases or whether the discretionary, case-by-case approach suggested by Latham LJ is correct.

69 *Hussain v UK* [1996] 22 EHRR 1.

70 *R (on the application of O'Connell) v Parole Board and Secretary of State for the Home Department* [2007] EWHC 2591 (Admin) para 24. It should be noted that the finding that article 5(4) is engaged for this was subsequently overruled by the Court of Appeal following the House of Lords' judgment in *R (on the application of Black) v Secretary of State for Justice* [2009] UKHL 1.

Content of written representations

10.72 Although it is not possible to be prescriptive about the contents of representations as each case will require very careful individual consideration, as a general guide written representations should aim to cover the following matters:

- *Inform the Board at the outset of the direction/recommendation that the prisoner is seeking.* This will help focus attention on relevant matters. For example, if the prisoner is only seeking a move to open conditions and not release, it will mean that the review is unlikely to be delayed or hampered if the dossier does not contain full details of a proposed release plan.

  If the prisoner is seeking an oral hearing in a case where a move to open conditions or release is not being sought, an explanation should be included as to why the oral hearing is required and what purpose it will serve with reference to the factors contained in paragraph 6 of the Bench Book (above).
- *Address any factual errors or concerns that the prisoner has about the contents of the historical details,* such as previous convictions or the details of progress in custody. If the errors are minor and are unlikely to be relevant to the outcome of the review, it may be worth noting them very briefly as a matter of record. If the errors or disputed records are material to the outcome of the review, more detailed representations may be required. This is also the opportunity to submit any material that will support the prisoner's account of historical events.
- *Comment on the current reports on behaviour, paying particular attention to the risk factors identified in the case and the extent to which these have been addressed or, alternatively, should not be treated as indicators of future risk.* This part will normally form the main substance of the representations and will need to be very carefully drafted with reference to the aims being sought by the prisoner and the recommendations of the reports. In cases where the prisoner is happy with the reports and there is nothing contentious in them, it is usually advisable to keep these comments fairly short. However, in cases where the reports do not agree with each other, or where the prisoner is unhappy with all of the reports, these may need to be extensive.

  It is necessary to consider the nature of the contact the report writer has had with the prisoner and the basis of the report writer's expertise when drafting this part of the representations. A prison probation officer who has had extensive contact with a prisoner might, for example, be better placed to make an accurate risk assessment than a home probation officer who has had just one visit and is working mainly from historical records. An assessment of risk factors made by a psychologist is very likely to carry more weight than a risk assessment prepared by the medical officer or the prisoner's personal officer. Conversely, an assessment of custodial behaviour made by a wing manager who has day-to-day contact with the prisoner will probably be more accurate than an assessment made the psychologist.

- It is essential to *direct the Board to the real risk factors in any given case.* A prisoner may receive negative reports based on difficult prison behaviour, but this might not be relevant to the assessment of risk. Similarly, concerns about trustworthiness and compliance with licence conditions might not be sufficiently serious to impede release where there is no evidence that the prisoner poses any ongoing danger to the public.
- *If independent reports have been prepared at this stage, these should be enclosed and an explanation made as to why they are being relied upon.* In cases where these reports disagree with expert reports contained in the dossier, an explanation should be given as to why the Board should prefer the independent expert's assessment. This may be based on the greater experience or expertise of the author of the independent report or simply because the approach of the independent report is more realistic.
- *Any additional material that the prisoner wishes the Board to consider,* such as work references, offers of employment, letters from family members or certificates of attendance on courses. These should be enclosed, and the relevance of this material in terms of risk and rehabilitation issues should be drawn to the attention of the Board.
- *Final submissions on legal considerations,* such as how the test for release has been applied by report writers and the weight that the Board should give to evidence.

Distribution

10.73 All written representations, both at this stage and in the future, should be sent to the Parole Board and copied to the relevant casework team at PPCS.[71] As the Secretary of State is also a party to the review, it is

71 See the details of the casework teams at LRRS in appendix G.

important to make sure that PPCS is copied into all correspondence with the Board at all times.

Consideration on the papers

Options and decisions

10.74 PBR rule 11 requires the Parole Board to consider the case by a single member panel without a hearing. The options available to the panel are either to refer the case to an oral hearing[72] or to make a provisional decision that the prisoner is unsuitable for release.[73] If the decision is that the case should proceed to an oral hearing, directions will be issued by the single member at this stage. The next stage of the procedure where an oral hearing is to take place is dealt with in chapter 11. In either event, the decision must be notified to the parties within one week of the date of the decision.[74]

10.75 The PBR state that in any case where the single member panel has made a provisional decision that the prisoner is unsuitable for release, the prisoner can request an oral hearing.[75] As a matter of strict statutory construction, the practice of referring the case to an oral hearing to consider suitability for open conditions or other matters is not provided for in the PBR, but as it is within the discretion of the Board to do so, this practice overrides the crude reading of this provision. Where a negative decision has been reached on the papers and communicated to the prisoner, the prisoner has four weeks in which to apply for an oral hearing[76] and if no notification is sent, then the decision becomes final.[77]

10.76 Where an application is to be made for an oral hearing, the factors set out in paragraphs 10.69–10.71 above should be borne in mind. The question of whether an oral hearing is likely to produce any benefit will be very fact specific. To balance against the possible benefits of the oral hearing is the delay that is caused to the case. A single member's decision may be notified to the prison as long as three

72 PBR r11(2)(a).
73 PBR r11(2)(b).
74 PBR r11(3).
75 PBR r12(1).
76 PBR r12(2).
77 PBR r12(3).

months before PBR envisage that the oral hearing will take place.[78] If the paper decision is accepted, the review will conclude at this point. The prisoner will then normally have the time set for the next review subject to the statutory two-year maximum period between reviews. In contrast, if the oral hearing goes ahead and a more favourable decision is not made, the prisoner's review cycle will be put back by the additional period that has been spent waiting for that hearing. There is also the likelihood that the extra time waiting for the hearing will be 'dead time' during which the prisoner may not be doing anything to progress through the sentence.

10.77 The final factor to consider is the merits test that must be applied under the CDS public funding scheme. Advocacy assistance, the public funding available for oral parole hearings, is subject to both means and merit testing. It is essential to be able to demonstrate that there is a real benefit to the client in proceeding to an oral hearing in order to authorise this funding. However, in any case where the Board agrees to an oral hearing it is likely that the benefit test will be met as the Board itself will have taken the view that a significant issue requires determination.

Transfers of prisoners during the review

10.78 The transfer of a prisoner once a review has commenced can cause disruption to the review process and transfers will not normally be authorised. There may, however, be exceptional security, compassionate or disciplinary reasons for such a move to take place, including where it is necessary to allow offending behaviour courses to be completed.[79] If a transfer does take place during the review, the sending prison will normally retain responsibility for completing reports as staff there will have a better knowledge of the prisoner, although in some cases the receiving prison may accept responsibility. If agreement cannot be reached, then the sending prison has to take responsibility.[80] Transfers after the parole hearing has been fixed will be extremely rare as this will result in considerable delay.

78 In fact, the time taken to list an oral hearing can vary enormously and at times, when the Board has a significant backlog of cases, the wait for a hearing has been as long as 12 months.

79 PSO 6010 para 2.5.1.

80 PSO 6010 para 2.5.2.

CHAPTER 11

Oral hearing procedure

continued

Pre-hearing preparation

ICM directions

11.1 When a case is referred for an oral hearing, directions will be made at this time to aid the progression of the case, pursuant to the general power to make directions in PBR rule 8. Directions should be served on all parties – PPCS, the prison and the prisoner – although there has sometimes been a tendency for the Board to omit to send directions to prisoners and their representatives. The ICM process has a pro forma for directions and the first matter to be addressed will be the contents of the dossier. If there are any reports missing or additional reports required, a direction will be made of them to be prepared within a particular timeframe and added to the dossier.[1] The panel may require historical reports, such as old psychological assessments, or further current information such as security reports, to be added.

11.2 At this stage, it is important to check the pro forma directions to ascertain whether or not the panel has approved the listing of the case before these directions are complied with. The procedure had envisaged that cases would not be listed until all reports were ready and so many panels would not certify cases as being ready for listing until the reports had been added. However, if the reports are relatively minor or where there are likely to be lengthy delays before the hearing date in any event, the case should be put forward for listing with the reports to be added within a fixed period of time. If the ICM directions have not approved the case for listing until the additional material is provided, then an application should be made for the case to be approved for listing in any event to avoid there being a further delay built into the review period.

11.3 The ICM directions should also consider what witnesses will be required and directions made for their attendance. The reason why this step is taken at this stage is to provide the maximum possible notice period to the relevant witness and to give the witness the opportunity to provide dates to avoid. This is intended to prevent hearings being ineffective through witnesses being unavailable.

Directions applications

11.4 The ICM directions are made by the Board on their own motion, but it is possible for either party to make a request for formal directions pursuant to PBR rule 8. Where the case has not yet been assigned

1 The full list of required reports is contained in chapter 10.

to a particular panel, a duty member of the Board can deal with the application. It may be necessary to seek directions relating to the disclosure of further relevant material in the possession of the Prison Service, such as further evidence from prison or probation staff or even security reports, particularly where there are disputed allegations. The application should be served upon PPCS and it is usually sensible to copy this also to the case manager at the prison itself.

11.5 When applying for directions, particularly when seeking a direction that will require the disclosure of additional material or the preparation of a fresh report, it is essential to explain the evidential purpose behind the request and the reasons why it will help facilitate the assessment of risk and suitability for release. A common example is where reports refer to undisclosed security material alleging misbehaviour, or where reference is made to an historical report that has not been previously disclosed to the prisoner.

11.6 In the event that there is substantial disagreement between the parties, or where complex legal or factual matters arise in the application, the chair may decide to convene an oral directions hearing. Oral directions hearings will usually be held where it is most convenient for the chair – either in the courthouse where the chair is sitting (if it is a judicial member) or at the Parole Board itself. At least 14 days' notification of the directions hearing date should be given,[2] but it will often be in the interests of all parties for the hearing to be convened more quickly. The representative of the prisoner and the Secretary of State (usually someone from PPCS) will be present, but the prisoner will not unless unrepresented. There is no formal procedure to be followed for the hearing and the chair will usually ask the party making the application to make submissions and then the other party to respond. Where the application does raise legal arguments, it is always sensible to prepare a written summary of the argument and to have copies of any cases or other materials relied upon available for all the parties. Wherever possible, these should be served well ahead of the hearing to avoid delays on the day itself.

11.7 Written decisions containing any directions made by the chair – whether after considering written applications or after an oral hearing – should be served on the parties 'as soon as practicable'.[3] Surprisingly, this has proven to be a major failing by the Parole Board over the years, with case managers often failing to send prisoners' representatives copies of the written decisions, although they do

2 PBR r8(5).
3 PBR r8(9).

usually send them to PPCS. This is possibly symptomatic of the very slow progress towards the recognition of the Parole Board as a court, and the consequent requirement for its administration to be of the quality one would expect from other courts, rather than an off-shoot of the functions of the Prison Service. This is a further reason why it is sensible to identify the named case manager in each case so that there is a point of contact to chase decisions and notifications.

The hearing date

11.8 The actual hearing date will normally be fixed no later than six weeks before it takes place, with the listings team arranging hearings at the start of each month (ie a meeting at the start of January will seek to list hearings for March). This timing coincides with the date on which a panel is appointed to the case and the dossier is sent to the chair of the panel. If the hearing is to be at a prison where there are a large number of cases to be heard, the panel may be at the prison for two to three days, and the hearing will be scheduled for any of those days. If a 'floating' date of this type is given and there is a particular reason why one of the days is more suitable than another (eg for witnesses to attend or the availability of an advocate), the case manager should be informed immediately so that efforts can be made to try to accommodate that date. The precise listing with the start time of the case is usually sent out around a week before the hearing itself.

Witness requests

11.9 The PBR state that requests for the attendance of witnesses should be made within six weeks of the hearing date and require that all witness requests should include the name, address and occupation of the witness and the substance of the evidence that the witness will give at the hearing.[4] In the vast majority of cases, the witness will be one of the report writers in the dossier or an independent expert who has written a report for the hearing. If the independent expert's report has not previously been served on the Board and PPCS, then it should be sent at this stage to coincide with the witness requests. As the witnesses will nearly always have written some form of report, it is not necessary to repeat the contents of their evidence. Instead, it is advisable to set out what the purpose of the oral evidence will be and the reasons why oral evidence is needed to enable the panel

4 PBR r15(1).

to reach a decision on the case. There will be cases where there are relevant witnesses who have not prepared any form of report, such as family members with whom the prisoner intends to live on release. In those cases, slightly more detail about the nature of the evidence to be given will be needed. It should be remembered that witness requests can be made by both the prisoner and PPCS.

11.10 The Parole Board's *Oral Hearings Guide for Chairs* (the Guide) advises that witness requests will normally be granted so as to ensure the prisoner does not have the perception that his/her access to justice is being impeded.[5] This is not, however, an open invitation for every witness to be approved and panels are reminded that consideration has to be given to the substance of the evidence and the overall length of the hearing. It is not considered good practice to have too many witnesses because of the impact this will have on the length of the hearing. As a very rough rule of thumb, the general advice is:

- independent experts and family members should normally be permitted to attend;
- witnesses who have prepared evidence that is unfavourable to the prisoner should always be allowed to attend;
- witnesses who can make a further contribution to risk assessment should always be allowed to attend;
- if the prisoner is in an open prison, the home probation officer should usually be required to attend;
- witnesses who have written favourable reports and whose evidence is not likely to be in dispute should only be allowed if they can materially add to the evidence in the dossier;
- the offender manager should be required to attend where release is being considered or it is a recall case but, otherwise, their attendance is not routinely required, except in IPP cases where the offender manager has primary responsibility for risk assessment under the offender management model (see chapter 8). If it becomes clear during a hearing that the risk is low enough for release to be considered, the Guide advises that the hearing is adjourned;[6]
- children should not normally be called to give evidence, not least because of the problems that arise for them to actually attend a hearing.[7] Where children are called, detailed guidance on the arrangements for them to give evidence is set out below.

5 Oral Hearings Guide, para 34.

6 Annex 11 para 10.

7 Ibid, annex 11 para 7.

11.11 Prison psychological assessments are very often prepared by trainee psychologists, supervised by a chartered psychologist. Usually, there is no difficulty in the trainee attending to give evidence. However, if the trainee wants the supervisor to be present, that is permitted and the panel chair is advised to issue an 'invitation' to that person to attend as this makes it clear that the discretion as to whether attendance is appropriate rests with the supervisor.[8]

11.12 Once the chair of the panel has considered the requests, notification should be given to the parties of the permitted witnesses. If the request is refused, reasons should be given for that decision.[9] When considering these requests, the chair is also permitted to make a decision as to whether to require any other witnesses not already dealt with at the ICM stage or in the parties' requests to attend. If the parties making the witness requests have not sought the attendance of a witness whom the panel chair considers should give evidence, it is open to the chair to make a direction for the witness to attend. If the panel chair does decide a further witness should be called, written notification must be sent to the parties containing the name, address and occupation of the witness and the substance of the evidence it is proposed to adduce.[10]

11.13 In one of the early drafts of the amendments to the PBR, a new rule 15(5) was inserted instructing the chair to give consideration to whether it is desirable and practical for the witness to give evidence other than by appearing in person. That proposed addition was intended to allow for witnesses to give evidence by video link, the aim being to save the costs and inconvenience caused by witnesses travelling to the prison, and also to allow for vulnerable witnesses to give their evidence without coming into contact with the prisoner. The Probation Service had also been lobbying for permission to give their evidence by video link. Although this amendment did not formally become part of the PBR, the Guide instructs panel chairs that 'the use of video link should be considered, especially for external probation officers and, in exceptional circumstances, it might be acceptable for evidence to be given over a conference telephone or another mechanism by which all parties can hear the witness'.[11]

8 Ibid, annex 11 para 12.
9 PBR r15(3).
10 PBR r15(2).
11 The Guide, annex 11 para 3.

Securing the attendance of witnesses

11.14 It is the responsibility of the person who has sought permission for a witness to attend to ensure that witness is present at the hearing. This means that when a request for a witness to attend is made on behalf of a prisoner and is granted, it will fall to the prisoner's legal representative to notify each witness of the hearing date and time and that their attendance is required. Technically, this remains the responsibility of the prisoner even if the witness is a hostile witness (such as a prison psychologist or probation officer) and the prisoner has requested their attendance to cross-examine them on the contents of the report. However, as a matter of practice, since the introduction of ICM the Board has become far more efficient at forwarding directions for witnesses to attend directly to the appointed case manager at the prison and the probation officer and PSO 6010 makes it clear that 'the expectation is that NOMS staff directed to give evidence at a Parole Board hearing will comply'.[12]

11.15 Historically, the home probation officer (offender manager) was often the most difficult witness to persuade to attend the hearing. This problem seems to have been largely cured by a probation directive emphasising the importance of attendance at parole hearings,[13] combined with the more effective procedures for giving notice of the requirement to attend. In those rare cases where there is still some doubt about their attendance, it is advisable to send a fax directly to the witness's work address providing notification of the hearing details and asking for confirmation that they will attend the hearing.

11.16 Where the chair of the panel has requested the attendance of a witness, the Board's advice to panels is that it is preferable for witnesses to attend voluntarily. The standard form of wording that is recommended in letters to witnesses is as follows:

> The Board directs that [name of witness] shall attend the hearing to give evidence. The witness should note that the proceedings will be as informal as possible, but that the Board will nevertheless sit as a court. Non-attendance is only permitted in compelling circumstances and the Board does have the power to enforce attendance by way of a witness summons. Full reasons must be given by anyone unable to attend.[14]

11.17 The Court of Appeal has issued guidance on the appropriate lines of responsibility for securing the attendance of reluctant witnesses

12 Paragraph 1.9.2.

13 PC 45B/2004.

14 The Guide, para 35.

whose evidence is hostile to a prisoner and this indicated that the Board should direct the Secretary of State (through PPCS) to notify the witness and to obtain a witness summons from the court if necessary.[15] The Board has no power to issue a witness summons itself.[16] This means that any party wishing to summons a witness to the hearing must make use of the power of the county court and High Court to issue a witness summons in aid of a tribunal pursuant to Civil Procedure Rule 34.4. In order to make such an application it is necessary to provide the court with evidence confirming that the Parole Board has directed the attendance of the witness at the hearing and evidence as to why a summons is considered to be necessary. In cases where the witness is one the Board itself has directed should attend or where the witness is required to give evidence to support the Secretary of State's case, even if their attendance has been requested by the prisoner, PPCS will be directed to apply for the summons. This situation is most likely to arise with non-professional witnesses, such as members of the public or other prisoners who have provided evidence that the Secretary of State proposes to rely upon against the prisoner. In cases where the witness is a professional, such as a psychologist or probation officer who has since left their job, there is no reason why the prisoner's representative should not apply for the witness summons if their attendance has been requested by the prisoner.

11.18 The use of witness summonses is extremely rare in the parole context.[17] The Parole Board's internal guidance suggests that panel chairs should have in mind the following considerations when deciding whether a reluctant witness should be required to attend:

- A witness should only be summonsed where their oral evidence is crucial to the outcome of the case.
- Where a witness is reluctant, a panel chair should always consider the alternative of written evidence.
- It is never appropriate to compel a minor to attend.
- The likely outcome should be considered. Although a witness can be compelled to attend, the witness cannot be compelled to give evidence. It may be pointless directing the Secretary of State to compel attendance if the witness will ultimately refuse to give evidence.

15 See *R (on the application of Brooks) v Parole Board* [2004] EWCA Civ 80.

16 One of the criticisms of the amendments to the PBR was that the Board was not given this power.

17 It was precisely because this is so unusual that none of the parties in the *Brooks* case (as above) were really sure about what to do.

11.19 Although these guidelines only apply to situations where the Board is being asked to direct the Secretary of State to obtain a witness summons, they are also useful points for prisoners' representatives to bear in mind when making a decision on whether to summons a reluctant witness.

Observers

11.20 Parties to the hearing may apply for observers to be present at the hearing.[18] The application is usually made at the same time as applications for the attendance of witnesses and it is required that the procedure in PBR rule 15 is followed. The chair of the panel should seek to obtain the consent of the prison governor before authorising the attendance of observers.

11.21 Applications for observers to attend usually fall into three categories:

(a) Prisoners may wish to apply for a close friend or family member, or even a personal officer, to attend to provide support. Prisoners making such an application should be reminded that the hearing is likely to go over the details of the index offence and general offending history. Some prisoners may actually find it inhibiting to talk about these matters in front of family members, especially if the offences are sexual or particularly violent.
(b) The prison or PPCS may ask for new staff, such as trainee lifer managers to attend, to give them a greater insight into the parole process and to learn how to present cases on behalf of the Secretary of State.
(c) The Parole Board might ask for new or trainee members to attend for the same reasons. Occasionally, a request may be made for academic researchers to attend.

11.22 When considering such requests, the chair should have regard to the numbers of persons likely to be at the hearing and the need for the prisoner to feel at ease. Although there is no provision in the PBR for prisoners to veto requests for observers made by the Board or LRRS, panel chairs are usually very mindful of the need for prisoners to feel comfortable at the hearing and will take very seriously any objection raised by a prisoner to the attendance of an observer. Issues relating to the Data Protection Act 1998 may well arise if an observer were to attend against the prisoner's wishes.

18 PBR r16.

Attendance of victims

11.23 The Parole Board is required to comply with the Code of Practice for Victims of Crime[19] and this includes the obligation to consider representations and any evidence that might be relevant to risk,[20] The process for obtaining written representations from victims is dealt with in chapter 10, and following consultation with stakeholders, in September 2009 the Board issued detailed guidance on the role of victims and the procedures to be followed where a victim wishes to attend hearing in person. The Board now accepts that victims can also be permitted to attend the hearing itself.[21]

11.24 The guidance defines a victim as: 'Someone who was harmed or who has suffered physical or emotional damage as a result of the offence or offences'. The procedures for attendance at a hearing are as follows:

- The victim may request to be present and have the statement read on his or her behalf; request to be present and read it in person; request to read the statement via Live-Link or record it on audio/video tape or DVD and have it played to the panel (only if facilities are available). Normally, a request to attend in person will be granted.
- The statement should be concise and normally not take more than about ten minutes. The audio/video tape or DVD must be limited to a reading by the victim of the written statement. The written statement must accompany the audio/video tape or DVD. The panel chair will have the power to limit the number of victim statements. The Ministry of Justice will be responsible for providing facilities for the playing of audio/video/DVD recordings and for the provision of Live-Link.
- A victim under 18 years of age will not normally be allowed to attend the hearing in person but may have the statement read on his or her behalf or request to read the statement via Live-Link or record it on audio/video tape or DVD and played to the panel (if facilities are available).
- The statement and any recording must be sent by the Ministry of Justice to the Board at least 28 days before the date fixed for the panel hearing. The statement will be considered by the panel

19 www.homeoffice.gov.uk/documents/victims-code-of-practice?view=Binary, para 2.1.

20 Ibid, para 12.

21 This is available at: www.paroleboard.gov.uk/victims_and_families/practice_guide_on_victim_participation/.

chair and directions may then be given, for example to remove any irrelevant material from the statement.

- If it appears to the panel chair that the statement contains new information potentially relevant to the prisoner's risk, the panel chair may request the Secretary of State to submit evidence relating to the matter and/or may direct that that information will only remain within the statement if the victim attends the panel hearing as a witness in order to give evidence (and potentially to be cross-examined) in relation to it.
- Either party may make written representations to the panel chair in relation to the statement or to any of the directions.
- It should be clearly understood by victims that normally the statement and any recording thereof will be disclosed to the prisoner and his/her legal representative in its final form. If the victim wishes to object to such disclosure, written notification with reasons should be provided to the Ministry of Justice when the statement is sent and the Ministry of Justice may make the appropriate non-disclosure application to the Board (and thus to the panel chair). The application will be decided by the panel chair in accordance with rule 6(2) of the Parole Board Rules 2004 (as amended).

11.25 The Secretary of State must take responsibility for meeting the victim and keeping them apart from the prisoner while in the prison. The prisoner can choose whether or not to attend during the presentation of the victim personal statement and cannot be forced to be present. The normal practice is for the victim to read the statement to the panel at the start of the hearing and they will not be allowed to add anything to the contents of the written statement. Once the statement has been read, the victim will be asked to leave and there is no room for questioning of the victim. The victim may apply to be accompanied by a supporter, normally the victim liaison officer or a family member or friend.

Final preparation for the hearing

11.26 If a hearing date has no previously been fixed, the PBR require that at least three weeks' notice should be given, although a shorter time can be given with the consent of the parties.[22] The parties are supposed

22 PBR r17(2).

to be consulted before the hearing is fixed,[23] but this rarely happens as most parole hearings are fixed with reference to the dates at which panels are scheduled to visit particular prisons. It is only in the rare cases where a hearing is particularly complex and is being fixed to take place on its own that the parties are routinely consulted.

11.27 Although there is rarely any consultation on the fixing of hearing dates, case managers are extremely helpful in trying to minimise any difficulties that might arise. In cases where the panel is sitting at the prison over several days, requests for a case to be fixed on a particular date or time are treated sympathetically. The general provision in the PBR to allow the chair to vary the timetable so long as it does not cause prejudice to the parties does mean that unless genuine prejudice is going to arise from a listing that is late or where there has been no consultation, it is unlikely that it will be possible to have the hearing date altered.

11.28 The general power to vary the timetable set out in the PBR ensures that there is a great deal of flexibility, which permits late requests for witnesses, the late submission of documents or late requests for directions. Panel chairs will almost always be willing to deal with additional issues as they arise and it is extremely rare for applications to be refused simply because they are made outside of the time limits. The chair is far more likely to be concerned with ensuring that the hearing will be effective and that all evidence and material relevant to a fair and accurate risk assessment is available.

11.29 At this stage, the areas where additional directions are most likely to be needed are:

- additional witness requests where there have been late reports, including late expert reports;
- special measures for vulnerable or reluctant witnesses, including ensuring that video conferencing facilities are available if required and making sure that any special measures for vulnerable witnesses are in place;
- making directions for interpreters to be present if necessary for either the prisoner or any witnesses;[24]
- assessing whether there is any need to change the location of the hearing for security or practical reasons.

11.30 Prisoners' representatives should ensure that they have checked whether any additional directions should be sought and that all the

23 PBR r17(1).

24 This is normally the responsibility of the prison.

witnesses whose attendance they have requested are aware of the hearing date and can attend. If the representative is concerned that the case cannot proceed as crucial material is unavailable or there is a difficulty with witness attendance, it is possible to apply for a deferral (see below). At one point the Board considered implementing a system for the parties to file 'certificates of readiness' before hearings could take place and even prepared a form that was available on their website. Following the implementation of the ICM procedures and the generic parole process in PSO 6010, this was abandoned.

The Secretary of State's view

11.31 There is no requirement in the PBR for the Secretary of State to provide a view, although this is common practice. PSO 6010 envisages that where a view is to be put forward, it will be provided at a relatively early stage, some eight weeks after the case is first listed.[25] Alternatively, if no view is to be issued, the Board should be notified at this time. In practice, this date is rarely met and the view is usually disseminated far closer to the hearing itself. The view is prepared by PCCS and will explain how the Secretary of State views the case, whether release or a move to open conditions is being opposed and the reasons for that view. The quality of these views will vary enormously depending on who has prepared it. Sometimes they run to more than a page and contain detailed comments on the evidence. In other cases they will only be a perfunctory paragraph that does not engage with the facts of the case at all.

Applications for a deferral

11.32 Once an oral parole hearing has started, there may be reasons arising at the hearing that require it to be adjourned and resumed at a later date. An adjournment requires the same panel to continue hearing the case and must be distinguished from a deferral. If it becomes apparent before the hearing has commenced that there are difficulties that are likely to prevent the panel from reaching a fair decision, an application should be made for the hearing to be deferred. There is no specific provision for this in the PBR and no reported case-law on this issue, so the guidance on how to apply for deferrals and how the

25 PSO 6010 para 1.10.3.

Board treats such requests is taken from practical experience and the Guide issued by the Board to panel members.

11.33 Although the Board's internal Guide provides a summary of current procedure, it is possible that the House of Lords decision in *R (on the application of James (formerly Walker), Lee and James) v Secretary of State for Justice*[26] could impact on these decisions in time and so this must be borne in mind when making applications. One of the article 5(4) challenges in that case was that a review where the parole reports are inadequate does not allow for an effective review of detention and so is in breach of the Convention right. The Lords were troubled by this argument and Lord Simon Brown in the main speech said:

> The appellants' argument is a strong one. What is the point of having a Parole Board review of the prisoner's dangerousness once his tariff period expires unless the Board is going to be in a position then to assess his safety for release?

11.34 Ultimately, however, he decided that all that the Board required to have a meaningful review that met the obligations of article 5(4) was the basic parole dossier. If the Board was unable to order release without receiving further information, this would mean that there was enough evidence for the prisoner to remain detained and so article 5(4) would not be breached. It is possible that this approach will give the Board licence to press ahead with reviews, even where information is sparse, providing the skeleton dossier has been prepared and disclosed.

Applications before the review has begun

11.35 If a case has been referred to the Board but the review has not yet begun (ie the case has not been listed under PBR rule 5) an application for a deferral should be made to the oral hearings team at the Board and it will normally be processed without any reference to a judicial member of the Board. The application should explain why the request has been made and the length of time for which the prisoner wishes the case to be deferred. The presumption operated by the Parole Board in these cases is that the request to defer should be accepted.[27]

26 [2009] UKHL 22.

27 The Guide, para 56.

Applications after the review has commenced

11.36 If the review has started but it is in the early stages and has not been allocated to a panel, applications to defer should be made in writing to the oral hearings team and these will be referred to an ICM member for consideration. The member should consider whether:

- additional written or oral information is needed for the review and, if so, whether it will be available within a short and specific time; and
- this information will have a material bearing on the outcome.[28]

11.37 If the ICM member grants a deferral, directions for further case management should be given. Where it is decided that a deferral should not be granted , written reasons should be given for the decision. If the deferral is approved, a letter should be sent to all parties confirming the period of deferral, specifying what information is missing, who should provide it and the time period in which it should be made available.

Applications after the case has been allocated to a panel

11.38 In this instance, the request must be referred to the chair of the panel. The chair will have in mind the same considerations as the ICM member. Generally, it proves harder to obtain a deferral the further into the review the case has reached. Although the reasons to be applied by the Board do not change, it has been suggested that as the costs to the Board increase enormously once the case has been referred to a panel, there is a greater reluctance to defer cases once they have reached this stage.

11.39 It is implicit in the guidance issued by the Board to panel members that deferrals should be allowed where relevant material is unavailable that will become available in a reasonably short period of time.[29] The Guide suggests in the following circumstances, a deferral will not normally be granted:

- where the prisoner is about to commence a course, or wishes to complete a course, and a report is unlikely to be available within three months. The judge/chair will take into account the normal requirement of the Board that a successfully completed course may not be of use without a period of monitoring subsequently to

28 Ibid, para 57.

29 Although the Lords' decision in *James and others*, above, may alter this approach.

see if lessons learned can be put into practice. This will depend on the subject of the course;

- where a prisoner is approaching the end of a course but where the outcome is unlikely to be a material factor. For example, where multiple risk factors are present and it is clear to the duty judge/ chair that the course report will have little effect on the panel's decision;
- to enable a transfer to another establishment to take place for courses or therapy to begin. Timescales here are very uncertain and are likely to delay the case for many months, or even years;
- where a prisoner recently arrived in open conditions wishes to be assessed for, and complete, home leaves and/or undertake booster work. Prisoners in open conditions will not be permitted to take unescorted leave until they have been assessed by the Prison Service. Unless evidence is available to say that reports will be written within a short period of time, the process is likely to take at least six months.
- in some cases where a prisoner wants to await the outcome of criminal proceedings. This often occurs in recall cases. The duty judge/chair should consider the reports and decide whether there is sufficient material about the alleged incident(s) to enable the panel to reach a decision, with the benefit of oral evidence, whether the *risk* of further offences is acceptable, regardless of whether a crime has actually been committed. Remember, the Board is not required to adopt the criminal standard of proof;
- where the Secretary of State does not wish to be represented, or has not put in a view.[30]

11.40 The suggestion that that deferrals pending the outcome of criminal charges should usually be refused is highly contentious and is arguably very difficult to sustain. Although the Board operates to a lower standard of proof than the criminal courts,[31] it is very difficult to see how a fair inquiry can take place before the criminal trial and how an accurate assessment of risk can be made until it is known whether a criminal offence has been committed. This is far more likely to be an issue in recall hearings and is explored further in that context (see chapter 13).

30 Paragraph 62.

31 See the discussion of evidence at oral hearings, below.

11.41 Cases where the application is likely to be granted are:

- where the prisoner is about to complete offence-related work and the report will be available soon and it is likely to affect the outcome;
- where a material witness is unable to attend on the date of the panel. This type of request will require the chair to consider the excuse given by the witness and decide whether it is reasonable or not;
- in most cases where the prisoner needs more time to obtain legal representation. Indications are that the courts will afford the prisoner a lot of leeway in this area;
- where a prisoner in open conditions has completed most of what is required but is nearing the end of a crucial course; or needs to complete a limited number of home leaves; or where the release plan is not yet in place but is likely to be soon.

11.42 If a deferral application is refused, it is still possible to renew this application at the start of the oral hearing itself. As a matter of good practice, the panel should be notified in advance that the application is being renewed and it should be made at the commencement of the hearing and before any evidence has been taken. If evidence has been taken, technically the case can no longer be deferred but must be adjourned. This is a far more difficult procedural step, as an adjournment will normally require that the same panel reconvenes to rehear the case when it resumes. It is necessary to have the same panel as otherwise the panel making the final decision will not have heard all the relevant evidence.

11.43 When an application for a deferral is granted, the chair should issue a deferral letter. The letter should contain directions for the provision of missing information, who should provide it and a deadline for the submission of the material. One of the parties, either the Secretary of State or the prisoners' representative, should be directed to send a copy of the deferral letter to the relevant report writer or witness.

Location of proceedings

11.44 The PBR provide for the oral hearing to be held at the prison where the prisoner is detained, although the chair can direct the hearing is held elsewhere, providing the Secretary of State consents.[32] There

32 PBR r18(1).

is an obvious efficacy in holding the hearing where the prisoner is detained as the majority of the witnesses are likely to be from the prison and there will be no need to consider security issues arising from moving the prisoner to a different location.

11.45 As the number of oral hearings has increased over the years, the Parole Board has explored the possibility of having hearings outside the prison where the prisoner is detained or alternative methods of giving evidence such as through video links. Consideration has been given to having parole hearings at regional trial centres but no formal amendment has been made to the PBR to allow this.

11.46 The PBR also require that the hearings are held in private.[33] The reasons for this are partly tied to the security concerns of making hearings held inside prisons (especially high security prisons) open to the public and partly to ensure that the privacy of victims is properly protected. A challenge to this was found to be inadmissible by the European Court of Human Rights in 2000.[34] Arguably, there may be cases where the presumption that the hearings should be conducted in private could be displaced, but it is difficult to envisage circumstances where this might arise.

11.47 The precise location of the hearing will vary greatly from prison to prison. Some prisons set aside a large room for the hearing itself, with side rooms for witnesses and private consultation with the client. Other prisons have the most basic of facilities, for example holding hearings in the middle of draughty gyms with poor consultation facilities. It is possible that conditions could be so poor that they could undermine the ability to hold a fair hearing.[35] Somewhat surprisingly, PSO 6010 does not contain any guidance to prisons on the facilities that should be made available at oral hearings. The Guide issued by the Board states that instructions are sent to each prison confirming that a quiet and private room is needed for the hearing, with a table large enough for 9 or 10 people to sit around it and space for witnesses and observers.[36] Two waiting rooms in the immediate vicinity should be provided, one for the prisoner and representative and one for the Secretary of State's representative and any witnesses.

33 PBR r18(2).

34 *Hirst v UK* [2001] CLR 919 – the case was successful in challenging the interval set between parole reviews, but the part of the application challenging the holding of parole hearings in private was dismissed at the admissibility stage.

35 At Stocken hearings were held in a sectioned-off corner of the visits room at one stage, which did not provide the appropriate privacy or general environment for a judicial hearing.

36 Chapter 5 para 1.

Refreshments are to be provided for the Board – but not necessarily for participants – toilets should be available nearby and photocopying facilities made available for the copying of late papers. If the facilities are not adequate, a complaint will be sent to the governor by the Board so that this can be addressed for future hearings.

The persons present at the hearing

11.48 The physical arrangements for the hearing have all the persons sitting around a table or with witnesses and observers seated in the hearing room. Witnesses do not give evidence on oath and the members of the panel should be addressed as 'sir' or madam'. Other than the prisoner and his/her legal representative, the following persons will be present at the hearing.

The panel

11.49 The panel will consist of between one and three members of the Parole Board.[37] For all cases involving a mandatory or discretionary life sentence or a sentence of detention at HMP, the panel must contain a sitting or retired judge. Therefore, hearings for IPP prisoners do not need a judicial or even a legally qualified member to hear the case. As the number of cases heard has expanded exponentially, the pressure to increase the numbers of members of the Parole Board has led to a relaxation of these requirements. It used to be a requirement that all panels had three members for cases involving lifers and IPP prisoners and that one member of the panel was required to have held a legal qualification as a barrister or solicitor for at least five years. This requirement was abolished by the amendments to the PBR in April 2009.

11.50 The other two members of the panel are drawn from the lay members of the Parole Board. In the early days when all panels were for discretionary lifers, it was a requirement that one panel member should be a psychiatrist. It is still very common for one member to hold a psychiatric or psychological qualification, and in any case where psychiatric or psychological issues are relevant to the assessment of risk, this should always be the norm and the ICM directions should specify that a member with such a qualification is on the panel.

37 PBR r3(3).

The panel administrator

11.51 It is envisaged that in the majority of cases, a panel administrator will be present, but this is not always the case. The role of the administrator is to assist the panel with routine administration on the day (checking whether parties are ready, showing them to the room etc) and to make a written note of the hearing. For a while, oral hearings were tape recorded so that transcripts of evidence could be prepared. This practice was instituted in response to the requirement on panel chairs to keep a note of key points of evidence and points of law as well as giving written reasons for decisions[38] in case a challenge was made to the decision and a transcript of the evidence was required. This practice was halted as the number of hearings increased and requests for the tapes or transcripts began to rise. The panel administrator's note is therefore part of the record of the hearing that can be referred to in the event of a dispute at a later date. The administrator can offer advice to the Board on procedural matters but in no circumstances is allowed to make any comment on the outcome of the review.

11.52 If no panel administrator is available, this will not result in the hearing being postponed. This will simply increase the administrative burden on the panel itself and the need for other parties present to keep an accurate note of the proceedings.

The Secretary of State's representative

11.53 If the Secretary of State has provided a written view, this will normally be represented at the hearing by the lifer manager of the prison where the hearing takes place or a public protection advocate from PPCS.[39] In particularly complex cases, PPCS may instruct the Treasury Solicitor and a barrister may be instructed. A public protection advocate or legal representatives will attend in all recall cases as the prison in which the lifer is held may not know anything about his/her case and may not even have a lifer department.

11.54 There are cases where the lifer manager does not agree with the Secretary of State's view on the case. It is not uncommon for a lifer manager to be in favour of a progressive transfer or release, only for the Secretary of State to oppose this view. In those circumstances, the lifer manager may be needed to give evidence and

38 *R v Parole Board ex p Gittens* (1994) *Times* 3 February.

39 PSO 6010 paras 1.13.2–3.

cannot present the case. In any event, good practice dictates that the lifer manager should not present a case where he/she disagrees with the Secretary of State and if no public protection advocate has been sent, another member of staff at the prison should be nominated to represent the Secretary of State.[40] Interestingly, where the lifer governor agrees with the Secretary of State's view it is envisaged that this person can both present the case and give evidence. In those cases, the panel should ascertain whether the parties have any objection and whether they themselves consider it appropriate to proceed.[41]

The prisoner's representative

11.55 The PBR permit a prisoner to be represented by any person they have authorised except for:

- any person liable to be detained under the Mental Health Act 1983;
- any person serving a sentence of imprisonment;
- any person on licence;
- any person with a previous conviction for an imprisonable offence that remains unspent under the Rehabilitation of Offenders Act 1974.[42]

11.56 In cases where there is material being dealt with under the PBR rule 6(2) procedure, it should be borne in mind that rule 6(3) dictates that this can only be disclosed to a narrower group of people including a barrister, a solicitor, a medical practitioner or someone the panel considers suitable by virtue of their professional qualifications.

The witnesses

11.57 For the vast majority of hearings, all the witnesses will be present for the entire hearing. The reason for this is that the evidence given at the hearing might be relevant to the assessment of risk and so it is helpful for the witnesses to hear that evidence. However, the panel can permit a witness to leave once their evidence has been given.

40 PSO 6010 para 1.13.4.

41 The Guide, chapter 5 para 11.

42 PBR r5.

11.58 The exception to this general rule is when there are contested factual allegations, possibly matters that have already been the subject of a criminal trial or discontinued criminal charges and that the Board wishes to reinvestigate. In that instance, it may be appropriate for the evidence to be heard in a manner that more closely resembles the criminal trial process, with witnesses only entering the hearing to give their own evidence. This is most likely to arise when dealing with recall hearings and is a matter that should be raised at the directions stage if possible.

Observers

11.59 Observers will normally be present for the whole of the hearing.

Hearing procedure

An overview

11.60 Guidance as to how the hearing should be conducted is contained in PBR rule 19. Rule19(2) provides that:

> The panel shall avoid formality in the proceedings and so far as possible shall make its own enquiries in order to satisfy itself of the level of risk of the prisoner; it shall conduct the hearing in such manner as it considers most suitable to the clarification of the issues before it and generally to the just handling of the proceedings it.

11.61 A number of important principles that underpin the style of the hearing and inform judicial decisions on challenges to parole review can be taken from rule 19:

- the hearing should be as informal as possible;
- the panel has an inquisitorial role;
- the panel has flexibility as to how to conduct that inquiry.

11.62 There is room for some debate as to whether the proceedings should be adversarial or inquisitorial. Case-law from the European Court of Human Rights suggests that an adversarial hearing is a necessary guarantee of article 5(4) of the Convention in the parole context:

> The Court is of the view that, in a situation such as that of the applicant, where a substantial term of imprisonment may be at stake and where characteristics pertaining to his personality and level of maturity are of importance in deciding on his dangerousness, Article 5(4) requires an oral hearing in the context of an adversarial procedure

involving legal representation an the possibility of calling and questioning witnesses.[43]

11.63 It is possible that the reference to 'adversarial' in this context is not a term of art, but a recognition of the practice and procedure of the oral hearings process as it already existed in this country at the time of the judgment.[44] 'Adversarial' might arguably be a way of describing a process where there are two parties, both of whom are represented and can call and cross-examine witnesses. This would not undermine the distinction between the more stringent adversarial process that exists in the civil and criminal courts and the essentially inquisitorial nature of the parole hearing, which is seeking to make an assessment of risk rather than a precise finding of fact.

11.64 In cases where the Board is required to make a factual determination, the panel conducting the hearing is more likely to dispose of that part of the case in a manner that is closer to traditional criminal proceedings. As was outlined above, the procedure will often be varied and the order of the evidence will be changed to ensure that witnesses are only present for their own evidence; the panel is more likely to act as an arbiter between the parties. Where, as in most cases, the evidence is more concerned with reaching a decision as to what the correct assessment of risk is for an individual, although the evidence before the Board will be tested through cross-examination, the inquisitorial model is arguably more appropriate with the panel taking more of a lead in directing witnesses attendance,[45] asking questions and directing which evidence it wishes to hear.

11.65 The Guide issued to panel chairs makes it clear that the panel is required to ensure that witnesses, particularly the prisoner, are at their ease. Chairs are instructed to ensure that representatives do not 'badger' a witness and that witnesses are comfortable enough to give all the evidence that the panel needs to hear to reach a decision.[46]

43 *Hussain and Singh v United Kingdom* (1996) 22 EHRR 1 paras 59–60.

44 This case was where the European Court of Human Rights held that there should be an extension of the oral hearings process from discretionary lifers to HMP detainees.

45 Under the power in PBR r15(2).

46 Chapter 3 para 5.

Order of evidence

11.66 The PBR require the panel chair to explain at the outset how the panel intends to proceed and then to invite each party to present their view on the suitability for release.[47] Invariably, the Secretary of State's representative will first read out the written view and the prisoner's legal representative is then invited to comment on that view and explain what is being sought from the hearing: a release direction, a recommendation for open conditions or some other outcome.

11.67 In cases where a deferral is being sought, the application should be made at this stage before any evidence is heard. If it is a case where there have been late reports or late written submissions, it is also sensible to check at the outset that everyone at the hearing is working from the same documents.

11.68 The Guide issued to panel chairs advises that the Secretary of State's witnesses should normally be called to give evidence first.[48] The witness will be examined-in-chief by the Secretary of State, cross-examined by the prisoner's representative and then asked questions by the panel itself. Once all of these witnesses have been heard, in the vast majority of cases the first person to give evidence will be the prisoner. The prisoner's representative will ask questions. Once this examination-in-chief has concluded, the Secretary of State's representative then has the opportunity to put questions. The panel will then ask questions of the prisoner, although it is not uncommon for panel chairs to interject while evidence is being given. Finally, the prisoner's representative has a further opportunity to put questions to the client. This procedure is then repeated for all other witnesses.

11.69 It must be remembered that although this is the guidance given to panel members, the aim of the proceedings is to be flexible and so this can be varied as and when necessary.[49] For example, it is rare for the Secretary of State to ask for a witness' attendance, except at recall hearings and so many of the witnesses may have actually been called by the panel itself (especially since the ICM procedures requires decisions to be made at that stage about relevant witnesses). In such cases, a witness may have been called whose evidence is contested by the prisoner but who is not formally the Secretary of State's witness. It is always advisable to raise the order of the witnesses with the panel at the commencement of the hearing.

47 PBR r19(1).

48 Chapter 3 para 10.

49 See PBR r19(2) above.

Advocacy style

11.70 The evidence given by the prisoner is often crucial and so it is important for legal representatives to give a great deal of thought as to the questions they will put to their clients. The considerations to have in mind when preparing those questions are as follows:

- *Always discuss with the client the questions to be put to him/her in advance of the hearing.* It is essential that the client does not feel surprised or pressured when giving evidence.
- *Try to cover as much ground as possible that is relevant to the determination of the issues during the examination-in-chief.* A successful examination-in-chief will leave the panel with very little to ask the prisoner. A prisoner is likely to feel much more comfortable answering questions from his/her own lawyer, especially if it is understood why the question is being asked, than one put by a stranger.
- *Try to keep the evidence as focused and succinct as possible.* The key to this is the relevance test. In many cases, the panel will want the prisoner to provide an explanation of his/her offending history and an account of progression since that time. However, if it is clear from the evidence that the area of dispute is the suitability of a release plan, it may not be necessary to go over this history at all. Panels will often give an indication at the start of the hearing if there are areas they do not need to hear evidence on.
- *Always advise the prisoner that the panel, particularly the chair, may interject at any time.*

11.71 While there is no prescriptive advice to be given on a particular style of advocacy to adopt, the inquisitorial and informal nature of parole hearings does mean that a forensic, criminal court advocacy style is often inappropriate. For example, rather than trying to build up the background to a relevant point through a series of questions, it will usually be of more assistance to the panel to put points directly to the witnesses. Although the approach of panel chairs will vary, there is not the same blanket prohibition on leading witnesses, not least because in most cases the purpose of the hearing is not to examine contested factual matters. Obviously, in cases such as recall hearings where there is a contested factual matter, a more conventional advocacy style is likely to be appropriate.

Evidence

11.72 There are no formal rules of evidence for parole hearings. PBR rule 19(5) states:

> The panel may adduce or receive in evidence any document or information notwithstanding that such document or information would be inadmissible in a court of law, but no person shall be compelled to give any evidence or produce any document which he could not be compelled to give or produce on the trial of an action.

11.73 It should be noted from the outset that the criminal rules of evidence do not apply to parole hearings and that the criminal limb of article 6 of the European Convention on Human Rights has also been held not to apply.[50] Although there has been some room to explore whether the requirements of article 5(4) in this context are materially different from article 6, the view of the domestic courts has always tended towards allowing the Parole Board significant discretion to regulate how, and in what form, it receives evidence. In *R (on the application of Roberts) v Parole Board*,[51] the decision of the Lords was that the Board's primary statutory duty is to protect the public and that this does allow flexibility in determining procedure and receiving evidence. The safeguard for prisoners is that the Board must not adopt procedures that would effectively extinguish the right to a fair hearing. Although the Lords were divided on whether a particular procedure – in that case the adoption of a special advocate[52] – would cross the dividing line, the overall analysis emphasises the flexibility that the Board has in relation to evidential matters.

11.74 The PBR permit panels of the Parole Board to receive evidence that would not be admissible in a court of law.[53] A great deal of the evidence at parole hearings is in the form of hearsay evidence, whether written or oral. Where hearsay evidence is not contested or contentious, this is uncontroversial. One of the key evidential issues that has arisen over the years is whether contested hearsay evidence, especially in relation to disputed factual matters, is admissible.

50 There have been numerous cases on this issue, possibly the most authoritative recent discussion can be found in *R (on the application of Smith) v Parole Board* [2005] UKHL 1.

51 [2005] UKHL 45.

52 See above in the section on disclosure of evidence for a discussion on the implications of the *Roberts* case for the special advocate procedure.

53 For example, none of the evidence is given on oath.

11.75 Two decisions of the Court of Appeal firmly concluded that hearsay evidence is permissible at parole hearings, even in cases where the hearsay evidence is contested and contradicted by oral evidence. The issue identified for the panel by the Court of Appeal was not whether this evidence is admissible, but the degree of weight that is given to it. In *R (on the application of Sim) v Parole Board*[54] Keene LJ analysed the issue in the following manner:

> Merely because some factual matter is in dispute does not render hearsay evidence about it in principle inadmissible or prevent the Parole Board taking such evidence into account. It should normally be sufficient for the Board to bear in mind that that evidence is hearsay and to reflect that factor in the weight which is attached to it. However, like the judge below, I can envisage the possibility of circumstances where the evidence in question is so fundamental to the decision that fairness requires that the offender be given the opportunity to test it by cross-examination before it is taken into account at all. As so often, what is or is not fair will depend on the circumstances of the individual case.[55]

11.76 This was followed and applied to particular facts in *R (on the application of Brooks) v Parole Board.*[56] The facts of the case are worth considering, as they illustrate how a process that can appear fundamentally flawed by comparison with the criminal trial process has been deemed acceptable in parole reviews. The case concerned a discretionary lifer who had been recalled to prison following allegations made by his partner that he had raped her. The allegations had been made to the Probation Service and repeated to the police, but the complainant had declined to pursue criminal charges and indicated to the prisoner's solicitors that she wished to withdraw the charges. She declined to attend the parole hearing[57] but evidence was given about her allegations by the interviewing probation officer and the written statements were available. The panel went on to find the rape had occurred on the balance of probabilities. The Court of Appeal held that the review had been conducted fairly, Kennedy LJ commenting:

54 [2003] EWCA Civ 1845.

55 Para 57.

56 [2004] EWCA Civ 80.

57 Part of the case was concerned with whether appropriate steps had been taken to secure her attendance – this is discussed in the section on securing the attendance of witnesses above at paras 11.14–11.19.

> I, like Keene LJ in *Sim* can envisage the possibility of circumstances where the evidence in question is so fundamental to the decision that fairness requires that the offender be given the opportunity to test it by cross-examination before it is taken into account at all. As Elias J indicated in the present case, that could require production of the complainant if someone in the position of [the complainant] was willing to testify, but as Keene LJ went on to point out, the requirements of fairness depend on the circumstances of the individual case, and in my judgment there was nothing unfair about the decision of this panel to proceed as it did. As I have made clear, neither the Parole Board nor the Secretary of State did anything to inhibit the claimant's opportunity to test by cross-examination the allegations of [the complainant] before those allegations were taken into account, but in the particular circumstances of this case that opportunity was not worth much, and the claimant's solicitor was entitled to decide not to pursue it more than she did.[58]

11.77 As the Board operates to the civil standard of proof rather than to the criminal standard when dealing with factual findings, there is no prohibition on the evidence that has been considered during criminal proceedings being reheard at a parole hearing with the lower standard of proof applied. The courts have cautiously approved the approach applied in cases decided under the Children Act 1989, whereby a criminal acquittal is not considered determinative and does not preclude the tribunal from making its own inquiry applying the civil standard of proof. The leading Children Act authority on this subject is *Re H (minors) (sexual abuse: standard of proof)*[59] in which Lord Nicholls explained the duty as follows:

> When assessing the probabilities the court will have in mind as a factor, to what ever extent is appropriate in the particular case, that the more serious the allegation the less likely it is that the event occurred and, hence, the stronger should be the evidence before the court concludes that the allegation is established on the balance of probability.[60]

11.78 The Children Act analogy has always been considered apposite in the parole context, as the predominant statutory requirement to protect the best interests of the child is mirrored by the Board's primary duty to protect the public. Despite this, there has been some judicial reservation as to whether this can be transposed to the parole process in its

58 Para 37.

59 [1996] AC 563 at 586.

60 At 586.

entirety.[61] In *Re D v Life Sentence Comrs for Northern Ireland*[62] the evidential issues were explored in the context of a prisoner who had been recalled in Northern Ireland under a system largely analogous to the system in England and Wales. The Lords held that greater cogency of evidence was needed in cases where the allegations are more serious, an analysis that they thought properly applied the principles established in *Re H (Minors Sexual Abuse: Standard of Proof)*.[63] They went on to confirm that there is a single standard of proof in civil matters (ie the balance of probabilities) and it is the application of that standard that is flexible. Thus for a more serious allegation, it is not the standard of proof that changes but the strength or quality of the evidence needed to prove the allegation. The discussion on the standard of proof in the speech of Lord Brown is particularly interesting as he explores the practical difficulties that arise from trying to separate out the need for 'more cogent evidence' from actually applying a different standard of proof. He suggested that in certain civil cases it might be more appropriate to apply the criminal standard although, interestingly, he seems quite content to exclude parole from the category that requires the criminal standard, even when dealing with disputed factual allegations amounting to criminal behaviour.[64]

11.79 The flexibility that a panel has when receiving evidence was illustrated in the case of *R (on the application of Gardner) v Parole Board*[65] where it was held that the Board did not act unlawfully when excluding the prisoner from part of a hearing when his wife was giving evidence in support of allegations against him, and in circumstances where she expressed herself as unwilling to give evidence if he was in the same room, even though the Rules did not include any express provision for this. The prisoner's advocate was able to be present, and was allowed time to take instructions on the evidence given, so the witness could be cross-examined. Following the House of Lords'

61 See, for example, Elias J in *R (on the application of Sim) v Parole Board* [2003] EWHC 152 (Admin) at paras 76–78 in the Administrative Court, although this was not an issue raised on the appeal. In contrast, in the *Brooks* case in the Court of Appeal, the Board did adopt the *H* approach and this was not criticised by the court.

62 [2008] UKHL 33.

63 [1996] AC 563.

64 See also *R (on the application of Wyles) v Parole Board* [2006] EWHC 493 (Admin) where the practical application of this approach permitted the Board to make a finding that a prisoner had not committed an assault but that his general behaviour surrounding the incident gave rise to sufficient cause for concern to justify his recall.

65 [2006] EWCA 122 (Admin).

decision in *Roberts* (above), it was held that the Board has inherent power to adopt such a procedure, and moreover there was no breach of article 5(4) of the ECHR in doing so, the court citing the flexibility allowed by the ECtHR in article 6 cases.[66]

11.80 Although the admissibility of evidence will be fact-specific, the most succinct summary of the guidelines the Board will apply can be found in *R v Parole Board ex p Watson*:[67]

> In exercising its practical judgment the Board is bound to approach its task under the two sections in the same way, balancing the hardship and injustice of continuing to imprison a man who is unlikely to cause serious injury to the public against the need to protect the public against a man who is not unlikely to cause to such injury. In other than a clear case this is bound to be a difficult and very anxious judgment. But in the final balance the Board is bound to give preponderant weight to the need to protect innocent members of the public against any significant risk of serious injury.[68]

New confidential evidence

11.81 The submission of confidential material usually happens before the hearing itself (see the discussion on disclosure above). If, however, during the course of the hearing the Secretary of State's representative seeks to introduce evidence that is not to be disclosed to the prisoner under PBR rule 6, the panel should ask everyone except for the two representatives and the panel administrator to leave the room. The panel will have to determine why the application is being made and why it is being made at such a late stage. The prisoner's representative must be allowed the chance to read the material and to make representations on disclosure, subject of course to the prisoner approving this course of action. Once representations have been received, the panel will need to make a decision on disclosure pursuant to rule 8(2)(d) and the two representatives should be called to the room for the decision to be conveyed. As rule 8(3) permits an appeal to be made to the chair of the Parole Board within seven days, if either party indicates that they wish to appeal, the hearing will need to be adjourned (or deferred if no evidence has yet been taken) to allow that appeal to take place.

66 Eg, *Doorson v Netherlands* (1996) 22 EHRR 330.

67 [1996] 1 WLR 906.

68 At 916H – the judgment was given by Lord Bingham when he was Master of the Rolls and so has even greater force.

Disruptive behaviour

11.82 The Board does not have any powers to hold persons in contempt. The PBR do permit the panel to exclude any persons present at the hearing who are behaving in a disruptive manner. Once excluded, the chair of the panel can place conditions before permitting a return.[69]

Children and young persons

11.83 Occasionally children and young persons may be present at oral hearings, either as witnesses or as prisoners. In whatever capacity the child appears, particular care needs to be taken to ensure that his/her evidence can be adduced as effectively and fairly as possible.

11.84 In so far as child witnesses are concerned, the panel will need to be satisfied that the witness is competent to give evidence, namely that they have the ability to understand questions and to give answers that can be understood. Ordinarily this will be a matter for the chair of the panel to consider as a preliminary issue when making directions for the attendance of witnesses. The burden of proof lies with the party seeking to call the child to give evidence and is on balance of probabilities. Where a child or young person does attend to give evidence, panels are reminded to consider directions for 'special measures' subject to available facilities at the prison concerned.

11.85 When hearing evidence from a child witness or prisoner, the panel should have regard to the key principles of the Practice Direction issued by the Lord Chief Justice in relation to trials of children and young persons in the Crown Court. The overriding principle is that the hearing itself should not expose the child or young person to avoidable intimidation, humiliation or distress and that all possible steps should be taken to assist the young person in understanding and participating in the proceedings. The young person should have the opportunity to have legal representation and, so far as possible, the ordinary hearing process should be adapted to meet those ends. Modifications to the hearing process may include:

- enabling the young person to see the hearing room prior to giving evidence in order that he/she can familiarise himself/herself with it;
- permitting the young person, if he/she wishes, to sit with members of his/her family in a place that permits easy informal communication with the young person's legal representative and others;

69 PBR r19(4).

- the panel should explain the proceedings to the young person in terms he/she can understand;
- the hearing should be conducted according to a timetable that takes full account of a young person's inability to concentrate for long periods. Frequent and regular breaks will often be appropriate;
- a more informal approach to the proceedings may be required, including addressing the young person by his/her first name.

Adjournments

11.86 Panels have the power to adjourn hearings after the evidence has commenced if it is considered that further information might be needed to enable a final determination to be reached. The most common situations where this is likely to occur are where the release plan has not been properly prepared or the evidence suggests that amendments to the release plan might be necessary.

11.87 When a panel adjourns, the case should normally be relisted before the same panel on a later date. This is different from a deferral where the case can be considered by an entirely new panel. This distinction is made because if evidence has already been received, then the same panel members will need to reconvene in order to be able to reach a decision on risk. New panel members would not usually be able to reach this assessment if they have not heard all the evidence.

11.88 The point of the hearing at which a panel adjourns is important. If the panel reaches a decision on risk and then adjourns for reports on the release plan, it is not permitted to reopen the risk issue. In one case where this happened, at the resumed hearing PPCS and the probation service persuaded the panel that their initial risk assessment was incorrect and the provisional release direction was rescinded.[70] The High Court quashed this decision of the Parole Board, accepting the argument that the Board was functus officio on the issue of risk assessment and that it could not reopen this issue unless new factual material was available. Fresh submissions and argument were insufficient. Following this decision, most panels will refrain from making a determination on risk at the time of the adjournment, not least because the nature of the release plan may be intimately tied to the management of risk in the community.

70 *R v Parole Board ex p Robinson* (1999) *Independent* 8 November.

Concluding the hearing

11.89 At the conclusion of the evidence, the chair of the panel will invite the Secretary of State's representative to make any closing comments or submissions. The prisoner's representative will then also be given this opportunity. It is always the case that the prisoner should be given the last word.

11.90 The Secretary of State's representative will, in the vast majority of cases, simply repeat the view that was provided in writing at the start of the hearing. The representative will not have the authority to depart from that view[71] and it is only in cases where the initial view was neutral that there might be scope for a more focused view to be provided on consideration of the evidence.

11.91 The closing comments made on behalf of the prisoner provide an opportunity to draw out any important themes from the evidence and to make legal submissions on the interpretation of that evidence or the appropriate test to be applied. It is important that submissions are made on all relevant points, but this does have to be tempered with the need not to alienate the panel by reminding them of legal principles with which they will be familiar. It is a question of judgment in each case, although some panels will provide an indication of their views on a case and the areas that are still causing them concern. In hearings where a great deal of evidence has been taken from the home probation officer about the precise licence conditions, this can be an indication that the panel are minded to release.

11.92 Once the final submissions have been made, the panel will inform the participants that a decision will be made within 14 days.[72] There may occasionally be cases where the 14 days permitted does not always meet the requirements for a speedy determination of the need for continued detention,[73] although if there are reasons why this period of time is problematic, this will need to be raised with the panel at the conclusion of the hearing. It will be conveyed to the prisoner, the representative, PPCS and the governor. The parties will then be asked to leave the room and wait in a room nearby while

71 PSO 6010 para 1.13.4.

72 PBR r20: this change to the PBR doubled the time for the decision to be made from 7 to 14 days.

73 In *R (on the application of Hirst) v Secretary of State for the Home Department* [2005] EWHC 1480 (Admin) a delay of 14 days on the part of the Secretary of State in providing reasons for a recall decision was held to breach article 5(4) due to the subsequent delays this had on the review of the recall.

the panel assess whether any further evidence or submissions are needed. If the panel is satisfied that it has all the evidence it needs, the participants will be permitted to leave.

The decision

11.93 The test that the Board is required to apply on release is the statutory test in the Crime (Sentences) Act 1997 section 28(6)(b) that:

> the Board is satisfied that it is no longer necessary for the protection of the public that the prisoner should be confined.

11.94 The precise nature and ambit of this test is discussed at length in chapter 9. The concern here is with the procedural aspects of the final decision made by the Board, whether this is release or otherwise.

11.95 The PBR require decisions to be recorded in writing with reasons and sent to the parties within 14 days of the hearing, or two days in determinate recall cases. Panel decisions must be unanimous and, if agreement cannot be reached, the panel will be dissolved by the chair of the Board and a new panel appointed.[74] The Board often used to send decisions to prison in the internal prison post, which can be slow and often leads to the decision not arriving at the prison until after the 14-day period has elapsed, but it is now more common for decisions to be sent by email. The decision will usually be sent to the lifer manager or lifer clerk to be passed onto the prisoner. This can introduce further delay if the prison does not deal with this promptly. It is always sensible for representatives to contact the Board on the 14th day to have a copy faxed or emailed if it has not arrived and to arrange for the client to telephone that afternoon to find out the result.

11.96 The case-law that developed in relation to paper parole reviews where article 5(4) was not engaged emphasised the duty of the Board to give clear and cogent reasons for its decisions. This common law test is now one of the requirements of the PBR and remains a general principle of good administrative practice. Inadequate reasons can be a basis for a legal challenge and so decisions should be checked to ensure that the reasons:

- focus on the question of risk;
- address the test for release and the Secretary of State's directions;

74 PBR r10: this replaces the previous provision that permitted majority decisions.

- identify the matters in favour of and against release;
- explain how the panel have weighed the varying evidence and reached a conclusion.

11.97 The internal guidance provided by the Board to panel members on the drafting of reasons is as follows:[75]

> Reasons should be clear, accurate and concise. Simple, short sentences are best. However, the courts have criticised the terseness of some reasons which leaves them open to misconstruction and misunderstanding. Reasons should, therefore:
> - concisely cover the issues and leave the prisoner in no doubt how the panel arrived at its decision;
> - avoid jargon. For example, what does 'address offending behaviour' really mean? It means different things in different cases. Panels must say exactly what factors contributed to the 'offending behaviour';
> - avoid absolutes where possible. For example, 'no evidence that the prisoner has addressed ...' does not necessarily mean the problem has not been worked on and invites the prisoner to point to some evidence however slight, which shows the contrary. 'There is insufficient evidence ...' is preferable. Similarly, it is better not to say, eg, 'the prisoner has had 5 adjudications'. This invites an argument over the correct number. It is preferable to use the 'several' or 'a number of'.

11.98 The Board has become more prescriptive about the format of reasons in recent years and the Guide now provides a very comprehensive structure for the drafting of decisions and the structure that should be followed. The guidance is:[76]

> **Guidance to accompany the Framework for Reasons**
>
> **1. Decision of the panel**
> - Panels may wish to use this section to briefly set out the purpose of the hearing or panel relevant to the point during sentence when the case is being considered e.g. To determine suitability for early release on licence [DCR] or To determine suitability for transfer to open conditions [Lifer].
> - In this section, panels may want to adopt the wording of the Secretary of State's referral or the test to be applied. For example: 'The Panel considered your case at an oral hearing on (date) and was satisfied that it is no longer necessary for the protection of the public that you should be detained and therefore decided that you should be released on life licence with the conditions listed below.

75 The Guide, Chapter 4 para 26.

76 Ibid, Annex G.

This decision was based on the following reasons' [Lifer or IPP] or 'The panel considered your case based on the dossier papers on (date) and concluded that the level of risk which you present cannot be safely managed in the community during the early release period. Parole is therefore refused' [DCR].

2. **Evidence considered by the panel**

- In this section, panels may find it helpful to confirm the standard dossier contents were received by all parities and list additional documents submitted on the day of the hearing to ensure clarity regarding all evidence considered.
- Panels may find it helpful to list the witnesses who gave oral evidence including names and role.
- Aspects of the oral evidence which are relevant to risk could be incorporated here or incorporated into sections 3, 4 or 5 where relevant. The panel can decide where best to include evidence which forms part of the analysis, thereby minimising the amount of descriptive evidence needed.
- This is an opportunity to refer to the prisoner's representations, Secretary of State's view and victim statement. One alternative would be to cover these views in section 8.
- Panels may want to address the issue of non-disclosable material here. Guidance can be found in the Oral Hearings Guide and Members Handbook.

3. **Analysis of offending**

- This section is the opportunity to outline the historical evidence of offending. Panels may wish to rely on documents such as judge's sentencing remarks, previous convictions and details of the index offence in Pre-Sentence Reports, witness statements or findings of fact e.g. where offender has admitted offences for which they were not convicted.
- In this section panels may find it helpful to identify the type of offending for which the panel has to determine the level of risk.
- Psychological psychiatric or medical considerations relevant to risk could be highlighted here or in section 4.
- Consideration could be given to the impact on the victim and their family in this section.
- Evidence of unconvicted offending could helpfully be addressed here.

4. **Factors which increase or decrease risk of re-offending and harm**

- Panels may find it helpful to comment on each of the risk factors which the panel have identified (rather than relying solely on those listed in the dossier) based on the analysis of information in section 3, highlighting patterns and identifying the characteristics of the individual and the circumstances which appear to be related to their offending behaviour.

- Psychological psychiatric or medical considerations relevant to risk could be highlighted here or in section 3.

5. **Evidence of change during sentence**

- This section is an opportunity to comment on changes in the prisoner's circumstances, relationships, insight into offending, attitude and behaviour in custody (e.g. adjudications, MDTs) and including completion of relevant interventions to reduce risk (not limited to OBPs).
- Panels may find it helpful to highlight indicators of increasing as well as decreasing risk.
- Panels may wish to draw on evidence of release on temporary licence (ROTL), absconds and periods in open conditions to assess response to trust, compliance and ability to apply knew skills in a more realistic setting.

6. **Panel's assessment of current risk of re-offending and serious harm**

- In this section, panel could refer to and make a judgment on actuarial/structured risk assessments
- Panels may find it helpful to consider the imminence of re-offending in this section
- All risk factors identified by the panel could helpfully be addressed individually in this section, for example indicating whether there has been sufficient change such as cessation of substance misuse, continuing influence such as attitudes supportive of violence or opportunities to manage risk effectively in future such as by way of 'no contact' licence conditions.
- When evaluating the evidence, panels could use this section to convey the relative weight given to key facts or opinions in arriving at their decision.
- The panel may want to comment here on whether all relevant risk and protective factors have been addressed in the evidence.

7. **Risk management plan (where release is being considered)**

- In this section, the panel may find it helpful to confirm that all risk factors identified by the panel have been addressed within the risk management plan (RMP).
- The panel may want to comment on likely compliance of offender with RMP, relying on evidence of ROTL, previous breaches and positive engagement with supervising probation officer.
- This section can be omitted when the panel is not considering release e.g. referral for a pre-tariff expiry lifer.
- Panels may want to comment on protective factors here.

8. **Conclusion: Level of risk and suitability for release/open conditions**

- This is an opportunity to identify outstanding areas of risk
- This section provides the opportunity to link the assessment of

risk to the relevant test (reference Secretary of State's Directions) including considering the relevant parole period over which risk is being considered.

- The Secretary of State and Legal Representatives' views could be addressed here.
- The balancing of evidence and arguments for and against release or open conditions which has been conducted throughout the reasons can be summarised in this section.
- In relevant cases, the panel could use this section to state whether or not risk is manageable in open conditions or the community.
- The panel could include the final decision of the panel based on evidence and logical development of reasons.

9. **Licence conditions (where required)**

- This section is an opportunity to highlight those conditions over and above the standard conditions on a licence. Links could be made between conditions and the risk assessment to demonstrate necessary and proportionate. In addition, victim concerns can be addressed here.
- Members may wish to refer to relevant sections of the Members Handbook and Oral Hearing Guide.

Additional Guidance
Panels can, where appropriate, adopt conclusions of previous panels set out in earlier decision letters, thereby reducing the need to repeat detailed information. Panels wishing to do this may want to check that those reading the current reasons have access to these earlier decision letters.

Processing decisions made by the Board

11.99 The Board has the power to direct release[77] but, as noted in chapter 9, all other powers are advisory only. Where release has been directed, the duty to process the direction, to draw up the life licence and physically to organise the release rests with PPCS.

11.100 PPCS policy used to be to aim to process release directions within five working days, but PSO 6010 no longer contains a timetable for this to happen save to explain that the prisoner must be released on tariff expiry if so directed.[78] Obviously, PPCS are under a duty to act speedily in accordance with article 5(4). The precise time it will take physically to release a prisoner will depend on the circumstances of the release arrangements in each case. Where release is directed to

77 C(S)A 1997 s28(5).
78 PSO 6010 para 1.15.1.

a home address, all that needs to be done is for PPCS to liaise with the probation service and draw up the licence. If release is to a hostel, it will only be able to take place when the hostel has a bed for the prisoner. It is to be hoped that the timescale is known at the hearing itself, but sometimes this is impossible to predict and, in the worst cases, prisoners can wait for four to six weeks for a bed to be available.

11.101 If the Board has recommended a move to open conditions, PPCS make the final decision on this recommendation on behalf of the Secretary of State. Once again, there used to be a recommended time limit of six weeks to reach this decision, but this time period is no longer set out in PSO 6010. The decision is usually made by a senior caseworker at PPCS on behalf of the Secretary of State, although in high profile or contentious cases ministerial approval will be sought. The final decision will be sent to the prisoner with a memorandum explaining whether it has been accepted or not and, if it has not, the reasons for rejecting the recommendation. The memorandum will also set out the time when the next parole review will take place. Where the Board has not directed release or recommended a move to open conditions, PPCS simply notify the prisoner of when the next review will take place.

Timing between reviews

11.102 PPCS retains the responsibility for setting the timing between reviews, even though the courts have stated that it would be more sensible for this power to be exercised by the Board.[79] The statutory requirement is for a review to take place at least every two years. As the rationale behind the requirement for article 5(4) reviews is that the person subject to the sentence is susceptible to change, the decision as to how long the gap should be between reviews is case sensitive.[80] The legal rationale for this restriction is discussed in chapter 9.

11.103 There have been a number of cases decided by the ECtHR in relation to the interval between reviews for lifers and many of these are summarised in the leading domestic case of *R (on the application of MacNeil) v Discretionary Lifer Panel*.[81] In *MacNeil*, an argument was

79 *R (on the application of Day) v Secretary of State for the Home Department* [2004] EWHC 1742 (Admin).

80 For a general background on the ECtHR view of the requirements of article 5(4) see *Herczegalvy v Austria* (Series A No 244) and *Sanchez-Reisse v Switzerland* (Series A No 107).

81 [2001] EWCA Civ 448.

made that the statutory two-year interval breaches article 5(4), but this argument was rejected. Instead, the Court of Appeal considered that an individual assessment was needed on the facts of the individual case to determine whether an earlier review was needed. It was held that the two-year review ordered was lawful in light of the prisoner's history of absconding and drug abuse and his subsequent poor behaviour following the parole decision.

11.104 The ECtHR appears to be slightly more purposive in determining the appropriate interval between reviews and in *Oldham v UK*[82] a two-year review period was held to be unlawful as all the relevant coursework had been completed in eight months. The manner in which the issue should be approached was explained by the ECtHR in *Hirst v UK*[83] where it was explained that the very nature of the life sentence is such that the prisoner is liable to change and so reviews have to be set with the possibility of maturity, development and change in mind.[84] The decision goes on to note that the Secretary of State sought to defend the action on the grounds that if there had been further development that had not been expected, an earlier review could be ordered at that stage. This principle has subsequently been accepted as the correct approach in domestic law meaning that it is possible for a prisoner to ask the Secretary of State to advance a review if there are developments justifying an earlier hearing.[85]

11.105 The appropriate method for the courts to take when determining these issues is to reach a primary decision on what is required in the case rather than to simply make a reasonableness assessment, this duty arising partly because the initial decision is being taken by the executive and partly because it is a Convention right that is at stake.[86] Furthermore, in keeping with the cases addressing the provision of relevant offending behaviour programmes and the mechanisms for hearing cases, the decision on the appropriate timing is an objective question to be answered without reference to resources.[87] The

82 (2001) 31 EHRR 34.

83 (2001) Crim LR 919.

84 Further ECtHR cases relating to domestic decisions can be found in *Blackstock v UK* (above); *AT v UK* (1995) 20 EHRR CD 50; *Curley v UK* (2001) 31 EHRR 14; *Waite v UK* (2003) 36 EHRR 54.

85 See *R (on the application of Ashford) v Secretary of State for Justice* [2008] EWHC 2734 (Admin), where the Court held that the appropriate question to be determined was whether the prisoner's progress justified an earlier consideration of his case, before proceeding to dismiss the claim on the merits.

86 See *McNeill* above.

87 *R (on the application of Loch) v Secretary of State for Justice* [2008] EWHC 2278 (Admin).

appropriate remedies for delays, either in relation to failure to set the correct timing between reviews or because of failures on the part of the Board in actually concluding reviews within the requisite period, are discussed in chapter 14.

Lifers facing deportation

11.106 In cases where the lifer is to be deported, the Board can direct release from the life sentence but does not have jurisdiction to interfere with any decision made by the immigration authorities to detain. In the majority of cases, lifers being deported will be released from closed prison conditions (see chapter 8). In those cases, it will be normal for the immigration authorities to seek to continue the detention pending the physical deportation. In the rarer cases where the lifer has already been moved to open conditions and is released from there, it may be far more difficult for detention on immigration grounds to be justified.

11.107 The physical process of arranging deportation can be lengthy, even where the deportation is not contested. Arrangements are dealt with by the Criminal Casework Team of the UK Borders Agency. They will require proof of citizenship, such as a passport or birth certificate, to enable the receiving state to agree to accept the return of the prisoner. The physical arrangements will involve making a booking with an airline, which will nearly always require the prisoner to be escorted, and then finding a date on which escorts are available. Even in cases where it has been possible to arrange for the documentation issues confirming nationality to be resolved promptly, it can still take several weeks for the physical flight arrangements to be resolved. Unreasonable delay in arranging for physical removal can render detention unlawful,[88] and it is impermissible to have a rebuttable presumption that people will continue to be detained in such circumstances.[89]

88 *R v Governor of Durham Prison ex p Singh (Hardial)* [1984] 1 WLR 704.

89 *Abdi v Secretary of State for the Home Department* [2008] EWHC 3166 (Admin).

CHAPTER 12

Licences

continued

Introduction

The purpose of licence supervision

12.1 While licence conditions form part of the sentence of the criminal court, the purpose of their enforcement is not to punish.[1] Licences, even for determinate sentence prisoners, are therefore primarily preventative. Those released on licence are supervised by the Probation Service,[2] who also will be responsible for initiating enforcement action where the conditions of the licence are broken. Both those serving determinate and indeterminate sentences are released on a licence that contains a set of standard conditions. As it is probation officers who have the responsibility for the supervision of licences, they also play a large part in determining which conditions, beyond the standard conditions, should be imposed in any particular case.

Limits on what licences can contain

12.2 Licence supervision can impose significant restrictions on the offender's life in the community. As will be seen below, licence conditions can, among other things, exclude the offender from specified geographical areas, determine who he/she can live with and place restrictions on the kinds of employment that can be undertaken. The courts have therefore recognised that the imposition of licence conditions is capable of engaging the offender's right to private and family life under article 8 of the European Convention on Human Rights (ECHR).[3]

12.3 It will not be every licence condition that will engage article 8 (for example the requirement to report to the supervising officer), but many will. Obvious examples are those conditions that restrict the offender's ability to maintain ties with close family members, or those that prevent him/her from continuing in their chosen profession or from living in his/her own home.

12.4 Where licence conditions do constitute interference with article 8 rights, the question then arises as to whether the interference is for

1 *R (on the application of Smith) v Parole Board* [2005] UKHL 1 para 40 where Lord Bingham stated that 'a challenge to revocation of a licence may lead to detention imposed to protect the public but it cannot lead to punishment' in deciding that the Parole Board was not determining a 'criminal charge' within the meaning of article 6 of the European Convention on Human Rights (ECHR) when considering recall.

2 CJCSA 2000 s1.

3 See *R (on the application of Craven) v Home Secretary and Parole Board* [2001] EWHC Admin 850.

one of the purposes set out in article 8(2) and whether it is proportionate. Guidance to the Probation Service states that:

> In addition a condition must comply with Article 8 of the ECHR (the right to respect for private and family life). To be compatible with that right **a condition must be a necessary and proportionate measure for the purposes of ensuring public safety and/or prevention of crime.** In this context, 'necessary' means that the measure adopted must be the appropriate way of managing a particular risk; and 'proportionate' means that the restriction on the offender's liberty is the minimum required to manage the risk and that no other, less intrusive, means of addressing the risk is available or appropriate. It should be noted that the standard licence conditions already contain sufficient authority to manage most risks in the community.[4]

Clearly the greater the risk the offender is assessed as posing to the public, the more restrictive will be the licence conditions that are permitted.

12.5 Although courts, when examining the lawfulness of licence conditions, will be required to come to their own view as to whether they disproportionately interfere with Convention rights,[5] they will also give considerable weight in making such assessments to the view of the Probation Service:

> The licence conditions and assessment of risks to the public, on which they are based, are matters of fine judgment for those in the prison and the probation service experienced in such matters not for the courts. The courts must be steadfastly astute not to interfere save in the most exceptional case.[6]

12.6 As licence conditions are preventative, they must bear a relationship to the kind of risk to the public that the sentence in question was imposed to address. Therefore conditions imposed on the basis of material errors of fact taken into account in assessing the risk (such as

4 PC 29/2007 para 12.

5 *R (on the application of Daly)* [2001] 2 AC 532 which contains the appropriate standard of review in cases concerning Convention rights.

6 *R (on the application of Carman) v Secretary of State for the Home Department* [2004] EWHC 2400 (Admin) para 33. This statement, while indicating the courts' approach, clearly overstates the deference that the courts should have to decisions regarding licences where article 8 rights are engaged. The court has to decide the question whether any interference is justified under article 8(2), and this should not rely on any test of 'exceptionality': *Huang v Secretary of State for the Home Department* [2007] UKHL 11. For a more measured rejection of a proportionality challenge in this context see *R (on the application of Gunn) v Secretary of State for Justice and Nottinghamshire MAPPA Board* [2009] EWHC 1812 (Admin) para 10.56 below.

the number of convictions the sentence relates to) may render conditions unlawful.[7]

12.7 Licence conditions should only be reasonably imposed. For example, additional licence conditions may include a requirement to address offending behaviour, by attending community-based programmes (see para 12.24 below). However, an offender who does not admit his/her guilt cannot be required to complete a course that is only open to those who accept guilt.[8] In practice, the wording of such conditions is normally vague enough to be interpreted as requiring offenders to comply with assessments for courses.

12.8 In accordance with normal public law principles, policies on the supervision of licence conditions should not be applied inflexibly. For example, in relation to the standard condition that those on licence should not travel abroad, the Probation Service previously had a policy[9] that stated that in relation to determinate sentence prisoners permission for such travel should only be granted in exceptional compassionate circumstances, and not for holiday, business or recreation. Following a legal challenge the policy was amended to include clarification that, in exceptional circumstances, travel abroad could be allowed for such purposes.[10]

Liaison with other organisations to inform licence conditions

12.9 Multi agency public protection arrangements (MAPPA), if applicable to the offender, will inform any licence conditions recommended by the Probation Service, especially for high risk prisoners.[11] As noted in

7 *R (on the application of Carman) v Secretary of State for the Home Department* [2004] EWHC (Admin) 2400.

8 *R (Wilkes) v Home Secretary* [2001] EWHC 210 (Admin); although in *R (on the application of Taplin) v Parole Board* [2004] EWHC 515 (Admin), where a prisoner had pleaded guilty to a sexual offence but had been inconsistent during his sentence as to whether he admitted guilt, the judge doubted whether it was unreasonable to require the offender to attend a community sex offender treatment programme.

9 In PC 16/2005.

10 See now PC 4/2006. A challenge to a decision under the amended policy to refuse to allow an offender to travel abroad to take up employment failed in *R (on the application of Mehmet) v London Probation Board* [2007] EWHC 2223 (Admin) in a case that shows that the courts will be reluctant to interfere with the Probation Service's assessment as to what constitutes exceptional circumstances.

11 See *The Joint National Protocol on the Supervision, Revocation and Recall of Offenders agreed between the Probation, Police and Prison Services* Part 6. The Protocol forms part of the Prison Service's Public Protection Manual and is appended to PC 05/2009.

chapter 10 there is real concern over the degree to which the MAPPA process may influence the Board as to which licence conditions are to be imposed, when its hearings have so little in the way of procedural safeguards (see further paras 10.54–10.57 below).

12.10 The policy states that in respect of those identified as posing a high or very high risk of harm under OASys, MAPPA level 2 and 3 cases, 'serious organised criminals', those identified as prolific and priority offenders (PPOs) and national intelligence model ('NIM') targets, the Probation Service will make a formal request to the police for any information or intelligence that may impact upon what may be appropriate licence conditions.[12] This process should take place no later than 28 days prior to release.[13]

Consultation with victims

12.11 Since the first victim's charter was introduced in 1996, the Probation Service has been required, where this is requested by the victim, both to inform victims as to when prisoners convicted of the more serious offences are released on licence, and also to consult on whether the victim wishes to make representations as to appropriate licence conditions.

12.12 This duty is now a statutory one[14] on the local probation board or trust for where the prisoner is to be released, where an offender receives a sentence of 12 months or more for a sexual or violent offence. The duty is to take all reasonable steps to ensure that if the victim wants to make representations about licence conditions, these are forwarded to whoever is responsible for the setting of them. The victim is also entitled to information about what supervision arrangements are in place and such other information as the Probation Board considers appropriate to provide.[15]

12.13 This duty is now reinforced by a code of practice[16] describing the minimum services that criminal justice agencies should provide to victims of crime, which has now replaced the victim's charter. This states that consider:

> The Parole Board must consider any representations that victims have offered to the Probation Service on the conditions to be included

12 National Protocol, para 6.4.

13 National Protocol, para 6.1.

14 DVCVA 2004 s35.

15 DVCVA 2004 s35(7).

16 www.homeoffice.gov.uk/documents/victims-code-of-practice.

> in the release licences of prisoners serving sentences subject to consideration by the Parole Board and reflect these considerations in the parole decisions. Conditions relating to the victim should be disclosed to the victim through the Probation Service, and where a licence condition has not been included, the Parole Board should provide an explanation for the non-inclusion.[17]

The Parole Board also has its own practice guide on involvement of victim's in the parole process (see paras 2.14–2.16 and 11.23–11.25 above).

12.14 It is clear that victims cannot insist on disproportionate or unreasonable licence conditions being imposed on released prisoners. What the courts have recognised is that, when deciding whether a licence condition that interferes with an offender's rights under article 8(1) of the ECHR can be justified under one of the grounds in article 8(2), this can necessitate balancing the offender's rights with those of the victim. So a condition excluding an offender from entering a prescribed area imposed to minimise the risk of contact with the victim can be justified as protecting 'the rights and freedoms of others'.[18] However, such conditions have to be proportionate, or the minimum necessary interference to meet the stated aim. Any exclusion zone and any terms that allow the offender access to it must be carefully tailored to address the real risk of contact with victims balanced against the impact on the offender's private and family life.[19]

Enforcement of licences

12.15 For sentences of less than four years for offences committed before 1 January 1999,[20] breaches of licence conditions are punished by the courts. The only other situation where enforcement involves prosecution rather than executive recall is where prisoners released from 'return to custody' orders imposed under section 116 of the Prosecution of Offenders Act 2000 of less than 12 months breach the conditions of their three-month licence.[21]

17 Victims' Code of Practice, para 12.2.

18 *R (Craven) v Home Secretary and Parole Board* [2001] EWHC 850 (Admin), where the court considered that 'a democratic society should be sensitive to the emotional harm caused to victims of crime'.

19 Following the *Craven* case, guidance was issued to the Probation Service on exclusion zones – initially in PC 28/2003; see now PC 29/2007 paras 18–19.

20 When the CDA 1998 repealed CJA 1991 s38.

21 CJA 1991 s40A. See also para 5.26.

Licences and determinate sentences

12.16 All prisoners serving determinate sentences will be released on licence except:

- those serving sentences of less than 12 months whenever imposed (except offenders who are under 22 at the date of release who are on three months' minimum supervision,[22] or those released from a 'return to custody' order of less than 12 months[23]);
- CJA 1967 'existing prisoners' released at the two-thirds point; and
- recalled prisoners released at sentence expiry.

Summary of length of licences

12.17
- *CJA 1967 cases (those sentenced before 1 October 1992)* – If released early, the licence expires at the two-thirds point.
- *CJA 1991 ACR cases and DCR cases (those sentenced on or after 1 October 1992 for offences committed before 4 April 2005 to terms of at least 12 months)* – The licence expires at the three-quarter point, subject to recall,[24] unless the prisoner is a DCR prisoner released automatically at the halfway point, in which case the licence lasts for the entire sentence.
- In relation to *sexual offences committed prior to 30 September 1998* the court can order that the licence lasts for the whole of the sentence in any event.[25]
- *CJA 2003 standard determinate sentences (12 months and over for offences committed on or after 4 April 2005)* – Licences will always run until sentence expiry.[26]
- *Extended sentences under CJAs 1991 and 2003 impose an extra period of supervision on licence to be served in the community* – Offenders are on licence until the end of the extension period.

CJA 1991 determinate sentence prisoners

12.18 The initial release dates, and licence expiry dates, for CJA 1991 prisoners were preserved when the relevant parts of the CJA 2003 were

22 CJA 1991 s65.
23 CJA 1991 s40A.
24 CJA 1991 s37(1).
25 PCC(S)A 2000 s86.
26 Section 249(1).

brought into force.[27] The position has changed with the coming into force of the CJIA 2008, which trades automatic release for DCR prisoners who have not been convicted of specified sexual or violent offences[28] with the imposition of licence supervision for the entirety of the sentence. For prisoners released on licence under CJA 1991 provisions there is a duty to comply with the conditions specified in the licence, and the Secretary of State is empowered to make rules for the regulating of licence supervision.[29]

CJA 2003 determinate sentence prisoners

12.19 Under the CJA 2003 fixed term prisoners, including extended sentence prisoners, are released on licence[30] and the licences last for the whole of the sentence.[31] The conditions that can be attached to these sentences are authorised by section 250, which empowers the Secretary of State to prescribe standard and additional licence conditions by statutory instrument (see below). When exercising the power to prescribe licence conditions the Secretary of State must have regard to:

- the protection of the public;
- prevention of reoffending; and
- securing the successful reintegration of the prisoner into the community.[32]

12.20 Prisoners released under the CJA 2003 provisions, as with those released under the CJA 1991, are required to comply with such conditions as are specified in the licence.[33]

Content of licences

12.21 In summary, where the Parole Board has responsibility for deciding whether a prisoner is released early, it is also consulted about appropriate licence conditions. In cases where prisoners are automatically released, the responsibility lies with the governor of the holding

27 Criminal Justice Act (Commencement No 8 and Transitional and Saving Provisions) Order 2005 SI No 950 Sch 2 para 19.

28 Contained in CJA 2003 Sch 15.

29 CJA 1991 s37(4).

30 CJA 2003 ss244 and 247, respectively.

31 CJA 2003 s249.

32 CJA 2003 s250(8).

33 CJA 2003 s252.

prisons to set the licence conditions on behalf of the Secretary of State.[34]

12.22 Although for CJA 2003 cases the licence conditions that can be imposed are specified by the Act and statutory instrument (see below), guidance to the Probation and Prison Services confirms that the same standard and additional licence conditions can be imposed on CJA 1991 cases.[35]

Standard conditions

12.23 Licences will require the offender to report to the supervising officer immediately. In addition, all licences will contain standard conditions. For CJA 2003 cases the standard licence conditions are statutorily prescribed under section 250 of the Act.[36] For other determinate sentences the standard licence conditions are similar and set out in PC 29/2007.[37] The standard conditions require the prisoner:

(a) to keep in touch with their supervising officer in accordance with any instructions that they may be given;
(b) if required, to receive visits from their supervising officer at their home/place of residence (eg approved premises);
(c) permanently reside at an address approved by the supervising officer and to notify him or her in advance of any proposed change of address or any proposed stay (even for one night) away from that approved address;
(d) undertake only such work (including voluntary work) approved by the supervising officer and to notify him or her in advance of any proposed change;
(e) not to travel outside the UK unless otherwise directed by the supervising officer (permission for which will be given in exceptional circumstances only) or for the purpose of complying with immigration deportation/removal;
(f) to be well behaved, not to commit any offence and not to do anything that could undermine the purpose of supervision, which is to protect the public, prevent the prisoner from reoffending and help the prisoner to resettle successfully into the community.

34 See guidance in PC 29/2007 and PSO 6000 chapter 14.

35 See, for example, PC 29/2007 para 2.

36 Criminal Justice (Sentencing) (Licence Conditions) Order 2005 SI No 648.

37 Paragraph 3.

Additional licence conditions

12.24 The Probation Service can also recommend additional licence conditions from a prescribed list.[38] The additional licence conditions are:

- *contact requirement* – to attend appointments with a named psychiatrist/psychologist/medical practitioner;
- *prohibited activity requirement* – for example, not to work with persons under a specified age, or not to access the internet without approval;
- *residency requirement* – a stronger version of the standard requirement;
- *prohibited residency* – for example, not to stay in the same household as a child under a specified age without approval;
- *prohibited contact requirement* – for example, not to contact a named victim without approval;
- *programme requirement* – for example, to comply with requirements specified by the Probation Service to address offending behaviour;
- *curfew requirement* – electronic monitoring is available for those identified as MAPPA level 3 cases, including critical public protection cases;[39]
- *exclusion requirement* – not to enter a specified area;
- *supervision requirement* – for example, reporting regularly to a police station, or notifying probation officer of any developing relationship;
- *non-association requirement* – for example, not to associate with specified offenders.

The polygraph condition pilot

12.25 The Offender Management Act (OMA) 2007 sections 28-29 permits the imposition of a polygraph condition (a requirement to submit to 'lie-detector' tests) for those convicted of specified sexual offences.[40] This can apply to those convicted of any custodial sentence including

38 Section 250(4)(b) and SI No 648 art 3, and guidance in PC 29/2007, annex A and PSO 6000 chapter 14.

39 See PC 29/2007 paras 20–22. The power to impose such conditions comes from CJCSA 2000 s62: see guidance in PC 115/2001. In non-'critical' cases, electronic monitoring is only available in the pilot areas of Hampshire, Nottinghamshire and West Yorkshire.

40 OMA s28(4) – namely those sexual offences contained in CJA 2003 Sch 15: see appendix D.

life sentences.[41] The power to impose the requirement has not been generally introduced, but is subject to a pilot being conducted and scheduled to conclude on 31 March 2012.[42]

12.26 The standard wording of the polygraph condition is:

> To comply with any instruction given by your supervising officer requiring you to attend for a polygraph session, to participate in polygraph sessions and examinations as instructed by or under the authority of your supervising officer, and to comply with any instruction given to you during a polygraph session by the person conducting the polygraph session.[43]

Setting and varying licence conditions

Responsibility and procedures

12.27 The general rule is that where the Parole Board is responsible for making the decision to release a prisoner, it also has the statutory duty to set the licence conditions. Where release is automatic it is the governor of the releasing prison who has the responsibility, although the governor will not in practice insert any additional conditions beyond the standard unless requested to do so by the prisoner's offender manager.[44] Usually the Parole Board will set conditions at the same time as considering suitability for release. This will be after the prisoner has had disclosure of reports and a chance to make representations. In such circumstances there are unlikely to be concerns over whether licence conditions have been set in a procedurally unfair manner.

12.28 Once the prisoner has been released there is a power to vary licence conditions (see further paras 12.50–12.52 below). The policies on the exercise of this power do not make it clear what procedural safeguards should be put in place before such decisions are made. In practice those on licence are sometimes told of changes to their licence conditions without having been given any warning, disclosure or a chance to make representations.

41 OMA 2007 s28(3).

42 OMA (Commencement No 3) Order 2009 SI No 32; see also PSI 4/2009. The pilot is being run in the West Midlands, West Mercia, Warwickshire, Staffordshire, Lincolnshire, Leicestershire, Derbyshire, Nottinghamshire and Northamptonshire probation areas. A challenge that the imposition of such a condition breached article 8 failed in *C v Secretary of State for Justice* [2009] EWHC 2671 (Admin).

43 PSI 4/2009 para 15.

44 See, for example, PSO 6000 para 14.1.3.

12.29 A decision to vary licence conditions may impose restrictions on family contact, employment or place of residence. Accordingly fairness requires at least a minimum level of disclosure to the offender of the material that is to be put before the decision-maker (either a MAPPA meeting, the releasing governor or the Parole Board) so that representations can be submitted.[45] As noted above such decisions may well interfere with the offender's rights under Article 8 of the Convention. Article 8 also embodies a procedural aspect that requires decision-makers to act fairly[46] and this would also support the necessity for a minimum of disclosure with an opportunity to make representations in this context.[47]

CJA 1991 ACR and CJA 2003 SDS cases

12.30 For CJA 1991 ACR cases (ie sentences of 12 months or more but less than four years imposed in respect of offences committed before 4 April 2005) and CJA 2003 SDS cases (sentences of 12 months or more in respect of offences committed on or after that date) the licence is issued by the individual prison by the governor on behalf of the Secretary of State, who must also approve any additional licence conditions recommended by the Probation Service.[48] There is no Parole Board involvement, as release for these classes of prisoner is automatic.

12.31 If the Probation Service requests any licence conditions not included within the standard or additional conditions set out above, the governor must consult with PPCS, which will have the responsibility for deciding whether any such exceptional licence conditions can be added to the licence.[49]

12.32 Licence conditions can be varied by application to the governor of the releasing prison.[50]

45 By application of the well known principles in *R v Secretary of State for the Home Department ex p Doody* [1994] 1 AC 531, although obviously this principle may be tempered where there is an urgent need to protect the public: see, for example, *R v Chief Constable of the North Wales Police ex p Thorpe* [1999] QB 396, 427–8.

46 *W v UK* (1987) 10 EHRR 29.

47 See, for example, in the context of disclosure of convictions *W v Chief Constable of Northumbria* [2009] EWHC 747 (Admin). See further para 10.56.

48 PC 29/2007 annex C; PSO 6000 chapter 14 para 14.4.

49 PSO 6000 para 14.4.1.

50 PC 29/2007 annex C; PSO 6000 para 14.8.1.

CJA 1991 DCR cases

12.33 Since the coming into force of the relevant sections of the CJIA 2008 DCR prisoners are now treated differently depending on whether they have been convicted of sexual or violent offences contained in Schedule 15 to the CJA 2003. Those not serving sentences for such offences are released automatically. Those who are still have discretionary release at the halfway point decided by the Parole Board (see chapter 5). In keeping with the general rule that it is only where the Board has responsibility for release that it is responsible for determining licence conditions, where prisoners are released automatically their licence conditions will be set by the governor of the releasing prison.[51]

12.34 For DCR prisoners whose offences are contained in Schedule 15 to the CJA 2003, and whose cases fall to be considered by the Board, licence conditions beyond the standard conditions can only be imposed after consultation with the Parole Board.[52] The request for additional conditions should be made by the Probation Service in the report prepared for the parole dossier, and should only be from the set of additional conditions set out above.[53] The Board will set out any recommended conditions in its decision recommending release, and if release is not recommended the decision will confirm whether any additional licence conditions should be imposed at the NPD (when the prisoner is automatically released at the two-thirds point).

12.35 If the prisoner has not applied for parole and it is considered that additional conditions should be imposed, a report can be forwarded to the Parole Board for consideration as to whether such conditions should be imposed.[54] For DCR prisoners serving sentences of less than 15 years, the Board's decision on additional conditions is binding. For those serving 15 or more years, the Board's decision, as with release decisions, is considered by the Secretary of State, who makes the final decision.

12.36 Requests to vary the licence conditions of DCR cases where release is automatic at the halfway point will be made to the governor of the releasing prisoner. The Parole Board does not have to be

51 PSI 17/2008 para 18, which also confirms that it is the responsibility of offender managers to request any additional licence conditions beyond the standard conditions, as in other cases where the governor sets licence conditions.

52 CJA 1991 s37(5) and (6) and PSO 6000 para 14.3.1.

53 PC 29/2007 annex C.

54 See PSO 6000 chapter 6.

involved.[55] However, if the request for variation or amendment of the conditions involves a condition that is not included in the standard list of additional conditions (see above) then this should be referred to the PPCS.[56]

12.37 For DCR prisoners whose release still falls to be considered by the Board because of the nature of their sentence, requests to vary licence conditions by the Probation Service should still be sent to the PPCS, which will ensure that they are forwarded to the Parole Board for consideration.[57]

Extended sentences

12.38 CJA 2003 extended sentence cases, where the sentence was imposed before 14 July 2008, are dealt with in a similar way to DCR cases where the sentence is of 15 years or more, in that additional licence conditions must be approved by the Parole Board but the final decision on which conditions will be added rests with the Secretary of State.[58] In cases where the sentence was imposed on or after 14 July 2008 (and so release is automatic rather than reliant on a decision of the Board) then the imposition and variation of licence conditions will be subject to similar processes as apply for SDS cases.

12.39 With CJA 1991 extended sentences the length of the custodial term, together with the type of offence, is decisive. If it is less than four years, or for longer but not for a sexual or violent offence contained in Schedule 15 to the CJA 2003, the offender is treated as an ACR prisoner for the purpose of the setting of licence conditions. If the sentence is for four or more years and for a Schedule 15 offence, the prisoner is treated as a DCR prisoner convicted of such an offence and additional conditions will be the responsibility of the Board.[59]

Judicial recommendations

12.40 For sentences where release will be under the CJA 2003, the sentencing court can now recommend further conditions 'which in its view should be included in any licence granted to the offender'.[60] Those

55 PC 12/2008 para 11.

56 PSI 17/2008 para 18.

57 PSO 6000 para 14.3.1, and there is a standard form for the probation request see PC 29/2007 annex C.

58 PSO 6000 para 14.7.2.

59 CJA 1991 s44(2).

60 CJA 2003 s238(1).

responsible for issuing licences must have regard to such recommendations, although it is accepted that circumstances may change during the currency of a sentence to such a degree that the recommendation may be no longer relevant, or in fact be counter productive. In such cases the Probation Service will consult with the PPCS to seek authority to omit the judicial recommendation. If the PPCS feels it appropriate to omit the condition, it will inform the sentencing judge of this.[61] If a judicial recommendation as to a licence condition relating to a victim is not to be included, the reasons for this should be explained to the victim.[62]

Effect of recall on licences

12.41 The effect of recall on licences is only relevant to CJA 1991 cases as the SDS licence always lasts until sentence expiry, and indeterminate sentence licences (with the exception of the licence in relation to the indeterminate sentence for public protection) last for life (see below).

12.42 For determinate sentences administered under the CJA 1991 (where the offence was committed before 4 April 2005) the situation is complicated. When the relevant provisions of the CJA 2003 were brought in to force on 4 April 2005 the wording of the relevant commencement order[63] was at best confusing and led to significant litigation. Eventually, although it was clarified that those serving CJA 1991 sentences in the community were liable to be recalled under the provisions of the CJA 2003,[64] the courts confirmed that for those serving CJA 1991 sentences the new provisions did not affect either automatic release dates, or length of licences.[65]

12.43 Where an offender serving a CJA 1991 sentence is recalled before between on or after 4 April 2005 but before 14 July 2008 (the date of the coming into force of the relevant provisions of the CJIA 2008), if the Parole Board does not direct release, there is an automatic entitlement to release at the three-quarter point. Such release is

61 PSO 6000 para 14.9.2; PC 29/2007 para 32.

62 PC 29/2007 para 33.

63 CJA 2003 (Commencement No 8 and Transitional and Saving Provisions) Order 2005 SI No 950 Sch 2.

64 *R (on the application of Buddington) v Secretary of State for the Home Department* [2006] EWCA Civ 280; see further chapter 13.

65 *R (on the application of Stellato) v Secretary of State for the Home Department* [2007] 2 AC 70.

unconditional for those sentenced for offences committed before 30 September 1998,[66] and on licence to sentence expiry for those sentenced for offences committed after that date.[67]

12.44 Recall on or after 14 July 2008 is different. Now all CJA 1991 prisoners are liable to be detained until sentence expiry unless released by the Board, and whenever released the licence lasts until sentence expiry.[68]

12.45 While there is evident unfairness in increasing the proportion of a sentence during which an offender may be subject to licence conditions, it has been held that such changes will not breach article 7 of the ECHR (the prohibition on retrospective penalties).[69] Neither do they interfere with the sentence of the court so as to breach the fair trial provisions of article 6.[70]

Indeterminate sentences

Statutory basis of licence supervision

12.46 All indeterminate sentence prisoners, when their release is directed by the Parole Board, are released on licence.[71] Licences remain in force until the offender's death[72] with the exception of the sentence imposed for public protection under the CJA 2003 (see below). Indeterminate sentence prisoners are placed under a duty to comply with the conditions contained in the licence and the Secretary of State is empowered to make rules relating to supervision.[73]

Responsibility for setting licence conditions

12.47 Although licences for indeterminate sentence prisoners are prepared by the PPCS on behalf of the Secretary of State, conditions can only

66 The date of the coming into force of the CDA 1998; see *Stellato* above.

67 *Gibson v Secretary of State for Justice* [2009] QB 204.

68 CJA 1991 s50A, inserted by the CJIA 2008 and in effect only for recalls from 14 July 2008: CJIA 2008 Sch 27 para 12.

69 *R (on the application of Uttley) v Secretary of State for the Home Department* [2004] UKHL 38.

70 *R (on the application of Poku) v Secretary of State for Justice* [2009] EWHC 1380 (Admin); *R (on the application of Salami and Robinson)* [2009] EWHC 2251 (Admin).

71 C(S)A 1997 s28(5).

72 C(S)A 1997 s31(1).

73 C(S)A 1997 s31(2).

be imposed in accordance with the recommendations of the Parole Board.[74] In practice, lifers are released on licences containing the standard conditions and any additional conditions the Parole Board specifies in its decision directing release.

Contents of life licences – standard conditions

12.48 Although, as noted above, licences must be imposed in accordance with recommendations of the Board, there are seven standard licence conditions that PPCS has indicated should be included in indeterminate licences. These now largely mirror the determinate sentence standard conditions:[75]

1. He/she shall place himself/herself under the supervision of whichever supervising officer is nominated for this purpose from time to time.
2. He/she shall on release report to the supervising officer so nominated, and shall keep in touch with that officer in accordance with that officer's instructions.
3. He/she shall, if his/her supervising officer so requires, receive visits from that officer where the licence holder is living.
4. He/she shall reside only where approved by his/her supervising officer.
5. He/she shall undertake work, including voluntary work, only where approved by his/her supervising officer and shall inform that officer of any change in or loss of such employment.
6. He/she shall not travel outside the United Kingdom without the prior permission of his/her supervising officer.
7. He/she shall be well behaved and not do anything which could undermine the purposes of supervision on licence which are to protect the public, by ensuring that their safety would not be placed at risk, and to secure his/her successful reintegration into the community.

Additional conditions

12.49 These are also imposed in accordance with recommendations of the Board. Although, unlike with determinate sentences, there is no prescribed list of additional conditions, such conditions will have to be lawful and otherwise not disproportionately interfere with the offend-

74 C(S)A 1997 s31(3).
75 See PC 29/2007, para 5.

er's ECHR rights. In practice, the Board will generally only impose additional conditions in line with those approved for recommendation by the Probation Service for determinate sentence prisoners (see paras 12.23–12.24 above). The polygraph condition is also available for life sentences in the areas where it is being piloted (see para 12.25 above).

Variation and cancellation of indeterminate sentence licences

12.50 After release licence conditions can be varied. The process is that the Probation Service should send a request, which has to be endorsed by an assistant chief officer grade, to PPCS. This will be referred to the Parole Board and, if agreed, the PPCS will issue the amended licence.[76] Clearly the offender should normally be given an opportunity to make representations as to any proposed amendment and should be given reasons for decisions (see para 12.28 above).

12.51 Those serving the indeterminate sentence of imprisonment for public protection imposed under the CJA 2003 can, after ten years of supervision in the community, apply to the Parole Board, which has the power to order that the licence ceases to have effect where it is satisfied that it is no longer necessary for the protection of the public.[77]

12.52 In all other cases, the licence lasts until the offender's death. However, consideration may be given to cancelling the supervision element (although this does not affect the offender's liability to recall) of the life licence after a minimum of four years, or ten years for sex offenders. Such cases will be dealt with by application to PPCS, based on reports from the offender manager, that will need to show 'sustained progress' in the community.[78] The supervision requirement can be reimposed if further incidents suggesting this may be necessary come to the attention of the Probation Service.[79] PPCS will need to consult with the Board before varying or cancelling any licence condition.[80]

76 PC 5/2009 para 8.
77 C(S)A 1997 s31A(4).
78 PC 5/2009 para 9.
79 See PSO 4700 para 14.6.
80 C(S)A 1997 s31(3).

CHAPTER 13

Recall to prison

continued

Introduction

13.1 It has always been recognised that the consequences of being returned to prison from a state of liberty will have a greater impact on the offender than a refusal of initial release. Even when release on licence, including for those serving life sentences, was seen purely as a matter of clemency at the discretion of the executive, a distinction was been made between processes to determine initial release, and those applicable to licence revocation.[1] Both under the European Convention on Human Rights (ECHR) and common law it has been recognised that loss of liberty, even where conditional, requires the highest standards of fairness.

13.2 Not all licence breaches will justify a recall to custody, even for those serving determinate sentences. However, there is a distinction between indeterminate and extended sentences on the one hand, where the grounds for recall must have a 'causal link' with the purpose of the sentence to be lawful,[2] and the position with determinate sentence prisoners. The grounds upon which offenders on licence can be recalled to custody will therefore vary according to the sentence that has been imposed.

- For determinate sentence prisoners (not including extended sentence prisoners during the extension period) the Secretary of State has issued directions to the Parole Board as to recall (see para 13.40 below), which set out the factors that the Board is required to consider when determining whether to direct re-release.
- For CJA 1991 extended sentence prisoners, as the sentence is imposed to protect the public from further sexual or violent re-offending, it is only where the offender's behaviour during the extension period demonstrates a substantial risk of further such offending that recall can be justified.[3]
- For CJA 2003 extended sentence prisoners during the extension period, and all indeterminate sentence prisoners, as the sentence is imposed to protect the public from offences of serious harm, it

1 When the Parole Board was created by the CJA 1967, unlike with other decisions, reasons for recall were required to be given to prisoners, and the Home Secretary was bound to accept recommendations for their release: CJA 1967 s62.

2 *Stafford v UK* (2002) 35 EHRR 32; *R (on the application of Sim) v Parole Board* [2003] EWCA Civ 1845.

3 *R (on the application of Sim) v Parole Board* [2003] EWHC 152 (Admin) paras 42–45.

is only where the offender's behaviour demonstrates a substantial risk of such harm that recall can be justified.[4]

- Notwithstanding specific behaviour indicative of risk to the public, those on licence may be recalled if their behaviour suggests that supervision has fundamentally broken down (making the risk unmanageable in the community).[5]

Legal assistance

13.3 Prisoners can be assisted in relation to making written representations to the Board under the CDS advice and assistance scheme. If the initial written representations are rejected then representation can be provided at the oral hearing under the advocacy assistance scheme as with indeterminate sentence cases.

Determinate sentence recalls

Recall procedure

13.4 The procedure adopted in the recall of determinate sentence prisoners has been radically changed in recent years. First there was the decision of the House of Lords in *R v Parole Board ex p Smith and West*,[6] which confirmed that recalled determinate sentence prisoners would commonly be entitled to an oral hearing. For a while after this judgment the Board's practice was to grant an oral hearing in all cases where one was requested. This has now changed and the Board has adopted a policy that prisoners have to make representations as to why fairness requires a hearing (see para 13.36 below). The provisions relating to recall contained in the CJA 2003 were then overhauled from 14 July 2008 by the CJIA 2008 which introduced the fixed-term recall, and amended the Board's powers and duties when making decisions.

The legal framework of recall

13.5 Since 4 April 2005 all determinate sentence prisoners, irrespective of the date the relevant offences were committed, are recalled under

4 *R v Parole Board ex p Watson* [1996] 1 WLR 906.

5 *R (Sim) v Parole Board* [2003] EWHC 152 (Admin) para 44.

6 [2005] UKHL 1. For fuller discussion see chapter 1.

section 254 of the CJA 2003. It is the Secretary of State who has the power to revoke the licence and recall the offender to prison.[7] This marks a change from the previous power to recall under the CJA 1991[8] where, except in urgent cases,[9] the Secretary of State was under a duty to consult the Parole Board before recalling an offender.[10] Now the initial recall decision is entrusted wholly to the executive, a change that has also been made in respect of indeterminate sentence prisoners.

Prisoners recalled on or after 4 April 2005

13.6 The commencement order that brought the CJA 2003 recall provisions for determinate sentence prisoners into force[11] appeared on the one hand to remove the old power to recall under the CJA 1991,[12] but then failed to make those who had been released prior to its coming into force liable to recall at all.[13]

13.7 Following a legal challenge by a prisoner released on licence before 4 April 2005 to his recall after that date[14] a further statutory instrument was brought into force to clarify that section 254 was intended to apply to CJA 1991 prisoners whenever they were released.[15] When the issue was considered by the court it held that, although the draftsman did not 'deserve any prizes' for its wording, the intention of Parliament must have been to allow for the recall of prisoners released prior to 4 April 2005. Therefore the original commencement order should be construed as permitting the recall of this class of prisoner.[16]

7 CJA 2003 s254(1).

8 See CJA 1991 s39(1).

9 CJA 1991 s39(2).

10 And even in urgent cases it was the practice to consult the Board on an extra-statutory basis as soon as possible after the recall.

11 Commencement Order No 8 2005 SI No 950 – see above.

12 SI 2005 No 950 Sch 1 para 44(k).

13 See SI 2005 No 950 Sch 2 para 23 – which applied the CJA 2003 recall power under s254 only to a CJA 1991 prisoner 'who falls to be released *after* 4th April 2005' (emphasis added).

14 *R (on the application of Buddington) v Secretary of State for the Home Department* [2005] EWHC 2198 (QB) – a challenge also to the further effect of the commencement order of making those originally released under the CJA 1991 when recalled liable to detention until sentence expiry – see chapter 12.

15 Criminal Justice Act 2003 (Commencement No 8 and Transitional and Saving Provisions) Order 2005 (Supplementary Provisions) Order 2005 SI No 2122 – in force from 29 July 2005.

16 Criminal Justice Act 2003 (Commencement No 8 and Transitional and Saving Provisions) Order 2005 (Supplementary Provisions) Order 2005 SI No 2122 para 33. The Court of Appeal upheld the decision in [2006] EWCA Civ 280.

13.8 CJA 1991 prisoners who are recalled between 4 April 2005 and 14 July 2008 retain their original automatic release and licence expiry dates. If not released on a referral to the Parole Board they must be released at the three-quarters point of the sentence, unconditionally if their offence was committed before 30 September 1998, and on licence if the offence was committed after that date but before 4 April 2005.[17]

Prisoners recalled on or after 14 July 2008

13.9 Where prisoners have been recalled on or after this date a new framework applies:

- The PPCS considers the Probation Service recommendation for recall and makes a decision as to whether the licence should be revoked and the prisoner recalled to prison.[18]
- Where the sentence is not for a sexual or violent offence and the prisoner has not been recalled previously, the PPCS on behalf of the Secretary of State will make a decision as to whether they should be subject to a fixed-term recall (FTR) of up to 28 days.[19]
- Where not eligible for an FTR the prisoner will be subject to a standard recall. They will remain in prison until sentence expiry unless either the Parole Board or the Secretary of State decide they can be released earlier.[20]
- Extended sentence prisoners are not eligible for FTR, and can only be released prior to sentence expiry where the Parole Board directs.[21]

13.10 The provisions of the CJIA 2008 removed the entitlement of CJA 1991 prisoners to automatic release at the three-quarter point of the sentence, and the right to those convicted of offences committed before 30 September 1998 to unconditional release at that point.[22] Now all determinate sentence prisoners once recalled are liable to be detained

17 See the table on page 76.

18 CJA 2003 s254(1).

19 CJA 2003 ss225A–225B.

20 CJA 2003 s255C – and the application of this regime to CJA 1991 prisoners who previously would have had an entitled to release, either unconditionally or on licence depending on the date of the offence, has been held not to be an unlawful interference with the sentence of the court so as to breach article 6 – *R (on the application of Salami) v Parole Board, R (on the application of Robinson) v Secretary of State for Justice* [2009] EWHC 2251 (Admin).

21 CJA 2003 s255D.

22 CJA 1991 s50A.

until the sentence expiry date. If released earlier the licence similarly is extended to SED.[23]

The recommendation for recall

Fixed-term recall

13.11 In practice it is the supervising probation officer, or offender manager, who will initiate procedures leading to recall. Guidance to the Probation Service highlights the need for probation staff to identify those who may be *eligible* and *suitable* for FTR.[24] The guidance confirms that offenders are *eligible* for FTR unless:[25]

- they are serving any kind of extended sentence;
- they are serving a sentence for an sexual or violent offence listed in Schedule 15 to the CJA 2003;[26]
- they have already been recalled before their automatic release date from home detention curfew or compassionate release; or
- they have already been released after FTR on the same sentence.

13.12 An offender is *suitable* for FTR only where the Secretary of State 'is satisfied that he will not present a risk of serious harm to members of the public if he is released at the end of that [28-day] period'.[27] 'Serious harm' means 'death or serious personal injury, whether physical or psychological'.[28] Probation Service guidance states that no offender should be considered suitable for FTR if assessed as presenting a high or very high risk of harm.[29] The test for suitability for FTR relates to a markedly more serious level of risk to the public than the generalised grounds for recall (see directions to the Board at paras 13.40–13.45 below). So where an offender's behaviour demonstrates a risk of further non-violent offending, such as theft, then they should be considered suitable for FTR if recalled.

23 The CJIA 2008 therefore gave statutory effect to what the Secretary of State argued was the intention when the CJA 2003 was enacted on 4 April 2005, an argument which failed in *Stellato*. *R (on the application of Young) v Secretary of State for Justice* [2009] EWHC 2875 (Admin) confirmed that the new legislation has achieved the intention.

24 PC 14/2008 para 8.

25 CJA 2003 s255A(2); PC 14/2008 para 11.

26 See appendix D.

27 CJA 2003 s255A(5).

28 CJA 2003 s255A(13).

29 PC 14/2008 para 13.

13.13 Where the offender manager decides the offender is eligible for FTR, that they are assessed as either low or medium risk of serious harm at the point of recall, and that this level of risk is not likely to be adversely affected by 28 days in custody, the request for recall report[30] should be completed and forwarded to the PPCS[31] by email within 24 hours of the decision to recall.[32] The PPCS, on behalf of the Secretary of State, makes the decision as to whether the recall will be an FTR.

Standard recall

13.14 Standard recall will be used where the offender is not eligible for FTR for one of the reasons set out in para 13.11 above, or where they pose a high risk of serious harm. Where this is the case the offender manager completes the same request for recall report.[33] Again this should be emailed to PPCS within 24 hours of the decision to recall. The request should be processed by PPCS within 24 hours of receipt.[34] The police have a target of arresting standard recall offenders within 96 hours of the revocation of the licence.

Emergency recall

13.15 Where the probation service believes that there is current evidence that the offender presents 'very high risk of serious harm, or whose supervision has broken down to the point where re-offending is imminent, regardless of the potential for harm to the public posed by that re-offending',[35] an emergency recall should be requested.[36] Again the same report form is used and should be processed by PPCS within two hours of receipt, and the police have a target of arrest of 48 hours from revocation.[37] PPCS has an out of hours rota system for processing emergency recalls in particularly serious cases.

The request for recall report

13.16 There is detailed guidance on the completion of the request for recall report at Annex E of PC 14/2008. This states:

30 PC 14/2008 annex E.
31 PC 14/2008 para15.
32 PI 04/2009.
33 PC 14/2008 annex E.
34 PC 14/2008 paras 22–23.
35 PC 14/2008 annex F.
36 PC 14/2008 para 24.
37 PC14/2008 para 26.

In detailing the breach and its circumstances, you must show the deterioration in behaviour/compliance, which leads you to assess that the risk of serious harm, or re-offending has increased to an unacceptable level. Whilst the seriousness of the breach is a factor, its importance lies in how it demonstrates the breakdown of supervision and increasingly risky behaviour of the offender.

13.17 The Probation Service National Standards 2005[38] stated that breach action could be initiated where there had been 'one unacceptable failure' to comply with licence conditions where appropriate, and if such action is not initiated a formal written warning should be given. This approach clearly drove the increase in recalls. The most recent available guidance to the Probation Service is now contained in the Offender Management National Standards (OMNS) 2007 and makes it clear that recall action in urgent cases must be based on a greater risk to the public.[39] In non-urgent cases a failure to comply with licence supervision should only precipitate recall action where the failure is indicative of:[40]

- a serious, gross, wilful or fundamental refusal to comply or a breakdown of the licence; or
- a significant rise in the risk of serious harm or likelihood of reoffending presented by the offender; or
- in relation to a post-release licence there have already been two written warnings issued in the preceding 12 months.

13.18 Any decision to recall must be endorsed by an assistant chief officer grade.[41]

Where the licensee faces further criminal charges

13.19 Where the licensee has been charged with further offences, the Probation Service guidance suggests that supervising officers should:

explain the behaviour surrounding the charge, and other behaviour/concerns which lead to your assessment and recommendation for recall. It is not enough to state that the good behaviour condition in the licence has been breached by the further charges, which may be dropped at a later stage. Arrest need not always lead to a request for recall. An offender may be arrested, having been in a place at a time

38 See PC 15/2005.

39 OMNS 2007 2f.3.

40 OMNS 2007 2f.4.

41 *Joint National Protocol –Supervision , Revocation and Recall of Offenders Released on Licence*, March 2007, para 8.3; PSO 6000 chapter 7 para 6.4.

when an offence has been committed by others, and there may not be any evidence on which to charge the offender.[42]

13.20 Further alleged offences can create difficulties in advising prisoners as the Parole Board assumes that even if criminal proceedings in respect of fresh allegations have not concluded, it is nevertheless usually possible to consider whether recall is appropriate in light of evidence of the offender's behaviour, short of that relating to the new charges themselves. It has been held that the mere fact of a further charge and pending prosecution cannot on its own justify recall on the basis of a risk of reoffending[43] but it is likely to be the case that the Board will need to consider the evidence upon which the new charges are based in order to come to a proper assessment of risk.[44] Where the new charge does have a bearing on the risk assessment it is difficult to see how the Board can fairly deal with it in advance of the criminal trial without prejudicing the prosecution.

13.21 Although agreeing to a deferral of the Parole Board hearing pending the outcome of the prosecution will inevitably lead to delay, this course may be advisable where a decision of the Board upholding the recall will potentially result in long periods of further detention.

13.22 If the Board does uphold recall in advance of the hearing of any further charges by the criminal courts, and the prisoner is subsequently found not guilty, then the Secretary of State retains the discretion to rerefer the original recall decision to the Board where he considers that there is a realistic prospect that a different view may be taken by the Board.[45] The Prison and Probation Services, the police and the Home Office have agreed a joint protocol relating to the supervision and recall of offenders,[46] which states that prosecutions should not be discontinued purely because an offender has been recalled to custody and in fact the commission of an offence while on licence 'is a significant public interest factor in support of a charge'.[47]

42 PC 14/2008 annex F.

43 *R (on the application of Broadbent) v Parole Board* [2005] EWHC 1207 (Admin) para 26.

44 Ibid, para 29; *R (on the application of Brooks) v Parole Board* [2004] EWCA Civ 80.

45 *R (on the application of Francis and Clarke) v Secretary of State for the Home Department* [2004] EWHC 2143 (Admin) para 49.

46 Last revised in March 2007 and most recently appended to PI 04/2009.

47 National Protocol, para 8.7.

Consideration of the recall request by the PPCS

13.23 The decision as to whether to recall the offender, and whether this will be an FTR lies with the PPCS. As noted above the decision as to whether to recall will be made by the PPCS within 24 hours of the receipt of the report from the probation service, or two hours in emergency cases.[48]

13.24 If PPCS officials make the decision to recall, on either an FTR or standard recall, the revocation order will be sent to:[49]

- the supervising probation officer, or equivalent;
- New Scotland Yard for entry onto the police national computer;
- the nominated police force communication centre;
- the releasing/holding prison.

13.25 Once the revocation has been issued, if the offender is not already in custody (for example, having been recalled following arrest for a new offence) he/she is deemed to be 'unlawfully at large' until returned to prison.[50] The offender can then be arrested without warrant.[51] The National Protocol states that the police 'will then take steps to ensure the speedy arrest of the individual'.[52] Time spent unlawfully at large is not then taken into account when calculating release dates and the eventual sentence expiry date.[53] The offender does not need to be aware of the revocation of licence to be unlawfully at large.[54] Following arrest, recalled offenders will be taken to the nearest remand prison.[55]

13.26 The fact that the executive decision to recall will be referred to the Board means that it will only be in exceptional cases that the Administrative Court will review the initial recall decision.[56] This is because the referral to the Board is the appropriate remedy for the recall decision, and because the Board 'is in a better position than the court to

48 See also PSO 6000 chapter 7 para 6.2. This chapter of the PSO was radically amended by PSI 29/2008 on the coming into force of the relevant sections of the CJIA 2008.

49 PSO 6000 chapter 7 para 7.1.

50 CJA 2003 s254(6).

51 Prison Act 1952 s49(1).

52 Para 9.3.

53 Prison Act 1952 s49(2) – see guidance in PSO 6650 chapter 7.

54 *R (on the application of S) v Secretary of State for the Home Department* [2003] EWCA Civ 426.

55 PSO 6000 chapter 7 para 8.1.

56 In *Gulliver* (see footnote 89 below) Sir Igor Judge raised the possibility of a revocation decision-making process 'so subverted' that judicial review or habeas corpus proceedings may be appropriate as the Board would not be able to provide an adequate remedy: para 45.

assess where the balance should lie between, on the one hand, the risk to the public, and, on the other, the interests of the prisoner'.[57]

13.27 The courts have made a distinction between the recall to prison and the actual return to prison. Accordingly, in situations where the reference to the Parole Board is dependent on the making of representations, such representations can be made before the prisoner is physically back in custody. Reliance on this distinction may be appropriate in cases where the decision to recall is clearly erroneous.[58]

After the return to prison

13.28 As soon as a prison receives a recalled prisoner it must notify the PPCS on a prescribed form.[59] The prisoner should be informed of the reasons for the revocation of licence and of the right to make representations.[60] In FTR cases the prisoner must be informed that he will be released on licence at the end of the 28-day period.[61] PPCS should issue a representations pack within 24 hours of receipt of the notification that the prisoner has arrived back in prison. The prison should then immediately supply the pack to the prisoner, making sure that the process for making representations is understood.[62]

Referral to the Parole Board

13.29 Prior to the coming into force of the relevant sections of the CJIA 2008 on 14 July 2008 all determinate sentence prisoners had their cases referred to the Parole Board,[63] and only the Board could direct the release of the prisoner before any automatic release date. This

57 *R (on the application of Hare) v Secretary of State for the Home Department* [2003] EWHC 3336 (Admin); see also *R (on the application of Biggs) v Secretary of State for the Home Department* [2002] EWHC 1012 (Admin), which also confirmed that [PPCS] is entitled to rely on the probation report in making the decision to recall and generally is not required to make further inquiries as to the facts behind the recommendation.

58 *Roberts v Secretary of State for the Home Department* [2006] 1 WLR 843. This case also confirmed that at the time it was decided that in such cases the Secretary of State had a power to decide whether to rescind a revocation decision in light of such representations. This aspect of the case is now irrelevant as in recalls after 14 July 2008 the Secretary of State now has a statutory power to re-release.

59 At PSO 6000 chapter 7 appendix A.

60 CJA 2003 s254(2); PSO 6000 chapter 7 para 10.1.

61 CJA 2003 s225B(1)(a).

62 PSO 6000 chapter 7 para 10.2.

63 This provision in CJA 2003 s254(3) was removed by the CJIA 2008.

position has now changed except for all types of extended sentence prisoners (see para 13.54 below).

13.30 Whether the recall is an FTR or standard recall in determinate sentence cases the Secretary of State now has a power to re-release recalled prisoners on licence at any time, where satisfied that 'it is not necessary for the protection of the public that he should remain in prison'.[64]

13.31 In FTR cases the recall is only referred to the Parole Board if the prisoner makes representations after receiving the recall pack.[65] If the Board does not have time to consider the case within the 28-day period the prisoner must be released on licence in any event.[66] If the Parole Board is able to consider the case in time, where it recommends release this decision is binding on the Secretary of State.[67] All prisoners, including those serving CJA 1991 sentences are released on licence to sentence expiry from FTR.[68] Although in principle fairness may require the Board to consider whether an oral hearing is necessary before making a decision to refuse to release a prisoner on an FTR, it is difficult in practical terms to see how the Board would be able to manage this administratively before the automatic release date.

13.32 In standard recall cases the PPCS must refer the case to the Parole Board when the prisoner makes representations, or where no representations are made after he/she has been back in prison for more than 28 days.[69]

Parole Board process – standard recall

13.33 In standard recall cases where the prisoner makes representations, or more than 28 days have elapsed since the prisoner has been returned to prison, the PPCS refers the case to the Board. The recall pack and any further reports that are submitted to the Parole Board should be disclosed to the prisoner unless the standard grounds for withholding information[70] apply.[71]

64 CJA 2003 ss225B and 225C.
65 CJA 2003 s255B(4).
66 CJA 2003 s255B(1)(b); PSO 6000 chapter 7 para 12.7.
67 CJA 2003 s255B(5).
68 CJA 1991 s50A; PSO 6000 chapter 7 para 12.9.
69 CJA 2003 s255C(4).
70 See para 6.10.
71 PSO 6000 chapter 6 para 14.3.

13.34 There is a timetable for the determination of standard recalls. As the timetable shows, the procedure is that the Board initially considers the case on the papers. If prisoners require the assistance of a legal representative in the process it is important that they contact one immediately on return to prison. The representative will then be able to request a copy of the recall pack from the relevant PPCS casework section and assist in submitting the representations to the Board. Clearly where the circumstances of the recall involve disputed facts, representatives may need time to obtain witness or other evidence. In such cases a request should be put to the Board that a final decision is not made until there has been a proper opportunity to make representations.

13.35 After recall the offender manager is required to produce a further report, the review for re-release by the PPCS/Parole Board.[72] The purpose of this form is to 'enable the PPCS and the Parole Board, at either paper or oral hearing, to make an informed decision on the risk presented by the offender, having in mind any representations made by the offender against recall, and whether or not the offender should be released'.[73] In determinate sentence recall cases the report must be sent to PPCS within 14 days of the return to custody[74] and it should contain:[75]

- a review of the assessments;
- any further information relevant to the offender's risk;
- a risk management/sentence plan;
- a clear recommendation on release based on the evidence and the offender manager's judgment on the offender's manageability in the community.

Timetable for consideration of standard determinate sentence recall[76]

Day 1 Return to custody of recalled prisoner. Notification to PPU by establishment of receipt of recalled prisoner. PPCS issues recall dossier to establishment. PPCS notifies supervising probation officer of return to custody of prisoner, and gives provisional panel date for review by Parole Board. The parole clerk must ensure the dossier is served on the prisoner immediately and that they understand that they have a right to make representations to the Parole Board.

72 The form is at PC 14/2008 annex H.
73 PC 14/2008 annex F.
74 PC 14/2008 para 49.
75 PC 14/2008 para 50.
76 From PSO 6000 chapter 7, as amended by PSI 29/2008.

The establishment has 5 working days in which to confirm to PPCS whether the prisoner intends to make representations, and to advise of legal representative details.

Day 5 Annex A [prisoner's intention to make representations] in recall dossier to be returned to PPCS.

Day 14 Prisoner's representations submitted to PPCS. Report for Review submitted to PPCS by the Probation Service, and simultaneously to the establishment, for disclosure to the prisoner. Report for Review and representations to be added to the recall dossier by PPCS and the complete dossier is sent to the Parole Board.

Day 19 Any additional/late representations made by the prisoner in response to the Report for Review must be submitted to PPCS by no later than 10.00 am on day 19.

Day 20 Parole Board Panel sits. PPCS notified of the outcome and the result is notified to establishment and Probation Service. Establishment notifies the prisoner; where the Board recommends release, the establishment must put arrangements in place to give effect to the recommendation.

Oral hearings

13.36 Although the decision of the House of Lords in *Smith and West* did not suggest that fairness would *always* require the Board to consider determinate sentence recall cases at an oral hearing,[77] the immediate response of the Board was to offer one whenever requested by the prisoner. Where an oral hearing is held for normal determinate sentence recalls (other than extended sentences) the Board's practice is for this to be before a single member. The provision of oral hearings in all cases obviously put an additional strain on the Board's resources. This led to a change of policy from February 2007:[78]

> We have taken legal advice and the Parole Board is now in a position to implement the judgement more strictly in accordance with their Lordships' comments. There will be no prejudice to those whose reasons for requesting an oral hearing are genuinely in line with the judgement and they will continue to receive one, time permitting.
>
> With immediate effect, therefore, the Parole Board will require reasons from the prisoner when applying for an oral hearing. These will be considered on a case by case basis and an oral hearing will not be granted simply because the prisoner asks for one. Applications will

77 See para 13.4.

78 www.paroleboard.gov.uk/policy_and_guidance/smith_and_west/.

be granted only where it appears to the Parole Board that a hearing is necessary and falls within the ambit of the House of Lords' ruling.

13.37 Clearly prisoners and their representatives when submitting written representations in the recall process should give consideration as to whether fairness requires an oral hearing. If so, the representations should state that the Board should not make a final decision to refuse release without convening one. The relevant extracts from the *Smith and West* decision are set out earlier in this book[79] and should be consulted when considering the content of such representations. The most obvious cases are where important facts going to the assessment of risk are in dispute, or where there is conflicting professional or expert opinion, or a need to question further the probation officer who recommended the recall.

Procedure and the Parole Board Rules

13.38 The PBR 2004 as amended do not apply to recalled determinate sentence prisoners, although the Board treat such recalls in a similar way, with some modifications. The main difference is that recall hearings in relation to determinate sentence prisoners (not including those serving extended sentences) will be heard by a single member rather than a panel of three. Even though the PBR do not apply, prisoners and their representatives should approach hearings in the same way as for indeterminate sentence cases. For example, where needed, requests for directions as to further disclosure or for attendance of witnesses should be sought.

13.39 The recall hearing for a determinate sentence prisoner will be largely the same in terms of procedure as those for lifers, and similar considerations will apply in terms of preparation and evidence, bearing in mind the different test for release that will apply (see below). The Secretary of State can be represented at the hearing although this is far less common than at recall hearings for extended sentence and indeterminate sentenced prisoners.

The test applied when considering recall

13.40 In the recall of normal determinate sentence prisoners the test for release does not rely on risk of commission of offences of a particular type (unlike with extended and indeterminate sentence prisoners: see below). The matters to be considered by the Board when considering

79 See para 1.46.

whether to re-release are contained in the statutory directions given by the Secretary of State.[80] Whenever giving directions to the Board the Secretary of State is required to have regard to:

- the need to protect the public from serious harm from offenders; and
- the desirability of preventing the commission by them of further offences and of securing their rehabilitation.[81]

13.41 Such directions are issued periodically as the statutory framework changes. However, strangely, at the time of writing it is unclear as to which are the appropriate directions. When the relevant sections of the CJA 2003 came into force in April 2005 the Secretary of State issued directions on recall of determinate sentence prisoners.[82] When the relevant parts of the CJIA 2008, which significantly altered the Board's powers in respect of recalls from 14 July 2008, came into force new directions were contained in an annex to PSI 29/2008.[83] These clarified, for example, that in considering recalls from that date the Board would no longer be responsible for setting the date of future reviews and that the Board would also need to consider the position of FTR cases where representations have been made. However, it seems that these were not at that time formally served on the Board and, at the date of writing, still have not been. Although the two sets of directions do have significant differences, both suggest that the Board needs to consider risk to the public in terms of the likelihood of the prisoner reoffending and whether any risk management plan prepared by the Probation Service is sufficient to manage such risk. Until the new directions are formally served on the Board (and it is possible that they will be amended again before being served) then it is the 2005 directions that apply.

13.42 Both the 2005 and 2008 directions have a different emphasis to those in force previously,[84] which indicated that the type of reoffending that might justify recall needed to involve a risk to public safety, and also suggested that *any* licence breaches could justify recall. By contrast, the 2005 directions state that when determining whether to release a prisoner the Board 'should satisfy itself that the prisoner presents an acceptable risk to public safety and that adequate risk

80 Now under CJA 2003 s239(6).

81 CJA 2003 s239(6)(a)–(b).

82 See appendix F.

83 See appendix F. It is understood that the directions were planned to be served in December 2009.

84 From 2002 to 2005.

management arrangements are in place', and elsewhere 'the assumption is that the Parole Board will seek to re-release the prisoner or set a future release date in all cases where it is satisfied that the risk can be safely managed in the community'. The 2008 directions require the Board to consider, among other matters, 'whether the risk management plan is adequate to manage effectively any potential risk of serious harm or of imminent re-offending'. This change of emphasis in the new directions means that cases involving challenges to recalls under the old regime should be treated with caution.[85]

13.43 In deciding whether any developments since release justify recall, the Board is not solely concerned with examining the reasons given by the PPCS for making the recall decision.[86] Although when determinate sentence prisoners are released automatically there does not have to be an assessment by the Board that risk has increased since the initial release to justify recall (as there has to be with lifers, or those previously released on the Board's recommendation), it would seem to be implicit in the statutory scheme that there has to be some further behaviour by the offender, or new information, that gives rise to concern.[87] This is also reflected in current Probation Service guidance.[88] It is, however, now clear that even where the Board considers that the facts leading to recall involved no breach of licence conditions, if on consideration of all the material before it at the time it comes to make its decision it considers that the prisoner poses an unacceptable risk, then it is entitled to refuse to recommend release.[89]

85 For example, *R (on the application of Morecock) v Parole Board* [2004] EWHC (Admin), where the court accepted that recall could be justified where there was no risk to public safety, and *R (on the application of Buxton) v Parole Board* [2004] EWHC 1930 (Admin), which held that in deciding whether there was an 'unacceptable' risk the Board was not required to balance compassionate factors in the prisoner's favour, if these were not relevant to the level of assessed risk. It also held that the Board did not have to consider whether recall would breach the prisoner's Convention rights under articles 3 and 8.

86 See *R (on the application of Jackson) v Parole Board* [2003] EWHC 2437 (Admin), although compare with *Rodgers v Brixton Prison Governor* [2003] EWHC 1923 (Admin), where a recall was held invalid for failing to give the right reasons at the right time.

87 *R (on the application of Irving) v Parole Board* [2004] EWHC 2863 (Admin). See also comments of Sedley LJ in *R (on the application of West) v Parole Board* [2002] EWCA Civ 1641 para 43 that recall 'in the case of a short-term prisoner ... results from an assessment of risk to the public in the light of new developments; in the case of the discretionary release of a long-term prisoner it represents a revision in the light of developments of the Board's earlier assessment of risk'.

88 See paras 13.17 above.

89 *R (on the application of Gulliver) v Parole Board* [2007] EWCA Civ 1386.

13.44 The courts have also suggested that there is a distinction to be drawn between the statutory period during which an offender is liable to recall, and the obligation to adhere to the requirements of supervision. In *Re Rodgers*[90] the offender had wrongly been informed that his licence would expire before the statutory date. While this did not affect the liability to recall on the basis of risk to the public, it did render unlawful a decision to recall purely for failing to comply with supervision requirements.

13.45 The applicable test in extended sentence cases is dealt with below.[91]

The Parole Board decision

Recalls before 14 July 2008

13.46 Where the recall pre-dates relevant provisions of the CJIA 2008 coming into force, if the Board does not recommend immediate release,[92] it has the following options where there are more than 12 months to serve before the automatic release date:

- it must either fix a future date for the prisoner's release on licence;[93] or
- fix a date for the prisoner's next review by the Board,[94] which must be no more than 12 months from the Board's decision.[95] At subsequent reviews the Board has the same range of powers as on the first referral.[96]

13.47 Although it is unlikely that there are any such prisoners still awaiting the first consideration of their case by the Board, there will be determinate sentence prisoners in the system whose recall pre-dated 14 July 2008. The responsibility for setting the further review dates for such prisoners therefore still remains with the Board.

13.48 It is also important to remember that where recall does pre-date 14 July 2008 that prisoners sentenced to offences committed prior to 4 April 2005 will retain their entitlement to automatic release at the three-quarter point, unconditionally where the offence was

90 [2003] All ER (D) 156 (Mar).

91 See paras 13.54–13.59.

92 Which is binding on the Secretary of State: CJA 2003 s254(4).

93 CJA 2003 s256(1)(a) which must be given effect to by the Home Secretary – s256(4).

94 CJA 2003 s256(1)(b).

95 CJA 2003 s256(2).

96 CJA 2003 s256(5).

committed before 30 September 1998, on licence if afterwards.[97] This includes those DCR prisoners given automatic release on or after 9 June 2008, but recalled *before* the new recall provisions came into force on 14 July 2008.[98]

Recalls on or after 14 July 2008

13.49 In a standard recall where the Board recommends immediate release on licence, the Secretary of State must give effect to the recommendation.[99] As with an FTR the Secretary of State also retains a new separate power from 14 July 2008[100] to release a recalled prisoner on licence at any time.[101] Where the recall is on or after 14 July 2008, if the Board does not recommend immediate release, it must:

- fix a future date for the prisoner's release on licence, which must not be any later than 12 months from the decision;[102] or
- 'determine the reference by making no recommendation for release'.[103]

13.50 Accordingly, where the Board refuses to release the prisoner it no longer decides when the next review should take place. Since the changes brought into effect by the CJIA 2008 this power has reverted to the Secretary of State, who must refer the prisoner's case back to the Board no later than 12 months after the first decision.[104] The Board does have a power to recommend that a referral should be made.[105] Where a referral is made the Board has similar powers as on the initial recall referral, that is either recommending immediate release, release at a future date (both of which are binding on the Secretary of State[106]), or making no recommendation.[107] Where there is no recommendation for release, the need for further reviews at no more than yearly intervals is continued.[108]

97 See the guidance at paras 16.1–16.14 of PSI 29/2008.
98 Paras 17.1–17.4 of PSI 29/2008.
99 CJA 2003 s255C(5).
100 CJA 2003 s255C(2).
101 See para 12.44 above.
102 CJA 2003 s256(1)(a) and 256(2) as amended.
103 CJA 2003 s256(1)(b).
104 CJA 2003 s256A(1) – and a referral can be made at any time prior to the 12-month anniversary: s256A(2).
105 CJA 2003 s256A(3).
106 CJA 2003 s256A(5).
107 CJA 2003 s256A(4).
108 CJA 2003 s256A(1).

Release on HDC and recall

13.51 As noted above the Parole Board does not play a role in considering the recall of HDC prisoners recalled in relation to the tagging conditions.[109] The CJA 1991 provides that where a prisoner serving a sentence imposed for an offence committed before 4 April 2005 is released on HDC, where the curfew condition is breached, or where electronic monitoring is no longer possible, the offender can be recalled solely in relation to the curfew condition.[110] This provision is preserved for HDC recalls after 4 April 2005 for CJA 1991 cases.[111] In these circumstances the recall is reviewed by the Secretary of State[112] and, if upheld, the prisoner is released at the normal automatic release date.[113] Release is on licence to the original three-quarter point of the sentence.[114]

13.52 If the offender's behaviour during the HDC licence period was in breach of other licence conditions, recall can be effected in the normal way[115] and the recall referred to the Parole Board in accordance with the procedure outlined above.

13.53 The drafting of the CJA 2003 is confusing in that the power to recall those on HDC licence where the offence dates from 4 April 2005 appears to relate to failure to comply with 'any condition' in the licence,[116] not just the curfew condition. This wording raised an issue as to whether the Secretary of State also had the power to recall those on HDC under the general section 254 powers. If not, it would have had the bizarre effect of requiring him to recall those on HDC, even where the grounds raised serious public safety concerns, under provisions that would then necessitate automatic release at the normal halfway point.[117] The courts confirmed that both powers of recall exist.[118] The position under the CJA 2003 is, therefore, as in CJA 1991 cases, to enable those on HDC both to be recalled on grounds

109 See chapter 5.

110 CJA 1991 s38A.

111 See Criminal Justice Act 2003 (Commencement No 8 and Transitional and Saving Provisions) Order 2005 SI No 950 Sch 2 para 19, and this is of course the only ground of recall for those serving sentences of under 12 months.

112 CJA 1991 s38A(3).

113 CJA 1991 s33A.

114 CJA 1991 s37(1).

115 Now under CJA 2003 s254.

116 CJA 2003 s255(1)(a).

117 CJA 2003 s244.

118 *R (on the application of Ramsden and Naylor) v Secretary of State for the Home Department* [2006] EWHC 3502 (Admin).

relating to the curfew condition (which will not affect re-release at the halfway point of the sentence) and for other licence breaches (which will allow detention beyond that point and a review by the Board).[119]

Recall of extended sentence prisoners

Article 5 and extended sentences

13.54 From 4 April 2005 all extended sentence offenders (under both the CJA 1991 and 2003) are subject to the same statutory framework of recall as other determinate sentence prisoners.[120] This is subject to two qualifications. Firstly they are not eligible for FTR, and secondly must in all circumstances have their cases referred to the Board.[121] Any recommendation to release is binding on the Secretary of State.[122] Similarly extended sentence prisoners are also entitled to at least annual reviews where not released on the initial referral.[123]

13.55 However, there are important differences in how the Board has to approach these recalls. This is because the extended sentence is not like a normal determinate sentence, but is rather a hybrid between a determinate and indeterminate sentence.

13.56 The extension period that follows the custodial term is not imposed as punishment, and the statutory presumption is that it will be served in the community (as the extension period begins at what would otherwise be the LED for CJA 1991 cases, and at the end of the custodial period in CJA 2003 cases). As the extension period is purely preventative, the legality of detention during it requires the supervision of a court-like body under article 5(4) of the Convention, as the degree to which an offender poses a risk to the public is clearly susceptible to change. Without such supervision there is a risk of arbitrary detention, as whether custody is actually necessary to protect the public during the extension period cannot be anticipated by the sentencing court.[124]

13.57 As article 5 applies to the recall of extended sentence prisoners during the extension period, there must be a causal link between the

119 See PSO 6000 chapter 7 para 4.9, which proceeds on this basis.
120 CJA 2003 s254.
121 CJA 2003 s255D.
122 CJA 2003 s255D(2).
123 CJA 2003 s256.
124 *R (Sim) v Parole Board* [2004] 2 WLR 1170.

grounds for recall and the imposition of the sentence. This gives rise to differing tests the Board must apply when considering CJA 1991 cases as against CJA 2003 cases. Extended sentences imposed for offences committed before 4 April 2005 can be imposed for sexual and violent offences where the court is satisfied that the licence period applicable to what would be the commensurate sentence is inadequate to prevent the commission of further offences and to secure rehabilitation.[125] A CJA 1991 extended sentence prisoner's recall can only be in accordance with article 5 by reference to a risk that further sexual or violent offences may be committed.[126]

13.58 By contrast, the CJA 2003 extended sentence is only imposed where the sentencing court makes a finding that the offender poses a risk of 'serious harm'.[127] In these cases the test on recall is therefore a 'serious harm' one as with the indeterminate sentences. Further, recall may be justified where the risk has become unmanageable in the community.

13.59 An important distinction between extended sentences and indeterminate sentences is that, as noted above, the former are released automatically at the end of the custodial period. This means that the Board must also approach these recalls on the basis that the 'default position' is the offender's liberty, and so must be positively satisfied that detention is necessary to protect the public.[128]

13.60 If extended sentence prisoners are released at the first opportunity by the Board's recommendation (halfway through the custodial term) then they may be on licence for some time before the extension period begins, and so there may be recalls of extended sentence prisoners where the Board is entitled to apply the same test as for other determinate sentence prisoners. In practical terms it may be difficult to apply different tests for recalled extended sentence prisoners depending on when they were recalled. The Board's practice in relation to CJA 1991 cases appears to have been to apply the *Sim* test even if at the date of hearing the custodial term had not expired.

13.61 However, this is not evident from the guidance in PSO 6000, which suggests that in extended sentence recall cases the Board is to apply the same directions as in normal determinate sentence

125 PCC(S)A 2000 s85.

126 *R (Sim) v Parole Board* [2003] EWHC 152 (Admin) para 44.

127 CJA 2003 ss227(1)(b), 228(1)(b).

128 *R (Sim) v Parole Board* [2004] 2 WLR 1170 para 51 where the Court of Appeal upheld a Human Rights Act 1998 s3 construction of the statutory test to give this effect.

cases.[129] This is also evident by the PPCS practice of including a set of the directions in dossiers for extended sentence prisoners. This is misleading for cases involving recalls or detention during the extension period for the reasons outlined above, and the Board should be reminded of this when considering cases.[130]

Extended sentences and the Parole Board Rules

13.62 The Parole Board Rules when amended in 2009 were not expressed as covering the recall of determinate or extended sentence prisoners recalled under the 2003 provisions.[131] The Board will consider the case initially on the papers and, in light of any representations (see the procedure above), will determine whether an oral hearing is required. Where the Board decide that an oral hearing is required then the case will follow a timetable similar to that that applies to lifers[132] (see para 13.80 below). PBR r3 permits panels at oral hearings to consist of 1–3 members. The Secretary of State will normally be represented at the recall hearing by a PPA from the PPCS. Oral recall hearings for extended sentence prisoners were given first priority by the Board when listing, as with indeterminate sentence recalls.[133]

Further annual reviews

13.63 If the Parole Board does not direct release there is an entitlement to further reviews at least annually as with other determinate sentence cases[134] if there is sufficient time before the automatic release date (at the end of the extension period for CJA 1991 cases, and at sentence expiry for CJA 2003 cases). The process should begin 26 weeks after the Board's confirmation of the initial recall with the preparation of the dossier.[135] The practice of the Parole Board is no longer automatically

129 PSO 6000 para 8.6.2.

130 The Board's own bench book does clarify that extended sentences are subject to a different test for release.

131 PBR 2(1).

132 See *ICM oral hearings general guidance*, Parole Board, July 2008, Part 6.

133 Parole Board, *Oral Hearing listing prioritisation framework*, March 2009, www.paroleboard.gov.uk/policy_and_guidance/oral_hearing_listing_prioritisation_framework/ – although in November 2009 this policy was amended to give priority to 'due date' of hearing, whatever the type of referral.

134 See para 13.50 above.

135 PSO 6000 para 8.9.1.

to hold oral hearings at the annual reviews but to require the prisoner to give reasons as to why their case should not be considered on the papers when making initial representations. Where it does decide to hold an oral hearing the timetable from that decision will be similar to that which applies to recalls.[136]

Recalls and 'return to custody' orders

13.64 Those subject to the provisions of the CJA 1991 (including those serving sentences of less than 12 months for offences committed on or after 4 April 2005)[137] remain 'at risk' of being ordered to return to prison on sentencing for a new offence committed before the sentence expiry date of the first sentence, to a maximum of the period between the commission of the new offence and the sentence expiry of the first.[138] This is a power separate to the recall provisions and the use of one does not preclude the other. However, because of the possible severity of the impact on the prisoner, it has been held that where a prisoner has been recalled, the sentencing court should take this into account when deciding whether and for how long to order a return to prison, and similarly that any order to return should be a relevant factor in deciding whether to recall.[139] Such return to custody orders, however, are not available for DCR prisoners released automatically on licence to SED at the halfway point, as they are treated as if their licence was imposed under the CJA 2003.[140]

The recall of those serving indeterminate sentences

13.65 In the year 2008–09 there were 1,646 life or indeterminate sentenced prisoners under active supervision in the community. Of these 89 were recalled during that year, or 5.4 per cent – a slight reduction on the previous years figures.[141]

136 *ICM oral hearings general guidance*, Part 6.

137 Criminal Justice Act 2003 (Commencement No 8 and Transitional and Saving Provisions) Order 2005 SI No 950 Sch 2 para 29.

138 PCC(S)A 2000 s116.

139 *R (on the application of Akhtar (T'Herah)) v Secretary of State for the Home Department* [2001] EWHC 38 (Admin).

140 PSI 17/2008 para 20.

141 *Parole Board annual report* 2008–09.

The decision to recall

13.66 The PPCS, on behalf of the Secretary of State, is given the power revoke the licence and recall those serving indeterminate sentences in the community.[142] The CJIA 2008 from 14 July 2008 removed the statutory provisions that provided the power to the Board to recommend whether lifers should be recalled in non-urgent cases. Recall for lifers is now always solely a decision of the executive as with determinate sentence cases. All recall cases must now be referred to the Parole Board.[143]

13.67 There used to be an extra-statutory process in urgent cases of referring the decision to the Board for a review, before the 'formal', statutory referral process that leads to an oral hearing is activated (see below). Again this was not a process the lifer played a part in. If as a result of this referral the Board recommended release such a recommendation was not binding on the Secretary of State, unlike a direction under the formal referral process.[144]

13.68 When an indeterminate sentence prisoner is recalled, the Board is required in accordance with article 5(4) to consider whether the detention is lawful. The procedure whereby the executive makes the decision to recall without any judicial input, and then refers the matter to the Board for review, does not breach article 5.[145]

13.69 The process leading to recall is similar to determinate sentence cases (see above). The Probation Service are required to complete the same request for recall report[146] and send it to the PPCS, and subsequently the review of release form, although this must be sent within four weeks, rather than 14 days, of the return to custody.[147] The differences are that in indeterminate cases all recall requests are treated as urgent, and probation officers are reminded that recall requires there to be an unacceptable risk of commission of offences leading to serious harm.[148]

142 Crime (Sentences) Act (C(S)A) 1997 s32(1).

143 C(S)A 1997 s32(4).

144 *R v Secretary of State for the Home Department ex p Cummings* [2001] EWCA Civ 45, CA, unreported. Further, this extra-statutory role in the executive decision to recall has been held not compromise the Board's impartiality when considering the formal referral: *R v Parole Board ex p Watson* [1996] 1 WLR 906.

145 *R (on the application of Hirst) v Secretary of State for the Home Department* [2006] EWCA Civ 945, which rejected the contention that article 5(4) required greater judicial supervision of the decision to recall itself.

146 At PC 14/2008 annex E.

147 PC 14/2008 paras 64–68.

148 Ibid, para 64.

Further criminal charges/prosecution

13.70 The comments on further criminal charges in relation to determinate sentences[149] also apply to indeterminate sentences. There is a real risk that an approach that endeavours to ignore a further charge, while purporting to make an assessment of risk based upon the behaviour surrounding it, will have unfair results (and may result in a finding that is implicitly taken as a finding of guilt whatever subsequently occurs in relation to the prosecution of the criminal charge). While individual cases may be different, it will often be advisable to seek a deferral pending the disposal of the criminal charge.

The effect of recall

13.71 Once the licence has been revoked, the offender is unlawfully at large until returned to custody.[150] On arrest the offender will be returned to the nearest local prison.[151] Whether the prisoner remains at the local prison or is transferred elsewhere pending the review will depend upon the outcome of the local prison's liaison with the PPCS as to the suitable allocation.[152]

Referral to the Board

13.72 The recalled prisoner has to be informed of reasons for the recall and of the right to make representations to the Parole Board.[153] Reasons must be given promptly.[154] The statute previously stated that it was only where prisoners made representations that their case was referred to the Board. In fact the practice was always to refer. From 14 July 2009 the Crime (Sentences) Act has been amended to clarify that recalled lifers' cases are always referred to the Board.[155]

149 See 13.19 above.

150 C(S)A 1997 s32(6).

151 Joint National Protocol, para 9.6.

152 PSI 26/2006 para 37.

153 C(S)A 1997 s32(3).

154 *Hirst* (note 145 above) held that the duty in article 5(2) was also applicable in this context and that a failure to give reasons for eight days breached this requirement.

155 C(S)A 1997 s32(4).

The test for release

13.73 Once the recall is referred to the Parole Board, it has the power to direct the prisoner's release and the Secretary of State has to give effect to that direction.[156] The test for release on recall is the same as for initial release and so the Board will be considering whether the circumstances leading to recall show that the prisoner poses a substantial risk of committing further offences of serious harm.[157]

13.74 The Board in applying this test on recall is not solely bound to consider the validity of the reasons given by the Secretary of State for recall. For example, the Board can uphold a recall, not for the reasons given in the revocation decision, but because of other behaviour that comes to light before the hearing. As those serving indeterminate sentences will previously have satisfied the Board that they were eligible for release, there must be relevant new material to justify the reconsideration of the risk they pose to the public before they can be recalled.[158] If there is no new information of concern and the original reasons for recall are held to be invalid, this would mean that the Board would not lawfully be able to uphold the recall.

13.75 While risk to the public is the issue, if the prisoner's conduct means that supervision arrangements have fundamentally broken down so that the risk to the public is effectively unmanageable in the community, then this may also justify recall.[159]

The recall hearing and the Parole Board Rules

13.76 The PBR 2004 as amended apply to recalled indeterminate sentenced prisoners.[160] In recognition of the need to consider recall cases expeditiously, the normal timetable is not applicable and any time limits should be set by the panel chair taking into account both 'the desirability of the Board reaching an early decision in the prisoner's case

156 C(S)A 1997 s32(5).

157 *R v Parole Board ex p Watson* [1996] 1 WLR 906; the grounds for detention must have a 'causal link' with the purpose of the sentence, which is to detain dangerous offenders: *Stafford v UK* (2002) 35 EHHR 32.

158 Ibid at 916D.

159 *R (on the application of Sim) v Parole Board* [2003] EWHC 152 (Admin) para 44.

160 PBR 2004 r2(i).

and the need to ensure fairness'.[161] For the same reason, rules 11–13, which deal with provisional decisions before a single member without a hearing do not apply to recalls.[162] However recall hearings are now subject to the ICM process (see paras 13.78–13.80 below).

13.77 The contents of a dossier prepared for a recall hearing are prescribed in Schedule 2 to the PBR. The dossier should specifically contain the Probation Service's reports that led to the revocation of the licence, the Secretary of State's reasons for recall and details of any Parole Board decisions recommending recall. These will be appended to the dossier prepared for the hearing that directed the prisoner's release, and the Board's decision directing release.

13.78 Further guidance on indeterminate recall cases, which the Board will routinely refer to an oral hearing, is contained in the ICM – General Guidance document. This states:[163]

> Recall cases have an extremely challenging deadline and the Board must hear the case as soon as possible. Under such circumstances the turnaround on delivery of the dossier and ICM assessment needs to be very quick. This means that any Directions issued will need to be complied with as a priority in order that the case can be heard swiftly. In view of the limited time involved, the Board will not issue an initial notification and only an exact notification will be sent, once a date for the hearing has been established.

13.79 The ICM guidance also sets out guidance on contents of recall dossiers. The following documents are mandatory for recall dossiers:

- request for revocation of licence report prepared by the offender manager;
- pre-sentence report;
- list of previous convictions;
- copy of the licence (and details of any conditions added post-release);
- copy of court form 5089 (judicial requirements) (where relevant);
- witness evidence (where relevant);
- charge sheets/police evidence (where relevant);
- breach report/request for recall report;
- assessment of risk and risk management plan/review of re-release report.

161 PBR r24(2)(a).
162 PBR r24(1)(a).
163 Part 8.

13.80 The same guidance also suggests that the following 11-week process should be followed, and expedited where possible, for all recall cases:

- Week 11 PPCS refer the case to the Board and supply basic dossier. The Board submits dossier to an ICM member for assessment and directions are issued, if required.
- Week 10 The Board issues directions to the PPCS, setting a maximum deadline of four weeks for compliance.
- Week 6 (latest) All directions should be complied with and the full paginated dossier sent to the Board who resubmit to ICM member for further assessment, if necessary.
- Week 5 (latest) The Board allocates a slot onto an existing panel if available, or sets up a new panel if resources allow. The Board issues exact notification to all parties.
- Week 4 (latest) The Board sends the dossier to all panel members.
- Week 0 Hearing takes place.

13.81 In some cases even adherence to this timetable may be insufficient to satisfy the requirement for a hearing to be 'speedy' under article 5(4). For example the duty was breached in a case where a recalled lifer, whose mental state was 'fragile' and deteriorating due to his detention, had a hearing listed 59 days after his recall. The judge was also critical of the lack of procedures to ensure that in appropriate cases the need for expedition was not considered by members of the Board, but by untrained staff.[164]

13.82 Oral hearings to determine the recall of indeterminate sentence prisoners are also given first priority in listing by the Board.[165]

13.83 Often the Probation Service report leading to the recall will rely on unsubstantiated evidence, or multiple hearsay statements, in support of the recall. It will rarely include first-hand evidence of any allegations that have led to the recall, and will often provide very little in the way of detail. However, as noted above,[166] as the notion of a 'burden of proof' is largely irrelevant in the parole context it is not enough for the prisoner to say that recall has not been justified because of the quality of the evidence.

13.84 Accordingly, it is important for representatives to ensure that, if the allegations in the recall dossier are contested, that PPCS and

164 *R (on the application of Cooper) v Parole Board* [2007] EWHC 1292 (Admin).

165 Parole Board, *Oral hearing listing prioritisation framework*, March 2009,www.paroleboard.gov.uk/policy_and_guidance/oral_hearing_listing_prioritisation_framework/ – although see the amendment to this policy.

166 See paras 9.13–9.33.

the Probation Service are required to provide proper evidence to substantiate them, so that this may be properly challenged at the hearing. This may necessitate an early request for directions from the Board,[167] within the above process, requiring PPCS to obtain further documents, witness evidence or to arrange for the attendance of witnesses for cross-examination.[168] However, as with other oral hearings[169] there is no prohibition on hearsay evidence before the Board and the issue will normally be as to weight rather than admissibility.[170]

13.85 Recall hearings are likely to involve more contested facts than those considering initial release and this will impact upon the approach the panel will adopt. In most cases, rather than the lifer manager or governor from the holding prison representing the Secretary of State, a PPA from the PPCS will attend the hearing or, in serious cases, counsel instructed by the Treasury Solicitor may attend. Recall hearings are often more adversarial and panels should be encouraged to adopt a more exacting approach to evidence (for example, witnesses of contested facts should not be present in the hearing before giving evidence). The PPCS will in all cases ask the supervising probation officer or offender manager to attend the hearing to give evidence as to the circumstances of recall.

13.86 The recall decision may be associated with the breakdown of the release plan, such as the loss of a hostel place. In preparation for the recall hearing it is important to remember that as well as challenging the basis of recall, the Board will want to know, if minded to direct release, what the release plan will be. If the material in the dossier does not include sufficient details of a release plan, then a direction should be sought from the Board for a further report from the Probation Service. As the supervising probation officer will normally have recommended recall, it can prove difficult to persuade the Probation Service to put a release plan in place. Although a local probation board is under a duty to ensure that there is sufficient provision for

167 PBR 2004 r8.

168 Including where necessary by securing attendance by witness summons from the court under Civil Procedure Rules (CPR) 34.4 – see *R (on the application of Brooks) v Parole Board* [2004] EWCA Civ 80 para 32.

169 See chapter 10 and *R (on the application of Sim) v Parole Board* [2003] EWCA Civ 1845 para 57.

170 Although in at least one case a recall decision has been quashed due to the failure of the Board to make findings of fact based on hearsay rather than direct oral testimony: *R (on the application of Headley) v Parole Board* [2009] EWHC 663 (Admin).

providing accommodation in hostels to those on licence[171] this does not impose a duty owed to individual prisoners.[172]

Decisions

13.87 If the Parole Board directs release[173] the PPCS, on behalf of the Secretary of State, must give effect to the direction.[174] Decisions, as with those relating to initial release, must be given to the parties within 14 days of the end of the hearing.[175] If the decision is for release, the PPCS aim to make arrangements for release and issue the licence within five working days. If release is refused, it will be for PPCS to decide on the timing of the next review, which cannot be more than two years from the Parole Board decision.[176] As with tariff expiry decisions, if the decision is not to release it may be necessary to make representations as to the timing of the next review if, for example, it is clear that anticipated offending behaviour work can be completed in a short period. It is not open to the Board, if it does not direct release, to recommend a transfer to open conditions unless the recall referral specifically requests advice on this issue.[177] If an open recommendation is to be sought, then a request will need to be made to the PPCS for this issue to be referred to the Board.

171 Criminal Justice and Court Services Act 2000 s5(1)(a).

172 *R (on the application of Irving) v London Probation Board* [2005] EWHC 605 (Admin) – where permission to bring a claim for judicial review was refused in circumstances where the had Board upheld a recall because the Probation Service could not provide accommodation suitable for the offender.

173 C(S)A 1997 s32(5).

174 C(S)A 1997 s32(5) refers to the Board directing 'immediate release' – this means that if release cannot be given effect to *immediately* then the direction may not be binding on the Home Secretary (see *R v Home Secretary ex p Gunnell* [1998] Crim LR 170 and *R v Home Secretary ex p De Lara* (HC 22.3.95, unreported).

175 PBR 20.

176 C(S)A 1997 s28(7)(b).

177 *R (on the application of Mills) v Secretary of State for the Home Department and the Parole Board* [2005] EWHC 2508 (Admin): evidence to the court was that referrals only exceptionally make such requests.

CHAPTER 14

Remedies

Non-judicial remedies

14.1 There may be actions or omissions during the course of a parole review, which are not decisions of the Board itself, that the prisoner will want to challenge. For example, there may be inclusion in the dossier by the parole clerk, or OMU, of material that should not be there, or an unreasonable delay by the PPCS in referring a case to the Board. While actions or omissions of the personnel at the individual prison, probation officers and those of the National Offender Management Service (NOMS) officials can ultimately be challenged in judicial review proceedings (see para 14.12 below), there are also complaints procedures that the courts will usually expect to be used before proceeding to litigation.[1]

Prison Service complaints procedure

14.2 Detailed guidance on the Prison Service complaints procedure has been issued.[2] The complaints procedure covers decisions or failings of departments within NOMS, such as PPCS. If the complaint is in relation to something that has occurred at the prison, then the prisoner should, in the first instance, submit a COMP 1 form, which should be freely available on the wing, to which there should normally be a response within three days for normal complaints.[3] If the prisoner remains unhappy with the response, then he/she can submit a COMP 1A form within seven days of the first response. This should be responded to by someone at a higher level than issued the first response,[4] within seven days for normal complaints. If still dissatisfied, the prisoner can, on the same COMP 1A within seven days, complain to the governor, on whose behalf there should be a response within seven days. Where the matter is particularly 'sensitive or serious', a complaint on COMP 2 can be made directly to the governor.[5]

14.3 If the matter does not relate to a failing at the prison, then it is a 'reserved subject' and the complaint should be dealt with by the appropriate department at Prison Service headquarters or NOMS.[6] So

1 *R (on the application of Cowl) v Plymouth City Council* [2001] EWCA Civ 1935.

2 PSO 2510.

3 See PSO 2510 chapter 13 for time limits.

4 PSO 2510 para 8.4.2.

5 PSO 2510 chapter 9.

6 See PSO 2510 chapter 10.

complaints about the PPCS should be treated as reserved subjects and forwarded to them for a response.

14.4 Going through the Prison Service complaints procedure is a prerequisite of making a complaint to the Prisons and Probation Ombudsman (see para 14.9 below). However, if a solicitor has raised the issue complained of with the establishment and has received a response on behalf of the governor or on behalf of the relevant decision-maker at Prison Service headquarters or the PPCS, then this will normally be accepted by the Ombudsman as sufficient to trigger the acceptance of a complaint to his office if the matter is otherwise within his remit.

Probation Service complaints

14.5 The Probation Service covers complaints made by those under probation supervision, or the victim of someone under such supervision.[7] Complaints in relation to matters more than a year old will not normally be investigated. The process is started by making a complaint in writing to the relevant probation area's chief officer. Within five working days of receiving the letter, the chief officer should respond to say how the complaint will be dealt with and give a timeframe for a response.

14.6 If the complainant is not satisfied with the response, he/she can write to appeal within 15 working days to the secretary of the local probation board. The appeal should be looked at by a panel, including at least one Board member, and the outcome will normally be sent within 20 working days of the receipt of the appeal. A complaint can then be made to the Prisons and Probation Ombudsman.

Parole Board complaints procedure

14.7 The Board has a complaints procedure;[8] however, this is not for challenging Board decisions,[9] although it appears that it could be used to complain about administrative failings in handling referrals. Complaints should generally be made within six months. If the complaint cannot be dealt with by the person receiving the complaint, it will be treated as a formal complaint and investigated with a response

7 See Probation Service, 'Making a Complaint', www.probation.homeoffice.gov.uk/output/page81.asp.

8 Available on the Board's website, www.paroleboard.gov.uk/contact/complaints/.

9 Ibid, para 1.5.

normally given within 20 working days.[10] If the complainant remains dissatisfied, there is an appeal to the chief executive, which should be resolved within three months of the start of the process.[11] If still dissatisfied, the complainant should be informed of his/her right to complain to the Parliamentary Ombudsman,[12] although such complaints need to be referred through a member of parliament.

14.8 Complaints about Parole Board decisions are dealt with by the Casework Team of the Parole Board Secretariat, who will respond to concerns raised directly about decisions, and to letters sent by solicitors on prisoners' behalf.

The Prisons and Probation Ombudsman

14.9 The Prisons and Probation Ombudsman has no jurisdiction over the Parole Board and cannot deal with complaints about its decisions. The Ombudsman will, however, consider complaints where either the prison or probation complaints process has been exhausted.[13] A complaint must be made to the Ombudsman within three months of the final reply in the Prison or Probation Service complaints procedure.[14]

14.10 If the complaint to the Prison or Probation Service has not received a response, the Ombudsman may investigate the complaint when the failure to respond reaches six weeks in relation to the Prison Service, or 45 working days in relation to the Probation Service.[15] Unless the delay is the fault of the Prison or Probation Service (by, for example, failing to respond to a complaint), the Ombudsman will not investigate a complaint where the matter complained of is more than 12 months old.[16]

14.11 The Ombudsman has a target date of 12 weeks for the completion of investigations into complaints (although the office will aim to deal with urgent complaints more quickly). If the complaint is upheld the Ombudsman can make a recommendation to the Director General of NOMS or the Secretary of State depending on the subject-matter of the complaint. Even though there is no duty to accept the Ombuds-

10 Para 12.3.
11 Para 12.5.
12 Para 8.16.
13 www.ppo.gov.uk/about-us/terms-of-ref/index.html.
14 Terms of reference, para 21.
15 Terms of reference, para 20.
16 Terms of reference, para 22.

man's recommendations, they are accepted in the vast majority of cases. The Ombudsman reviews the merits of decisions, not just the fairness of procedures.

Judicial remedies

Judicial review

14.12 Decisions of the Parole Board are outside the remit of the Prisons and Probation Ombudsman. If a prisoner tries to submit a complaint about a Parole Board decision under the Prison Service complaints procedure this will be forwarded to the Board, but this will rarely result in the Board agreeing to reconsider the matter or requesting a rereferral by the Secretary of State.

14.13 In practice, the only remedy available to challenge decisions of the Board is judicial review (JR). A detailed analysis of the law and practice relating to JR is outside the scope of this book. However, it is important to note the following:

- In a claim for JR the court is not generally considering an appeal against the merits of a decision, but rather the lawfulness of the decision-making process. The court will, to the degree that is appropriate on the facts, come to its own view as to whether there has been a breach of rights under the European Convention on Human Rights (ECHR).[17]
- A consequence of this is that the court will rarely resolve disputed issues of fact and will normally consider cases solely on consideration of the relevant papers (although in exceptional cases witness evidence may be called).
- Remedies in JR claims are discretionary, which means that even where there are good grounds, the court may refuse relief if, for example, the claimant has acted unreasonably (such as by failing to make full and frank disclosure of all material facts), or where relief would be academic, or perhaps most importantly, where the claimant has failed to make use of an adequate alternative remedy (although the court will consider in individual circumstances whether, for example, the applicable complaints procedure is adequate).

17 However, this does not involve a review of the merits, but of whether the Board was entitled to come to its view on risk: *R (on the application of Wyles) v Parole Board* [2006] EWHC 493 (Admin) para 32.

- In relation to Parole Board decisions the court will start from the premise that the Board is the expert body set up by statute in order to assess the risk posed to the public by offenders (see para 14.19 below).

Procedure

14.14 JR is governed by Part 54 of the Civil Procedure Rules (CPR) 1998.[18] The pre-action protocol for judicial review requires claimants to send a letter before claim setting out the reasons why it is alleged that the decision is unlawful and giving a time limit for a response (normally 14 days, but this can be less in urgent cases). This is to try to ensure that defendants have an opportunity to respond to claims before they are issued at court so as to avoid unnecessary litigation. Compliance with the pre-action protocol does not affect the time limit for issuing the claim.

14.15 JR claims must be issued in the Administrative Court Office promptly, and in any event within three months of the decision complained of, unless there is good reason for the delay.[19] The claim form (N461) must be served on the defendant and any interested party within seven days of issue.[20] In urgent cases, claimants can ask for expedition by filing, together with the claim form, an urgent consideration form (N463). The defendant, within 21 days of service of the claim form, should serve an acknowledgement of service.[21] A judge will then consider on the papers whether permission for the claim to proceed should be given. If permission is not given, then the claimant can request a hearing to renew the application.[22] If permission is granted, then the defendant should file grounds for resisting the claim and any evidence in support within 35 days of service of the order giving permission.[23] The claim will then proceed to a full hearing. At the hearing the court has the power to issue:

- *a mandatory order* – an order requiring the public body to do something. For example, where there has been unlawful delay by

18 See the DCA CPR homepage for the Rules and pre-action protocols: www.dca.gov.uk/civil/procrules_fin. See also guidance on JR claims on Court Service website: www.hmcourts-service.gov.uk/cms/1220.htm.

19 CPR 54.5.

20 CPR 54.7.

21 CPR 54.8.

22 CPR 54.12.

23 CPR 54.14.

the PPCS in referring a matter to the Parole Board or in arranging the release of a prisoner following the Board's direction, or by the prison in producing the dossier;

- *a prohibiting order* – an order preventing the public body from doing something, for example to prevent the Board proceeding to determine a matter by use of an unlawful procedure;[24]
- *a quashing order* – an order quashing the public body's decision. This is the most common order sought in Parole Board cases. It has the effect of requiring the Board to make a further decision. The court in JR proceedings will not substitute its own view;
- *a declaration* – where the court sets out in its decision a principle of law, or what the respective rights of the parties are;
- *injunctions* – an order prohibiting or requiring a body to do something – normally sought on an interim basis;
- *damages* – a claim for damages, including damages under the Human Rights Act (HRA) 1998, can be sought in JR claims, although this cannot be the only purpose of the claim. Damages can only be awarded if they could have been awarded in an ordinary claim, so a private law cause of action (such as negligence or false imprisonment) or right to damages under the HRA has to be established;[25]
- *interim and other relief* – the court has the power to order interim remedies, normally an interim injunction[26] and there is inherent jurisdiction to grant bail, or to grant a stay.[27]

Who is the right defendant?

14.16 If the decision is one of the Board, as it has its own legal identity, it is the appropriate defendant. If the decision is within the remit of the holding prison (for example, in failing to disclose a dossier) then the defendant will be the governor of the holding prison. If the decision

24 See, for example, *R (on the application of Roberts) v Parole Board* [2005] UKHL 45, although such challenges will be exceptional as the court will normally want to consider the legality of any procedure in the context of the Board's final decision: see *R (on the application of Hirst) v Parole Board* [2002] EWHC 1592 (Admin).

25 In this context a claim for damages is most likely to arise where there has been a breach of requirement for a speedy review under article 5(4).

26 CPR 25.2.

27 CPR 54.10.

is made by the PPCS (for example, a refusal to accept the recommendation of the Board to transfer a lifer to an open prison) then, as those bodies make decisions on behalf of the Secretary of State, the correct defendant is the Secretary of State for Justice. It will often be the case that there is more than one defendant, for example where there is not only a challenge to the Parole Board decision, but also to the PPCS decision on the timing of the subsequent review.

Grounds for seeking judicial review

14.17 This is a large and complex area, but in the parole context a brief outline of the grounds upon which JR might be sought is:

- where there is an error of law (for example where the Board applies the wrong test for release, or acts outside of its statutory powers, takes into account irrelevant matters or fails to consider relevant ones);
- where there is procedural impropriety, that is unfairness in the decision-making process (for example, failure to disclose documents to enable representations to be made, refusal to call relevant witnesses or giving inadequate reasons);
- where the decision is irrational, that is so unreasonable as to be unsustainable, or where there is an abuse of power;
- where the body in question has breached the requirement to act compatibly with rights under the ECHR.[28]

14.18 There is obviously a considerable degree of overlap between these categories.

Particular considerations in Parole Board decisions

The Board as an expert body

14.19 The starting point for the court will be that the Parole Board has been entrusted by parliament to make the sometimes difficult decisions as to when prisoners should be released. This means that there will be occasions where, although the court may express a view that the decision in question is not one that it would have made, the Board's decision will be upheld.

14.20 By way of illustration, in one instance a prisoner serving a ten-year sentence imposed for drug offences challenged a refusal of

28 HRA 1998 s6.

parole. By the time of his review he was in an open prison, engaged in community work and was supported in his application by both the prison and home probation officers. The Parole Board refused parole on the basis that he had not attended a formal offending behaviour course, notwithstanding the fact that this was not considered necessary by the report writers. The judge, in refusing the claim for judicial review, stated:

> The panel reached a decision which is not the one which I would have reached if I had been in their position. That, however, is nothing to the point. The Parole Board have both experience and expertise in making decisions of this character which judges lack. Furthermore, the decision in question has been entrusted by Parliament to the Parole Board, not the judiciary.[29]

Reasons

14.21 The Board is required to give reasons for its decisions.[30] Where there is a duty to give reasons, the courts require them to be 'proper, adequate and intelligible'.[31] In relation to parole decisions in respect of determinate sentence prisoners where statutory directions have been issued, the courts have held that the reasons given must:

> focus on the question of risk to which their decision is directed. Full account must be taken, as they affect any individual prisoner, of the matters listed in the Secretary of State's directions ... the Board should identify in broad terms the matters judged by the Board as pointing towards and against a continuing risk of offending and the Board's reasons for striking the balance as it does. Needless to say the letter should summarise the considerations which have in fact led to the final decision. It would be wrong to prescribe any standard form of decision letter and it would be wrong to require elaborate or impeccable standards of draftmanship.[32]

How the Board approaches denial of guilt

14.22 This has been the subject of a large amount of litigation and there is a common misapprehension that those that deny guilt are refused parole for that reason. The courts have held that, as the Board is carrying out an assessment of risk, the fact that the prisoner does not

29 *R v Parole Board ex p Blake* HC (2000) 23 February, unreported, para 54.

30 See Parole Board Rules r20 and PSO 6000 para 5.19.

31 *In re Poyser and Mills' Arbitration* [1964] 2 QB 467.

32 *R v Parole Board ex p Oyston* (2000) *Independent* 17 April, CA.

accept guilt of the offence will be a relevant, but not decisive, consideration. The Court of Appeal has approved this summary of the correct approach:

(a) The Parole Board must assume the prisoner's guilt of the offence or offences of which the prisoner has been convicted.
(b) The Board's first duty is to assess the risk to the public that the prisoner might commit further offences if the prisoner is paroled.
(c) It is therefore unlawful for the Board to deny a recommendation for parole *solely on the ground* that the prisoner continues to deny his/her guilt.
(d) But in some cases, particularly cases of serious persistent violent of sexual crime, a continued denial of guilt will almost inevitably mean that the risk posed by the prisoner to the public or a section of the public if the prisoner is paroled either remains high or, at least, cannot be objectively assessed. In such cases the Board is entitled (perhaps obliged) to deny a recommendation.[33]

14.23 Denial of guilt does not necessarily prevent the offender completing accredited offending behaviour courses (see chapter 4), and in any event the prisoner may demonstrate a reduced risk of reoffending in other ways than by completion of courses (for example a commitment to avoid a lifestyle associated with offending). Prisoners who maintain their innocence can, however, face insuperable problems. In one case where the prisoners were convicted of terrorist offences, the Board refused to consider evidence as to the likelihood of them committing further such offences because they maintained their innocence. The reason was that in the face of their stance, the question of whether the offences had a political motivation could not be determined, despite the nature of the offences being self-evidently political.[34]

Successful challenges

14.24 As challenges to the merits of the decision will rarely be successful, it is in cases where there has been a failure to apply the appropriate test, or there have been procedural failings, that claims for judicial review are likely to be more successful. Examples of such cases where there have been successful challenges by way of judicial review of Parole Board decisions are:

33 *R v Parole Board ex p Oyston* (2000) *Independent* 17 April, CA.

34 *R (on the application of Botmeh and Alami) v Parole Board and Secretary of State for Justice* [2008] EWHC 1115 (Admin).

- *where the Board's reasons are inadequate.* For example by failing to indicate that a significant matter in the prisoner's favour has been taken into account;[35]
- *where the Board misapplies any statutory directions it is required to follow.* For example, when required by directions to balance the risk to the public against the benefits to the prisoner in its decision making, the Board must indicate how competing factors have been balanced.[36] This does not mean that the Board has specifically to refer to the directions, as long as it is evident from its decision as a whole that the required balancing act has been carried out;[37]
- *where the Board makes its decision on the assessment of risk on the basis of factually inaccurate material in the dossier material.*[38] However the court is only likely to intervene where errors of fact may have been material to the decision;[39]
- *where the Board has breached the requirements of procedural fairness,* for example where it considers material as part of the review that was not disclosed to the prisoner[40] or improperly admits hearsay evidence.[41]

Timings of reviews, delays and remedies under article 5

14.25 Where article 5 is engaged (once the minimum term is expired for indeterminate sentence prisoners, or during the extension period for extended sentence prisoners), there is a requirement under article 5(4) for the initial review to be speedy and, where further reviews are necessary, for them to be carried out at reasonable intervals.[42] Practical issues as to the timing of reviews is dealt with above.[43] Where

35 Ibid.

36 *R (on the application of Tinney) v Parole Board* [2005] EWHC 863 (Admin) and, in the context of lifers moving to open conditions, *R (on the application of Gordon) v Parole Board* [2001] ACD 47, QBD; *R v Parole Board ex p Hart* (2000) 24 May, HC.

37 *R (on the application of Atkinson) v Parole Board* [2008] EWHC 1215 (Admin); *R (on the application of Alvey) v Parole Board* [2008] EWHC 311 (Admin).

38 *R v Parole Board ex p Higgins* (1998) 22 September HC – where the offence was wrongly described in the dossier.

39 *R (on the application of Morton) v Parole Board* [2009] EWHC 188 (Admin).

40 For example, see *R (AT) v Parole Board* [2004] EWHC 515.

41 *R (on the application of Headley) v Parole Board* [2009] EWHC 663 (Admin).

42 *Herczegalvy v Austria* (1992) 15 EHRR 437.

43 Paragraphs 11.102–11.105.

this requirement is breached, there is a right to compensation under article 5(5). One of the main issues indeterminate sentence prisoners require advice about is the timing between reviews when release has not been directed. These decisions are made by PPCS, not the Parole Board. Although there is a statutory requirement for a review every two years, the actual review period must be set by reference to what needs to be achieved before a further review would be appropriate. It must be borne in mind that the need for article 5(4) reviews is premised on the fact that levels of dangerousness change over time and so the time between reviews must be tailored to monitor these changes.

14.26 There is a great deal of authority in the European Court of Human Rights and domestically on when delay in the review will breach article 5(4), for example:

- An indeterminate prisoner's review must take place before or on the date of minimum term expiry.[44]
- Where after a first review the Parole Board recommended a 12-month review, but one was not held for 19 months there is a breach.[45]
- Where a discretionary lifer completed further offending work in eight months, but a review was not held for two years, there was a breach as the interval between reviews needs to be tailored so that the time between reviews can be justified by considerations of 'rehabilitation and monitoring'.[46]

These decisions do not mean that the 'standard' two-year review between indeterminate sentence reviews will always breach article 5(4), as each case must be considered on its own facts.[47]

14.27 Despite these decisions, there has been some confusion in the domestic courts as to when delay may breach article 5(4) either in the consideration of initial and periodic reviews, or on recall. This confusion has been caused by the House of Lords decision in *R (on the application of James, Lee and Wells) v Secretary of State for Justice*.[48] That case established that article 5(4) was not breached by the Board

44 *R (Noorkoiv) v Home Secretary* [2002] EWCA Civ 770.

45 *AT v UK* (1995) 20 EHRR CD 59.

46 *Oldham v United Kingdom* (36273/97) (2001) 31 EHRR 34; see also *Hirst v UK* [2001] Crim LR 919; *Curley v UK* (2001) 31 EHRR 14; *Waite v United Kingdom* (53236/99) (2003) 36 EHRR 54.

47 *R (on the application of MacNeill) v HMP Lifer Panel* [2001] EWCA Civ 448.

48 [2009] UKHL 22.

having insufficient evidence as to risk before it. However in discussing this issue Lord Hope commented:

> It is open to it to decide how much information it needs, to conclude that for whatever reason the information that is available for the time being is inadequate and to set its own timetable for the information that it needs to be made available. It is entitled to expect co-operation from those who are responsible for the management of the sentence in meeting its requirements. But a failure to meet them does not of itself mean that there will be a breach of article 5(4). As in the case of article 5(1)(a), it will only be if the system which the statutes have laid down breaks down entirely because the Parole Board is denied the information that it needs for such a long period that continued detention has become arbitrary that the guarantee that article 5(4) provides will be violated and the prisoner will be entitled to a remedy in damages.[49]

14.28 This has been relied upon by the Board to assert that the 'speedy review' requirement of article 5(4) will only be breached where the system breaks down entirely. This analysis has been accepted in some cases in the Administrative Court.[50] The better view is that Lord Hope was not directly considering the issue as to whether delay in holding a hearing may on the individual facts of the case, breach the requirement for a speedy review. For example, in a case heard shortly after the Lords decision Collins J commented:

> I confess that for my part I have some difficulty in following precisely what Lord Hope was intending to cover in that last sentence. The reality is that Article 5(4) requires a speedy hearing to determine the lawfulness of the detention. It may well be that in a given case the hearing will, and will inevitably, decide that the detention is lawful. That does not mean that the hearing itself can be deferred beyond a period that can be properly regarded as speedy. Equally, there is jurisprudence, and not least the decision of the House of Lords in *D v Secretary of State for Northern Ireland intervening* [2008] 1 WLR 1499, that delays in having a hearing which result from the Parole Board's own reasonable actions, for example requiring further information, and indeed, so far as the Parole Board is concerned, independently of any attack upon the system as a whole, in dealing with the matter in accordance with the resources that it has, provided that it does the best it can. 'Speedy' does not indicate a particular period, and I accept entirely that it is fact sensitive. What may be required in a particular case may not be required in another, depending upon the circumstances.

49 Paragraph 21.

50 For example, *R (on the application of Faulkner) v Secretary of State for Justice* [2009] EWHC 1507 (Admin).

But, one has to see in an individual case what has been the cause of the delay.[51]

14.29 This accords with a similar approach adopted in a large number of cases decided before the decision of the House of Lords. Article 5(4) will be breached in individual cases short of systemic breakdown, where for example there are delays due to administrative failures or delays by either the Board, or the Ministry of Justice (where the fault lies with either the prison or the PPCS), or delay in hearings due solely to lack of resources (at the time of writing the main cause of delays in listing cases). In relation to the Board's inability to list cases due to lack of judicial members, Collins J further commented in the same case, which was heard in June 2009, that as the Board were evidently taking steps to remedy the problem that prisoners should not bring claims for judicial review to force the Board to list their cases in the absence of 'special circumstances' as this would merely mean that those who litigated would jump the queue.[52] This of course does not prevent claims for damages being brought once a hearing had been held if there has been an article 5(4) breach. The position as to the Board's ability to list hearings is obviously likely to develop, as will the degree to which judicial review is an appropriate remedy in these cases, especially where there is delay in listing notwithstanding a very strong case for release.

14.30 The amount of damages for delays in holding effective hearings under article 5(4) will vary, as there is an obvious distinction between cases where the delay has actually delayed the prisoner's release, and those where it does not – where the Board decide that the prisoner should remain detained at the end of the process. In the latter cases the court will normally expect there to be contemporaneous evidence of real frustration and distress caused by the delay.[53] The frustration and distress must be significant, 'of such intensity that it would in itself justify an award of compensation for non-pecuniary damage'.[54] This approach has been followed in the parole context in *R (on the application of Bernard) v Secretary of State for the Home Department*

51 *R (on the application of Betteridge) v Parole Board* [2009] EWHC 1638 (Admin) para 22. This approach has been followed in, for example, *R (on the application of Pennington) v Parole Board* [2009] EWHC 2296 (Admin) and *R (on the application of Alcock) v Parole Board* [2009] EWHC 2401 (Admin).

52 *Betteridge* para 31.

53 *R (on the application of KB) v Mental Health Review Tribunal (Damages)* [2003] EWHC 193 (Admin).

54 Ibid, para 73.

and The Parole Board[55] and *R (on the application of Downing) v Parole Board.*[56] The Board's current position is to deny liability to pay compensation except where delay has postponed release; this is likely to be the subject of further litigation. Delay may be caused by the prison (failing to prepare/disclose dossier), the Secretary of State (delay in disclosure or in referral to the Board), or by the Board itself (delay in listing) and any challenge must be careful to identify correctly the party responsible.

14.31 Where a period of prolonged detention can be directly attributable to a breach of article 5, the courts have held that it is appropriate to look at damages in relation to the comparable tort of false imprisonment when deciding the level of compensation.[57] In one case, LRRS delayed the disclosure of a dossier to a recalled lifer for 14 days without any good reason. The lifer was eventually released after the parole hearing. The entire review process took three months from the date of the recall to release and the lifer received £1,500 compensation for the 14-day delay.[58]

55 [2005] EWHC 452 (Admin).

56 [2008] EWHC 3198 (Admin).

57 *KB* above; this approach was the subject of some criticism by House of Lords in *R v Home Secretary ex p Greenfield* [2005] UKHL 14, although that case involved article 6.

58 *R (on the application of Hirst) v Secretary of State for the Home Department* [2005] EWHC 1480 (Admin).

APPENDICES

APPENDIX A

The Parole Board Rules 2004 (as amended)[1]

Made 2004
Coming into force 1st April 2009

ARRANGEMENT OF RULES

PART I: Introduction

PART II: General

PART III: Proceedings without a hearing

PART IV: Proceedings with a hearing

PART V: Miscellaneous

1 Amended by the Parole Board (Amendment) Rules 2009.

SCHEDULES

The Secretary of State, in exercise of the powers conferred on him by section 32(5) of the Criminal Justice Act 1991, hereby makes the following Rules:

PART I: Introduction

Title, commencement and revocation

1. (1) These Rules may be cited as the Parole Board Rules 2004 and shall come into force on 1st August 2004.
(2) The Parole Board Rules 1997 are hereby revoked.

Application and interpretation

2. (1) Subject to rule 24, these Rules apply where a prisoner's case is referred to the Board by the Secretary of State under section 28(6)(a), 28(7) or 32(4) of the 1997 Act, or under section 39(4) or 44A(2) of the 1991 Act, at any time after the coming into force of these Rules.
(2) In these Rules, unless a contrary intention appears –
'Board' means the Parole Board, continued by section 32(1) of the 1991 Act;
'Chairman' means the chairman of the Board appointed under paragraph 2 of Schedule 5 to the 1991 Act;
'chair' means the chairman of a panel appointed under rule 3(5);
'governor' includes a director of a contracted out prison;
'ICM member' means a member of the Board accredited by the Board to manage cases in accordance with the Board's intensive case management system.
'oral panel' means those members of the Board constituted in accordance with rule 3(3);
'panel' means those members of the Board constituted in accordance with rule 3 and having conduct of the case;
'parties' means the prisoner and the Secretary of State;
'prison' includes a young offender institution or any other institution where the prisoner is or has been detained;
'single member panel' means that member of the Board constituted in accordance with rule 3(1);
'the 1991 Act' means the Criminal Justice Act 1991; and
'the 1997 Act' means the Crime (Sentences) Act 1997.

PART II: General

Appointment of panels

3. (1) The Chairman shall appoint one member of the Board for the purpose of conducting proceedings in relation to a prisoner's case without a hearing pursuant to rule 11.

(3) Where a hearing is required in relation to a prisoner's case, the Chairman shall appoint one or more members of the Board to form a panel for the purpose of conducting proceedings with a hearing. In respect of a hearing in the case of a prisoner serving an automatic life sentence, a mandatory life sentence, a discretionary life sentence, or a sentence during Her Majesty's pleasure, the oral panel shall consist of or include a sitting or retired judge.

(4) In relation to any prisoner's case, no member shall be appointed to more than one of the panels formed under paragraph (1) or (3) above.

(5) The Chairman shall appoint one member of each panel to act as chair of that panel. In relation to any panels comprising two or more members formed under paragraph (3) above that include a sitting or retired judge, that person shall act as chair of the panel.

Listing the case for hearing

4. The Board shall list the case and shall notify the parties of the date when the case was so listed within 5 working days thereafter.

Representation

5. (1) Subject to paragraph (2), a party may be represented by any person who he has authorised for that purpose.

(2) The following are ineligible to act as a representative –

(a) any person liable to be detained under the Mental Health Act 1983,

(b) any person serving a sentence of imprisonment,

(c) any person who is on licence having been released under Part III of the Criminal Justice Act 1967, under Part II of the 1991 Act, under Chapter 6 of Part 12 to the Criminal Justice Act 2003 or under Part II of the 1997 Act, or

(d) any person with a previous conviction for an imprisonable offence which remains unspent under the Rehabilitation of Offenders Act 1974.

(3) Within 5 weeks of the case being listed, a party shall notify the Board and the other party of the name, address and occupation of any person authorised in accordance with paragraph (1).

(4) Where a prisoner does not authorise a person to act as his representative, the Board may, with his agreement, appoint someone to act on his behalf.

Information and reports by the Secretary of State

6. (1) Within 8 weeks of the case being listed, the Secretary of State shall serve on the Board and, subject to paragraph (2), the prisoner or his representative –

(a) the information specified in Part A of Schedule 1 to these Rules,

(b) the reports specified in Part B of that Schedule, and

(c) such further information as the Secretary of State considers to be relevant to the case.

(2) Any part of the information or reports referred to in paragraph (1) which, in the opinion of the Secretary of State, should be withheld from the prisoner on the grounds that its disclosure would adversely affect national security,

the prevention of disorder or crime or the health or welfare of the prisoner or others (such withholding being a necessary and proportionate measure in all the circumstances of the case), shall be recorded in a separate document and served only on the Board together with the reasons for believing that its disclosure would have that effect.

(3) Where a document is withheld from the prisoner in accordance with paragraph (2), it shall, unless the chair of the panel directs otherwise, nevertheless be served as soon as practicable on the prisoner's representative if he is –
(a) a barrister or solicitor,
(b) a registered medical practitioner, or
(c) a person whom the chair of the panel directs is suitable by virtue of his experience or professional qualification;

provided that no information disclosed in accordance with this paragraph shall be disclosed either directly or indirectly to the prisoner or to any other person without the consent/authority of the chair of the panel.

Evidence of the prisoner

7. (1) Within 12 weeks of the case being listed, the prisoner shall serve on the Board and the Secretary of State any representations about his case that he wishes to make.

(2) Any other documentary evidence that the prisoner wishes to adduce at a hearing of his case shall be served on the Board and the Secretary of State at least 14 days before the date of the hearing.

Directions

8. (1) Subject to paragraph (4), an ICM member may at any time prior to the appointment of a panel, and the chair of such panel may at any time after the panel is appointed give, vary or revoke such directions as he thinks proper to enable the parties to prepare for the consideration of the prisoner's case or to assist the panel to determine the issues.

(2) Such directions may in particular relate to –
(a) the timetable for the proceedings,
(b) the varying of the time within which or by which an act is required by these Rules to be done,
(c) the service of documents,
(d) as regards any documents which have been received by the Board but which have been withheld from the prisoner in accordance with rule 6(2), whether withholding such documents is a necessary and proportionate measure in all the circumstances of the case, and
(e) the submission of evidence.

(3) Within 7 days of being notified of a direction under paragraph (2)(d), either party may appeal against it to the Chairman, who shall notify the other party of the appeal; the other party may make representations on the appeal to the Chairman whose decision shall be final.

(4) Directions under paragraph (1) may be given, varied or revoked either –
(a) of the ICM member's or the chair of the panel's own motion, or
(b) on the written application of a party which has been served on the other party and which specifies the direction that is sought;

but in either case, both parties shall be given an opportunity to make written representations or, after a panel has been appointed and where the chair of the panel thinks it necessary, and subject to paragraph (7)(b), to make oral submissions at a preliminary hearing fixed in accordance with paragraph (5).

(5) Where the chair of the panel decides to hold a preliminary hearing, he shall give the parties at least 14 days' notice of the date, time and place fixed for that hearing.

(6) A preliminary hearing shall be held in private and information about the proceedings and the names of any persons concerned in the proceedings shall not be made public.

(7) Except in so far as the chair of the panel otherwise directs, at a preliminary hearing –
   (a) the chair of the panel shall sit alone, and
   (b) the prisoner shall not attend unless he is unrepresented.

(8) The power to give directions may be exercised in the absence of the parties.

(9) Notice of any directions given, varied or revoked under this rule shall be served on the parties as soon as practicable thereafter.

Adjournment

9. (1) The panel may at any time adjourn proceedings to obtain further information or for such other purposes as it may think appropriate.

(2) Before adjourning proceedings, the panel may give such directions as it thinks fit to ensure the proceedings can be resumed and the application considered as soon as possible.

(3) Before an oral panel resumes any hearing which was adjourned without a further hearing date being fixed, it shall give the parties not less than 3 weeks notice, or such shorter notice to which all parties may agree, of the date, time and place of the resumed hearing.

Panel decisions

10.(1) Where a panel has been constituted under rule 3(3), any decision of the majority of the members of the panel shall be the decision of the panel.

(2) A panel that is unable to reach a decision in accordance with paragraph (1) shall be dissolved by the Chairman, who shall then appoint a new panel.

PART III: Proceedings without a hearing

Consideration by single member panel

11.(1) Within 14 weeks of the case being listed, a single member panel shall consider the prisoner's case without a hearing.

(2) The single member panel must either –
   (a) decide that the case should receive further consideration by an oral panel, or
   (b) make a provisional decision that the prisoner is unsuitable for release.

(3) The decision of the single member panel shall be recorded in writing with reasons, and shall be provided to the parties within a week of the date of the decision.

Provisional decision against release

12.(1) In any case where the single member panel has made a provisional decision under rule 11(2)(b) that the prisoner is unsuitable for release, the prisoner may request an oral panel to give consideration to his case with a hearing.

(2) Where the prisoner does so request consideration of his case with a hearing,

he must serve notice to that effect giving full reasons for the request on the Board and the Secretary of State within 19 weeks of the case being listed.

(3) If no notice has been served in accordance with paragraph (2) after the expiry of the period permitted by that paragraph, the provisional decision shall become final and shall be provided to the parties within 20 weeks of the case being listed.

Provisional decision in favour of release: consideration by three member paper panel

Consideration by an oral panel

13. In any case where the single member panel has referred the case to an oral panel for further consideration under rule 11(2)(a) or where a hearing has been ordered pursuant to a request under rule 12(2), the case must be considered by an oral panel within 26 weeks of the case having been originally listed.

PART IV: Proceedings with a hearing

General provisions

14.(1) This Part of the Rules applies in any case where a decision pursuant to rule 11(2)(a) has been made, or where a hearing has been ordered pursuant to a request under rule 12(2), or in any case referred to the Board under section 32(4) of the 1997 Act or under section 39(4) or 44A(2) of the 1991 Act.

(3) The prisoner shall, within 23 weeks of the case being listed, notify the Board and the Secretary of State whether he wishes to attend the hearing.

(4) Any reference in this Part of the Rules to a 'panel' is to an oral panel.

Witnesses

15.(1) Where a party wishes to call witnesses at the hearing, he shall make a written application to the Board, a copy of which he shall serve on the other party, within 20 weeks of the case being listed, giving the name, address and occupation of the witness he wishes to call and the substance of the evidence he proposes to adduce.

(2) Where the Board wishes to call witnesses at the hearing, the chair of the panel should notify the parties, within 21 weeks of the case being listed, giving the name, address and occupation of the witness it wishes to call and the substance of the evidence it proposes to adduce.

(3) The chair of the panel may grant or refuse an application under paragraph (1) and shall communicate his decision to both parties, giving reasons in writing for his decision in the case of a refusal.

(4) Where a witness is called under paragraphs (1) or (2), it shall be the duty of the person calling the witness to notify the witness at least 2 weeks before the hearing of the date of the hearing and the need to attend.

Observers

16. A party may apply, in accordance with the procedure set out in rule 15(1) and (3), to be accompanied at the hearing by such other persons, in addition to any representative he may have authorised, as he wishes to support him or to observe the proceedings; but before granting any such application the Board shall obtain the agreement of –

(a) the governor where the hearing is held in a prison,

(b) in any other case, the person who has the authority to agree.

Notice of hearing

17.(1) The hearing shall be held within 26 weeks of the case being listed, but when fixing the date of the hearing the Board shall consult the parties.

(2) The Board shall give the parties at least 3 weeks notice of the date, time and place scheduled for the hearing or such shorter notice to which the parties may agree.

Location, privacy of proceedings

18.(1) The hearing shall be held at the prison or other institution where the prisoner is detained, or such other place as the chair of the panel, with the agreement of the Secretary of State, may direct.

(2) The hearing shall be held in private.

(3) In addition to witnesses and observers previously approved pursuant to rules 15 and 16, the chair of the panel may admit to the hearing such other persons on such terms and conditions as he considers appropriate.

(4) The parties may not challenge at the hearing the attendance of any witness or observer whose attendance has previously been approved pursuant to rules 15 and 16.

Hearing procedure

19.(1) At the beginning of the hearing the chair of the panel shall explain the order of proceeding which the panel proposes to adopt, and shall invite each party present to state their view as to the suitability of the prisoner for release.

(2) The panel shall avoid formality in the proceedings and so far as possible shall make its own enquiries in order to satisfy itself of the level of risk of the prisoner; it shall conduct the hearing in such manner as it considers most suitable to the clarification of the issues before it and generally to the just handling of the proceedings it.

(3) The parties shall be entitled to appear and be heard at the hearing and take such part in the proceedings as the panel thinks fit; and the parties may hear each other's evidence, put questions to each other, call any witnesses who the Board has authorised to give evidence in accordance with rule 15, and put questions to any witness or other person appearing before the panel.

(4) The chair of the panel may require any person present at the hearing who is, in his opinion, behaving in a disruptive manner to leave and may permit him to return, if at all, only on such conditions as the chair may specify.

(5) The panel may adduce or receive in evidence any document or information notwithstanding that such document or information would be inadmissible in a court of law, but no person shall be compelled to give any evidence or produce any document which he could not be compelled to give or produce on the trial of an action.

(6) The chair of the panel may require the prisoner, any witness appearing for the prisoner, or any other person present, to leave the hearing where evidence is being examined which the chair of the panel, in accordance with rule 8(2)(d) (subject to any successful appeal under rule 8(2)), previously directed should be withheld from the prisoner as adversely affecting national security, the prevention of disorder or crime or the health or welfare of the prisoner or others.

(7) After all the evidence has been given, the prisoner shall be given a further opportunity to address the panel.

The decision

20. The panel's decision determining a case shall be recorded in writing with reasons, signed by the chair of the panel, and provided in writing to the parties not more than 14 days after the end of the hearing; the recorded decision with reasons shall only make reference to matters which the Secretary of State has referred to the Board.

PART V: Miscellaneous

Time

21. Where the time prescribed by or under these Rules for doing any act expires on a Saturday, Sunday or public holiday, the act shall be in time if done on the next working day.

Transmission of documents etc.

22. Any document required or authorised by these Rules to be served or otherwise transmitted to any person may be transmitted by electronic means, sent by pre-paid post or delivered –

(a) in the case of a document directed to the Board or the chair of the panel, to the office of the Board;

(b) in any other case, to the last known address of the person to whom the document is directed.

Irregularities

23. Any irregularity resulting from a failure to comply with these Rules before the panel has determined a case shall not of itself render the proceedings void, but the panel may, and shall, if it considers that the person may have been prejudiced, take such steps as it thinks fit, before determining the case, to cure the irregularity, whether by the amendment of any document, the giving of any notice, the taking of any step or otherwise.

References to the Board following recall

24.(1) Where the Secretary of State refers a prisoner's case to the Board under section 32(4) of the 1997 Act or section 39(4) of the 1991 Act to consider a recall:

(a) rules 11 to 13 shall not apply; and

(b) subject to the above, these Rules shall only apply where the prisoner has made representations against recall and subject to the modifications in paragraph (2).

(2) The modifications referred to in paragraph (1) are as follows:

(a) any references to periods of time set out in these Rules shall apply as if they were references to such period of time as the chair of the panel shall in each case determine, taking into account both the desirability of the Board reaching an early decision in the prisoner's case and the need to ensure fairness to the prisoner; and

(b) rule 6 shall apply as if the references in paragraph (1)(a) and (b) of that rule to the information and reports specified in Schedule 1 were references to the information and reports set out in Schedule 2.

Transitional provision

25. The revocation by these Rules of the Parole Board Rules 1997 does not affect their operation in relation to any referral of a prisoner's case made to the Board before the coming into force of the revocation.

The amendments made by these Rules do not apply in relation to any hearing which begins prior to 1 April 2009. For the avoidance of doubt, any hearing which begins prior to 1st April 2009, and is adjourned to 1 April 2009 or later, is a hearing to which the amendments made by these Rules do not apply.

Home Office
Parliamentary Under-Secretary of State
2004

SCHEDULE 1: INFORMATION AND REPORTS FOR SUBMISSION TO THE BOARD BY THE SECRETARY OF STATE ON A REFERENCE TO THE BOARD UNDER SECTION 28(6)(a) OR (7) OF THE 1997 ACT OR SECTION 44A(2) OF THE 1991 ACT

Rule 6(1)

PART A: INFORMATION RELATING TO THE PRISONER

1. The full name of the prisoner
2. The date of birth of the prisoner.
3. The prison in which the prisoner is detained and details of other prisons in which the prisoner has been detained, the date and reasons for any transfer.
4. The date the prisoner was given the life sentence or extended sentence, details of the offence and any previous convictions.
5. The comments, if available, of the trial judge in passing sentence.
6. Where applicable, the conclusions of the Court of Appeal in respect of any appeal by the prisoner against conviction or sentence.
7. The parole history, if any, of the prisoner, including details of any periods spent on licence during the currency of the life sentence or extended sentence.

PART B: REPORTS RELATING TO THE PRISONER

1. Pre-trial and pre-sentence reports examined by the sentencing court on the circumstances of the offence.
2. Reports on a prisoner while he was subject to a transfer direction under section 47 of the Mental Health Act 1983.
3. Current reports on the prisoner's risk factors, reduction in risk and performance and behaviour in prison, including views on suitability for release on licence as well as compliance with any sentence plan.
4. An up-to-date home circumstances report prepared for the Board by an officer of the supervising local probation board, including information on the following where relevant:
   (a) details of the home address, family circumstances, and family attitudes towards the prisoner;
   (b) alternative options if the offender cannot return home;
   (c) the opportunity for employment on release;
   (d) the local community's attitude towards the prisoner (if known);
   (e) the attitudes and concerns of the victims of the offence (if known);
   (f) the prisoner's attitude to the index offence;
   (g) the prisoner's response to previous periods of supervision;
   (h) the prisoner's behaviour during any temporary leave during the current sentence;

(i) the prisoner's attitude to the prospect of release and the requirements and objectives of supervision;
(j) an assessment of the risk of reoffending;
(k) a programme of supervision;
(l) a view on suitability for release; and
(m) recommendations regarding any non-standard licence conditions.

SCHEDULE 2: INFORMATION AND REPORTS FOR SUBMISSION TO THE BOARD BY THE SECRETARY OF STATE ON A REFERENCE TO THE BOARD UNDER SECTION 32(4) OF THE 1997 ACT OR SECTION 39(4) OF THE 1991 ACT

Rules 6(1) and 24(2)(b)

PART A: INFORMATION RELATING TO THE PRISONER

1. The full name of the prisoner.
2. The date of birth of the prisoner.
3. The prison in which the prisoner is detained and details of other prisons in which the prisoner has been detained, the date and reasons for any transfer.
4. The date the prisoner was given the life sentence or extended sentence, details of the offence and any previous convictions.
5. The parole history, if any, of the prisoner, including details of any periods spent during the currency of the life sentence or extended sentence.
6. In the case of a referral under section 32(4) of the 1997 Act, the details of any life sentence plan prepared for the prisoner which have previously been disclosed to him.
7. The details of any previous recalls of the prisoner including the reasons for such recalls and subsequent re-release on licence.
8. The statement of reasons for the most recent recall which was given to the prisoner under section 32(3)(b) of the 1997 Act or section 39(3)(b) of the 1991 Act.
9. The details of any memorandum which the Board considered prior to making its recommendation for recall under section 32(1) of the 1997 Act or section 39(1) of the 1991 Act, or confirming the Secretary of State's decision to recall under section 32(2) of the 1997 Act or section 39(2) of the 1991 Act, including the reasons why the Secretary of State considered it expedient in the public interest to recall that person before it was practicable to obtain a recommendation from the Board.

PART B: REPORTS RELATING TO THE PRISONER

1. The reports considered by the Board prior to making its recommendation for recall under section 32(1) of the 1997 Act or section 39(1) of the 1991 Act, or its confirmation of the Secretary of State's decision to recall under section 32(2) of the 1997 Act or section 39(2) of the 1991 Act.
2. Any reports considered by the Secretary of State in deciding to recall under section 32(2) of the 1997 Act or section 39(2) of the 1991 Act.
3. In the case of a referral under section 39(4) of the 1991 Act, any pre-sentence report examined by the sentencing court on the circumstances of the offence.
4. Any other relevant reports.

APPENDIX B

The statutory framework of the Parole Board

Criminal Justice Act 2003 s239 and Schedule 19

The Parole Board

239 (1) The Parole Board is to continue to be, by that name, a body corporate and as such is –

(a) to be constituted in accordance with this Chapter, and

(b) to have the functions conferred on it by this Chapter in respect of fixed-term prisoners and by Chapter 2 of Part 2 of the Crime (Sentences) Act 1997 (in this Chapter referred to as 'the 1997 Act') in respect of life prisoners within the meaning of that Chapter.

(2) It is the duty of the Board to advise the Secretary of State with respect to any matter referred to it by him which is to do with the early release or recall of prisoners.

(3) The Board must, in dealing with cases as respects which it makes recommendations under this Chapter or under Chapter 2 of Part 2 of the 1997 Act, consider–

(a) any documents given to it by the Secretary of State, and

(b) any other oral or written information obtained by it;

and if in any particular case the Board thinks it necessary to interview the person to whom the case relates before reaching a decision, the Board may authorise one of its members to interview him and must consider the report of the interview made by that member.

(4) The Board must deal with cases as respects which it gives directions under this Chapter or under Chapter 2 of Part 2 of the 1997 Act on consideration of all such evidence as may be adduced before it.

(5) Without prejudice to subsections (3) and (4), the Secretary of State may make rules with respect to the proceedings of the Board, including proceedings authorising cases to be dealt with by a prescribed number of its members or requiring cases to be dealt with at prescribed times.

(6) The Secretary of State may also give to the Board directions as to the matters to be taken into account by it in discharging any functions under this Chapter or under Chapter 2 of Part 2 of the 1997 Act; and in giving any such directions the Secretary of State must have regard to–

(a) the need to protect the public from serious harm from offenders, and

(b) the desirability of preventing the commission by them of further offences and of securing their rehabilitation.

(7) Schedule 19 shall have effect with respect to the Board.

SCHEDULE 19: THE PAROLE BOARD: SUPPLEMENTARY PROVISIONS

Section 239(7)

Status and capacity

1 (1) The Board is not to be regarded as the servant or agent of the Crown or as enjoying any status, immunity or privilege of the Crown; and the Board's property is not to be regarded as property of, or held on behalf of, the Crown.

(2) It is within the capacity of the Board as a statutory corporation to do such things and enter into such transactions as are incidental to or conducive to the discharge of –

(a) its functions under Chapter 6 of Part 12 in respect of fixed-term prisoners, and

(b) its functions under Chapter 2 of Part 2 of the Crime (Sentences) Act 1997 in relation to life prisoners within the meaning of that Chapter.

Membership

2 (1) The Board is to consist of a chairman and not less than four other members appointed by the Secretary of State.

(2) The Board must include among its members –

(a) a person who holds or has held judicial office;

(b) a registered medical practitioner who is a psychiatrist;

(c) a person appearing to the Secretary of State to have knowledge and experience of the supervision or after-care of discharged prisoners; and

(d) a person appearing to the Secretary of State to have made a study of the causes of delinquency or the treatment of offenders.

(3) A member of the Board –

(a) holds and vacates office in accordance with the terms of his appointment;

(b) may resign his office by notice in writing addressed to the Secretary of State;

and a person who ceases to hold office as a member of the Board is eligible for re-appointment.

Payments to members

3 (1) The Board may pay to each member such remuneration and allowances as the Secretary of State may determine.

(2) The Board may pay or make provision for paying to or in respect of any member such sums by way of pension, allowances or gratuities as the Secretary of State may determine.

(3) If a person ceases to be a member otherwise than on the expiry of his term of office and it appears to the Secretary of State that there are special circumstances that make it right that he should receive compensation, the Secretary of State may direct the Board to make to that person a payment of such amount as the Secretary of State may determine.

(4) A determination or direction of the Secretary of State under this paragraph requires the approval of the Treasury.

Proceedings

4 (1) Subject to the provisions of section 239(5), the arrangements relating to meetings of the Board are to be such as the Board may determine.

(2) The arrangements may provide for the discharge, under the general direction

of the Board, of any of the Board's functions by a committee or by one or more of the members or employees of the Board.

(3) The validity of the proceedings of the Board are not to be affected by any vacancy among the members or by any defect in the appointment of a member.

Staff

5 (1) The Board may appoint such number of employees as it may determine.

(2) The remuneration and other conditions of service of the persons appointed under this paragraph are to be determined by the Board.

(3) Any determination under sub-paragraph (1) or (2) requires the approval of the Secretary of State given with the consent of the Treasury.

(4) The Employers' Liability (Compulsory Insurance) Act 1969 (c 57) shall not require insurance to be effected by the Board.

6 (1) Employment with the Board shall continue to be included among the kinds of employment to which a scheme under section 1 of the Superannuation Act 1972 (c 11) can apply, and accordingly in Schedule 1 to that Act (in which those kinds of employment are listed) at the end of the list of Other Bodies there shall continue to be inserted –

'Parole Board.'

(2) The Board shall pay to the Treasury, at such times as the Treasury may direct, such sums as the Treasury may determine in respect of the increase attributable to this paragraph in the sums payable under the Superannuation Act 1972 out of money provided by Parliament.

Financial provisions

7 (1) The Secretary of State shall pay to the Board–

(a) any expenses incurred or to be incurred by the Board by virtue of paragraph 3 or 5; and

(b) with the consent of the Treasury, such sums as he thinks fit for enabling the Board to meet other expenses.

(2) Any sums required by the Secretary of State for making payments under sub-paragraph (1) are to be paid out of money provided by Parliament.

Authentication of Board's seal

8 The application of the seal of the Board is to be authenticated by the signature of the Chairman or some other person authorised for the purpose.

Presumption of authenticity of documents issued by Board

9 Any document purporting to be an instrument issued by the Board and to be duly executed under the seal of the Board or to be signed on behalf of the Board shall be received in evidence and shall be deemed to be such an instrument unless the contrary is shown.

Accounts and audit

10 (1) It is the duty of the Board–

(a) to keep proper accounts and proper records in relation to the accounts;

(b) to prepare in respect of each financial year a statement of accounts in such form as the Secretary of State may direct with the approval of the Treasury; and

(c) to send copies of each such statement to the Secretary of State and the Comptroller and Auditor General not later than 31st August next following the end of the financial year to which the statement relates.

(2) The Comptroller and Auditor General shall examine, certify and report on each statement of accounts sent to him by the Board and shall lay a copy of every such statement and of his report before each House of Parliament.

(3) In this paragraph and paragraph 11 'financial year' means a period of 12 months ending with 31st March.

Reports

11 The Board must as soon as practicable after the end of each financial year make to the Secretary of State a report on the performance of its functions during the year; and the Secretary of State must lay a copy of the report before each House of Parliament.

APPENDIX C

The release and recall of life/ indeterminate sentenced prisoners

Crime (Sentences) Act 1997 ss28, 30–32, 34 (as amended)

Chapter II: Life sentences

Release on licence

Duty to release certain life prisoners

28(1A) This section applies to a life prisoner in respect of whom a minimum term order has been made; and any reference in this section to the relevant part of such a prisoner's sentence is a reference to the part of the sentence specified in the order.

(1B) But if a life prisoner is serving two or more life sentences–

(a) this section does not apply to him unless a minimum term order has been made in respect of each of those sentences; and

(b) the provisions of subsections (5) to (8) below do not apply in relation to him until he has served the relevant part of each of them.

(5) As soon as –

(a) a life prisoner to whom this section applies has served the relevant part of his sentence,

(b) the Parole Board has directed his release under this section,

it shall be the duty of the Secretary of State to release him on licence.

(6) The Parole Board shall not give a direction under subsection (5) above with respect to a life prisoner to whom this section applies unless –

(a) the Secretary of State has referred the prisoner's case to the Board; and

(b) the Board is satisfied that it is no longer necessary for the protection of the public that the prisoner should be confined.

(7) A life prisoner to whom this section applies may require the Secretary of State to refer his case to the Parole Board at any time –

(a) after he has served the relevant part of his sentence; and

(b) where there has been a previous reference of his case to the Board, after the end of the period of two years beginning with the disposal of that reference; and

(c) where he is also serving a sentence of imprisonment or detention for a term, after he has served one-half of that sentence;

and in this subsection 'previous reference' means a reference under subsection (6) above or section 32(4) below.

(8) In determining for the purpose of subsection (5) or (7) above whether a life prisoner to whom this section applies has served the relevant part of his sentence, no account shall be taken of any time during which he was unlawfully at large within the meaning of section 49 of the Prison Act 1952

(8A) In this section 'minimum term order' means an order under–
(a) subsection (2) of section 82A of the Powers of Criminal Courts (Sentencing) Act 2000 (determination of minimum term in respect of life sentence that is not fixed by law), or
(b) subsection (2) of section 269 of the Criminal Justice Act 2003 (determination of minimum term in respect of mandatory life sentence).

Power to release life prisoners on compassionate grounds

30 (1) The Secretary of State may at any time release a life prisoner on licence if he is satisfied that exceptional circumstances exist which justify the prisoner's release on compassionate grounds.

(2) Before releasing a life prisoner under subsection (1) above, the Secretary of State shall consult the Parole Board, unless the circumstances are such as to render such consultation impracticable.

Licences and recall

Duration and conditions of licences

31 (1) Where a life prisoner, other than a prisoner to whom section 31A below applies, is released on licence, the licence shall, unless previously revoked under section 32 below, remain in force until his death.

(1A) Where a prisoner to whom section 31A below applies is released on licence, the licence shall remain in force until his death unless–
(a) it is previously revoked under section 32(1) or (2) below; or
(b) it ceases to have effect in accordance with an order made by the Secretary of State under section 31A below.

(2) A life prisoner subject to a licence shall comply with such conditions as may for the time being be specified in the licence; and the Secretary of State may make rules for regulating the supervision of any description of such persons.

(2A) The conditions so specified shall include on the prisoner's release conditions as to his supervision by–
(a) an officer of a local probation board appointed for or assigned to the local justice area within which the prisoner resides for the time being or (as the case may be) an officer of a provider of probation services acting in the local justice area within which the prisoner resides for the time being;
(b) where the prisoner is under the age of 22, a social worker of the local authority within whose area the prisoner resides for the time being; or
(c) where the prisoner is under the age of 18, a member of a youth offending team established by that local authority under section 39 of the Crime and Disorder Act 1998.

(3) The Secretary of State shall not include on release, or subsequently insert, a condition in the licence of a life prisoner, or vary or cancel any such condition, except in accordance with recommendations of the Parole Board.

(4) [*Repealed.*]

(5) The power to make rules under this section shall be exercisable by statutory instrument which shall be subject to annulment in pursuance of a resolution of either House of Parliament.

(6) In relation to a life prisoner who is liable to removal from the United Kingdom (within the meaning given by section 259 of the Criminal Justice Act 2003), subsection (2) above shall have effect as if subsection (2A) above were omitted.

Imprisonment or detention for public protection: termination of licences

31A(1) This section applies to a prisoner who–

(a) is serving one or more preventive sentences, and

(b) is not serving any other life sentence.

(2) Where –

(a) the prisoner has been released on licence under this Chapter; and

(b) the qualifying period has expired,

the Secretary of State shall, if directed to do so by the Parole Board, order that the licence is to cease to have effect.

(3) Where –

(a) the prisoner has been released on licence under this Chapter;

(b) the qualifying period has expired; and

(c) if he has made a previous application under this subsection, a period of at least twelve months has expired since the disposal of that application,

the prisoner may make an application to the Parole Board under this subsection.

(4) Where an application is made under subsection (3) above, the Parole Board–

(a) shall, if it is satisfied that it is no longer necessary for the protection of the public that the licence should remain in force, direct the Secretary of State to make an order that the licence is to cease to have effect;

(b) shall otherwise dismiss the application.

(5) In this section –

'preventive sentence' means a sentence of imprisonment for public protection under section 225 of the Criminal Justice Act 2003 or a sentence of detention for public protection under section 226 of that Act (including such a sentence of imprisonment or detention passed as a result of section 219 or 221 of the Armed Forces Act 2006);

'the qualifying period', in relation to a prisoner who has been released on licence, means the period of ten years beginning with the date of his release.

Recall of life prisoners while on licence

32 (1) The Secretary of State may, in the case of any life prisoner who has been released on licence under this Chapter, revoke his licence and recall him to prison.

(3) A life prisoner recalled to prison under this section–

(a) may make representations in writing with respect to his recall; and

(b) on his return to prison, shall be informed of the reasons for his recall and of his right to make representations.

(4) The Secretary of State shall refer to the Parole Board the case of a life prisoner recalled under this section.

(5) Where on a reference under subsection (4) above the Parole Board directs the immediate release on licence under this section of the life prisoner, the Secretary of State shall give effect to the direction.

(6) On the revocation of the licence of any life prisoner under this section, he shall be liable to be detained in pursuance of his sentence and, if at large, shall be deemed to be unlawfully at large.

Interpretation of Chapter II

34 (1) In this Chapter 'life prisoner' means a person serving one or more life sentences and includes a transferred life prisoner as defined by section 273 of the Criminal Justice Act 2003.

(2) In this section 'life sentence' means any of the following imposed for an offence, whether committed before or after the commencement of this Chapter, namely –

(a) a sentence of imprisonment for life;

(b) a sentence of detention during Her Majesty's pleasure or for life under section 90 or 91 of the Powers of Criminal Courts (Sentencing) Act 2000; and

(c) a sentence of custody for life under section 93 or 94 of that Act

(d) a sentence of imprisonment for public protection under section 225 of the Criminal Justice Act 2003 (including one passed as a result of section 219 of the Armed Forces Act 2006), and

(e) a sentence of detention for public protection under section 226 of that Act (including one passed as a result of section 221 of the Armed Forces Act 2006);

(f) a sentence of detention for life under section 209 of the Armed Forces Act 2006;

(g) a sentence under section 218 of that Act (detention at Her Majesty's pleasure).

(3) [*Repealed.*]

(4) Where a person has been sentenced to one or more life sentences and to one or more terms of imprisonment, nothing in this Chapter shall require the Secretary of State to release the person in respect of any of the life sentences unless and until the Secretary of State is required to release him in respect of each of the terms.

APPENDIX D

The initial release and impact of recall on Criminal Justice Act 1991 determinate sentence prisoners (offences committed before 4 April 2005)

Criminal Justice Act 1991 ss33–37ZA, 39, 43–44A, 50–51; Criminal Justice Act 2003 Sch 15

CRIMINAL JUSTICE ACT 1991

New arrangements for early release

Duty to release short-term and long-term prisoners

33 (1) As soon as a short-term prisoner has served one-half of his sentence, it shall be the duty of the Secretary of State –

(a) to release him unconditionally if that sentence is for a term of less than twelve months; and

(b) to release him on licence if that sentence is for a term of twelve months or more.

(1A) As soon as a long-term prisoner has served one-half of his sentence, it shall be the duty of the Secretary of State to release him on licence.

(1B) Subsection (1A) does not apply to a long-term prisoner if the offence or one of the offences in respect of which he is serving the sentence is specified in Schedule 15 to the Criminal Justice Act 2003 (specified violent offences and specified sexual offences).

(1C) The reference in subsection (1B) to an offence specified in Schedule 15 to the Criminal Justice Act 2003 includes a reference to–

(a) an offence under section 70 of the Army Act 1955, section 70 of the Air Force Act 1955 or section 42 of the Naval Discipline Act 1957 as respects which the corresponding civil offence (within the meaning of the Act in question) is an offence specified in that Schedule, and

(b) an offence under section 42 of the Armed Forces Act 2006 as respects which the corresponding offence under the law of England and Wales (within the meaning given by that section) is an offence specified in that Schedule.

(1D) Section 48 of the Armed Forces Act 2006 (attempts, conspiracy etc) applies for the purposes of subsection (1C)(b) as if the reference in subsection (3)(b) of that section to any of the following provisions of that Act were a reference to subsection (1C)(b).

(2) As soon as a long-term prisoner to whom subsection (1A) does not apply has served two-thirds of his sentence, it shall be the duty of the Secretary of State to release him on licence.

(3) As soon as a short-term or long-term prisoner who–
(a) has been released on licence under this Part; and
(b) has been recalled to prison under section 39(1) and (2) below,
would (but for his release) have served three-quarters of his sentence, it shall be the duty of the Secretary of State to release him on licence.

(4) [*Repealed.*]

(5) In this Part –
'long-term prisoner' means a person serving a sentence of imprisonment for a term of four years or more;
'short-term prisoner' means a person serving a sentence of imprisonment for a term of less than four years.

Duty to release prisoners: special cases

33A(1) As soon as a prisoner–
(a) whose sentence is for a term of less than twelve months; and
(b) who has been released on licence under section 34A(3) or 36(1) below and recalled to prison under section 38A(1) or 39(1) or (2) below,
would (but for his release) have served one-half of his sentence, it shall be the duty of the Secretary of State to release him unconditionally.

(2) As soon as a prisoner –
(a) whose sentence is for a term of twelve months or more; and
(b) who has been released on licence under section 34A(3) below and recalled to prison under section 38A(1) below,
would (but for his release) have served one-half of his sentence, it shall be the duty of the Secretary of State to release him on licence.

(3) In the case of a prisoner who–
(a) has been released on licence under this Part and recalled to prison under section 39(1) or (2) below; and
(b) has been subsequently released on licence under section 33(3) or (3A) above and recalled to prison under section 39(1) or (2) below,
section 33(3) above shall have effect as if for the words 'three-quarters' there were substituted the words 'the whole' and the words 'on licence' were omitted.

34 [*Repealed*].

Power to release short-term prisoners on licence

34A(1) Subject to subsection (2) below, subsection (3) below applies where a short-term prisoner is serving a sentence of imprisonment for a term of three months or more.

(2) Subsection (3) below does not apply where –
(a) the sentence is an extended sentence within the meaning of section 85 of the Powers of Criminal Courts (Sentencing) Act 2000;
(b) the sentence is for an offence under section 1 of the Prisoners (Return to Custody) Act 1995;
(c) the sentence was imposed under paragraph 4(1)(d) or 5(1)(d) of Schedule 3 to the Powers of Criminal Courts (Sentencing) Act 2000 in a case where

the prisoner had failed to comply with a requirement of a curfew order;

(d) the prisoner is subject to a hospital order, hospital direction or transfer direction under section 37, 45A or 47 of the Mental Health Act 1983;

(da) the prisoner is subject to the notification requirements of Part 2 of the Sexual Offences Act 2003:

(e) the prisoner is liable to removal from the United Kingdom for the purposes of section 46 below;

(f) the prisoner has been released on licence under this section at any time and has been recalled to prison under section 38A(1)(a) below;

(g) the prisoner has been released on licence under this section or section 36 below during the currency of the sentence, and has been recalled to prison under section 39(1) or (2) below;

(h) the prisoner has been returned to prison under section 116 of the Powers of Criminal Courts (Sentencing) Act 2000 at any time; or

(j) the interval between –

(i) the date on which the prisoner will have served the requisite period for the term of the sentence; and

(ii) the date on which he will have served one-half of the sentence,

is less than 14 days.

(3) After the prisoner has served the requisite period for the term of his sentence, the Secretary of State may, subject to section 37A below, release him on licence.

(4) In this section 'the requisite period' means–

(a) for a term of three months or more but less than four months, a period of 30 days;

(b) for a term of four months or more but less than eighteen months, a period equal to one-quarter of the term;

(c) for a term of eighteen months or more, a period that is 135 days less than one-half of the term.

(5) The Secretary of State may by order made by statutory instrument–

(a) repeal the words 'aged 18 or over' in subsection (1) above;

(b) amend the definition of 'the requisite period' in subsection (4) above; and

(c) make such transitional provision as appears to him necessary or expedient in connection with the repeal or amendment.

(6) No order shall be made under subsection (5) above unless a draft of the order has been laid before and approved by a resolution of each House of Parliament.

Power to release long-term and life prisoners

35 (1) After a long-term prisoner has served one-half of his sentence, the Secretary of State may, if recommended to do so by the Board, release him on licence.

(1A) Subsection (1) does not apply to a long-term prisoner to whom section 33(1A) applies.

(2)–(3) [*Repealed.*]

Power to release prisoners on compassionate grounds

36 (1) The Secretary of State may at any time release a short-term or long-term prisoner on licence if he is satisfied that exceptional circumstances exist which justify the prisoner's release on compassionate grounds.

(2) Before releasing a long-term prisoner under subsection (1) above, the Secretary of State shall consult the Board, unless the circumstances are such as to render such consultation impracticable.

Duration and conditions of licences

37 (1) Subject to subsections (1A), (1B), (2) and (8) below, where a short-term or long-term prisoner is released on licence, the licence shall, subject to any revocation under section 39(1) or (2) below, remain in force until the date on which he would (but for his release) have served three-quarters of his sentence.

(1A) Where a prisoner is released on licence under section 33(3) or (3A) above, subsection (1) above shall have effect as if for the reference to three-quarters of his sentence there were substituted a reference to the whole of that sentence.

(1B) Where a prisoner whose sentence is for a term of twelve months or more is released on licence under section 33A(2) or 34A(3) above, subsection (1) above shall have effect as if for the reference to three-quarters of his sentence there were substituted a reference to the difference between–

(a) that proportion of his sentence; and

(b) the duration of the curfew condition to which he is or was subject.

(2) Where a prisoner whose sentence is for a term of less than twelve months is released on licence under section 34A(3) or 36(1) above, subsection (1) above shall have effect as if for the reference to three-quarters of his sentence there were substituted a reference to one-half of that sentence.

(3) [*Repealed.*]

(4) A person subject to a licence under this Part shall comply with such conditions as may for the time being be specified in the licence; and the Secretary of State may make rules for regulating the supervision of any description of such persons.

(4A) The conditions so specified may in the case of a person released on licence under section 34A above whose sentence is for a term of less than twelve months, and shall in any other case, include on the person's release conditions as to his supervision by–

(a) an officer of a local probation board appointed for or assigned to the petty sessions area within which the person resides for the time being; or

(b) where the person is under the age of 18 years, a member of a youth offending team established by the local authority within whose area the person resides for the time being.

(5) The Secretary of State shall not include on release, or subsequently insert, a condition in the licence of a long-term prisoner, or vary or cancel any such condition, except after consultation with the Board.

(6) For the purposes of subsection (5) above, the Secretary of State shall be treated as having consulted the Board about a proposal to include, insert, vary or cancel a condition in any case if he has consulted the Board about the implementation of proposals of that description generally or in that class of case.

(7) The power to make rules under this section shall be exercisable by statutory instrument which shall be subject to annulment in pursuance of a resolution of either House of Parliament.

(8) This section does not apply in relation to a long-term prisoner to whom section 33(1A) applies (provision as to the duration and conditions of licences for such prisoners being made by section 37ZA).

Duration and conditions of licences under section 33(1A) etc

37ZA(1)Where a long-term prisoner is released on licence under section 33(1A), the licence shall (subject to any revocation under section 254 of the 2003 Act) remain in force for the remainder of the sentence.

(2) Section 250(1), (4) and (8) of the 2003 Act apply in relation to a licence under section 33(1A) of this Act as they apply in relation to a licence under Chapter 6 of Part 12 of the 2003 Act in respect of a prisoner serving a sentence of imprisonment for a term of twelve months or more.

(3) A person subject to a licence under section 33(1A) must comply with such conditions as may for the time being be specified in the licence.

(4) The reference in section 254(1) of the 2003 Act to a person who has been released on licence under Chapter 6 of Part 12 of that Act includes a reference to a person released on licence under section 33(1A).

(5) In this section, 'the 2003 Act' means the Criminal Justice Act 2003.

Recall of long-term and life prisoners while on licence

39 (1) If recommended to do so by the Board in the case of a short-term or long-term prisoner who has been released on licence under this Part, the Secretary of State may revoke his licence and recall him to prison.

(2) The Secretary of State may revoke the licence of any such person and recall him to prison without a recommendation by the Board, where it appears to him that it is expedient in the public interest to recall that person before such a recommendation is practicable.

(3) A person recalled to prison under subsection (1) or (2) above –

(a) may make representations in writing with respect to his recall; and

(b) on his return to prison, shall be informed of the reasons for his recall and of his right to make representations.

(4) The Secretary of State shall refer to the Board –

(a) the case of a person recalled under subsection (1) above who makes representations under subsection (3) above; and

(b) the case of a person recalled under subsection (2) above.

(5) Where on a reference under subsection (4) above the Board—

(a) [*Repealed.*]

(b) recommends in the case of any person,

his immediate release on licence under this section, the Secretary of State shall give effect to the recommendation.

(5A) In the case of a prisoner to whom section 44A below applies, subsections (4)(b) and (5) of that section apply in place of subsection (5) above.

(6) On the revocation of the licence of any person under this section, he shall be liable to be detained in pursuance of his sentence and, if at large, shall be deemed to be unlawfully at large.

Special cases

Young offenders

43 (1) Subject to subsections (4) and (5) below, this Part applies to persons serving sentences of detention in a young offender institution, or determinate sentences of detention under section 91 of the Powers of Criminal Courts (Sentencing) Act 2000, as it applies to persons serving equivalent sentences of imprisonment.

(2) [*Repealed.*]

(3) References in this Part to prisoners, or to prison or imprisonment, shall be construed in accordance with subsection (1) above.

(4) In relation to a short-term prisoner under the age of 18 years to whom subsection (1) of section 33 above applies, that subsection shall have effect as if it required the Secretary of State –

(a) to release him unconditionally if his sentence is for a term of twelve months or less; and

(b) to release him on licence if that sentence is for a term of more than twelve months.

(5) In relation to a person under the age of 22 years who is released on licence under any provision of this Part other than section 33(1A), section 37(4A) above shall have effect as if the reference to supervision by an officer of a local probation board included a reference to supervision by a social worker of a local authority social services department.

Extended sentences for sexual or violent offenders

44 (1) This section applies to a prisoner serving an extended sentence within the meaning of section 85 of the Powers of Criminal Courts (Sentencing) Act 2000.

(2) Subject to the provisions of this section and section 51(2D) below, this Part, except section 40A, shall have effect as if the term of the extended sentence did not include the extension period.

(3) Where the prisoner is released on licence under this Part, the licence shall, subject to any revocation under section 39(1) or (2) above, remain in force until the end of the extension period.

(4) Where, apart from this subsection, the prisoner would be released unconditionally–

(a) he shall be released on licence; and

(b) the licence shall, subject to any revocation under section 39(1) or (2) above, remain in force until the end of the extension period.

(5) The extension period shall be taken to begin as follows–

(a) for the purposes of subsection (3) above, on the date given by section 37(1) above;

(b) for the purposes of subsection (4) above, on the date on which, apart from that subsection, the prisoner would have been released unconditionally.

(6) Sections 33(3) and 33A(1) above and section 46(2) below shall not apply in relation to the prisoner.

(7) For the purposes of sections 37(5) and 39(1) and (2) above the question whether the prisoner is a long-term or short-term prisoner shall be determined by reference to the term of the extended sentence.

(8) In this section 'extension period' has the same meaning as in section 85 of the Powers of Criminal Courts (Sentencing) Act 2000.

Re-release of prisoners serving extended sentences

44A(1) This section applies to a prisoner serving an extended sentence within the meaning of section 85 of the Powers of Criminal Courts (Sentencing) Act 2000 who is recalled to prison under section 39(1) or (2) above.

(2) Subject to subsection (3) below, the prisoner may require the Secretary of State to refer his case to the Board at any time.

(3) Where there has been a previous reference of the prisoner's case to the Board (whether under this section or section 39(4) above), the Secretary of State shall not be required to refer the case until after the end of the period of one year beginning with the disposal of that reference.

(4) On a reference –

(a) under this section; or

(b) under section 39(4) above,

the Board shall direct the prisoner's release if satisfied that it is no longer necessary for the protection of the public that he should be confined (but not otherwise).

(5) If the Board gives a direction under subsection (4) above it shall be the duty of the Secretary of State to release the prisoner on licence.

Transfer by order of certain functions to Board

50 (1) The Secretary of State, after consultation with the Board, may by order made by statutory instrument provide that, in relation to such class of case as may be specified in the order, the provisions of this Part specified in subsections (2) or (3) below shall have effect subject to the modifications so specified.

(2) In section 35 above, in subsection (1) for the word 'may' there shall be substituted the word 'shall';

(3) In section 37 above, in subsection (5) for the words 'after consultation with the Board' there shall be substituted the words 'in accordance with recommendations of the Board', and subsection (6) shall be omitted.

(4) [*Repealed.*]

(5) No order shall be made under this section unless a draft of the order has been laid before and approved by resolution of each House of Parliament.

Prisoners recalled under section 254 of Criminal Justice Act 2003

50A(1) This section applies to a person who is –

(a) released on licence under any provision of this Part, and

(b) recalled to prison under section 254(1) of the 2003 Act (recall of prisoners while on licence).

(2) Nothing in the following provisions of this Part (which authorise or require the Secretary of State to release prisoners) applies in relation to the person –

(a) section 33;

(b) section 33A;

(c) section 34A;

(d) section 35;

(e) section 43(4).

(3) Sections 254(2) and (6) and 255A to 256A of the 2003 Act (which authorise release on licence etc) apply in relation to a person to whom this section applies with the modifications specified in subsection (4).

(4) Section 255A applies as if –

(a) the reference in subsection (2)(b) to section 246 or 248 of the 2003 Act were a reference to section 34A or 36 of this Act,

(b) the reference in subsection (11) to section 244 of the 2003 Act were a reference to section 33(1), (1A) or (2) of this Act,

(c) subsection (12) were omitted (provision to the same effect being made by section 51(2) of this Act, as it applies by virtue of subsection (9) below), and

(d) subsection (14) provided that 'term of imprisonment' included any sentence of detention mentioned in section 43(1) of this Act.

(5) The provisions of Chapter 6 of Part 12 of the 2003 Act specified in subsection (6) apply in relation to –
(a) a licence under that Chapter granted to a person to whom this section applies, and
(b) a licence under section 36 of this Act granted to such a person.

(6) The provisions of the 2003 Act specified in this subsection are–
(a) section 249 (duration of licence), as modified by subsection (7) below;
(b) section 250(1), (4) and (8) (licence conditions), as modified by subsection (8) below;
(c) section 252 (duty to comply with licence conditions).

(7) Section 249 of the 2003 Act applies–
(a) as if the reference in subsection (1) to a fixed-term prisoner were a reference to a person to whom this section applies, and
(b) as if for subsection (3) there were substituted –
'(3) Subsection (1) has effect subject to section 51(2) to (2D) of the Criminal Justice Act 1991 (treatment of consecutive and concurrent terms etc).'

(8) Section 250(4) of the 2003 Act applies as if the reference to a prisoner serving a sentence mentioned in that subsection were a reference to a person to whom this section applies.

(9) In relation to a person to whom this section applies, subsections (2) to (2D) of section 51 of this Act (treatment of consecutive and concurrent terms etc) apply as if any reference in those subsections to this Part of this Act included the provisions of the 2003 Act mentioned in subsections (3) and (6).

(10) Except as provided by subsections (7)(b) and (9), nothing in this Part applies in relation to the duration and conditions of –
(a) a licence under Chapter 6 of Part 12 of the 2003 Act granted to a person to whom this section applies, or
(b) a licence under section 36 of this Act granted to such a person.

(11) In this section, 'the 2003 Act' means the Criminal Justice Act 2003.

Interpretation of Part II

51 (1) In this Part –
'the Board''means the Parole Board;
'long-term prisoner' and 'short-term prisoner' have the meanings given by section 33(5) above (as extended by sections 43(1) and 45(1) above);
'sentence of imprisonment' does not include a committal in default of payment of any sum of money, or for want of sufficient distress to satisfy any sum of money, or for failure to do or abstain from doing anything required to be done or left undone.
'sexual offence' and 'violent offence' have the same meanings as in the Powers of Criminal Courts (Sentencing) Act 2000.

(2) For the purposes of any reference in this Part, however expressed, to the term of imprisonment to which a person has been sentenced or which, or part of which, he has served, consecutive terms and terms which are wholly or partly concurrent shall be treated as a single term if—
(a) the sentences were passed on the same occasion; or

(b) where they were passed on different occasions, the person has not been released under this Part at any time during the period beginning with the first and ending with the last of those occasions.

(2A) Where a suspended sentence of imprisonment is ordered to take effect, with or without any variation of the original term, the occasion on which that order is made shall be treated for the purposes of subsection (2) above as the occasion on which the sentence is passed.

(2B) Where a person has been sentenced to two or more terms of imprisonment which are wholly or partly concurrent and do not fall to be treated as a single term –

(a) nothing in this Part shall require the Secretary of State to release him in respect of any of the terms unless and until the Secretary of State is required to release him in respect of each of the others;

(b) nothing in this Part shall require the Secretary of State or the Board to consider his release in respect of any of the terms unless and until the Secretary of State or the Board is required to consider his release, or the Secretary of State is required to release him, in respect of each of the others;

(c) on and after his release under this Part he shall be on licence for so long, and subject to such conditions, as is required by this Part in respect of any of the sentences;

(d) [*Repealed.*]

(2C) Where a person has been sentenced to one or more terms of imprisonment and to one or more life sentences (within the meaning of section 34 of the Crime (Sentences) Act 1997), nothing in this Part shall—

(a) require the Secretary of State to release the person in respect of any of the terms unless and until the Secretary of State is required to release him in respect of each of the life sentences; or

(b) require the Secretary of State or the Board to consider the person's release in respect of any of the terms unless and until the Secretary of State or the Board is required to consider his release in respect of each of the life sentences.

(2D) Subsections (2B) and (2C) above shall have effect as if the term of an extended sentence (within the meaning of section 85 of the Powers of Criminal Courts (Sentencing) Act 2000) included the extension period (within the meaning of that section).

(3) [*Repealed.*]

(4) Section 161(4) of the Powers of Criminal Courts (Sentencing) Act 2000 (meaning of 'protecting the public from serious harm') shall apply for the purposes of this Part as it applies for the purposes of that Act.

CRIMINAL JUSTICE ACT 2003

SCHEDULE 15: SPECIFIED OFFENCES FOR PURPOSES OF CHAPTER 5 OF PART 12

Section 224

Part 1: Specified Violent Offences

1 Manslaughter.

2 Kidnapping.

3 False imprisonment.

4 An offence under section 4 of the Offences against the Person Act 1861 (soliciting murder).

5 An offence under section 16 of that Act (threats to kill).

6 An offence under section 18 of that Act (wounding with intent to cause grievous bodily harm).

7 An offence under section 20 of that Act (malicious wounding).

8 An offence under section 21 of that Act (attempting to choke, suffocate or strangle in order to commit or assist in committing an indictable offence).

9 An offence under section 22 of that Act (using chloroform etc to commit or assist in the committing of any indictable offence).

10 An offence under section 23 of that Act (maliciously administering poison etc so as to endanger life or inflict grievous bodily harm).

11 An offence under section 27 of that Act (abandoning children).

12 An offence under section 28 of that Act (causing bodily injury by explosives).

13 An offence under section 29 of that Act (using explosives etc with intent to do grievous bodily harm).

14 An offence under section 30 of that Act (placing explosives with intent to do bodily injury).

15 An offence under section 31 of that Act (setting spring guns etc with intent to do grievous bodily harm).

16 An offence under section 32 of that Act (endangering the safety of railway passengers).

17 An offence under section 35 of that Act (injuring persons by furious driving).

18 An offence under section 37 of that Act (assaulting officer preserving wreck).

19 An offence under section 38 of that Act (assault with intent to resist arrest).

20 An offence under section 47 of that Act (assault occasioning actual bodily harm).

21 An offence under section 2 of the Explosive Substances Act 1883 (causing explosion likely to endanger life or property).

22 An offence under section 3 of that Act (attempt to cause explosion, or making or keeping explosive with intent to endanger life or property).

23 An offence under section 1 of the Infant Life (Preservation) Act 1929 (child destruction).

24 An offence under section 1 of the Children and Young Persons Act 1933 (cruelty to children).

25 An offence under section 1 of the Infanticide Act 1938 (infanticide).

26 An offence under section 16 of the Firearms Act 1968 (possession of firearm with intent to endanger life).

27 An offence under section 16A of that Act (possession of firearm with intent to cause fear of violence).
28 An offence under section 17(1) of that Act (use of firearm to resist arrest).
29 An offence under section 17(2) of that Act (possession of firearm at time of committing or being arrested for offence specified in Schedule 1 to that Act).
30 An offence under section 18 of that Act (carrying a firearm with criminal intent).
31 An offence under section 8 of the Theft Act 1968 (robbery or assault with intent to rob).
32 An offence under section 9 of that Act of burglary with intent to–
(a) inflict grievous bodily harm on a person, or
(b) do unlawful damage to a building or anything in it.
33 An offence under section 10 of that Act (aggravated burglary).
34 An offence under section 12A of that Act (aggravated vehicle-taking) involving an accident which caused the death of any person.
35 An offence of arson under section 1 of the Criminal Damage Act 1971.
36 An offence under section 1(2) of that Act (destroying or damaging property) other than an offence of arson.
37 An offence under section 1 of the Taking of Hostages Act 1982 (hostage-taking).
38 An offence under section 1 of the Aviation Security Act 1982 (hijacking).
39 An offence under section 2 of that Act (destroying, damaging or endangering safety of aircraft).
40 An offence under section 3 of that Act (other acts endangering or likely to endanger safety of aircraft).
41 An offence under section 4 of that Act (offences in relation to certain dangerous articles).
42 An offence under section 127 of the Mental Health Act 1983 (ill-treatment of patients).
43 An offence under section 1 of the Prohibition of Female Circumcision Act 1985 (prohibition of female circumcision).
44 An offence under section 1 of the Public Order Act 1986 (riot).
45 An offence under section 2 of that Act (violent disorder).
46 An offence under section 3 of that Act (affray).
47 An offence under section 134 of the Criminal Justice Act 1988 (torture).
48 An offence under section 1 of the Road Traffic Act 1988 (causing death by dangerous driving).
49 An offence under section 3A of that Act (causing death by careless driving when under influence of drink or drugs).
50 An offence under section 1 of the Aviation and Maritime Security Act 1990 (endangering safety at aerodromes).
51 An offence under section 9 of that Act (hijacking of ships).
52 An offence under section 10 of that Act (seizing or exercising control of fixed platforms).
53 An offence under section 11 of that Act (destroying fixed platforms or endangering their safety).
54 An offence under section 12 of that Act (other acts endangering or likely to endanger safe navigation).

55 An offence under section 13 of that Act (offences involving threats).
56 An offence under Part II of the Channel Tunnel (Security) Order 1994 (offences relating to Channel Tunnel trains and the tunnel system).
57 An offence under section 4 of the Protection from Harassment Act 1997 (putting people in fear of violence).
58 An offence under section 29 of the Crime and Disorder Act 1998 (racially or religiously aggravated assaults).
59 An offence falling within section 31(1)(a) or (b) of that Act (racially or religiously aggravated offences under section 4 or 4A of the Public Order Act 1986).
60 An offence under section 51 or 52 of the International Criminal Court Act 2001 (genocide, crimes against humanity, war crimes and related offences), other than one involving murder.
61 An offence under section 1 of the Female Genital Mutilation Act 2003 (female genital mutilation).
62 An offence under section 2 of that Act (assisting a girl to mutilate her own genitalia).
63 An offence under section 3 of that Act (assisting a non-UK person to mutilate overseas a girl's genitalia).
63A An offence under section 5 of the Domestic Violence, Crime and Victims Act 2004 (causing or allowing the death of a child or vulnerable adult.
64 An offence of–
(a) aiding, abetting, counselling, procuring or inciting the commission of an offence specified in this Part of this Schedule,
(b) conspiring to commit an offence so specified, or
(c) attempting to commit an offence so specified.
65 An attempt to commit murder or a conspiracy to commit murder.

Part 2: Specified Sexual Offences

66 An offence under section 1 of the Sexual Offences Act 1956 (rape).
67 An offence under section 2 of that Act (procurement of woman by threats).
68 An offence under section 3 of that Act (procurement of woman by false pretences).
69 An offence under section 4 of that Act (administering drugs to obtain or facilitate intercourse).
70 An offence under section 5 of that Act (intercourse with girl under thirteen).
71 An offence under section 6 of that Act (intercourse with girl under 16).
72 An offence under section 7 of that Act (intercourse with a defective).
73 An offence under section 9 of that Act (procurement of a defective).
74 An offence under section 10 of that Act (incest by a man).
75 An offence under section 11 of that Act (incest by a woman).
76 An offence under section 14 of that Act (indecent assault on a woman).
77 An offence under section 15 of that Act (indecent assault on a man).
78 An offence under section 16 of that Act (assault with intent to commit buggery).
79 An offence under section 17 of that Act (abduction of woman by force or for the sake of her property).
80 An offence under section 19 of that Act (abduction of unmarried girl under eighteen from parent or guardian).

81 An offence under section 20 of that Act (abduction of unmarried girl under sixteen from parent or guardian).
82 An offence under section 21 of that Act (abduction of defective from parent or guardian).
83 An offence under section 22 of that Act (causing prostitution of women).
84 An offence under section 23 of that Act (procuration of girl under twenty-one).
85 An offence under section 24 of that Act (detention of woman in brothel).
86 An offence under section 25 of that Act (permitting girl under thirteen to use premises for intercourse).
87 An offence under section 26 of that Act (permitting girl under sixteen to use premises for intercourse).
88 An offence under section 27 of that Act (permitting defective to use premises for intercourse).
89 An offence under section 28 of that Act (causing or encouraging the prostitution of, intercourse with or indecent assault on girl under sixteen).
90 An offence under section 29 of that Act (causing or encouraging prostitution of defective).
91 An offence under section 32 of that Act (soliciting by men).
92 An offence under section 33 of that Act (keeping a brothel).
93 An offence under section 128 of the Mental Health Act 1959 (sexual intercourse with patients).
94 An offence under section 1 of the Indecency with Children Act 1960 (indecent conduct towards young child).
95 An offence under section 4 of the Sexual Offences Act 1967 (procuring others to commit homosexual acts).
96 An offence under section 5 of that Act (living on earnings of male prostitution).
97 An offence under section 9 of the Theft Act 1968 of burglary with intent to commit rape.
98 An offence under section 54 of the Criminal Law Act 1977 (inciting girl under sixteen to have incestuous sexual intercourse).
99 An offence under section 1 of the Protection of Children Act 1978 (indecent photographs of children).
100 An offence under section 170 of the Customs and Excise Management Act 1979 (penalty for fraudulent evasion of duty etc) in relation to goods prohibited to be imported under section 42 of the Customs Consolidation Act 1876 (indecent or obscene articles).
101 An offence under section 160 of the Criminal Justice Act 1988 (possession of indecent photograph of a child).
102 An offence under section 1 of the Sexual Offences Act 2003 (rape).
103 An offence under section 2 of that Act (assault by penetration).
104 An offence under section 3 of that Act (sexual assault).
105 An offence under section 4 of that Act (causing a person to engage in sexual activity without consent).
106 An offence under section 5 of that Act (rape of a child under 13).
107 An offence under section 6 of that Act (assault of a child under 13 by penetration).
108 An offence under section 7 of that Act (sexual assault of a child under 13).

109 An offence under section 8 of that Act (causing or inciting a child under 13 to engage in sexual activity).

110 An offence under section 9 of that Act (sexual activity with a child).

111 An offence under section 10 of that Act (causing or inciting a child to engage in sexual activity).

112 An offence under section 11 of that Act (engaging in sexual activity in the presence of a child).

113 An offence under section 12 of that Act (causing a child to watch a sexual act).

114 An offence under section 13 of that Act (child sex offences committed by children or young persons).

115 An offence under section 14 of that Act (arranging or facilitating commission of a child sex offence).

116 An offence under section 15 of that Act (meeting a child following sexual grooming etc).

117 An offence under section 16 of that Act (abuse of position of trust: sexual activity with a child).

118 An offence under section 17 of that Act (abuse of position of trust: causing or inciting a child to engage in sexual activity).

119 An offence under section 18 of that Act (abuse of position of trust: sexual activity in the presence of a child).

120 An offence under section 19 of that Act (abuse of position of trust: causing a child to watch a sexual act).

121 An offence under section 25 of that Act (sexual activity with a child family member).

122 An offence under section 26 of that Act (inciting a child family member to engage in sexual activity).

123 An offence under section 30 of that Act (sexual activity with a person with a mental disorder impeding choice).

124 An offence under section 31 of that Act (causing or inciting a person with a mental disorder impeding choice to engage in sexual activity).

125 An offence under section 32 of that Act (engaging in sexual activity in the presence of a person with a mental disorder impeding choice).

126 An offence under section 33 of that Act (causing a person with a mental disorder impeding choice to watch a sexual act).

127 An offence under section 34 of that Act (inducement, threat or deception to procure sexual activity with a person with a mental disorder).

128 An offence under section 35 of that Act (causing a person with a mental disorder to engage in or agree to engage in sexual activity by inducement, threat or deception).

129 An offence under section 36 of that Act (engaging in sexual activity in the presence, procured by inducement, threat or deception, of a person with a mental disorder).

130 An offence under section 37 of that Act (causing a person with a mental disorder to watch a sexual act by inducement, threat or deception).

131 An offence under section 38 of that Act (care workers: sexual activity with a person with a mental disorder).

132 An offence under section 39 of that Act (care workers: causing or inciting sexual activity).

133 An offence under section 40 of that Act (care workers: sexual activity in the presence of a person with a mental disorder).
134 An offence under section 41 of that Act (care workers: causing a person with a mental disorder to watch a sexual act).
135 An offence under section 47 of that Act (paying for sexual services of a child).
136 An offence under section 48 of that Act (causing or inciting child prostitution or pornography).
137 An offence under section 49 of that Act (controlling a child prostitute or a child involved in pornography).
138 An offence under section 50 of that Act (arranging or facilitating child prostitution or pornography).
139 An offence under section 52 of that Act (causing or inciting prostitution for gain).
140 An offence under section 53 of that Act (controlling prostitution for gain).
141 An offence under section 57 of that Act (trafficking into the UK for sexual exploitation).
142 An offence under section 58 of that Act (trafficking within the UK for sexual exploitation).
143 An offence under section 59 of that Act (trafficking out of the UK for sexual exploitation).
144 An offence under section 61 of that Act (administering a substance with intent).
145 An offence under section 62 of that Act (committing an offence with intent to commit a sexual offence).
146 An offence under section 63 of that Act (trespass with intent to commit a sexual offence).
147 An offence under section 64 of that Act (sex with an adult relative: penetration).
148 An offence under section 65 of that Act (sex with an adult relative: consenting to penetration).
149 An offence under section 66 of that Act (exposure).
150 An offence under section 67 of that Act (voyeurism).
151 An offence under section 69 of that Act (intercourse with an animal).
152 An offence under section 70 of that Act (sexual penetration of a corpse).
153 An offence of–
(a) aiding, abetting, counselling, procuring or inciting the commission of an offence specified in this Part of this Schedule,
(b) conspiring to commit an offence so specified, or
(c) attempting to commit an offence so specified.

APPENDIX E

The release of CJA 2003 determinate sentence prisoners (offences committed on or after 4 April 2005) and recall procedures for all determinate sentence prisoners

Criminal Justice Act 2003 ss244–256A[1]

Release on licence

Duty to release prisoners

244 (1) As soon as a fixed-term prisoner, other than a prisoner to whom section 247 applies, has served the requisite custodial period, it is the duty of the Secretary of State to release him on licence under this section.

(2) Subsection (1) is subject to section 245.

(3) In this section 'the requisite custodial period' means–

(a) in relation to a person serving a sentence of imprisonment for a term of twelve months or more or any determinate sentence of detention under section 91 or 96 of the Sentencing Act, one-half of his sentence,

(b) in relation to a person serving a sentence of imprisonment for a term of less than twelve months (other than one to which an intermittent custody order relates), the custodial period within the meaning of section 181,

(c) in relation to a person serving a sentence of imprisonment to which an intermittent custody order relates, any part of the term [which for the purposes of section 183 (as read with section 263(2) or 264A(2) in the case of concurrent or consecutive sentences) is not a licence period], and

(d) in relation to a person serving two or more concurrent or consecutive sentences [none of which falls within paragraph (c)], the period determined under sections 263(2) and 264(2).

Restrictions on operation of section 244(1) in relation to intermittent custody prisoners

245 (1) Where an intermittent custody prisoner returns to custody after being unlawfully at large within the meaning of section 49 of the Prison Act 1952 (c 52) at any time during the currency of his sentence, section 244(1) does not apply until –

1 Words substituted in sections 244-256A, from a date to be appointed, by Criminal Justice and Immigration Act 2008 Part 2.

(a) the relevant time (as defined in subsection (2)), or
(b) if earlier, the date on which he has served in prison the number of custodial days required by the intermittent custody order.

(2) In subsection (1)(a) 'the relevant time' means–
(a) in a case where, within the period of 72 hours beginning with the return to custody of the intermittent custody prisoner, the Secretary of State or the responsible officer has applied to the court for the amendment of the intermittent custody order under paragraph 6(1)(b) of Schedule 10, the date on which the application is withdrawn or determined, and
(b) in any other case, the end of that 72-hour period.

(3) Section 244(1) does not apply in relation to an intermittent custody prisoner at any time after he has been recalled under section 254, unless after his recall the Board has directed his further release on licence.

Power to release prisoners on licence before required to do so

246 (1) Subject to subsections (2) to (4), the Secretary of State may–
(a) release on licence under this section a fixed-term prisoner, other than an intermittent custody prisoner, at any time during the period of 135 days ending with the day on which the prisoner will have served the requisite custodial period, and
(b) release on licence under this section an intermittent custody prisoner when 135 or less of the required custodial days remain to be served.

(2) Subsection (1)(a) does not apply in relation to a prisoner unless–
(a) the length of the requisite custodial period is at least 6 weeks, and
(b) he has served–
(i) at least 4 weeks of that period, and
(ii) at least one-half of that period.

(3) Subsection (1)(b) does not apply in relation to a prisoner unless–
(a) the number of required custodial days is at least 42, and
(b) the prisoner has served–
(i) at least 28 of those days, and
(ii) at least one-half of the total number of those days.

(4) Subsection (1) does not apply where–
(a) the sentence is imposed under section 227 or 228,
(b) the sentence is for an offence under section 1 of the Prisoners (Return to Custody) Act 1995,
(c) the prisoner is subject to a hospital order, hospital direction or transfer direction under section 37, 45A or 47 of the Mental Health Act 1983,
(d) the sentence was imposed by virtue of paragraph 9(1)(b) or (c) or 10(1)(b) or (c) of Schedule 8 in a case where the prisoner has failed to comply with a curfew requirement of a community order,
(e) the prisoner is subject to the notification requirements of Part 2 of the Sexual Offences Act 2003,
(f) the prisoner is liable to removal from the United Kingdom,
(g) the prisoner has been released on licence under this section during the currency of the sentence, and has been recalled to prison under section 255(1)(a),
(h) the prisoner has been released on licence under section 248 during the currency of the sentence, and has been recalled to prison under section 254, or

(i) in the case of a prisoner to whom a direction under section 240 or 240A relates, the interval between the date on which the sentence was passed and the date on which the prisoner will have served the requisite custodial period is less than 14 days or, where the sentence is one of intermittent custody, the number of the required custodial days remaining to be served is less than 14.

(4A) In subsection (4)–

(a) the reference in paragraph (d) to a community order includes a service community order or overseas community order under the Armed Forces Act 2006; and

(b) the reference in paragraph (i) to a direction under section 240 includes a direction under section 246 of that Act.

(5) The Secretary of State may by order–

(a) amend the number of days for the time being specified in subsection (1)(a) or (b), (3) or (4)(i),

(b) amend the number of weeks for the time being specified in subsection (2)(a) or (b)(i), and

(c) amend the fraction for the time being specified in subsection (2)(b)(ii) or (3)(b)(ii).

(6) In this section–

'the required custodial days', in relation to an intermittent custody prisoner, means–

(a) the number of custodial days specified under section 183, or

(b) in the case of two or more sentences of intermittent custody which are consecutive, the aggregate of the numbers so specified, or

(c) in the case of two or more sentences of intermittent custody which are wholly or partly concurrent, the aggregate of the numbers so specified less the number of days that are to be served concurrently;

'the requisite custodial period' in relation to a person serving any sentence other than a sentence of intermittent custody, has the meaning given by paragraph (a), (b) or (d) of section 244(3);

'sentence of intermittent custody' means a sentence to which an intermittent custody order relates.

Release on licence of prisoner serving extended sentence under section 227 or 228

247 (1) This section applies to a prisoner who is serving an extended sentence imposed under section 227 or 228.

(2) As soon as–

(a) a prisoner to whom this section applies has served one-half of the appropriate custodial term,

(b) [*Repealed.*]

it is the duty of the Secretary of State to release him on licence.

(7) In this section 'the appropriate custodial term' means the period determined by the court as the appropriate custodial term under section 227 or 228.

Power to release prisoners on compassionate grounds

248 (1) The Secretary of State may at any time release a fixed-term prisoner on licence if he is satisfied that exceptional circumstances exist which justify the prisoner's release on compassionate grounds.

(2) Before releasing under this section a prisoner to whom section 247 applies, the Secretary of State must consult the Board, unless the circumstances are such as to render such consultation impracticable.

Duration of licence

249 (1) Subject to subsections (2) and (3), where a fixed-term prisoner is released on licence, the licence shall, subject to any revocation under section 254 or 255, remain in force for the remainder of his sentence.

(2) Where an intermittent custody prisoner is released on licence under section 244, the licence shall, subject to any revocation under section 254, remain in force–

(a) until the time when he is required to return to prison at the beginning of the next custodial period of the sentence, or

(b) where it is granted at the end of the last custodial period, for the remainder of his sentence.

(3) Subsection (1) has effect subject to sections 263(2) (concurrent terms) and 264(3) and (4) (consecutive terms) and subsection (2) has effect subject to section 264A(3) (consecutive terms: intermittent custody).

(4) In subsection (2) 'custodial period', in relation to a sentence to which an intermittent custody order relates, means any period which is not a licence period as defined by 183(3).

Licence conditions

250 (1) In this section–

(a) 'the standard conditions' means such conditions as may be prescribed for the purposes of this section as standard conditions, and

(b) 'prescribed' means prescribed by the Secretary of State by order.

(2) Subject to subsection (6) and section 251, any licence under this Chapter in respect of a prisoner serving one or more sentences of imprisonment of less than twelve months and no sentence of twelve months or more–

(a) must include–

(i) the conditions required by the relevant court order, and

(ii) so far as not inconsistent with them, the standard conditions, and

(b) may also include–

(i) any condition which is authorised by section 62 of the Criminal Justice and Court Services Act 2000 (electronic monitoring) or section 64 of that Act (drug testing requirements) and which is compatible with the conditions required by the relevant court order, and

(ii) such other conditions of a kind prescribed for the purposes of this paragraph as the Secretary of State may for the time being consider to be necessary for the protection of the public and specify in the licence.

(2A) If the sentence (or, if more than one, each sentence) that the prisoner is serving is one in relation to which no custody plus or intermittent custody order is in force, subsection (2) has effect as if there were omitted–

(a) paragraph (a)(i);

(b) the words 'so far as not inconsistent with them,' in paragraph (a)(ii); and

(c) the words from 'and which' in paragraph (b)(i).

(3) For the purposes of subsection (2)(a)(i), any reference in the relevant court order to the licence period specified in the order is, in relation to a prohibited activity requirement, exclusion requirement, residence requirement or super-

vision requirement, to be taken to include a reference to any other period during which the prisoner is released on licence under section 246 or 248.

(4) Any licence under this Chapter in respect of a prisoner serving a sentence of imprisonment or detention in a young offender institution for a term of twelve months or more (including such a sentence imposed under section 227) or any sentence of detention under section 91 of the Sentencing Act or section 228 of this Act–
 (a) must include the standard conditions, and
 (b) may include–
  (i) any condition authorised by section 62 or 64 of the Criminal Justice and Court Services Act 2000 or section 28 of the Offender Management Act 2007, and
  (ii) such other conditions of a kind prescribed by the Secretary of State for the purposes of this paragraph as the Secretary of State may for the time being specify in the licence.

(5) A licence under section 246 must also include a curfew condition complying with section 253.

(6) Where–
 (a) a licence under section 246 is granted to a prisoner serving one or more sentences of imprisonment of less than 12 months and no sentence of 12 months or more, and
 (b) the relevant court order requires the licence to be granted subject to a condition requiring his compliance with a curfew requirement (as defined by section 204),

that condition is not to be included in the licence at any time while a curfew condition required by section 253 is in force.

(7) The preceding provisions of this section have effect subject to section 263(3) (concurrent terms), section 264(3) and (4) (consecutive terms) and section 264A(3) (consecutive terms: intermittent custody).

(8) In exercising his powers to prescribe standard conditions or the other conditions referred to in subsection (4)(b)(ii), the Secretary of State must have regard to the following purposes of the supervision of offenders while on licence under this Chapter–
 (a) the protection of the public,
 (b) the prevention of re-offending, and
 (c) securing the successful re-integration of the prisoner into the community.

Licence conditions on re-release of prisoner serving sentence of less than 12 months

251 (1) In relation to any licence under this Chapter which is granted to a prisoner serving one or more sentences of imprisonment of less than twelve months and no sentence of twelve months or more on his release in pursuance of a decision of the Board under section 254 or 256, subsections (2) and (3) apply instead of section 250(2).

(2) The licence–
 (a) must include the standard conditions, and
 (b) may include–
  (i) any condition authorised by section 62 or 64 of the Criminal Justice and Court Services Act 2000, and

(ii) such other conditions of a kind prescribed by the Secretary of State for the purposes of section 250(4)(b)(ii) as the Secretary of State may for the time being specify in the licence.

(3) In exercising his powers under subsection (2)(b)(ii), the Secretary of State must have regard to the terms of the relevant court order (if any).

(4) In this section 'the standard conditions' has the same meaning as in section 250.

Duty to comply with licence conditions

252 (1) A person subject to a licence under this Chapter must comply with such conditions as may for the time being be specified in the licence.

(2) But where–

(a) the licence relates to a sentence of imprisonment passed by a service court,

(b) no custody plus order was made in relation to the sentence, or such an order was made but subsequently revoked, and

(c) the person is residing outside the British Islands,

the conditions specified in the licence apply to him only so far as it is practicable for him to comply with them where he is residing.

Curfew condition to be included in licence under section 246

253 (1) For the purposes of this Chapter, a curfew condition is a condition which–

(a) requires the released person to remain, for periods for the time being specified in the condition, at a place for the time being so specified (which may be premises approved by the Secretary of State under section 13 of the Offender Management Act 2007), and

(b) includes requirements for securing the electronic monitoring of his whereabouts during the periods for the time being so specified.

(2) The curfew condition may specify different places or different periods for different days, but may not specify periods which amount to less than 9 hours in any one day (excluding for this purpose the first and last days of the period for which the condition is in force).

(3) The curfew condition is to remain in force until the date when the released person would (but for his release) fall to be released on licence under section 244.

(4) Subsection (3) does not apply in relation to a released person to whom an intermittent custody order relates; and in relation to such a person the curfew condition is to remain in force until the number of days during which it has been in force is equal to the number of the required custodial days, as defined in section 246(6), that remained to be served at the time when he was released under section 246.

(5) The curfew condition must include provision for making a person responsible for monitoring the released person's whereabouts during the periods for the time being specified in the condition; and a person who is made so responsible shall be of a description specified in an order made by the Secretary of State.

(6) Nothing in this section is to be taken to require the Secretary of State to ensure that arrangements are made for the electronic monitoring of released persons' whereabouts in any particular part of England and Wales.

Recall after release

Recall of prisoners while on licence

254 (1) The Secretary of State may, in the case of any prisoner who has been released on licence under this Chapter, revoke his licence and recall him to prison.

(2) A person recalled to prison under subsection (1)–

(a) may make representations in writing with respect to his recall, and

(b) on his return to prison, must be informed of the reasons for his recall and of his right to make representations.

(6) On the revocation of the licence of any person under this section, he shall be liable to be detained in pursuance of his sentence and, if at large, is to be treated as being unlawfully at large.

(7) Nothing in this section applies in relation to a person recalled under section 255.

Recall of prisoners released early under section 246

255 (1) If it appears to the Secretary of State, as regards a person released on licence under section 246–

(a) that he has failed to comply with any condition included in his licence, or

(b) that his whereabouts can no longer be electronically monitored at the place for the time being specified in the curfew condition included in his licence,

the Secretary of State may, if the curfew condition is still in force, revoke the licence and recall the person to prison under this section.

(2) A person whose licence under section 246 is revoked under this section–

(a) may make representations in writing with respect to the revocation, and

(b) on his return to prison, must be informed of the reasons for the revocation and of his right to make representations.

(3) The Secretary of State, after considering any representations under subsection (2)(b) or any other matters, may cancel a revocation under this section.

(4) Where the revocation of a person's licence is cancelled under subsection (3), the person is to be treated for the purposes of section 246 as if he had not been recalled to prison under this section.

(5) On the revocation of a person's licence under section 246, he is liable to be detained in pursuance of his sentence and, if at large, is to be treated as being unlawfully at large.

Further release after recall: introductory

255A(1) This section applies for the purpose of identifying which of sections 255B to 255D governs the further release of a person who has been recalled under section 254 ('the prisoner').

(2) The prisoner is eligible to be considered for automatic release unless–

(a) he is an extended sentence prisoner or a specified offence prisoner;

(b) in a case where paragraph (a) does not apply, he was recalled under section 254 before the normal entitlement date (having been released before that date under section 246 or 248); or

(c) in a case where neither of the preceding paragraphs applies, he has, during the same term of imprisonment, already been released under section 255B(1)(b) or (2) or section 255C(2).

(3) If the prisoner is eligible to be considered for automatic release the Secretary

of State must, on recalling him, consider whether he is suitable for automatic release.

(4) For this purpose 'automatic release' means release at the end of the period of 28 days beginning with the date on which the prisoner is returned to prison.

(5) The person is suitable for automatic release only if the Secretary of State is satisfied that he will not present a risk of serious harm to members of the public if he is released at the end of that period.

(6) The prisoner must be dealt with–

(a) in accordance with section 255B if he is eligible to be considered for automatic release and is suitable for automatic release;

(b) in accordance with section 255C if he is eligible to be considered for automatic release but was not considered to be suitable for it;

(c) in accordance with section 255C if he is a specified offence prisoner or if he is not eligible to be considered for automatic release by virtue of subsection (2)(b) or (c);

(d) in accordance with section 255D if he is an extended sentence prisoner.

(7) The prisoner is an 'extended sentence prisoner' if he is serving an extended sentence imposed under section 227 or 228 of this Act, section 58 of the Crime and Disorder Act 1998 or section 85 of the Powers of Criminal Courts (Sentencing) Act 2000.

(8) The prisoner is a 'specified offence prisoner' if (not being an extended sentence prisoner) he is serving a sentence imposed for a specified offence within the meaning of section 224.

(9) The reference in subsection (8) to a specified offence (within the meaning of section 224) includes a reference to–

(a) an offence under section 70 of the Army Act 1955, section 70 of the Air Force Act 1955 or section 42 of the Naval Discipline Act 1957 as respects which the corresponding civil offence (within the meaning of the Act in question) is a specified offence, and

(b) an offence under section 42 of the Armed Forces Act 2006 as respects which the corresponding offence under the law of England and Wales (within the meaning given by that section) is a specified offence.

(10) Section 48 of the Armed Forces Act 2006 (attempts, conspiracy etc) applies for the purposes of subsection (9)(b) as if the reference in subsection (3)(b) of that section to any of the following provisions of that Act were a reference to subsection (9)(b).

(11) In subsection (2)(b) the 'normal entitlement date' means the date on which the prisoner would (but for his earlier release) have been entitled to be released under section 244.

(12) For the purposes of subsection (2)(c) terms of imprisonment which are consecutive and terms which are wholly or partly concurrent are to be treated as a single term if–

(a) the sentences were passed on the same occasion, or

(b) where they were passed on different occasions, the prisoner has not been released under this Chapter at any time during the period beginning with the first and ending with the last of those occasions.

(13) In subsection (5) 'serious harm' means death or serious personal injury, whether physical or psychological.

(14) In this section, 'term of imprisonment' includes a determinate sentence of

detention under section 91 or 96 of the Sentencing Act or under section 227 or 228 of this Act.

Automatic release

255B(1) A prisoner who is suitable for automatic release must–

(a) on his return to prison, be informed that he will be released under this subsection, and

(b) at the end of the 28 day period mentioned in section 255A(4) (or such other period as is specified for the purposes of that subsection), be released by the Secretary of State on licence under this Chapter (unless he has already been released under subsection (2)).

(2) The Secretary of State may, at any time after a prisoner who is suitable for automatic release is returned to prison, release him again on licence under this Chapter.

(3) The Secretary of State must not release a person under subsection (2) unless the Secretary of State is satisfied that it is not necessary for the protection of the public that he should remain in prison until the end of the period mentioned in subsection (1)(b).

(4) If a prisoner who is suitable for automatic release makes representations under section 254(2) before the end of that period, the Secretary of State must refer his case to the Board on the making of those representations.

(5) Where on a reference under subsection (4) relating to any person the Board recommends his immediate release on licence under this Chapter, the Secretary of State must give effect to the recommendation.

(6) In the case of an intermittent custody prisoner who has not yet served in prison the number of custodial days specified in the intermittent custody order, any recommendation by the Board as to immediate release on licence is to be a recommendation as to his release on licence until the end of one of the licence periods specified by virtue of section 183(1)(b) in the intermittent custody order.

Specified offence prisoners and those not suitable for automatic release

255C(1) This section applies to a prisoner who–

(a) is a specified offence prisoner,

(b) is not eligible to be considered for automatic release by virtue of section 255A(2)(b) or (c), or

(c) was eligible to be considered for automatic release but was not considered to be suitable for it.

(2) The Secretary of State may, at any time after the person is returned to prison, release him again on licence under this Chapter.

(3) The Secretary of State must not release a person under subsection (2) unless the Secretary of State is satisfied that it is not necessary for the protection of the public that he should remain in prison.

(4) The Secretary of State must refer to the Board the case of any person to whom this section applies–

(a) if the person makes representations under section 254(2) before the end of the period of 28 days beginning with the date on which he is returned to prison, on the making of those representations, or

(b) if, at the end of that period, the person has not been released under subsection (2) and has not made such representations, at that time.

(5) Where on a reference under subsection (4) relating to any person the Board recommends his immediate release on licence under this Chapter, the Secretary of State must give effect to the recommendation.

(6) In the case of an intermittent custody prisoner who has not yet served in prison the number of custodial days specified in the intermittent custody order, any recommendation by the Board as to immediate release on licence is to be a recommendation as to his release on licence until the end of one of the licence periods specified by virtue of section 183(1)(b) in the intermittent custody order.

Extended sentence prisoners

255D(1)The Secretary of State must refer to the Board the case of any extended sentence prisoner.

(2) Where on a reference under subsection (1) relating to any person the Board recommends his immediate release on licence under this Chapter, the Secretary of State must give effect to the recommendation.

Review by the Board

256 (1) Where on a reference under section 255B(4), 255C(4) or 255D(1) in relation to any person, the Board does not recommend his immediate release on licence under this Chapter, the Board must either–

(a) fix a date for the person's release on licence, or

(b) determine the reference by making no recommendation as to his release.

(2) Any date fixed under subsection (1)(a) must not be later than the first anniversary of the date on which the decision is taken.

(4) Where the Board has fixed a date under subsection (1)(a), it is the duty of the Secretary of State to release him on licence on that date.

Further review

256A(1)The Secretary of State must, not later than the first anniversary of a determination by the Board under section 256(1) or subsection (4) below, refer the person's case to the Board.

(2) The Secretary of State may, at any time before that anniversary, refer the person's case to the Board.

(3) The Board may at any time recommend to the Secretary of State that a person's case be referred under subsection (2).

(4) On a reference under subsection (1) or (2), the Board must determine the reference by–

(a) recommending the person's immediate release on licence under this Chapter,

(b) fixing a date for his release on licence, or

(c) making no recommendation as to his release.

(5) The Secretary of State–

(a) where the Board makes a recommendation under subsection (4)(a) for the person's immediate release on licence, must give effect to the recommendation; and

(b) where the Board fixes a release date under subsection (4)(b), must release the person on licence on that date.

APPENDIX F

The Secretary of State's directions to the Parole Board

Directions to the Parole Board under section 32(6) of the Criminal Justice Act 1991

Issued May 2004

Directions relating to the Release of Determinate Sentence Prisoners

1. In deciding whether or not to recommend release on license, the Parole Board shall consider primarily the risk to the public of a further offence being committed at a time when the prisoner would otherwise be in prison and whether any such risk is acceptable. This must be balanced against the benefit, both to the public and the offender, of early release back into the community under a degree of supervision which might help rehabilitation and so lessen the risk of re-offending in the future. The Board shall take into account that safeguarding the public may often outweigh the benefits to the offender of early release.
2. Before recommending release on parole licence, the Parole Board shall consider:
   (a) whether the safety of the public would be placed unacceptably at risk. In assessing such risk, the Board shall take into account;
      (i) the nature and circumstances of the index offence including any information provided in relation to its impact on the victim of the victim's family;
      (ii) the offender's background, including the nature, circumstances and pattern of any previous offending;
      (iii) whether the prisoner has shown by his attitude and behaviour in custody that he is willing to address his offending behaviour by participating in programmes or activities designed to address his risk, and has made positive effort and progress in doing so;
      (iv) behaviour during any temporary release or other outside activities;
      (v) any risk to other persons, including the victim, their family and friends;
      (vi) any medical, psychiatric or psychological considerations relevant to risk (particularly where there is a history of mental instability);
      (vii) if available, the indication of predicted risk as determined by a validated actuarial risk predictor:
      (viii) that a risk of violent or sexual offending is more serious than a risk of other types of offending;

(b) the content of the resettlement plan;
(c) whether the longer period of supervision that parole would provide is likely to reduce the risk of further offences being committed;
(d) whether the prisoner is likely to comply with the conditions of his licence and the requirements of supervision, taking into account occasions where he has breached trust in the past;
(e) the suitability of home circumstances;
(f) the relationship with the supervising probation officer:
(g) the attitude of the local community in cases where it may have a detrimental affect upon compliance; and
(h) representations on behalf of the victim in respect of licence conditions.

3. Each individual case shall be considered on its merits, without discrimination on any grounds.

Directions to the Parole Board under section 32(6) of the Criminal Justice Act 1991

Issued August 2004

Release and recall of life sentence prisoners

Introduction

1. The Secretary of State may refer to, and seek advice from, the Parole Board on any matters relating to the early release and recall to custody of those prisoners sentenced to imprisonment for life, custody for life, detention during Her Majesty's pleasure, and detention for life.
2. The Parole Board is empowered to direct the release, or re-release following recall to custody, of those life sentence prisoners (lifers) who have served the period of imprisonment necessary to satisfy the requirements of retribution and deterrence.
3. The Parole Board cannot direct the release of any lifer unless the following conditions are met:
   a) the Secretary of State has referred the case to the Parole Board for consideration of the prisoners suitability for release;
   b) the Parole Board is satisfied that it is no longer necessary for the protection of the public that the prisoner should be confined.
4. The test to be applied by the Parole Board in satisfying itself that it is no longer necessary for the protection of the public that the prisoner should be confined, is whether the lifer's level of risk to the life and limb of others is considered to be more than minimal.

Directions

5. Before directing a lifer's release under supervision on life licence, the Parole Board must consider:
   a) all information before it, including any written or oral evidence obtained by the Board;
   b) each case on its merits, without discrimination on any grounds;
   c) whether the release of the lifer is consistent with the general requirements and objectives of supervision in the community, namely;

- protecting the public by ensuring that their safety would not be placed unacceptably at risk;
- securing the lifers successful re-integration into the community.

6. In assessing the level of risk to life and limb presented by a lifer, the Parole Board shall consider the following information, where relevant and where available, before directing the lifer's release, recognising that the weight and relevance attached to particular information may vary according to the circumstances of each case:
   a) the lifers background, including the nature, circumstances and pattern of any previous offending;
   b) the nature and circumstances of the index offence, including any information provided in relation to its impact on the victim or victim's family;
   c) the trial judge's sentencing comments or report to the Secretary of State, and any probation, medical, or other relevant reports or material prepared for the court;
   d) whether the lifer has made positive and successful efforts to address the attitudes and behavioural problems which led to the commission of the index offence;
   e) the nature of any offences against prison discipline committed by the lifer;
   f) the lifers attitude and behaviour to other prisoners and staff,
   g) the category of security in which the lifer is held and any reasons or reports provided by the Prison Service for such categorisation, particularly in relation to those lifers held in Category A conditions of security;
   h) the lifer's awareness of the impact of the index offence, particularly in relation to the victim or victims family, and the extent of any demonstrable insight into his /her attitudes and behavioural problems and whether he/she has taken steps to reduce risk through the achievement of life sentence plan targets;
   i) any medical, psychiatric or psychological considerations (particularly if there is a history of mental instability);
   j) the lifer's response when placed in positions of trust, including any absconds, escapes, past breaches of temporary release or life licence conditions and life licence revocations;
   k) any indication of predicted risk as determined by a validated actuarial risk predictor model, or any other structured assessments of the lifers risk and treatment needs
   l) whether the lifer is likely to comply with the conditions attached to his or her life licence and the requirements of supervision, including any additional non-standard conditions;
   m) any risk to other persons, including the victim, their family and friends.
7. Before directing release on life licence, the Parole Board shall also consider:
   a) the lifer's relationship with probation staff (in particular the supervising probation officer), and other outside support such as family and friends;
   b) the content of the resettlement plan and the suitability of the release address;
   c) the attitude of the local community in cases where it may have a detrimental effect upon compliance;
   d) representations on behalf of the victim or victims relatives in relation to licence conditions.

Recall of life licensees

Introduction

8. When a lifer is released from custody, he/she becomes subject to a life licence for the rest of their lives and may be recalled to prison at any time if their behaviour gives cause for concern. The Secretary of State may revoke a life licence and recall the life licensee to prison on the recommendation of the Parole Board, or without such a recommendation where the Secretary of State considers this to be expedient in the public interest.
9. Supervision under life licence, including compliance with any conditions attached to the licence, is an integral part of the life sentence. It enables the level of risk to be assessed and managed in a way consistent with the objectives of supervision, in particular the protection of the public from harm.

Directions

10. In deciding whether or not to recommend the recall of a life licensee, the Parole Board must consider:
    a) all information before it;
    b) each case on its merits, without discrimination on any grounds;
    c) whether the lifers continued liberty would present an unacceptable risk of harm to other persons or be otherwise inconsistent with the general requirements and objectives of supervision in the community.
11. In assessing the level of risk presented by a life licensee as part of the above consideration, the Parole Board must address the following factors:-
    a) the extent to which the licensees continued liberty presents a risk of harm to a specific individual or individuals, or members of the public generally;
    b) the immediacy and level of such risk which the life licensee presents and the extent to which this is manageable in the community;
    c) the extent to which the licensee has failed previously to comply with licence conditions or the objectives of supervision, or is likely to do so in the future, and the effect of this on the immediacy and level of risk presented by the licensee;
    d) any similarity between the prisoners behaviour and that which preceded the index offence.
12. Following the revocation of a life licence and the licensees return to custody, the lifer will be informed of the reasons for the recall, and of their right to make representations and have these considered at an oral hearing.
    When considering the possible re-release of a lifer whose licence has been revoked, the Parole Board shall consider the case under the Directions for release and shall apply the same test of risk set out in those Directions.

Transfer of life sentence prisoners to open conditions

Introduction

1. A period in open conditions is essential for most life sentence prisoners (lifers). It allows the testing of areas of concern in conditions that more closely resemble those that the prisoner will encounter in the community often after having spent many years in closed prisons. Lifers have the opportunity to take resettlement leave from open prisons and, more generally, open conditions require them to take more responsibility for their actions.

2. The main facilities, interventions, and resources for addressing and reducing core risk factors exist principally in the closed lifer estate. In this context, the focus in open conditions is to test the efficacy of such core risk reduction work and to address, where possible, any residual aspects of risk.
3. A move to open conditions should be based on a balanced assessment of risk and benefits. However, the Parole Boards emphasis should be on the risk reduction aspect and, in particular, on the need for the lifer to have made significant progress in changing his/her attitudes and tackling behavioural problems in closed conditions, without which a move to open conditions will not generally be considered.

Directions

4. Before recommending the transfer of a lifer to open conditions, the Parole Board must consider:
   - all information before it, including any written or oral evidence obtained by the Board;
   - each case on its individual merits without discrimination on any grounds.
5. The Parole Board must take the following main factors into account when evaluating the risks of transfer against the benefits:
   a) the extent to which the lifer has made sufficient progress during sentence in addressing and reducing risk to a level consistent with protecting the public from harm, in circumstances where the lifer in open conditions would be in the community, unsupervised, under licensed temporary release;
   b) the extent to which the lifer is likely to comply with the conditions of any such form of temporary release;
   c) the extent to which the lifer is considered trustworthy enough not to abscond;
   d) the extent to which the lifer is likely to derive benefit from being able to address areas of concern and to be tested in a more realistic environment, such as to suggest that a transfer to open conditions is worthwhile at that stage.
6. In assessing risk in such matters, the Parole Board shall consider the following information, where relevant and where available, before recommending the lifers transfer to open conditions, recognising that the weight and relevance attached to particular information may vary according to the circumstances of each case:
   a) the lifer's background, including the nature, circumstances and pattern of any previous offending;
   b) the nature and circumstances of the index offence and the reasons for it, including any information provided in relation to its impact on the victim or victim's family;
   c) the trial judges sentencing comments or report to the Secretary of State, and any probation, medical, or other relevant reports or material prepared for the court;
   d) whether the lifer has made positive and successful efforts to address the attitudes and behavioural problems which led to the commission of the index offence;

e) the nature of any offences against prison discipline committed by the lifer;
f) the lifer's attitude and behaviour to other prisoners and staff;
g) the category of security in which the lifer is held and any reasons or reports provided by the Prison Service for such categorisation, particularly in relation to those lifers held in Category A conditions of security;
h) the lifers awareness of the impact of the index offence, particularly in relation to the victim or victim's family, and the extent of any demonstrable insight into his/her attitudes and behavioural problems and whether he/she has taken steps to reduce risk through the achievement of life sentence plan targets;
i) any medical, psychiatric or psychological considerations (particularly if there is a history of mental instability);
j) the lifer's response when placed in positions of trust, including any outside activities and any escorted absences from closed prisons;
k) any indication of predicted risk as determined by a validated actuarial risk predictor model or any other structured assessment of the lifer's risk and treatment needs.

7. Before recommending transfer to open conditions, the Parole Board shall also consider the lifers relationship with the Probation Service (in particular the supervising probation officer), and other outside support such as family and friends.

Directions to the Parole Board under section 239(6) of the Criminal Justice Act 2003

Issued April 2005

Where an offender is subject to a custodial sentence, the licence period is an integral part of the sentence, and compliance with licence conditions is required. In most cases the licences are combined with supervision by a probation officer, social worker or member of the Youth Offending Team (the exception to this is the use of Home Detention Curfew licences for adult prisoners serving a sentence of less than 12 months).

The objects of supervision are:

- to protect the public;
- to prevent reoffending;
- to ensure the prisoners successful reintegration into the community

Review of a decision taken by the Secretary of State to recall an offender

Section 254 of the Criminal Justice Act 2003 requires the Parole Board to review any decision taken by the Secretary of State to recall an offender to prison. The review will take place once the offender has been returned to custody. In determining whether the recall was appropriate, the Parole Board is entitled to take into account the information available at the time the recall decision was taken, together with any subsequent information, including representations made by or on behalf of the offender. The Parole Board should consider whether:

a) The prisoners continued liberty presents an unacceptable risk of a further offence being committed; or

b) The prisoner has failed to comply with one or more of his or her licence conditions; and that failure suggests that the objectives of probation supervision have been undermined.

In cases where the Parole Board believes that the initial decision to recall was inappropriate, the prisoner should be re-released as soon as it is practicable to do so. In determining when to re-release the prisoner, the Parole Board should satisfy itself that the prisoner presents an acceptable risk to public safety and that adequate risk management arrangements are in place.

Where a prisoner has been charged for an offence committed whilst subject to Home Detention Curfew licence, the Board shall additionally take into account that it is desirable for such a prisoner to be recalled to custody, unless it is clearly apparent that the conduct that has led the prisoner to being charged does not merit recall.

The Board's decision to re-release

The Board has powers to:

- release immediately;
- release at a specified future date;
- review the case again; and
- decline to release (only in cases where the prisoner has less than 12 months to serve before the sentence expires).

The assumption is that the Parole Board will seek to re-release the prisoner or set a future re-release date in all cases where it is satisfied that the risk be safely managed in the community. In making this assessment, the Board should take into account that a risk of sexual or violent offending is more serious than a risk of other types of offending.

In determining whether to set a re-release or review date, the Parole Board shall consider:

(a) Whether the risk management plan, prepared by the Probation Service is adequate to address any potential risk of harm or reoffending presented by the prisoner during the licence period.

(b) The likelihood, of the offender complying with the requirements of probation supervision should he or she be re-released during the licence period. In assessing the likelihood of compliance, the Board should consider the conduct of the offender during the licence period to date and the extent to which previous enforcement has influenced such conduct.

(c) The availability of a suitable release plan, the availability and timing of any offending behaviour work either in custody or in the community.

(d) The date on which the outcome of any pending prosecution will be known.

(e) Whether in the interests of public protection the prisoners long term rehabilitation would be better served if the offender were re-released whilst subject to probation supervision.

The Parole Board shall take into account the fact that prisoners who have been sentenced under the provisions of the Criminal Justice Act 1991 cannot be disadvantaged by the recall provisions of the Criminal Justice Act 2003.

Each individual case shall be considered on its own merits, without any discrimination on any unlawful grounds.

Direction to the Parole Board under section 239(6) of the Criminal Justice Act 2003[1]

Recall of determinate sentence prisoners

These directions apply in respect of determinate sentence offenders recalled to prison under section 254 of the 2003 Act on or after 14 July 2008.

Where an offender is subject to a custodial sentence, the licence period is an integral part of the sentence and compliance with licence conditions is required. In most cases the licences are combined with supervision by an offender manager, social worker or member of the Youth Offending Team (the exception to this is the use of Home Detention Curfew licences for adult prisoners serving a sentence of less than 12 months).

The objects of supervision are to:

- protect the public;
- prevent re-offending; and
- ensure the prisoner's successful reintegration into the community

Parole Board review of continued detention following a decision taken by the Secretary of State to recall an offender

Where an offender breaches the conditions of the licence, the Secretary of State can revoke the licence pursuant to section 254(1) of the 2003 Act. A recalled offender will be subject to one of the following sets of provisions of the 2003 Act (as amended by the Criminal Justice and Immigration Act 2008):

- the automatic release provisions (fixed term recall) of section 255B;
- the release provisions (standard recall) of section 255C; or
- the release provisions (extended sentence prisoners) of section 255D.

The 2003 Act requires the Parole Board to review the continued detention of an offender recalled by the Secretary of State in those cases where:

- the offender is subject to the fixed term recall provisions, has exercised the right to make representations against the decision to recall him/her to custody and has been referred to the Board under in accordance with section 255B(4);
- the offender is subject to a standard recall and has been in custody for 28 days or has made representations against the recall and has been referred to the Board in accordance with section 255C(4);
- the offender is an extended sentence prisoner and has been referred to the Board in accordance with section 255D(1).

In reviewing the offender's continued detention, the Parole Board may:

- recommend the offender's immediate release on licence;
- fix a date for the offender's future release on licence, within a year of the Board's decision; or
- determine the reference by making no recommendation as to the offender's release.

1 To be found at appendix K of PSI 29/2008, issued August 2008.

The Board is required to take into account all the information available at the time the recall decision was taken, together with any subsequent information, including representations made by or on behalf of the offender.

In particular, the Parole Board should consider:

(a) Any current risk assessments prepared by prison and probation staff, including whether the offender is assessed as presenting a high or very risk of serious harm.

(b) Whether the risk management plan, prepared by the Probation Service is adequate to manage effectively any potential risk of serious harm or of imminent re-offending.

(c) Whether, in light of the offender's previous response to supervision, the offender is likely to comply in future with the requirements of probation supervision for the duration of the licence period.

(d) The availability of suitable accommodation, as well as the availability and timing of any offending behaviour work either in or outside of custody or the date on which the outcome of any pending prosecution will be known.

(e) Whether the interests of public protection and the prisoner's long term rehabilitation would be better served if the offender were re-released whilst subject to probation supervision.

(f) Any representations on behalf of the victim in respect of licence conditions.

Each individual case should be considered on its own merits, without any discrimination on any grounds.

APPENDIX G

Useful addresses and contact details

The Parole Board for England and Wales
Grenadier House
99–105 Horseferry Road
London
SW1P 2DX

DX 155620, Victoria 17

Tel: 0845 251 2220
Fax: 0845 251 2221
Website: www.paroleboard.gov.uk

Oral hearings casework team

Team A

Altcourse	020 7217 0489
Ashfield	020 7217 0507
Ashwell	020 7217 0566
Aylesbury	020 7217 0566
Blantyre House	020 7217 0556
Brinsford	020 7217 0448
Buckley Hall	020 7217 0201
Bullingdon	020 7217 0038
Castington	020 7217 0507
Cookham Wood	020 7217 0489
Deerbolt	020 7217 0204
Dorchester	020 7217 0038
Drake Hall	020 7217 0038
Durham	020 7217 0201
East Sutton Park	020 7217 0566
Featherstone	020 7217 0201
Feltham	020 7217 0448
Garth	020 7217 0556
Gartree	020 7217 0489
Glen Parva	020 7217 0566
Grendon	020 7217 0038
Guys Marsh	020 7217 0507
Hindley	020 7217 0038
Hull	020 7217 0566
Huntercombe	020 7217 0448
Lancaster Castle	020 7217 0038
Lancaster Farms	020 7217 0038
Lewes	020 7217 0038
Lindholme	020 7217 0204
Lowdham Grange	020 7217 0566
Moorland	020 7217 0204
New Hall	020 7217 0489
Northallerton	020 7217 0448
Norwich	020 7217 0489
Parkhurst	020 7217 0507
Pentonville	020 7217 0204
Portland	020 7217 0566
Preston	020 7217 0201
Ranby	020 7217 0201
Reading	020 7217 0038
Rochester	020 7217 0566
Rye Hill	020 7217 0204
Send	020 7217 0038
Spring Hill	020 7217 0566
Stoke Heath	020 7217 0556
Swansea	020 7217 0489
Swinfen Hall	020 7217 0201

Wandsworth	020 7217 0507
Warren Hill	020 7217 0038
Werrington (YOI)	020 7217 0448
Wetherby	020 7217 0038
Wormwood Scrubs	020 7217 0556
Wymott	020 7217 0556

Team B

Acklington	020 7217 0155
Albany	020 7217 0193
Blundeston	020 7217 0185
Cardiff	020 7217 0194
Channings Wood	020 7217 0194
Dovegate	020 7217 0449
Dover	020 7217 0222
Downview	020 7217 0449
Elmley	020 7217 0222
Exeter	020 7217 0155
Ford	020 7217 0193
Gloucester	020 7217 0193
Haslar	020 7217 0222
High Down	020 7217 0155
Highpoint	020 7217 0449
Holloway	020 7217 0222
Holme House	020 7217 0191
Kennet	020 7217 0191
Kingston	020 7217 0185
Latchmere House	020 7217 0194
Leeds	020 7217 0449
Leicester	020 7217 0194
Lincoln	020 7217 0191
Low Newton	020 7217 0185
Maidstone	020 7217 0193
Manchester	020 7217 0185
Parc	020 7217 0155
Peterborough	020 7217 0193
Risley	020 7217 0191
Shepton Mallet	020 7217 0194
Stocken	020 7217 0449
Styal	020 7217 0155
Swaleside	020 7217 0222
Thorn Cross	020 7217 0038
The Verne	020 7217 0155
Wealstun	020 7217 0222
Whatton	020 7217 0191
Winchester	020 7217 0194

Team C

Askham Grange	020 7217 0129
Bedford	020 7217 0461
Belmarsh	020 7217 0509
Birmingham	020 7217 0129
Bristol	020 7217 0190
Brixton	020 7217 0509
Bronzefield	020 7217 0190
Camp Hill	020 7217 0129
Chelmsford	020 7217 0190
Coldingley	020 7217 0536
Dartmoor	020 7217 0461
Doncaster	020 7217 0229
Eastwood Park	020 7217 0229
Erlestoke	020 7217 0509
Everthorpe	020 7217 0129
Forston Hall	020 7217 0536
Frankland	020 7217 0536
Full Sutton	020 7217 0461
Haverigg	020 7217 0509
Hewell	020 7217 0129
Hollesley Bay	020 7217 0229
Kirkham	020 7217 0196
Kirlevington Grange	020 7217 0129
Leyhill	020 7217 0509
Littlehey	020 7217 0229
Liverpool	020 7217 0195
Long Lartin	020 7217 0196
Morton Hall	020 7217 0510
The Mount	020 7217 0196
North Sea Camp	020 7217 0461
Nottingham	020 7217 0229
Prescoed	020 7217 0536
Shrewsbury	020 7217 0129
Stafford	020 7217 0196
Standford Hill	020 7217 0536
Sudbury	020 7217 0196
Usk	020 7217 0536
Wakefield	020 7217 0190
Wayland	020 7217 0461
Whitemoor	020 7217 0129
Wolds	020 7217 0129
Woodhill	020 7217 0190

Paper hearings team (processing determinate sentence cases)
Tel (manager): 020 7217 0034
Tel (administrative support): 020 7217 0197 / 0209 / 0537 / 0198 / 0403
Fax: 020 7217 0339

Recalls team
Recalls on paper
Tel (manager): 020 7217 0203
Tel (administrative support): 020 7217 0271 / 0203 / 0549 / 0544
Fax: 020 7217 0339

Oral hearings for recall cases
Tel (manager): 020 7217 0215
Tel (case managers and administrators): 020 7217 0187 / 0124 / 0521 / 0106 / 0119 / 0296
Fax: 020 7217 0227

Post-Panel casework team
Responsible for all post-panel casework related to Parole Board decisions and recommendations, including judicial reviews and complaints regarding decisions.

Tel (manager): 020 7217 0217
Tel (caseworkers): 020 7217 0064 / 0174 / 0540 / 0436
Fax :020 7217 0342

Listings
Responsible for the listing and rescheduling of all oral hearings and allocating members to panels.

Tel (manager): 020 7217 0481
Tel (panel listings): 020 7217 0343
Tel (panel membership co-ordinator): 020 7217 0348
Fax: 020 7217 0338

National Offender Management Service
Public Protection Casework Section (PPCS)
8th floor, Cleland House
Page Street
London
SW1P 4LN

Oral hearings casework teams
Team B (East Midlands)

Ashwell, North Sea Camp, Rye Hill	020 7217 6831
Foston Hall, Glen Parva, Lowdham Grange, Morton Hall, Onley, Ranby	020 7217 2506
Leicester, Lincoln, Nottingham, Stockton, Wellingborough, Whatton	020 7217 6357
Sudbury	020 7217 2506

Team C (Eastern and London)

Bedford, Belmarsh, Peterborough, Whitemoor 020 7217 5552
Blundeston, Chelmsford, Holloway, Latchmere House, Littlehey 020 7217 6854
Brixton, Bronzefield, Feltham, Highpoint, Norwich, Warren Hill 020 7217 6800
Hollesley Bay, The Mount, Wayland 020 7217 6616
Pentonville, Wandsworth, Wormwood Scrubs 020 7217 1271

Team D (South East)

Albany, Coldingly, Cookham Wood, Ford, Rochester 020 7217 1163
Blantyre House, Dover, Elmley, Parkhurst 020 7217 1235
Bullingdon, Camp Hill, Downview, East Sutton Park, Huntercombe 020 7217 6201
Grendon, Lewes, Maidstone, Standford Hill 020 7217 6534

Team E (South Central)

Aylesbury, Haslar, High Down, Reading, Send 020 7217 1087
Kingston, Spring Hill, Woodhill, Winchester 020 7217 1273
Swaleside (surnames A-K) 020 7217 1272
Swaleside (surnames L-Z) 020 7217 6706

Team F (West Midlands)

Birmingham, Brinsford, Full Sutton, Stoke Heath, Swinfen Hall (surnames A-M) 020 7217 2794
Dovegate, Drake Hall, Hewell, Shrewsbury, Swinfen Hall (surnames N-Z) 020 7217 6273
Featherstone, Long Lartin, Stafford 020 7217 2799
Werrington (YOI) 020 7217 2796

Team G (North West)

Altcourse, Buckley Hall, Forest Bank, Haverigg, Preston 020 7217 1157
Garth 020 7217 2573
Hindley, Kennett, Kirkham, Lancaster Farms, Liverpool, Styal, Wymott 020 7217 1180
Lancaster Castle, Manchester, Risley, Thorn Cross 020 7217 2793

Team H (North East)

Acklington, Kirklevington Grange 020 7217 3655
Castington, Deerbolt, Durham, Holme House, Lowe Newton 020 7217 2578
Frankland 020 7217 1274

Team I (South West)

Ashfield, Bristol, Eastwood Park, Portland, Shepton Mallet 020 7217 6923
Dartmoor, Exeter, Parc, Prescoed, Usk 020 7217 6820
Cardiff, Channings Wood, Dorchester, Swansea, The Verne 020 7217 1257
Erlestoke, Gloucester, Guys Marsh, Leyhill 020 7217 2518

Team J (Yorkshire)

Askham Grange, Hull, Wakefield (surnames Q-Z), Wolds 020 8760 1839
Doncaster, Leeds, Lindholme, Moorland, New Hall, Northallerton 020 8760 1883
Everthorpe, Wakefield (surnames A-P), Wealstun, Weatherby 020 8760 1850

Recall teams for both determinate and indeterminate sentences
7th Floor
AMP House
Dingwall Road
Croydon
CR0 2LX

Tel (head of casework): 020 8760 1749
Tel (head of probation advisory team): 020 8774 0279
Tel (judicial reviews casework manager): 020 8760 1759

Recall team 1 (London)
Tel (casework manager): 020 8774 0264
Tel (senior caseworker): 020 8760 1712
Tel (probation advisory team): 020 8774 0224

Recall team 2 (Durham, Northumbria, Durham, Teesside)
Tel (casework manager): 020 8774 0264
Tel (senior caseworker): 020 8774 0227
Tel (probation advisory team): 020 8774 0224

Recall team 3 (Bedfordshire, Cambridgeshire, Essex, Hertfordshire, Norfolk, Suffolk)
Tel (casework manager): 020 8760 1851
Tel (senior caseworker): 020 8760 0233/020 8774 0234
Tel (probation advisory team): 020 8774 0273

Recall team 4 (Staffordshire, Warwickshire, West Mercia, West Midlands)
Tel (casework manager): 020 8760 1851
Tel (senior caseworker): 020 8760 1794
Tel (probation advisory team): 020 8774 0273

Recall team 5 (Humberside, North Yorkshire, South Yorkshire, West Yorkshire)
Tel (casework manager): 020 8774 0237
Tel (senior caseworker): 020 8760 1796
Tel (probation advisory team): 020 8774 0240

Recall team 6 (North Wales, South Wales, Dyfed-Powys, Gwent)
Tel (casework manager): 020 8774 0237
Tel (senior caseworker): 020 8760 1745
Tel (probation advisory team): 020 8774 0240

Recall team 7 (Derbyshire, Leicestershire & Rutland, Lincolnshire, Northamptonshire, Nottinghamshire)
Tel (casework manager): 020 8760 1724
Tel (senior caseworker): 020 8760 1722
Tel (probation advisory team): 020 8760 1731

Recall team 8 (Hampshire, Kent, Surrey, Sussex, Thames Valley)
Tel (casework manager): 020 8760 1724
Tel (senior caseworker): 020 8760 1854
Tel (probation advisory team): 020 8760 1731

Recall team 9 (Avon & Somerset, Devon & Cornwall, Dorset, Gloucestershire, Wiltshire)
Tel (casework manager): 020 8760 1837
Tel (senior caseworker): 020 8760 1747
Tel (probation advisory team): 020 8760 1838

Recall team 10 (Cheshire, Cumbria, Great Manchester, Lancashire, Merseyside)
Tel (casework manager): 020 8760 1837
Tel (senior caseworker): 020 8774 0296
Tel (probation advisory team): 020 8760 1838

HM Prison Service
HM Prison Service Headquarters
Cleland House
Page Street
London
SW1P 4LN

Website: www.hmprisonservice.gov.uk

Individual prison details are available at :
www.hmprisonservice.gov.uk/prisoninformation/locateaprison/

National Probation Service
NOMS Probation
1st Floor, Abell House
John Islip Street
London
SW1P 4LH

Website: www.probation.homeoffice.gov.uk

Details for local probation areas are available at:
www.probation.homeoffice.gov.uk/output/Page21.asp

Prisons and Probation Ombudsman
The Prisons and Probation Ombudsman
Ashley House
2 Monck Street
London
SW1P 2BQ

Tel: 020 7035 2876 or lo-call 0845 010 7938
Fax: 020 7035 2860
E-mail: mail@ppo.gsi.gov.uk
Website: www.ppo.gov.uk

Index

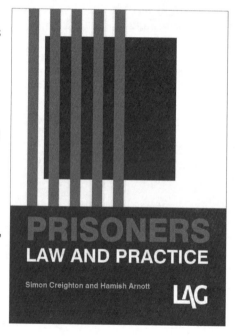